THE LAW OF
HARBOURS, COASTS AND
PILOTAGE

DOUGLAS & GEEN ON THE LAW OF HARBOURS COASTS AND PILOTAGE

BY

RICHARD DOUGLAS, O.B.E.

Former Legal Adviser to the National Ports Council 1964–1981
and British Ports Association 1981–1989
Consultant, Rees & Freres 1989–1995

PETER LANE

Partner, Rees & Freres
Solicitors and Parliamentary Agents

AND

MONICA PETO

Partner, Rees & Freres
Solicitors and Parliamentary Agents

FIFTH EDITION

LONDON   HONG KONG
1997

LLP Limited
Legal & Business Publishing Division
69–77 Paul Street
London EC2A 4LQ
Great Britain

SOUTH EAST ASIA
LLP Asia Limited
Room 1101, Hollywood Centre
233 Hollywood Road
Hong Kong

© R. P. A. Douglas, G. K. Geen, P. Lane & M. Peto 1997

British Library Cataloguing in Publication Data
A catalogue record for this book
is available from the
British Library

ISBN 1–85978–152–7

Typeset in 10/12 Plantin
by Interactive Sciences, Gloucester Ltd
Printed in Great Britain by
WBC Ltd, Bridgend,
Mid-Glamorgan

PREFACE TO THE FIFTH EDITION

There have not been many substantial changes in harbour law since the publication of the Fourth Edition and virtually none in pilotage law. However, there have been several important decisions by the High Court in these areas and the Merchant Shipping and Maritime Security Act 1997 includes a number of provisions which impinge on harbours. There have also been new sets of Regulations, and the consolidation of Merchant Shipping legislation by the Merchant Shipping Act 1995 has outdated many statutory references in the Fourth Edition.

However, the main considerations in our decision that a further edition was now required was the increasing environmental responsibilities of harbour authorities and their developing integration in the management of the coast. Coastal management is certainly an increasingly important subject.

The Fifth Edition therefore deals with the law of the coast as well as harbours and pilotage. The opportunity has also been taken to discuss some aspects of harbour law in more detail.

It should perhaps be emphasised that this book is concerned primarily with the law relating to public bodies acting under statutory powers, and Ministers of the Crown. Private transactions relating to the import or export of cargoes at harbours are discussed, if at all, only incidentally, as is the subject of fishing.

Certain of the provisions of the Merchant Shipping and Maritime Security Act 1997 have not, as at the date of going to press, been brought into force but it is understood that these will be the subject of a Commencement Order bringing them into force within the next few weeks.

June 1997   RICHARD DOUGLAS
                                                      PETER LANE
                                                      MONICA PETO

ABOUT THE AUTHORS

Richard Douglas O.B.E. is a solicitor. He was legal advisor to the National Ports Council from its establishment in 1964 until its abolition in 1981 and to the British Ports Association from 1981 to 1989. He was subsequently a consultant with Rees & Freres, Solicitors and Parliamentary Agents, from 1989 to 1995. He is the author of the first and second editions of *Harbour Law*. He collaborated with Captain Geen on the second edition of the *Law of Pilotage* and subsequently on the third and fourth editions of *The Law of Harbours and Pilotage*, a merger of *Harbour Law* and of the *Law of Pilotage*. He contributed to the fourth edition of *Halsbury's Laws of England* on "Ports and Harbours" (in collaboration with R.H.B. Sturt) and "Pilotage".

Peter Lane and **Monica Peto** are solicitors and parliamentary agents. They were formerly draftsmen at the office of the Parliamentry Counsel where they were engaged in the preparation of a variety of legislation including that relating to ports and local authorities. They are now partners in the firm of Rees & Freres and specialise in transport and planning law. They act for harbour authorities, local and other public bodies and commercial organizations, advising them on a wide range of harbour, coastal, planning and environmental matters. Their previous publications include *Blackstone's Guide to the Transport & Works Act 1992* and *Blackstone's Guide to the Environment Act 1995*.

Captain George Geen, M.Sc. (Wales), Extra Master, is a retired pilot for Associated British Ports (Swansea and Port Talbot). He was an officer in the Merchant Navy 1953–1964, and member of a pilotage authority for 17 years. He is the author of *The Law of Pilotage* (1977) and collaborated with R. P. A. Douglas on the second edition (1983). He also co-authored the third and fourth editions of *The Law of Harbours and Pilotage*.

CONTENTS

CONTENTS

CONTENTS

9. PREVENTION OF POLLUTION, ETC.

10. HARBOUR AUTHORITY FINANCES

11. SUBORDINATE LEGISLATION UNDER THE HARBOURS ACT 1964

CONTENTS

CONTENTS

17. COASTAL PROTECTION

CONTENTS

CONTENTS

CONTENTS

CONTENTS

BIBLIOGRAPHY

All references are to paragraph numbers

Para.

Abbot, Charles, *A Treatise of the Law relative to Merchant Ships and Seamen*, 2nd edn., London, 1804   20.5

Board of Trade, *Report of Departmental Committee on Pilotage* (Cd. 5571), London, 1911   19.14, 19.19, 19.23, 19.24

Coulson & Forbes on Waters and Land Drainage, 6th edn.   1.2, 1.9

Department of Trade, *Marine Pilotage in the United Kingdom, Report to the Secretary of State for Trade by the Steering Committee on Pilotage*, London, 1974   19.28

Department of Trade, *Report of the Advisory Committee on Pilotage to the Secretary of State for Trade on the content of future pilotage legislation*, London, 1977   19.31

Kent, James, *Commentaries on American Law*, vol. 3, 3rd edn., New York, 1836   21.18

MacLachlan's Treatise on the Law of Merchant Shipping, 7th edn., London, 1932   21.15

Marsden, *The Law of Collisions at Sea, British Shipping Laws*, vol. 4, 11th edn., London, 1961   21.17

Royal Commission, *Report from the Commissioners appointed to inquire into the Laws and Regulations relating to Pilotage in the United Kingdom* (1836), xxviii   19.10

Royal Commission, Canada, *Report of Royal Commission on Pilotage*, Ottawa, 1968   20.10, 21.20, 21.28, 21.68

Temperley, *Merchant Shipping Acts, British Shipping Laws*, vol. 2, 7th edn.   20.63

TABLE OF CASES

TABLE OF CASES

TABLE OF CASES

TABLE OF CASES

TABLE OF LEGISLATION

TABLE OF LEGISLATION

CHAPTER 1

HARBOURS AND HARBOUR AUTHORITIES GENERALLY

1.1 This book deals mainly, in its discussion of harbours, with the law relating to those harbours in Great Britain which are managed by harbour authorities under statutory powers (other than "fishery harbours" and "marine works" which are described below) for the purpose of providing a service to other persons. Much of the law relating to the harbours mentioned above also applies in relation to harbours of the kinds briefly referred to in paragraph 1.29 at the end of this chapter but this book does not discuss the law as it applies in particular to each of those kinds of harbour.

Meaning of "harbour" and "harbour authority"

1.2 In the case of *R. v. Hannam*[1] Lord Esher, M.R., said that a harbour in its ordinary sense was a place to shelter ships from the violence of the sea and where ships were brought to load and unload goods. He added that the quays were a necessary part of the harbour. In *Hunter v. Northern Marine Insurance Company*,[2] where the meaning of the word "port" was in issue, Lord Herschell said that: "A port is a place where a vessel can lie in a position of more or less shelter from the elements, with a view to the loading or discharge of cargo." At common law, therefore, "harbour" and "port" seem to be synonymous for most purposes although it appears on the authority of a treatise, *de Portibus Maris*, ascribed to Sir Matthew Hale, that a place which is a mere haven, natural or artificial, for the safe riding of ships (and has no facilities for loading or unloading goods) is also a "harbour".[3] Most questions which now arise on whether something is, or is within, a harbour involve consideration of one of the statutory definitions of "harbour" referred to below, all of which are in very wide terms, or the definition of the limits of a particular harbour contained in a local Act of Parliament or statutory order. A question which occasionally arises in relation to the definitions of "harbour" in public general

1. *R. v. Hannam* (1886) 2 T.L.R. 234.
2. *Hunter v. Northern Marine Ins. Co.* (1888) 13 App. Cas. 717.
3. See *Coulson & Forbes on Waters and Land Drainage*, 6th edn., p. 83.

1

statutes is whether a particular area of water is sufficiently enclosed or shel-
tered by land to be regarded as a harbour. This, of course, is a question of
fact.

1.3 For the purposes of the Merchant Shipping Act 1995 "harbour" is
defined in section 313 of that Act as including "estuaries, navigable rivers,
piers, jetties, and other works in or at which ships can obtain shelter, or ship
and unship goods or passengers"; but for the purposes of Chapter II of Part VI
of the 1995 Act, which deals with oil pollution, there is a separate definition
of "harbour in the United Kingdom" (paragraph 9.12 *post*) for the purposes of
that chapter.

1.4 For the purposes of the Harbours Act 1964 "harbour" is defined in
section 57(1) of that Act as "any harbour, whether natural or artificial, and any
port, haven, estuary, tidal or other river or inland waterway navigated by sea-
going ships, and includes a dock, wharf, and in Scotland a ferry or boat slip
being a marine work, . . . ". "Dock" is defined in the Harbours Act 1964 as "a
dock used by sea–going ships" and "wharf" as "any wharf, quay, pier, jetty or
other place at which sea-going ships can ship or unship goods or embark or
disembark passengers". It was held in the *Salt Union* v. *Wood*[4] that a "sea-going
ship" is a ship that in fact goes to sea and not merely one that could go to
sea.

1.5 The Harbours Act 1964 defines a harbour authority for the purposes of
that Act as "any person in whom are vested under this Act, by another Act or
by an order or other instrument (except a provisional order) made under
another Act or by a provisional order powers or duties of improving, maintaining or managing a harbour".

1.6 The definitions of "harbour" and "harbour authority" contained in the
Harbours Act 1964 have been adopted in various later statutes including the
Pilotage Act 1987 and the Ports Act 1991.

1.7 In the Merchant Shipping Act 1995 as amended by the Merchant
Shipping and Maritime Security Act 1997 "harbour authority" in relation to
a harbour generally means a "statutory harbour authority", defined as, in
relation to Great Britain, a harbour authority within the meaning of the
Harbours Act 1964 and, if there is no statutory harbour authority for the
harbour, the person (if any) who is the proprietor of the harbour or who is
entrusted with the function of managing, maintaining or improving the harbour (i.e., on a non-statutory basis). However, in Chapter II of Part VI of the
1995 Act, there is a separate definition of "harbour authority" (paragraph 9.12
post) for the purposes of that chapter.

1.8 Other important definitions of "harbour" or "harbour area" and "har-
bour authority" are contained in the Prevention of Pollution (Reception
Facilities) Order 1984 (paragraph 9.35 *post*) and the Dangerous Substances in
Harbour Areas Regulations 1987 (paragraphs 8.4 to 8.8 *post*).

---

4. *Salt Union* v. *Wood* [1893] 1 Q.B. 370.

Local statutory powers

1.9 Nearly all harbours with a significant degree of commercial or recreational use are managed under statutory powers. One reason for this is that, to quote from the Sixth Edition of *Coulson & Forbes on Waters and Land Drainage*, which refers to the authority of Hale: "The privilege of erecting ports at which customable goods may be landed and of taking dues and tolls as incident thereto is part of the royal prerogative and can only belong to a subject as a franchise by grant or prescription from the Crown or by Act of Parliament." Harbour authorities which rely on grant or prescription from the Crown are now very rare and do not include any major harbour authorities.

1.10 Another reason why statutory powers are necessary to manage a harbour is that the construction and maintenance of harbour works below high water mark may be open to challenge in the courts, unless such construction and maintenance is authorized by or under statute, on the grounds that the works interfere with the public right of navigation. Furthermore, harbour authorities for significant harbours need to have powers to regulate the activities of other persons using the harbour and in particular the movement and berthing of ships within the harbour. Adequate powers for these purposes can only be obtained by or under statute.

1.11 The local circumstances of the numerous harbours in Great Britain are extremely varied. This is perhaps one reason why harbour authorities still operate to a large extent under *local* statutory powers. The nature and functions of harbour authorities vary too. This aspect is dealt with in the next chapter. In the case of each harbour authority the limits of the harbour for which they are responsible are specified in their statutes. Different limits may sometimes be specified for different purposes.

1.12 Local statutory provisions under which a harbour authority manage their harbour may be contained in a local Act of Parliament or in subordinate legislation made under the Harbours Act 1964—the relevant enabling powers are described later. By virtue of the Private Legislation Procedure (Scotland) Act 1936 a private Bill cannot normally be promoted in relation to a harbour in Scotland. Instead application may be made to the Secretary of State for Scotland for a provisional order which, if made by him, is subject to confirmation by Parliament by means of a Confirmation Bill submitted to Parliament by the Secretary of State. Subsequent references in this book to local Acts of Parliament include references to Scottish provisional orders confirmed by Parliament. Some smaller harbours are still managed under powers conferred by provisional orders made and confirmed under the General Pier and Harbour Act 1861. As mentioned below, following the Transport and Works Act 1992 local Acts and Scottish provisional orders cannot now be used to achieve purposes which can be achieved by subordinate legislation under the Harbours Act 1964 and the *vires* for harbour revision and empowerment orders under that Act has been considerably extended. New local Acts and Scottish provisional orders dealing with harbour matters are therefore likely to be rare in future. The Transport and Works Act has also repealed the General Pier and Harbour Act 1861 and the General Pier and Harbour Act 1861 Amendment Act, which had become virtually obsolete.

1.13 Although the functions of harbour authorities vary, the form of local statutory harbour provisions generally follow broadly similar patterns. The Harbours, Docks and Piers Clauses Act 1847, which embodied the provisions normally included at that time in local harbour Acts so as to enable these to be incorporated by reference in future Acts without unnecessary repetition, contains a fairly comprehensive code of operational powers which includes powers for the harbour authority's harbour master to regulate a number of matters, including the movement and mooring of vessels, and confers quite wide powers for the harbour authority to make by-laws. Until recently the local Acts and orders of most harbour authorities incorporated the greater part of this operational code, often with some modifications, and new local harbour Acts and orders still frequently incorporate substantial parts of it. However, over the past 30 years or so new local measures, particularly in the case of major harbours, have often replaced old-fashioned provisions of the Clauses Act with modern powers, including, in particular, new powers to regulate vessels in the harbour and to make by-laws. These modern powers have tended to follow a common pattern. The more important of them, as well as some still common and effective provisions of the Clauses Act, are described later.

1.14 The statement that harbour authorities still operate mainly under powers contained in local Acts and orders needs to be qualified in the case of the few remaining nationalized harbours and the formerly nationalized harbours for which Associated British Ports are the harbour authority. The only harbour authority for nationalized harbours is now the British Waterways Board who manage their few small harbours to a large extent under powers contained in the Transport Acts of 1962 and 1968. Associated British Ports have a code of powers relating to all their harbours which is set out in Schedule 3 to the Transport Act 1981. These powers are similar to, but in some respects wider than, those of a nationalized harbour authority under the Transport Acts. A few provisions of those Acts continue to apply to Associated British Ports. However, in addition to the general powers referred to in this paragraph, local Acts and orders are also of considerable importance at the nationalized harbours and those of Associated British Ports.

Main public general statutes relating particularly to harbours

1.15 Prior to the Harbours Act 1964 there was little general legislation relating particularly to harbours. This was no doubt because, for reasons mentioned earlier, they were regarded as essentially local undertakings. The Merchant Shipping Act 1894, however, contained important provisions relating to harbours,[5] the Explosives Act 1875 and the Petroleum (Consolidation) Act 1928 each imposed on harbour authorities a duty to make by-laws (now repealed by the Dangerous Substances in Harbour Areas Regulations 1987) and the statutes consolidated in the Prevention of Oil Pollution Act 1971 also imposed important duties on harbour authorities. Legislation relating to pilotage was, and is, also of great importance to harbour authorities.

1.16 The Harbours Act 1964 stemmed from the recommendations contained in the Report of the Committee of Inquiry into the major ports of Great Britain published in 1962, usually known as the "Rochdale Report" from the name of the Chairman of the Committee, Viscount Rochdale. This Act was concerned mainly with the central organization of harbours. The status of harbour authorities as independent bodies was not greatly diminished and, as indicated above, they continue to operate mainly under local powers (subject to some qualification in the case of the nationalized and formerly nationalized harbours) but in this connection the Harbours Act included provisions for subordinate legislation which were intended to provide a cheaper and more expeditious alternative to private Bills. These provisions are described later. The one really important general power for harbour authorities contained in the Harbours Act was the power, also discussed later, to levy ship, passenger and goods dues.

1.17 The Harbours Act 1964 established the National Ports Council with mainly advisory powers although also with powers to promote training and research, initiate measures for the amalgamation or reconstitution of harbour authorities and the duty to determine objections to dues levied by harbour authorities. The Act also provided for major harbour development to be subject to control by the Secretary of State for Transport in the national interest and authorized the Secretary of State to make capital loans (and, originally, also grants) to harbour authorities. As indicated below, both the National Ports Council and the system for the control of major harbour development contained in the 1964 Act have now been abolished.

1.18 The Docks and Harbours Act 1966 conferred some important new general powers on harbour authorities. These included power for a harbour authority to acquire land by agreement for the purpose of any of their statutory powers or duties (section 38(1)) and power to carry out "harbour operations" as defined in the Harbours Act 1964 (except "the marking or lighting of a harbour or any part thereof" but as mentioned below a general power for that purpose has been conferred by section 201 of the Merchant Shipping Act 1995 which replaces section 38(2) of the Ports Act 1991). Section 37 of the Act of 1966 authorized a harbour authority to acquire by agreement any

5. The relevant provisions, so far as they are still extant, are now included in the Merchant Shipping Act 1995 which consolidated nearly all of the Merchant Shipping Acts and certain related statutes, except certain provisions of the Prevention of Oil Pollution Act 1971 relating to discharge of oil from land, which remain in force.

business or undertaking which consisted wholly or mainly of the carrying out of "harbour operations" and to subscribe for or acquire any securities of a body corporate which was wholly or mainly engaged or which it was proposed should become wholly or mainly engaged in carrying out "harbour operations". It appears that the reference in section 37 to subscribing for such securities means that a harbour authority can form a company for the purposes mentioned in section 37. The Transport and Works Act 1992 extended these purposes by substituting for the references in section 37 to "harbour operations" references to "activities relating to harbours". Section 37 of the Act of 1966, as amended by the Act of 1992, therefore confers very wide powers on harbour authorities including, it seems, power to form or acquire a company to carry out activities relating to harbours which may be beyond the powers of the harbour authority themselves (but as mentioned later a harbour authority cannot delegate any of their own functions to a company except where authorized to do so by a harbour revision order and such authorization cannot extend to basic harbour functions). Section 37 of the Docks and Harbours Act 1966 as at present in force is set out in Appendix A. The powers of harbour authorities to form and acquire companies is discussed in more detail in Chapter 13 *post.*

1.19 "Harbour operations" are defined in section 57(1) of the Harbours Act 1964 as—

    (a) the marking or lighting of a harbour or any part thereof;
    (b) the berthing or drydocking of a ship;
    (c) the warehousing, sorting, weighing or handling of goods on harbour land or at a wharf;
    (d) the movement of goods or passengers within the limits within which the person engaged in improving, maintaining or managing a harbour has jurisdiction or on harbour land;
    (e) in relation to a harbour (which expression for the purposes of this paragraph does not include a wharf)—
        (i) the towing, or moving of a ship which is in or is about to enter or has recently left the harbour;
        (ii) the loading or unloading of goods, or embarking or disembarking of passengers, in or from a ship which is in the harbour or the approaches thereto;
        (iii) the lighterage or handling of goods in the harbour; and
    (f) in relation to a wharf,—
        (i) the towing or moving of a ship to or from the wharf;
        (ii) the loading or unloading of goods, or the embarking or disembarking of passengers, at the wharf in or from a ship;[6]

"harbour land" is defined in section 57(1) as land adjacent to a harbour and occupied wholly or mainly for the purposes of activities there carried on and

---

6. "Harbour operations" are defined in slightly different terms in the Aviation and Maritime Security Act 1990 as amended by the Merchant Shipping and Maritime Security Act 1997; see paragraph 15.5 *post.*

"wharf" is defined in that section as any wharf, quay, pier, jetty or other place at which sea-going ships can ship or unship goods or embark or disembark passengers.

1.20 Parts I and II of the Transport Act 1981 provided, respectively, for the introduction of private capital into the harbour undertakings of the British Railways Board (then managed by their subsidiary Sealink) and the British Transport Docks Board. These undertakings are discussed in the next chapter. Part III of the Transport Act 1981 abolished the National Ports Council and made a number of consequential and other amendments to the Harbours Act 1964.

1.21 The Ports (Finance) Act 1985 repealed sections 9 and 10 of the Harbours Act 1964 which contained provisions for the control of major harbour development by the Secretary of State. It also, as described later, included important provisions relating to the borrowing powers of harbour authorities and the audit of their accounts.

1.22 The Dangerous Vessels Act 1985 contained powers for a harbour master to give directions prohibiting the entry into, or requiring the removal from, a harbour, of certain highly dangerous vessels. This Act is discussed in Chapter 6 *post*.

1.23 The Pilotage Act 1987, discussed in Chapter 20 *post*, abolished the former statutory pilotage system and made pilotage a function of harbour authorities.

1.24 Section 148 of, and Schedule 14 to, the Environmental Protection Act 1990 made important amendments to the Prevention of Oil Pollution Act 1971 in relation to pollution by foreign ships. These provisions are now included in Part VI of the Merchant Shipping Act 1995 which consolidated the statutes relating to marine pollution. This subject is discussed in Chapter 9 *post*.

1.25 Part III of the Aviation and Maritime Security Act 1990 contains provisions for the protection of, *inter alia*, harbour areas against "acts of violence". These provisions as amended by the Merchant Shipping and Maritime Security Act 1997 are described in Chapter 15 *post*.

1.26 Part I of the Ports Act 1991 provides for the privatization of port trusts other than the Port of London Authority. Part II of the Act provided for the privatization of the Port of London Authority's undertaking at Tilbury. These provisions are described in Chapter 12 *post*. Part III of this Act contained important provisions about lighthouses. These were repealed and substantially re-enacted by the Merchant Shipping Act 1995. The subject of lighthouses is discussed in Chapter 5 *post*.

1.27 Section 63 of, and Schedule 3 to, the Transport and Works Act 1992 extends the scope of section 37 of the Docks and Harbours Act 1966 (see paragraph 1.18 *ante*), enlarges the *vires* for harbour revision and empowerment orders under the Harbours Act 1964 and amends the procedure for making such orders (see Chapter 11 *post*). The Act also makes other amendments to the Harbours Act 1964 which are referred to later. It repeals section 62 of that Act which enabled private Bills and Scottish provisional orders to be used to achieve purposes which could be achieved by harbour revision and empowerment orders. It also repeals in whole or in part several obsolete harbour statutes. Section 63(3) of the Transport and Works Act amends the Coast Protection Act 1949 (see paragraphs 16.45 to 16.50 *post*). The Transport and Works Act 1992 also inserts in the Harbours Act 1964 a new section 48A which imposes on harbour authorities a duty to have regard to environmental considerations.

1.28 As mentioned above, the Merchant Shipping Act 1995 consolidated the Merchant Shipping Acts and related provisions, including some provisions of the Harbours Act 1964 (the scope of these Acts and provisions, although in part related to harbours, goes much wider). The Merchant Shipping and Maritime Security Act 1997 contained important provisions as respects pollution, including wide enabling powers for the Secretary of State to make regulations relating to reception facilities for ships' waste, and made a number of amendments in Part III of the Aviation and Maritime Security Act 1990.

Types of harbour not specifically dealt with

1.29 Before concluding this chapter it is proposed to refer briefly to the kinds of harbour with which this book is not primarily concerned. These are—

(a) Harbours managed otherwise than under statutory powers. This category includes (*inter alia*) wharves and jetties constructed and maintained by virtue of licences granted by harbour authorities under powers (referred to later) to license the construction of works below high water mark. Although no major harbours fall within this category it does include two or three not insignificant commercial ports, particularly the Port of Par.

(b) "Own-account" harbours. These are harbours (usually wharves or jetties) operated under statutory powers wholly or mainly for the export of goods manufactured by the operators (or their associated companies) or for the import of goods to be used by the operators for the purposes of their own business or those of associated companies. A typical example of such a harbour is a jetty managed by an oil company for their own purposes under powers conferred by a local Act of Parliament or a harbour empowerment order made under the Harbours Act 1964. A person managing such a harbour is, technically, a harbour authority for all statutory purposes and, if the harbour is a jetty or wharf, usually has a measure of control over a limited area of adjacent water.

(c) Fishery harbours. These do not comprise all those harbours which are concerned mainly with the fishing industry. Indeed the main fishing harbours are not within this category. A "fishery harbour" is defined in section 21(7) of the Sea Fish Industry Act 1951 for the purposes of that section as a small harbour ("harbour" being defined in that subsection as including any haven, cove or other landing place) which in the opinion of the Secretary of State for Transport and the Minister of Agriculture, Fisheries and Food is principally used by the fishing industry. Section 21 does not apply to Scotland and the harbours in question are therefore all in England and Wales. The harbours which at the beginning of 1951 were fishery harbours are named in Schedule 4 to the Sea Fish Industry Act 1951 and section 21(8) of that Act provides that a harbour shall not be deemed to have become, or ceased to be, a fishery harbour since the beginning of that year unless and until it is declared to have done so by an order made by the Minister of Agriculture, Fisheries and Food and the Secretary of State for Transport acting jointly. For the purposes of the Harbours Act 1964 and Part III of the Docks and Harbours Act 1966 "fishery harbour" has the same meaning as in section 21 of the Sea Fish Industry Act 1951. Most general enactments relating to harbours and harbour authorities apply to fishery harbours and the harbour authorities which manage them. But the responsible Minister for most purposes is the Minister of Agriculture, Fisheries and Food instead of the Secretary of State for Transport or, in the case of fishery harbours in Wales, the Secretary of State for Wales.

(d) Marine works. "Marine work" is defined for the purposes of the Harbours Act 1964 in section 57(1) of that Act as amended by the Local Government (Scotland) Act 1973. This definition also applies for the purposes of Part III of the Docks and Harbours Act 1966 and for the purposes of the Harbours, Piers and Ferries (Scotland) Act 1937. Briefly, a marine work as so defined is a harbour, ferry or boatslip in Scotland—

(i) which, in the opinion of the Secretary of State for Scotland and the Secretary of State for Transport (strictly, now, "in the opinion of the Secretary of State", since, technically, that office is indivisible) is principally used or required for the fishing industry; or

(ii) which, being situated in certain specified areas in the north of Scotland, is, in the opinion of the Secretary of State for Scotland and the Secretary of State for Transport principally used or required for the fishing or agricultural industries or the maintenance of communications between any place in those areas and any other place in Scotland.

Harbours, ferries or boatslips vested in certain specified bodies are excluded from the definition.

Again, most general enactments relating to harbours and harbour authorities apply to marine works and the harbour authorities responsible for them but the responsible Minister for most purposes is the Secretary of State for Scotland.

The Harbours, Piers and Ferries (Scotland) Act 1937 contains provisions for the acquisition, construction and maintenance of marine works by local authorities in Scotland.

(e) Dockyard ports. These are naval harbours. Their respective limits are defined by Orders in Council under the Dockyard Ports Regulation Act 1865. At each dockyard port the navigation both of Her Majesty's ships and others is subject to rules and regulations made by Order in Council under the Act of 1865. In respect of each such port there is a Queen's Harbour Master to superintend the execution of the Dockyard Ports Regulation Act and Orders in Council made thereunder. It is not uncommon for a dockyard port to be within, or overlap, the limits of a commercial harbour. In such cases the powers of the Queen's Harbour Master have precedence over those of the harbour authority. In practice, however, the Queen's Harbour Master and the harbour authority's harbour master generally liaise closely and it appears that such overlapping jurisdictions seldom give rise to serious difficulty.

CHAPTER 2

TYPES OF HARBOUR AUTHORITY

2.1 Although the variety of harbour authorities (that is to say, harbour authorities for harbours of the kind referred to in paragraph 1.1 above) is such that no precise classification is possible there are two main grounds on which distinctions can be made, namely—

(a) the functions performed by the harbour authority, and
(b) the nature of the body, e.g., nationalized undertaking, local authority, company or "port trust".

2.2 The main functions of harbour authorities, which are discussed later in some detail, may perhaps be classified, in general terms, as follows:

(a) the provision and maintenance of harbour facilities, i.e., quays, wharves, etc.;
(b) navigational safety functions, including lighting and buoying the harbour, the removal of wrecks and other obstructions and maintenance dredging;
(c) regulating the activities of other persons at the harbour including, in particular, regulating the movement and berthing of ships in the harbour by means of directions and by-laws and licensing dredging and the construction of works in the harbour by other persons;
(d) carrying out harbour operations including, in particular, cargo-handling activities;
(e) the provision of a pilotage service; and
(f) of increasing importance, the prevention of pollution and nature conservation, as described in Chapters 9 and 18 *post*.

2.3 Some harbour authorities, including most of the major ones, undertake all these classes of function. They include those harbour authorities, such as Associated British Ports at the Humber and Southampton, the Port of Tyne Authority[1] and the companies which, under the Ports Act 1991, have succeeded the Clyde Port Authority, the Forth Ports Authority, the Medway Ports

---

1. At the time of writing, the Port of Tyne Authority are the subject of proceedings initiated by the Secretary of State under the Ports Act 1991, for their compulsory privatization.

Authority and the Tees and Hartlepool Port Authority as harbour authorities for their respective harbours (Clydeport Ltd., Forth Ports PLC, Port of Sheerness Limited and Tees and Hartlepool Port Authority Limited), which are responsible for all kinds of harbour authority functions throughout a major estuary.

2.4 Following the recommendations of the Rochdale Report (see paragraph 1.16 *ante*), steps were taken in the 1960s and early 1970s towards the amalgamation of dock and conservancy functions in major estuaries but there are still some harbour authorities, of which the Harwich Haven Authority are a major example, which do not themselves provide harbour facilities but are engaged solely in conservancy functions and the regulation of shipping. Following the transfer of Tilbury Docks to a company (Port of Tilbury London Limited) under the Ports Act 1991 the Port of London Authority also falls within this category. Conversely, there are a few important harbour authorities, such as the Felixstowe Dock and Railway Company, which are mainly concerned with the management of docks and whose conservancy jurisdiction is limited to a relatively small area in the vicinity of their docks. Some smaller harbour authorities are concerned wholly or mainly with yachting and other recreational activities.

Associated British Ports

2.5 Turning to the various kinds of bodies which manage harbours under statutory powers, about a third of the harbours in Great Britain, including the great port of Southampton and the Humber ports, were, by virtue of the Transport Act 1962, vested in the British Transport Docks Board (BTDB) which were constituted by that Act. The harbours in question were formerly vested in the British Transport Commission to whom they had been transferred from the former railway companies by the Transport Act 1947, except that the undertakings of the former Humber and Southampton Conservancy Boards were transferred to the BTDB by harbour reorganization schemes under the Harbours Act 1964 (certain harbours were also transferred by such schemes or by local Act of Parliament from the BTDB to other harbour authorities).

2.6 On 31 December 1982, pursuant to section 5(1) of the Transport Act 1981, the BTDB were reconstituted under the name of "Associated British Ports". Under the provisions of Part II of the Transport Act 1981 Associated British Ports continue, as a statutory corporation, to manage their harbours under substantially the same powers as the BTDB. With a few exceptions, the provisions of the Transport Acts 1962 and 1968 no longer apply but a similar, and in some respects rather wider, code of powers for Associated British Ports is set out in Schedule 3 to the 1981 Act. The controls which, under the Transport Acts, the Secretary of State exercises over nationalized transport undertakings no longer apply to Associated British Ports and the financial provisions of those Acts, including borrowing and charging powers, have also ceased to apply. Schedule 3 to the 1981 Act includes borrowing powers for Associated British Ports and a power to charge for services and facilities. Associated British Ports charge ship, passenger and goods dues under section 26 of the Harbours Act 1964 (and combined charges under section 27A of that Act inserted by the Transport Act 1981) as do other harbour authorities.

2.7 Under Part II of the Transport Act 1981, Associated British Ports are controlled by a company, formed by the Secretary of State and registered under the Companies Act 1985, known as Associated British Ports Holdings plc in substantially the same way as if they were a wholly owned subsidiary of that company. In particular, under section 7(4) of the 1981 Act, the directors of Associated British Ports (of which there must be not less than five nor more than 13) are appointed by Associated British Ports Holdings plc for such period as that company may determine. Under Section 11(1) of the 1981 Act the directors of Associated British Ports must pay to Associated British Ports Holdings plc such sums as appear to the directors to be justified by the profits of Associated British Ports (this corresponding to the dividends which a subsidiary pays its holding company). But Associated British Ports Holdings plc has no power to give directions to the directors of Associated British Ports as respects the exercise of their powers and duties as a harbour authority.

2.8 The provisions of Part II of the Transport Act 1981, under which a statutory board with no share capital is to some extent controlled by a company formed and registered under the Companies Act 1948 (now replaced by the Companies Act 1985) but the directors of the board are, nevertheless, not subject to direction by the company, are thought to be unique. This concept was perceived as enabling the introduction of private capital and the commercial flexibility of a company formed under the Companies Act (Associated British Ports Holdings plc's memorandum of association enables it to carry out a wide variety of activities) to be reconciled with the principles usually associated with the carrying out of important powers and duties conferred and imposed by Parliament for public purposes. However, as mentioned later, it was not followed in the provisions for the privatization of port trusts under the Ports Act 1991.

Harbour authorities for other former railway ports

2.9 Not all the British Transport Commission's harbours were vested by the Transport Act 1962 in the BTDB. Several, broadly speaking the "packet ports" which at that time were mainly concerned with the transport of passengers to and from the Continent or Ireland, were vested in the British Railways Board (BRB) and a few small harbours at the seaward ends of canals were vested in the British Waterways Board (BWB). The latter are the only remaining nationalized harbours and the provisions of the Transport Acts as respects nationalized undertakings still apply to them.

2.10 The BRB's ports were managed, together with the Board's shipping services, by a subsidiary known as "Sealink". Section 2 of the Transport Act 1981 required that Sealink should form a company under the Companies Act 1948 and transfer to that company (which would be a subsidiary of Sealink) Sealink's harbour undertaking. This was done and, when BRB subsequently disposed of their security in Sealink, the harbours managed by Sealink Harbours Limited ceased to be nationalized and the relevant provisions of the Transport Acts 1962 and 1968 ceased to apply. In addition to local Acts and orders the provisions of Schedule 1 to the Transport Act 1981 applied to these harbours.

2.11 Most of these harbours have now been transferred by harbour revision orders under the Harbours Act 1964 to companies which are subsidiaries of Sea Containers Ltd.

Local authority ports

2.12 A number of harbours are managed by local authorities. These formerly included the major harbour of Bristol but this has now been transferred by harbour revision order to a company. Local authority ports include the new harbours developed at Scapa Flow in Orkney and Sullom Voe in the Shetlands for the exploitation of North Sea oil. The management of a harbour by a local authority has implications from the financial point of view in that the relevant local harbour legislation generally provides for payments and receipts in respect of the harbour undertaking to be carried to, and form part of, the general fund. Where the harbour undertaking have made a profit in any year the local authority are often enabled to set aside all or part of it as a reserve to meet future contingencies in connection with the undertaking but where the port loses money the deficit may be met from the council tax. Harbour authorities which are local authorities are, as such, exempt from corporation tax to which other harbour authorities are liable if they make a profit.

Statutory companies

2.13 The harbour authorities for several harbours—including, in particular, Mersey, Manchester Ship Canal and Felixstowe—are companies constituted by local Acts of Parliament and not under the Companies Acts. The Mersey Docks and Harbour Company were established by the Mersey Docks and Harbour Act 1971 (which dissolved the former Mersey Docks and Harbour Board).

Port Trusts

2.14 Many harbour authorities in Great Britain are still bodies of the kind commonly known (the expression does not seem to have appeared in any statute or to have any judicial authority) as "port trusts". A port trust may perhaps be described as an *ad hoc* body created by, or under, statute for the purpose of managing a harbour and not having a share capital. Examples of port trusts are the Dover Harbour Board and the Port of Tyne Authority.[2] The Port of London Authority, the Harwich Haven Authority and the Milford Haven Port Authority, although their functions are mainly in the conservancy field, are also port trusts, and many small and medium harbours throughout Great Britain are managed by port trusts.

2.15 The constitutions of port trusts have been a subject of controversy for many years. Originally, most members of port trusts were elected or appointed by particular interests concerned with the harbour or by a Minister of the Crown on the recommendation of, or after consultation with, such interests which generally included shipowners, importers and exporters of goods through the port, local authorities in the area and dock labour.

2.16 After 1970 a different pattern was adopted for all the port trusts which were harbour authorities for major harbours and in several other cases. A typical example is the constitution of the Port of Tyne Authority as reconstituted by the Port of Tyne Authority (Constitution) Revision Order 1974 which is set out in Appendix B. The concept was a relatively small Board consisting of a majority of members appointed by the Secretary of State not representative of particular interests but drawn from a specified range of relevant knowledge and experience, together with the chief executive officer and several other executives appointed by the Board. In a few cases this concept was modified to give a measure of special treatment to local authorities or take account of special circumstances. With the privatization of a number of authorities for major ports, as indicated in paragraph 2.19 *post*, major harbour authorities constituted on these lines are no longer the norm. Only three of them remain and, if the Port of Tyne Authority are compulsorily privatized (see paragraph 2.19), the Port of London Authority (now a conservancy body) and the Dover Harbour Board, which may be privatized in the near future, will be the only ones left (although the constitution of the Milford Haven Port Authority is similar).

2.17 The "representative" basis of appointment mentioned in paragraph 2.15 *ante* has been retained for most small and medium port trusts. A question which is sometimes raised is whether a member appointed in this way, although not a delegate, has a duty to protect the interests by, or by reference to, whom he was appointed as well as to the harbour authority. In the authors'

---

2. At the time of writing, the Port of Tyne Authority are the subject of proceedings initiated by the Secretary of State under the Ports Act 1991 for their compulsory privatization.

view the only duty of such a member, in his capacity as a member of the port trust, is, at meetings of the Board, or committees of the Board, to seek to promote the best interests of the harbour authority. In short, such a member does not sit on the Board of the port trust as a representative. This is emphasized in cases where provisions of the Commissioners Clauses Act 1847 are incorporated with the local Acts of the port trust (although they seldom are in recent Acts and orders) by the Declaration which a member is required to make by section 12 of the Commissioners Clauses Act to faithfully and impartially, according to the best of his skill and judgment, execute all the powers and authorities reposed in him as a Commissioner by virtue of the harbour authority's statutes.

Companies Act companies

2.18 Until 1992 the only harbour authorities for important harbours which were companies formed under the Companies Act 1985 (as distinct from statutory companies) were Sealink Harbours Limited and companies to which their harbours had been transferred (see paragraphs 2.10 and 2.11 *ante*). As mentioned in paragraph 2.7 *ante* Associated British Ports are not themselves a company although they are the statutory subsidiary of a company formed under the Companies Act 1985.

2.19 However, pursuant to the provisions of Part I of the Ports Act 1991 (see Chapter 12 *post*), the undertakings of four major port trusts—the Clyde Port Authority, the Forth Ports Authority, the Medway Ports Authority and the Tees and Hartlepool Port Authority—have been transferred to companies formed under the Companies Act 1985. The same is true of the Port of Dundee Authority. The undertaking of the Ipswich Port Authority has been privatized compulsorily under the Ports Act 1991 and the Port of Tyne Authority is the subject of proceedings for compulsory privatization under that Act. Under Part II of the Ports Act 1991 (see Chapter 12, *post*) the Port of London Authority's dock undertaking at Tilbury has also been transferred to a company formed under the Companies Act 1985—Port of Tilbury London Limited. The majority of major harbour authorities are now, therefore, companies.

2.20 A harbour authority who are a company formed under the Companies Act 1985 will normally have numerous functions, or potential functions, under their memorandum of association in addition to their functions as a harbour authority. However, in their capacity as a harbour authority, they will be subject to the same statutory obligations, and have the same statutory powers, as if they were a port trust.

The Environment Agency

2.21 The Environment Agency, constituted under the Environment Act 1995, is the harbour authority for a few small harbours. The function in question was transferred to the Agency from the former National Rivers

Authority by section 2(1)(a)(vi) of the 1995 Act. These functions had previously been transferred to the NRA under provisions mentioned in section 2(1)(a)(vi). For example, in the case of the Harbour of Rye, immediately before 1 September 1989, the Southern Water Authority had functions (of a navigation authority, conservancy authority or harbour authority within the meaning of the Water Act 1989) which effectively made it a harbour authority for the purposes of the Harbours Act 1964. These functions were transferred to the NRA on 1 September 1989 by section 142(1) of the 1989 Act (that section has been repealed by the Water Consolidation (Consequential Provisions) Act 1991). By virtue of section 2(1)(a)(vii) of the Environment Act 1995 the Environment Agency has power to apply to Ministers for an order under Schedule 2 to the Water Resources Act 1991, transferring to it the functions of a navigation, conservancy or harbour authority. It is therefore possible for the Agency to become the harbour authority for additional harbours in the future.

CHAPTER 3

BASIC DUTIES, POWERS AND LIABILITIES OF HARBOUR AUTHORITIES

Permissive powers may impose duty

3.1 In order to ascertain the law relating to any particular harbour authority reference must be made to their local Acts and orders (as well as the general law). However, in addition to the fact that local enactments often follow a common pattern, there are certain basic principles which apply generally. The powers granted to a harbour authority by Parliament are in virtually all cases conferred for the purpose of providing a public service. Until recent years powers to construct and/or manage and maintain harbours were generally in permissive terms, but it is clear that even although the terms of a special Act of Parliament establishing a body for the purpose of carrying on an undertaking are permissive the statute may by implication impose a duty on the body concerned to establish and maintain the service in question. *Gardner* v. *London, Chatham and Dover Railway Co.*[1] and *Re Salisbury Railway and Market House Co.*[2] are cases in point.

Section 33 of Harbours, Docks and Piers Clauses Act 1847

3.2 The intention of Parliament to impose a duty to operate the harbour even where the harbour authority's statutory powers are generally in permissive terms can be inferred if the relevant Acts and orders incorporate section 33 of the Harbours, Docks and Piers Clauses Act 1847, or include a provision to the same effect, which is nearly always the case. This extremely important provision, which requires a harbour authority to keep their harbour open for commercial users, is discussed in detail in Chapter 4 *post*.

Section 40 of the Harbours Act 1964

3.3 Section 40(1) of the Harbours Act 1964 provides that a harbour authority shall have power to make the use of services and facilities provided by them at

---

1. *Gardner* v. *London, Chatham and Dover Railway Co.* (1867) L.R. 2 Ch. App. 201.
2. *Re Salisbury Railway and Market House Co.* [1967] 3 W.L.R. 651; 111 S.J. 495; [1967] 1 All E.R. 813.

their harbour, subject to such terms and conditions as they see fit, except with respect to charges as to which their discretion is limited by a statutory provision (whether by specifying, or providing for specifying, charges to be made, or fixing or providing for fixing charges, or otherwise). Section 40(2) provides that certain bodies, including the British Waterways Board, are not harbour authorities for this purpose.

3.4 It is submitted that the reference to services and facilities in this section has the same meaning as the references to services and facilities in the definition of "ship, passenger and goods dues" in section 57(1) of the Harbours Act 1964 and, on that basis, should be narrowly construed as referring only to ancillary matters and not to such matters as the provision of jetties or a dredged channel. The meaning of the references to services and facilities in the definition of "ship, passenger and goods dues" is discussed in paragraphs 10.23 to 10.25 *post*.

3.5 That point was not raised when the scope of section 40 was under consideration in the cases of *R* v. *Dover Harbour Board ex parte Peter Gilder & Sons* and *R* v. *Associated British Ports ex parte Plymouth City Council* which are discussed in detail in Chapter 4 *post* but, as mentioned in paragraph 4.14 *post*, it was held in those cases that section 40 is subservient to section 33 of the Harbours, Docks and Piers Clauses Act 1847.

General duties and powers of harbour authorities

3.6 In recent local harbour legislation the duties of the harbour authority concerned are usually expressly stated and this is now the case with nearly all major harbour authorities. The general duties and powers of Associated British Ports are stated in section 9 of the Transport Act 1981. This section is set out in Part I of Appendix C. Part II of Appendix C sets out section 5 of the Port of London Act 1968 (as amended by the Port of Tilbury Transfer Scheme 1991 made under Part II of the Ports Act 1991) which states the general powers and duties of the Port of London Authority. The special legislation of the harbour authorities for nearly all major commercial harbours now contain general statements of powers and duties in substantially similar terms.

3.7 Although the terms of these provisions—to take such action for the specified purposes as the harbour authority consider necessary or desirable or expedient—confer a discretion, this must be exercised reasonably and in good faith for the purpose which the relevant legislation was designed to achieve which is in virtually all cases the provision of port services and facilities to meet the needs of the public.

Closure of harbours

3.8 Where a harbour authority have a statutory duty to maintain their harbour, which it is submitted is nearly always the case, it would seem that the harbour cannot be closed and the undertaking discontinued except by means of an Act of Parliament. There may be some doubt about this in the case of a harbour authority which is a company. However, in the *Salisbury Railway and Market House* case referred to above[3] it was held that the company concerned, which, although created by statute, had registered under Part VIII of the Companies Act 1948 and had then gone into a members' voluntary winding up, could not, without statutory sanction, abandon its functions relating to the market house.

3.9 Under section 666 of the Companies Act 1985 an unregistered company may be wound up by the court in certain specified circumstances. There is no recent authority on whether an unregistered company with subsisting statutory duties can be wound up under this provision but having regard to the *Salisbury Railway and Market House* case it seems that the better view is that such a company cannot be completely wound up and dissolved except by Act of Parliament. This view seems to be supported by the judgments of the Court of Appeal in *Re Woking Urban District Council (Basingstoke Canal) Act 1911*.[4]

3.10 It has been suggested that a port trust is an unregistered company for the purposes of the Companies Act 1985 and that it is therefore arguably possible for a port trust to be wound up under section 666 of that Act. However, it does not appear that a port trust is in any sense a company. The contrary view would appear to involve the proposition that every body corporate is such. Thus, for example, local authorities and bodies such as the BBC would be liable to be wound up by the court. It seems unlikely that Parliament intended to achieve such a result.

3.11 It may indeed often be doubtful whether a harbour authority can close even a significant part of their harbour without statutory authority. In particular, where section 33 of the Harbours, Docks and Piers Clauses Act 1847 is not only incorporated with a harbour authority's special legislation in relation to their harbour as a whole but also with an Act or order which authorizes the construction of a specific dock or jetty, it would seem that, unless the authority's special legislation provides to the contrary, that facility cannot be closed without further legislation. In order to overcome this difficulty some harbour authorities have recently included in their special legislation a declaration that section 33 as incorporated with that legislation shall not be construed as derogating from the power of the harbour authority to discontinue any part of their undertaking. As mentioned in chapter 11 *post*, following the extension of the *vires* for harbour revision orders by the Transport and Works Act 1992, a harbour revision order may be used to close part (but not the whole) of a harbour.

---

3. *Ante*, fn. 2.
4. *Re Woking Urban District Council (Basingstoke Canal) Act 1911* [1914] 1 Ch. 300.

Doctrine of ultra vires

3.12 Harbour authorities are still, for the most part, bodies created by statute (although, as indicated above, some important harbour authorities are now companies formed under the Companies Act 1985) and as such subject to the doctrine of *ultra vires*, that is to say, they can only do what is expressly authorized by or under statute or such things as are reasonably incidental to what is expressly authorized. The case of the *Dundee Harbour Trustees v. Nicol*[5] arose from the Trustees seeking to diversify their activities by letting out boats for excursions. This was challenged by a commercial firm in that line of business who brought an action against them on the grounds that the Trustees had no power to undertake this activity. In giving judgment against the Trustees Lord Haldane said: "It is now well settled that the answer to the question whether a corporation created by statute has a particular power depends exclusively on whether that power has been expressly given to it or can be implied from the language used."

Acquisition and disposal of land

3.13 With regard to harbour authorities' powers for the acquisition and disposal of land, section 38(1) of the Docks and Harbours Act 1966 provides that a harbour authority may for the purpose of any of their statutory powers or statutory duties acquire by agreement any land wherever situated. Some harbour authorities already possessed such a power under their special legislation. Section 23 of the Harbours, Docks and Piers Clauses Act 1847 authorizes a harbour authority with whose special legislation the section is incorporated to "lease or grant the use or occupation of any warehouses, buildings, wharfs, yards, cranes, machines, or other conveniences provided by them for the purpose of this or the special Act, at such rents, and upon such terms and conditions as shall be agreed upon between the undertakers and the persons taking the same, providing that no such lease be granted for a longer term than three years". This section, which it will be noted authorizes the grant of leases for operational harbour purposes and not the disposal of surplus land, is sometimes incorporated with a modification omitting the limitation to a three years' term.

3.14 The special legislation of most harbour authorities for major harbours now contains a general power to dispose of land belonging to them in such manner, whether by way of sale, exchange, lease, the creation of any easement, right or privilege or otherwise, for such periods, upon such conditions and for such consideration as they think fit. Sometimes this power is limited, in terms, to land no longer required for the purposes of the harbour undertaking and would not therefore authorize the grant of a lease for operational harbour

---

5. *Dundee Harbour Trustees v. Nicol* [1915] A.C. 550.

purposes, e.g., the lease of a berth to the intent that the lessees will operate it. If section 23 of the Harbours, Docks and Piers Clauses Act 1847 is incorporated with a harbour authority's special legislation such leases can be granted under that provision and in a few cases—for example Article 31 of the Port of Tyne Reorganization Scheme 1967—the special legislation includes, in addition to a power to dispose of surplus land, a modern provision authorizing the harbour authority to grant operational leases. However, it would seem that, even in the absence of an express power for the purpose, a harbour authority with express general powers and duties to manage their harbour probably have implied power to grant leases, licences, etc, where they consider that this would be in the interests of the efficient and economical management of the harbour. (But where there is an express power to lease subject, as in section 23 of the 1847 Act in its unmodified form, to a limit on the term which may be granted, implied powers could not be relied on to grant a longer term: *cf. Glebe Sugar Refining Co. v. Trustees of Port and Harbour of Greenock.*[6])

3.15 Some harbour authorities for major harbours have power under their special legislation to make, and submit to the Secretary of State, orders for the compulsory acquisition of land which they require for the purposes of their harbour undertakings. For this purpose the Acquisition of Land Act 1981, which contains the standard procedural code for the compulsory purchase of land, is generally applied. The Transport Act 1962 confers powers for the compulsory acquisition of land on the harbour authorities for nationalized harbours. In the case of Associated British Ports such powers are now contained in paragraph 19 of Schedule 3 to the Transport Act 1981.

Ownership of bed of harbour

3.16 The property in the bed of a harbour is *prima facie* vested in the Crown. In some cases however it is vested in the harbour authority by grant or charter from the Crown or by prescription and occasionally it is so vested in another person. Most harbour authorities do not own the bed of their harbour and, although such ownership has advantages, particularly in relation to the construction of works below high water mark, it is certainly not essential for the management of a harbour.

No liability for nuisance where works authorized by statute

3.17 Although there appears to be no direct authority, there seems no reason to doubt that the principle established in *Hammersmith and City Railway Co. Ltd. v. Brand*[7] and discussed in *Allen v. Gulf Oil Refining Ltd.*[8] that where a

---

6. *Glebe Sugar Refining Co. v. Trustees of Port and Harbour of Greenock* [1921] 2 AC 66.
7. *Hammersmith and City Railway Co. Ltd v. Brand* (1869) L.R. 4 H.L. 171.
8. *Allen v. Gulf Oil Refining Ltd.* [1981] A.C. 1001.

body are authorized by statute to construct (and therefore by implication to use) works in a specific position they will not be liable for nuisance in respect of the use of those works reasonably and without negligence for the purpose envisaged by the statute, applies to harbour authorities. (However, in such cases a harbour authority may be liable to pay compensation under Part I of the Land Compensation Act 1973 where the value of an interest in land is depreciated by certain kinds of nuisance—the "physical factors" described in section 1(2) of the Land Compensation Act 1973—caused by the use of a work, e.g., a dock, the construction of which was specifically authorized by statute.)

Liability for negligence

3.18 It is well established that a harbour authority will be liable if they, or their servants, fail to exercise reasonable care and skill in carrying out the harbour authority's functions. In the Privy Council case of *East London Harbour Board v. Caledonian Shipping Co.*[9] the harbour authority were held to be liable for the negligence of their harbour master in directing the movement and mooring of vessels. In *Edwards v. Falmouth Harbour Commissioners*[10] the Falmouth Harbour Commissioners were held to be liable for the action of their harbour master who gave orders for a ship to be beached in such a manner that she was damaged. In *The Ratata*[11] Preston Corporation, as harbour authority for the Ribble, were held liable for damage caused by the failure of their servants to exercise reasonable care and skill in carrying out a towage operation. In *The Framlington Court*,[12] it was held that the PLA were responsible for the negligence of their dock-master in ordering the *Framlington Court*, under powers conferred on the dock-master by the Port of London Act 1920, to get under way when he was aware of an obstruction at the dock entrance (although in the event the plaintiffs failed because of contributory negligence on the part of the master of the *Framlington Court*—if the incident had occurred after the passing of the Law Reform (Contributory Negligence) Act 1945 the result would have been different). It seems clear that the fact that the negligence of a harbour master relates to the exercise of statutory powers vested, in terms, directly in him (see para 6.1 *post*) makes no difference to the vicarious liability of the harbour authority who employ him. See also in this connection *A. F. Henry and MacGregor v. Aberdeen Harbour Commissioners.*[13]

3.19 The duties of a harbour authority in carrying out conservancy functions are discussed in more detail in Chapter 5. It was held in *Mersey Docks and*

---

9. *East London Harbour Board v. Caledonian Shipping Co.* [1908] A.C. 271.
10. *Edwards v. Falmouth Harbour Commissioners* (1884) 54 L.J. Adm. 42.
11. *The Ratata* [1898] A.C. 513.
12. *The Framlington Court* (1936) 56 Ll.L.Rep. 200.
13. *A. F. Henry and MacGregor v. Aberdeen Harbour Commissioners* (1943) 76 Ll.L.Rep. 107.

Harbour Board Trustees v. *Gibbs*[14] that a harbour authority are liable for damage occasioned by their failure to take reasonable care that their dock (so far as they keep it open for public use) may be used by those who choose to navigate it without danger to their lives or property. But it appears from *Queen of the River Steamship Co.* v. *River Thames Conservators*[15] that a harbour authority are not liable for damage caused by an obstruction in their harbour which they are not aware of and could not reasonably be expected to be aware of.

Limitation of liability

3.20 Under section 191 of the Merchant Shipping Act 1995, a harbour authority may limit their liability (whether arising under common law or under statute) for loss or damage occurring on any distinct occasion to any vessel or vessels or to any goods, merchandise or other things whatsoever on board any vessel or vessels, unless the loss or damage resulted from their personal act or omission committed with the intent to cause such loss or damage or recklessly and with knowledge that such loss would probably result. It seems therefore that a harbour authority will always be entitled to limit their liability for such loss or damage as is mentioned above which results from an act or omission on the part of a servant or agent of the harbour authority.

3.21 Where a harbour authority are entitled to limit their liability as mentioned in the preceding paragraph the extent of that limitation turns on the tonnage of the largest registered British ship which, at the time when the loss or damage in question occurs, is, or within the previous five years has been, within the harbour authority's limits of jurisdiction (excluding any ship which is, or was, within that area by reason only that she was built or fitted out there, or that she took shelter within or passed through that area on a voyage between two places outside that area, or that she has loaded or unloaded mails or passengers within that area). The amount of that limitation is to be calculated by applying to this tonnage the formula for calculating limits of liability specified in paragraph 1(*b*) of Article 6 of the Convention on Limitation of Liability for Maritime Claims 1976 (which Convention, by virtue of section 185 of the Merchant Shipping Act 1995, has the force of law in the United Kingdom and is set out in Part I of Schedule 7 to that Act, related and incidental provisions being specified in Part II of that Schedule) read with the related provisions of that Convention and with those of Part II of Schedule 7 to the Merchant Shipping Act 1995. (In relation to pilotage, special provisions as to the limitations of a harbour authority's liability apply. These are specified in paragraphs 20.81 to 20.89 *post*).

3.22 Under section 74 of the Harbours, Docks and Piers Clauses Act 1847, which, or an equivalent provision, is nearly always incorporated in the special

14. *Mersey Docks and Harbour Board Trustees* v. *Gibbs* (1866) L.R. 1 H.L. 93.
15. *Queen of the River Steamship Co.* v. *River Thames Conservators* (1907) 96 L.T. 62.

legislation of harbour authorities, a shipowner is absolutely liable for damage caused by his ship to harbour works except, it appears from the decision of the House of Lords in *River Wear Commissioners* v. *Adamson*,[16] where this is due to an Act of God.

3.23 Under the Convention on Limitation of Liability for Maritime Claims 1976, as in force in the United Kingdom by virtue of the Merchant Shipping Act 1995, a shipowner whose ship damages harbour works may, unless it is proved that the damage resulted from his personal act or omission committed with the intent to cause the damage, or recklessly and with knowledge that the damage would probably result, limit his liability in accordance with the formula specified in paragraph 1(*b*) of Article 6 of the Convention which is related to the tonnage of the ship concerned.

3.24 The limits of liability specified in paragraph 1(*b*) of Article 64 of the 1976 Convention referred to in paragraphs 3.21 and 3.23 *ante* are expected to be replaced by the limits specified in Article 3(1)(*b*) of the Protocol of 1996 to amend that Convention. By virtue of section 10 of the Merchant Shipping and Maritime Security Act 1997 these changes in limits of liability may be effected by modifications made by Order in Council of Parts I and II of Schedule 7 to the Merchant Shipping Act 1995.

3.25 The 1976 Convention also provides that shipowners and salvors may, on a similar basis, limit their liability in respect of the costs of wreck removal. However, by virtue of paragraph 3 of Part II of Schedule 7 to the Merchant Shipping Act 1995, this provision will not apply unless the Secretary of State, by order, provides for the establishment of a fund to compensate harbour authorities for consequential reductions in the amounts recoverable by them in claims for such costs. No such order has yet been made.

16. *River Wear Commissioners* v. *Adamson* (1877) 2 App. Cas. 743.

CHAPTER 4

SECTION 33 OF THE HARBOURS, DOCKS AND PIERS CLAUSES ACT 1847

4.1 The local legislation of nearly all significant commercial harbour authorities incorporates section 33 of the Harbours, Docks and Piers Clauses Act 1847. In the few cases where it does not—for example, in the case of the Port of London Authority—the local legislation usually includes a substantive provision to the same effect.

4.2 Section 33 provides that:

"Upon payment of the rates made payable by this and the special Act (ie. the Act which incorporates section 33), and subject to the other provisions thereof, the harbour, dock and pier shall be open to all persons for the shipping and unshipping of goods and the embarking and landing of passengers."

(As indicated later, section 26 of the Harbours Act 1964, which authorizes harbour authorities to levy dues, provides that references to rates in provisions of the Harbours, Docks and Piers Clauses Act 1847 incorporated in a harbour authority's local legislation include references to charges imposed by that authority under section 26.)

4.3 Section 33 is therefore a key provision in harbour legislation. It applies both in relation to ships wishing to use the harbour, and to members of the public wishing to use the quays and jetties, for the purposes specified in the section. It has been considered in a number of cases. In the case of *Thoresen Car Ferries Ltd* v. *Weymouth and Portland Borough Council*,[1] Donaldson, J., said that a harbour authority's duty under section 33 was to keep their harbour open (to any person wishing to use it) subject to the rights of others to use it. No doubt this duty is subject to the physical limitations of the harbour. It was, however, held in that case that (even in the absence of such a power to appropriate particular facilities as is mentioned below) a harbour authority may by contract grant a regular user of the port, such as a ferry operator, a right to use the berth at certain times and will not be in breach of section 33 because other users are not able to use the berth at those times. But it was also held in this case that a harbour authority are not obliged to enter into a commitment that a berth will be available to a particular user at particular

1. *Thoresen Car Ferries Ltd* v. *Weymouth and Portland Borough Council* [1977] 2 Lloyd's Rep. 614.

times, even though, in the case of a user who wishes to provide a regular service at specified times, the use of the berth on any other basis may not be commercially practicable.

4.4 Other important cases on the interpretation of section 33 of the 1847 Act have generally emphasized that it should be given a wide construction. In *LNER* v. *British Trawlers Federation*[2] it was held that the marketing of fish when landed must be regarded as part of the process of shipping and unshipping within the meaning of section 33 and that access to the docks must include access with such a vehicle as the party seeking access deems necessary. Lord Macmillan said:

"The harbour is to be open to all for the purposes of unshipping goods. It is manifest that this must include the consequential purposes of removing the goods unshipped, and such removal necessitates the employment of the appropriate vehicles."

He pointed out that, by virtue of the definition in section 2 of the 1847 Act, "the harbour, dock or pier" included, for the purposes of section 33, works connected therewith.

4.5 In *J. H. Piggot and Son* v. *Docks and Inland Waterways Executive*[3] it was held that tugowners are entitled by section 33 in the ordinary course of their business to employ their tugs in providing towage services to vessels entering or leaving a harbour for the shipping or unshipping of goods and/or the embarking or landing of passengers. In the course of his judgment Sellers, J., said:

"For shipping and unshipping to take place in any commercial or business sense, it is necessary to employ skilled stevedores and labourers to load, discharge, trim, stow or otherwise handle the cargo on the ship and on the quay. In interpreting the section (section 33), I would hold that any of the persons providing any of the facilities which I have mentioned and the persons engaged in such activities are persons to whom a dock must be open if it is to be open for the shipping and unshipping of goods. I can see no real distinction between the contractor who, by his vehicles, brings in the goods for shipment or removes them after discharge, the tugowner who, by his tugs, brings in or takes out vessels engaged in the shipping and unshipping of goods and the shipowner who brings his ship to the port aided or unaided by tugs. They are all performing services without which goods cannot be shipped or unshipped by vessels using the port; and the section makes no discrimination between persons. Provided they resort to the docks for the shipping and unshipping of goods they are on an equality, and the shipowner does not appear to have any greater or better right than a stevedore or a haulage contractor or, I could add, a tug owner, though the rights of all are subject to the payment of the appropriate dues which the dock authority may prescribe and subject to any regulation and control which the authority may have power, expressly or impliedly, to exercise."

The judgment however appears to acknowledge that section 33 may not entitle tugowners to keep their tugs within the docks and that a by-law made by the

---

2. *LNER* v. *British Trawlers Federation* [1934] A.C. 279.
3. *J. H. Piggot and Son* v. *Docks and Inland Waterways Executive* [1953] 1 Q.B. 338.

harbour authority prohibiting tugs from plying for hire within the docks except with the licence of the harbour master might be valid.

4.6 In the Scottish case of *Peterhead Towage Services Ltd* v. *Peterhead Bay Authority*,[4] in which a by-law prohibiting towage operations in the harbour except with the consent of the harbour master was upheld, Lord Penrose took a more restrictive view of the interpretation of section 33. He said that the section:

"prevented, for example, the imposition of restrictive conditions preventing those prepared to make payments of the appropriate rates from taking free use of the harbour facilities for the purposes of shipping and unshipping goods and the embarking and landing of passengers."

But he went on to argue that this did not include tugowners because they were not directly engaged in these activities (which was the main argument put forward by the defendants in the *Piggot* case) and that the dues they paid were not related to goods or passengers. Lord Penrose distinguished the case of *J. H. Piggot and Son* v. *Docks and Inland Waterways Executive*, emphasizing that in that case the Executive was seeking indirectly to circumvent a prohibition on the pursuit of a monopoly in the provision of towing services by their own tugs. But, although this point was referred to by Sellers, J., in his judgment in the *Piggot* case, it does not seem to be relevant to his wide interpretation of section 33. The two cases are not perhaps easy to reconcile.

4.7 In *Garland and Flaxman* v. *Wisbech Corporation*,[5] a case which did not turn primarily on the construction of section 33, it was stated, *per curiam*, that section 33 is really dealing with the question of access to the installations in the geographical area of the harbour or pier. "It means that the public can go on to those premises for the purpose of doing, and there do, the things specified in the section, that is to say, shipping or unshipping of goods and embarking and landing passengers."

4.8 It seems clears that a by-law made by a harbour authority under such enabling powers as are mentioned in Chapter 7 *post* (Harbour by-laws) cannot derogate from section 33 of the 1847 Act as incorporated in the local legislation of the harbour authority concerned (although it can regulate the relevant activities). In *Dick and Another* v. *Badart Freres*,[6] where it was held that the right of access to an Authority's docks and quays under section 33 must include not only shipowners and owners of goods but also their respective servants, a by-law made under section 83 of the Harbours, Docks and Piers Clauses Act 1847 (see Chapter 7 *post*) to exclude lumpers was held to be invalid (but the judge observed that a by-law that lumpers should only be employed subject to good conduct might be within the powers of section 83 to regulate the conduct and duties of those employed in the dock). It would seem

4. *Peterhead Towage Services Ltd* v. *Peterhead Bay Authority* 1992 S.L.T. 593.
5. *Garland and Flaxman* v. *Wisbech Corporation* [1962] 1 Q.B. 151.
6. *Dick and Another* v. *Badart Freres* (1883) 10 QB 387.

that a by-law made under such enabling powers as are mentioned above which prohibited the loading or unloading of cargo at a quay or jetty to which section 33 applied, except with the permission of the harbour authority, would be *ultra vires*.

4.9 The local legislation of a number of harbour authorities, including most major ones, includes a provision which enables the authority to derogate from section 33 of the 1847 Act as incorporated in their legislation by appropriating particular facilities for specified purposes. An example of such a provision, which is in the usual form in modern harbour legislation, is included in the Dover Harbour Revision Order 1969 and is as follows:

"(1) Notwithstanding anything in any statutory provision of local application the Board (the Dover Harbour Board) may from time to time for the purposes of or in connection with the management of the Harbour set apart and appropriate any lands, works, buildings, machinery, equipment or other property of the Board for the exclusive, partial or preferential use and accommodation of any particular trade, person, vessel or class or vessels, of goods, subject to the payment of such charges and subject to such terms, conditions and regulations as the Board may think fit.
(2) No person or vessel shall make use of any lands, works, buildings, machinery, equipment or other property so set apart or appropriated without the consent of the harbour master or other duly authorised officer of the Board . . . ".

The words "Notwithstanding anything in any statutory provision of local application" at the beginning of paragraph (1) clearly bite on section 33 of the 1847 Act as incorporated in the local legislation of the harbour authority concerned but even where, as in some cases, these words do not occur, the power to derogate from section 33 is probably implicit. (It is also presumably implicit that paragraph (2) does not apply to persons or vessels in whose favour the appropriation has been made.) It should be noted that this power of appropriation can be exercised only for the purposes of, or in connection with, the management of the harbour to which it relates.

4.10 The scope of this power of appropriation was considered in the cases of *R. v. Dover Harbour Board ex parte Peter Gilder & Sons*[7] and *R. v. Associated British Ports ex parte Plymouth City Council*.[8] In each of these cases it was held that the harbour authority concerned were obliged by section 33 to keep their port open for the export of live animals for slaughter (or for any lawful trade which was within the physical capacity of the port). It was also held that, although an appropriation under this kind of power could derogate from section 33, neither of the harbour authorities concerned could lawfully exercise this power so as to avoid their obligation to accept this traffic.

4.11 In particular, it was held that an appropriation designed to exclude a particular trade from the port was not within the scope of the power to

---

7. *R. v. Dover Harbour Board, ex parte Peter Gilder & Sons* [1995] 3 All E.R. 37.
8. *R. v. Associated British Ports, ex parte Plymouth City Council* [1995] 3 All E.R. 37.

appropriate. It was also held that an appropriation under the power in question must be construed so as to derogate as little as possible from section 33.

4.12 A question raised in the proceedings but not decided by the court was how far an appropriation under this power can reserve a general discretion to the harbour authority or their officers as to what trades can use the appropriated facilities. It would seem, however, that although such a reservation of powers might be acceptable where it is ancillary to an exclusive appropriation for a specified use which will constitute the main use of the facilities so that the reservation relates merely to any spare capacity, it would be *ultra vires* if it was designed to reserve to the harbour authority substantial control over the traffic which may use the port. An appropriation of facilities for such purposes as the harbour authority might from time to time see fit would certainly be invalid.

4.13 The court took the view that an appropriation intended to create a reserve capacity was acceptable provided that it was genuinely calculated to conduce to the efficient functioning of the harbour.

4.14 In these cases the court also considered the relationship between section 40 of the Harbours Act 1964 (see paragraphs 3.3 to 3.5 *ante*), under which a harbour authority may make the use of their services and facilities subject to whatever terms and conditions they think fit (except as to charges), and section 33 of the 1847 Act as incorporated in a harbour authority's local legislation. The court held that section 40 is subservient to section 33 and may not be invoked inconsistently with the harbour authority's overriding duty under section 33. Section 40 "cannot be used as a backdoor means of closing the harbour to those who have a right of access under section 33. That would be to exercise the section 40 discretion for a clearly improper purpose."

CHAPTER 5

THE NAVIGATIONAL SAFETY FUNCTIONS OF HARBOUR AUTHORITIES

5.1 The navigational safety functions of harbour authorities comprise dredging to maintain the navigational channels, the provision of lights, buoys and beacons to mark the channels and give warning of dangers, and the removal of wrecks and other obstructions to navigation. The purpose of these functions is to secure safe and convenient navigation in the harbour and their performance often involves surveying the bed of the harbour and the preparation of maps and charts.

Dredging

5.2 The special legislation of most harbour authorities for major harbours authorizes the authority to deepen, dredge, scour and improve the bed and foreshore of the harbour and blast any rock in the harbour. Generally, any dredged material becomes the property of the harbour authority and may be used or disposed of as the authority think fit but such material must not be deposited below the level of high water except in such position as the Secretary of State may approve and subject to such conditions or restrictions as he may impose. As indicated in Chapter 16 *post* a provision of this kind removes the need to obtain consent under section 34 of the Coast Protection Act 1949 for the authorized dredging. Where the bed and foreshore of the harbour belong to the Crown, as is generally the case, the powers of the harbour authority are subject to the rights of the Crown, and the Crown Estate Commissioners normally require some payment by the harbour authority in respect of dredged material. Dredging in harbours and coastal waters is discussed in more detail in Chapter 16 *post*.

Lighthouses etc.

5.3 The law relating to the provision and maintenance of public lighthouses, buoys and beacons is now contained in Part VIII of the Merchant Shipping Act 1995 which consolidated the lighthouse provisions of the Merchant Shipping Act 1894, sections 31 to 34 of the Ports Act 1991 and provisions of the Harbours Act 1964 relating to dues levied by local lighthouse authorities other than harbour authorities. Section 223(1) of the 1995 Act defines "buoys and beacons" as including all other marks and signs of the sea and "lighthouse" as including any floating and other light exhibited for the guidance of ships, and also any sirens and any other description of fog signals, and also any addition to a lighthouse of any improved light, or any siren, or any description of fog signal. Under section 223(2) references in Part VIII of the 1995 Act to a lighthouse, buoy or beacon include its appurtenances, and under section 223(3) the Secretary of State may by order (the draft of which must be approved by resolution of each House of Parliament) provide that references or a particular reference to a buoy or beacon in Part VIII of the 1995 Act shall be construed as including, in such circumstances as are specified in the order, equipment of a kind so specified which is intended as an aid in the navigation of ships.

5.4 Section 195(1) of the 1995 Act provides that, subject to the subsequent provisions of Part VIII of the Act and the rights of any local lighthouse authority, the general lighthouse authorities are responsible for the superintendence and management of all lighthouses, buoys and beacons within their respective areas. Under section 193(1) of the 1995 Act, Trinity House ("the master wardens and assistants of the guild, fraternity or brotherhood of the most glorious and undivided Trinity and of St. Clement in the parish of Deptford Strond in the county of Kent, commonly called the corporation of the Trinity House of Deptford Strond") are the general lighthouse authority as respects England and Wales and the adjacent seas and islands; the Commissioners of Northern Lighthouses are the general lighthouse authority as respects Scotland and the adjacent seas and islands (and the Commissioners of Irish Lights are the general lighthouse authority as respects Northern Ireland and the adjacent seas and islands).

5.5 By virtue of section 193(2)(a) of the 1995 Act as amended by the Merchant Shipping and Maritime Security Act 1997—see paragraphs 4 to 9 and 11 of Schedule 6 to the 1997 Act which clarify the references to harbour authorities in Part VIII of the 1995 Act and note that the reference in section 206(5) of that Act continues to include harbour authorities operating otherwise than under statutory powers—each statutory harbour authority (a harbour authority within the meaning of the Harbours Act 1964) is the local lighthouse authority as respects their area. Under section 193(4)(b) that area is the area or areas inside the limits within which the authority's statutory power and duties as a harbour authority are exercisable (this form of words was intended to exclude any area within which a harbour authority exercise pilotage functions only but it may be arguable whether it succeeded in doing so). Section 201 of the 1995 Act provides that every statutory harbour authority shall have power to carry out harbour operations consisting of the marking or lighting of a harbour or any part of a harbour either within their area or on harbour land. "Harbour land" and "harbour operations" have the same meanings as in the Harbours Act 1964 (see paragraph 1.19 *ante*).

5.6 Section 193(2)(b) of the 1995 Act continues to specify as local lighthouse authorities the bodies which previously were such authorities without being statutory harbour authorities. By virtue of section 193(4) the reference to such local lighthouse authorities is to those which were such authorities for the purposes of the Merchant Shipping Act 1894. Having regard to the terms of section 634 of that Act such authorities must have had continuous authority over local lights etc. since 1894. It may be arguable that, for the purpose of the power for local lighthouse authorities who are not statutory harbour authorities to levy local light dues under section 210 of the 1995 Act (which re-enacted section 29 of the Harbours Act 1964), the definition of local lighthouse authority has been narrowed. This is because the definition of that expression in section 57(1) of the 1964 Act, which referred to any person having by law or usage authority over local lighthouses, buoys or beacons, appeared to speak from time to time. However, this point may be academic.

5.7 By virtue of section 31(3) of the Ports Act 1991 (repealed by the Merchant Shipping Act 1995) every harbour authority within the meaning of the Harbours Act 1964 were to be regarded as a local lighthouse authority within the meaning of section 634 of the Merchant Shipping Act 1894. Before the relevant provisions of the Ports Act 1991 came into force most such harbour authorities were already local lighthouse authorities. However, there were some exceptions. Also, a number of lighthouses and other navigational aids within the statutory limits of such harbour authorities were owned and operated by general lighthouse authorities. Section 32 of the 1991 Act provided for the general transfer from the general lighthouse authorities to harbour authorities within the meaning of the Harbours Act 1964 of such lighthouses, buoys and beacons as were held by one of the general lighthouse authorities as:

(a) were situated in the area of any such harbour authority or on land adjacent to the area, or any part of the area, of such an authority, and

(b) appeared to the general lighthouse authority concerned to be of benefit solely or mainly to ships within, or entering or leaving, that harbour authority's area.

5.8 Section 32 of the 1991 Act provided for each of the general lighthouse authorities to submit to the Secretary of State proposals for the transfer to harbour authorities within the meaning of the Harbours Act 1964 of lighthouses, buoys and beacons as mentioned above together with related property and included provisions for consultation and for the Secretary of State to modify proposals. The general transfer from the general lighthouse authorities to statutory harbour authorities of lighthouses, buoys and beacons situated within, or on land adjacent to, the areas of such harbour authorities and of benefit solely or mainly to ships within, or entering or leaving, the respective areas of such harbour authorities took effect on 1 April 1993—the day appointed for the purpose under section 32(8) of the Ports Act 1991. As a result virtually all such lighthouses, buoys and beacons are now vested in statutory harbour authorities. (The provisions of section 32 of the 1991 Act, though already spent, were re-enacted in the Merchant Shipping Act 1995, section 202 and Schedule 9; which however have been repealed by the Merchant Shipping and Maritime Security Act 1997.)

5.9 Under section 203 of the Merchant Shipping Act 1995 a general lighthouse authority may, with the consent of the Secretary of State, transfer to a statutory harbour authority any individual lighthouse, buoy or beacon, including its appurtenances, situated in, or on land adjacent to, the area of that authority if it appears to the general lighthouse authority that the lighthouse, buoy or beacon is of benefit solely or mainly to ships within, or entering or leaving, that harbour authority's area. This is presumably intended to deal with cases of this kind where circumstances have changed since the general transfer discussed above.

5.10 Under section 204 of the Merchant Shipping Act 1995 a local lighthouse authority may, with the consent of the Secretary of State, surrender or sell by agreement, to the general lighthouse authority within whose area they are situated any lighthouse, buoy or beacon including its appurtenances but when the local lighthouse authority concerned are a statutory harbour authority the Secretary of State is precluded from giving his consent to such sale or transfer unless he considers that the maintenance of the lighthouse, buoy or beacon is in the interests of general navigation.

5.11 A general lighthouse authority have power under section 197(1) of the 1995 Act to erect or place any lighthouse, buoy or beacon but section 197(2) and (3) prohibits them from exercising that power within the area of a statutory harbour authority except in pursuance of a direction by the Secretary of State which may be given only if the Secretary of State considers it appropriate to do so in the interests of general navigation.

5.12 Section 198 of the Merchant Shipping Act 1995 requires each general lighthouse authority to inspect all lighthouses, buoys and beacons provided by local lighthouse authorities (nearly all of which are statutory harbour authorities) within their area. Section 199 of that Act gives general lighthouse authorities firm control over the activities of local lighthouse authorities. Under this section a general lighthouse authority may, with the sanction of the Secretary of State, and after giving due notice, direct a local lighthouse authority to lay down buoys, or to remove or discontinue any lighthouse, buoy or beacon, or to make any variation in the character of any lighthouse, buoy or beacon, or the mode of exhibiting lights in any lighthouse, buoy or beacon. It is the duty of any local lighthouse authority to whom such a direction is given to comply with it. Under the same section a local lighthouse authority are prohibited from taking any action in this field without the sanction of the general lighthouse authority.

5.13 Sections 77 and 78 of the Harbours, Docks and Piers Clauses Act

1847, which are still incorporated with the special legislation of some harbour authorities (although the latter is never incorporated with modern legislation), contain provisions which overlap those of section 199 of the Merchant Shipping Act 1995. Section 77 requires the harbour authority to lay down such buoys for the guidance of vessels as they are directed to do by Trinity House (in England and Wales) or by the Commissioners of Northern Lighthouses (in Scotland). It differs from the corresponding provision of section 199 of the Merchant Shipping Act 1995 in that Trinity House or the Commissioners of Northern Lighthouses, as the case may be, do not have to obtain the sanction of the Secretary of State before giving a direction. Section 78, which, as mentioned above, is not in practice incorporated in modern legislation, prohibits the harbour authority from erecting any lighthouse or beacons, or exhibiting or permitting the exhibition of, any light, beacon or sea mark without the sanction in writing of Trinity House (in England and Wales) or the Commissioners of Northern Lighthouses (in Scotland). It appears to overlap the corresponding provisions of section 199 of the Merchant Shipping Act 1995 almost completely.

Powers to remove wrecks etc.

5.14 Nearly all harbour authorities have dual, and to some extent overlapping, powers to remove wrecks. Section 252 of the Merchant Shipping Act 1995 confer powers for this purpose on all harbour authorities. This section is set out in Part I of Appendix F but the special legislation of most harbour authorities extends and supplements its application. An example of this is section 46 of the Medway Ports Authority Act 1973 which is set out in Part II of Appendix F. Furthermore, the special legislation of nearly all harbour authorities contains a provision for the protection of Crown interests in wrecks on the lines of section 47 of the Medway Ports Authority Act 1973 which is set out in Part II of Appendix F (under section 308 of the Merchant Shipping Act 1995 that Act does not, except where specially provided, apply to Her Majesty's ships).

5.15 In addition to these wreck raising powers under the Merchant Shipping Act 1995 the special legislation of nearly all harbour authorities either incorporates section 56 of the Harbours, Docks and Piers Clauses Act 1847, which empowers the harbour authority's harbour master to remove wrecks or other obstructions which impede navigation, or includes powers to the same effect. Section 56 of the Harbours, Docks and Piers Clauses Act 1847 is set out in Part III of Appendix F. The special legislation of a few harbour authorities contains provisions in a rather different form from those referred to above. In particular, the special legislation of the Port of London Authority does not build on section 252 of the Merchant Shipping Act 1995 but contains wreck removal powers—sections 121 and 122 of the Port of London Act 1968 which are set out in Part IV of Appendix F—which combine most of the features of section 56 of the Harbours, Docks and Piers Clauses Act 1847 and section 252 of the Merchant Shipping Act 1995 as commonly modified.

5.16 The logic of the dual wreck raising powers of most harbour authorities appears to be that where the removal of a wreck is urgently necessary the harbour master can take action on his own initiative under section 56 of the Harbours, Docks and Piers Clauses Act 1847 (which extends to other obstructions and "any floating timber which impedes the navigation" as well as wrecks) but that where action is not urgently necessary, and particularly where there may be some doubt whether a wreck does impede navigation, it is more appropriate for the harbour authority to proceed under section 252 of the Merchant Shipping Act 1995. It seems that before taking action under that section, the harbour authority must themselves form an opinion that a vessel sunk, stranded or abandoned in their harbour or in or near any approach thereto, is, or is likely to become, an obstruction or danger to navigation.

5.17 Section 252 of the Merchant Shipping Act 1995, although, unlike section 56 of the Harbours, Docks and Piers Clauses Act, limited to wrecks, is wider in that it authorizes the harbour authority, in terms, not merely to remove, but to destroy, the vessel (in *The Crystal*,[1] Lord MacNaughton expressed doubt whether the power to "remove" contained in section 56 included power to destroy) and also to light or buoy a wreck pending its raising, removal or destruction.

5.18 There is also an important difference between the two sections in that section 56 of the Harbours, Docks and Piers Clauses Act 1847 imposes a liability on the owner of the wreck or other obstruction to repay the cost of removal whereas section 252 of the Act of 1995 only contains a power of sale. However, the standard supplement to the latter section exemplified by section 46 of the Medway Ports Authority Act 1973 enables the harbour authority to recover from the owner of the wreck any expenses reasonably incurred by the harbour authority under section 252 of the Merchant Shipping Act 1995 which are not reimbursed out of the proceeds of the sale (if any).

5.19 In the case of *The Crystal* referred to above it was held that, although section 56 of the Harbours, Docks and Piers Clauses Act 1847 makes the owners of the wreck personally liable for the expenses of removal (even in the absence of negligence), the owners of the ship at the time when she becomes an obstruction will not be so liable if they abandon her before the harbour authority incur expense because "owner" in section 56 means the person who was the owner at the time when expenses were incurred by the harbour authority. The standard provision supplementing section 252 of the Merchant Shipping Act 1995, in relation to particular harbour authorities, removes this possible difficulty so far as that section is concerned by defining "owner" as the person who was the owner of the vessel at the time of her sinking, stranding or abandonment.

1. *The Crystal* [1894] A.C. 508.

5.20 In the case of *Dee Conservancy Board* v. *McConnell*[2] it was held that where a ship becomes a wreck through the negligence of her owners or their servants the owners are liable at common law for the reasonable cost of removing the obstruction (the common law liability not being displaced by the harbour authority's statutory remedies) and cannot therefore escape liability by abandoning the wreck before the harbour authority incur expenditure.

Conservancy duties of harbour authorities

5.21 The duties of a harbour authority in the conservancy field have been considered in several cases. In *St. Just Steam Ship Co. Ltd.* v. *Hartlepool Port and Harbour Commissioners*,[3] the issue was whether the Commissioners were liable for damage caused to a ship by a submerged wreck which the Commissioners thought had been dispersed but the continued existence, and position, of which (the judge found) they should have been aware of. In that case Mr Justice Wright (as he then was) said:

In those circumstances the law is now well established. The liability of the Commissioners in such a case does not directly depend upon the terms of the private Act. It depends on the special relations arising *de novo* as each ship enters the jurisdiction of the port, and it is a duty which has been very clearly expressed in a number of cases which is said to be analogous to the ordinary common law duty existing as between invitor and invitee; and it has been clearly expressed in the well known case of the *Mersey Docks and Harbour Board Trustees* v. *Gibbs*.[4]

5.22 In *Mersey Docks and Harbour Board Trustees* v. *Gibbs*,[5] which arose out of damage caused to a vessel entering one of the Mersey Board's docks by a bank of mud which had been allowed to accumulate there, Lord Westbury said:

Where such a body is constituted by statute, having the right to levy tolls for its own profit, in consideration of making and maintaining a dock or canal, there is no doubt of the liability to make good to the persons using it any damage occasioned by neglect in not keeping the works in proper repair:

and later:

The common law in such a case imposes a duty upon the proprietors to take reasonable care, so long as they keep it open for the public use of all who may choose to navigate it, that they may do so without danger to their lives or property.

5.23 In *The Neptun (Owners)* v. *Humber Conservancy Board*,[6] which arose from a ship stranding in the River Humber and subsequently becoming a total

2. *Dee Conservancy Board* v. *McConnell* [1928] 2 K.B. 159.
3. *St. Just Steam Ship Co. Ltd.* v. *Hartlepool Port and Harbour Commissioners* (1929) 34 Ll.L. Rep. 344.
4. *Mersey Docks and Harbour Board Trustees* v. *Gibbs* (1866) L.R. 1 H.L. 93.
5. (1866) L.R. 1 H.L. 93.
6. *The Neptun (Owners)* v. *Humber Conservancy Board* (1937) 59 Ll.L. Rep. 158; 54 T.L.R. 195.

loss, Langton, J., endorsed the statements of the law in *Mersey Docks and Harbour Board Trustees* v. *Gibbs*[7] and *St. Just Steam Ship Co. Ltd.* v. *Hartlepool Port and Harbour Commissioners.*[8] He held that the duty of a buoyage and beaconage authority was analogous to that existing between invitor and invitee, and was to take reasonable care, so long as the authority kept the navigable highway open for the public use of all who chose to navigate it, that they might do so without danger to their lives or property. He observed in the course of his judgment that this duty

cannot be stated exactly as being a relation of invitor or invitee, since it is difficult to imagine the Board extending to the public an invitation to use the highway which *ex concessi* is already their legal right. Nevertheless, . . . the common law duty is the same as that owed by an invitor to an invitee, and it is not necessary to invent any particular single term to indicate the relationship between a public custodian and an individual who pays for the use and the work performed by such a custodian.

5.24 In the course of his judgment in *The Neptun* case,[9] Mr Justice Langton (with whom two Elder Brethren of Trinity House had sat as nautical assessors) made some interesting comments on the more detailed conservancy obligations of a harbour authority (it appears from his judgment that, having regard to the nature of the bed of the River Humber, the question of dredging did not arise). He said:

It remains, perhaps, to outline briefly the scope of the obligations of a buoyage and beaconage authority. For this purpose I have relied upon the services of the Elder Brethren. Neither they nor myself would wish this short schedule of duties to be considered as necessarily exhaustive, but in the complete absence of any assistance in this matter such as I should have expected to have received from the Humber Conservancy Board it has become necessary to lay down what I conceive to be a minimum of their obligations. A fair and useful method of approach to this subject seemed to me to be to ask my advisers what they, as experienced shipmasters entering the Humber without knowledge of its channels, would expect at the hands of the buoyage and beaconage authority appointed to lay down the marks for the navigation of the river. Speaking as shipmasters, and incidentally also as persons with no small knowledge of the special work connected with buoyage and beaconage, they tell me that they would expect as follows:—

(1) That the authority should have sounded and found the best navigable channel in the river.

(2) That having found it the authority should have placed sea marks of the nature of light-vessels, floats or buoys in the positions where they would be of the best advantage to navigation.

(3) That by night such sea marks should be provided with adequate lights to enable the channel to be easily found and properly kept by a vessel using it.

(4) That the authority had re-sounded the channel as and when opportunity presented itself.

7. (1866) L.R. 1 H.L. 93.
8. (1929) 34 Ll.L. Rep. 344.
9. *Ante*, fn. 6.

(5) In view of the quickly shifting character of the river bed, that the authority had kept a vigilant watch upon the changes in the river bed and had altered, moved or renewed the sea marks in accordance with the changes ascertained.

(6) That records of the changes both in sounding and in movement of the marks should have been preserved for future reference and for the guidance of subsequent officials.

(7) That the authority should publish as conspicuously as possible such further information as would supplement the guidance given by sea marks.

For my part I accept unhesitatingly this comparatively short list of expectations as a fair statement of the minimum duties of a buoyage and beaconage authority upon a great and busy highway such as the Humber, and if one adds, upon the authority which I have quoted, that the Board should exercise reasonable care in the performance of all these duties I am of opinion that the legal position of the Humber Conservancy Board *vis-à-vis* the plaintiffs is defined with sufficient accuracy for present purposes.

5.25 In *The Tramontana II*[10] it was held that the defendants (the Ministry of Defence in respect of a Dockyard Port) having, in the exercise of their statutory powers, assumed responsibility for marking a wreck, owed a duty to all persons lawfully using the port to carry out that marking with reasonable skill and care.

5.26 The cases referred to in paragraphs 5.21 to 5.25 *ante* were decided before it became the practice to include in the special legislation of harbour authorities a statement of their general powers and duties. As indicated in paragraphs 3.6 and 3.7 *ante* such a provision, in relation to a harbour authority's conservancy functions, usually takes the form of an express duty to take such action as the harbour authority consider necessary or desirable for or incidental to the maintenance, operation, improvement and conservancy of their harbour.

5.27 Such a provision has not yet been judicially considered but it seems unlikely that the courts will hold that it abrogates, or overrides, a harbour authority's duty at common law to take reasonable care that those who lawfully use their harbour may do so in safety. The discretion conferred by such a statutory duty must be exercised reasonably and in good faith for the purpose for which it was conferred. On this basis a harbour authority would be bound to consider necessary any action which was required to satisfy their duty at common law.

---

10. *The Tramontana II* [1969] 2 Lloyd's Rep. 94.

CHAPTER 6

HARBOUR AUTHORITIES' POWERS TO REGULATE ACTIVITIES OF OTHER PERSONS AT HARBOURS AND CERTAIN OTHER REGULATORY PROVISIONS AFFECTING HARBOURS

6.1 An essential characteristic of the harbour authority for a significant harbour is their powers to regulate the activities of other persons there. For many harbour authorities their most important powers for this purpose are conferred by their by-laws. Harbour by-laws are discussed in the next chapter. The powers of a harbour authority to control shipping in the harbour are of particular importance. Certain powers for this purpose are vested directly in the harbour master since it is often necessary for him to take action at short notice and on his own initiative.

Section 52 of the Harbours, Docks and Piers Clauses Act 1847

6.2 Section 52 of the Harbours, Docks and Piers Clauses Act 1847, although (as indicated below) to some extent superseded, is still incorporated with the special legislation of most harbour authorities. It authorizes the harbour master to give directions—

For regulating the time at which and the manner in which any vessel shall enter into, go out of, or lie in or at the harbour, dock, or pier, and within the prescribed limits, if any, and its position, mooring or unmooring, placing and removing, whilst therein;

For regulating the position in which any vessel shall take in or discharge its cargo or any part thereof, or shall take in or land its passengers, or shall take in or deliver ballast within or on the harbour, dock or pier;

For regulating the manner in which any vessel entering the harbour or dock or coming to the pier shall be dismantled, as well for the safety of such vessel as for preventing injury to other vessels, and to the harbour, dock or pier, and the moorings thereof;

For removing unserviceable vessels and other obstructions from the harbour, dock or pier, and keeping the same clear;

For regulating the quantity of ballast or dead weight in the hold which each vessel in or at the harbour, dock or pier shall have during the delivery of her cargo, or after having discharged the same.

6.3 "The Harbour Master" is defined in section 2 of the Harbours, Docks and Piers Clauses Act 1847 so as to include, in addition to the harbour master himself, his assistants. The special legislation of most harbour authorities commonly defines the expression as including also any person authorized by the harbour authority to act in the capacity of harbour master.

6.4 Section 53 of the Harbours, Docks and Piers Clauses Act 1847 provides that—

The master of every vessel within the harbour or dock, or at or near the pier, or within the prescribed limits, if any, shall regulate such vessel according to the directions of the harbour master, made in conformity with this and the special Act; and any master of a vessel who, after notice of any such direction by the harbour master served upon him, shall not forthwith regulate such vessel according to such direction shall be liable to a penalty not exceeding twenty pounds.

This maximum penalty was increased to £50 by the Criminal Law Act 1977 and, by virtue of the Criminal Justice Act 1982, is now level 2 on the standard scale of fines introduced by that Act. The maximum penalty at a particular harbour may, however, depend on the terms of the local Act or order which incorporates section 53.

6.5 It was held in *The Excelsior*[1] that the master of a ship moored in a harbour, when directed by the harbour master to move her to a different berth, was required to comply with that direction even although, if that ship alone were to be considered, it would be injudicious to move the ship, it being the duty of the harbour master to consider the interests of all the shipping in the harbour.

6.6 The scope of section 52 of the Harbours, Docks and Piers Clauses Act 1847 was considered in the case of *The Guelder Rose*.[2] That case related to a direction at the harbour of Fowey that between the hours of sunrise and sunset certain vessels should proceed up the harbour at a pace not exceeding three miles an hour; that between sunset and sunrise they should anchor in a particular place specified by reference to a chart; that they should not at any time proceed above a specified point without the sanction of the harbour master; and that they should not at any time be moved within the limits of the harbour without notifying the harbour master, unless in either case they had a qualified pilot on board.

6.7 This direction was held to be *ultra vires* section 52. In relation to it Lord Justice Atkin said:

That does not appear to me to be in the least a matter for which jurisdiction was given to the harbour master. Speaking generally, it appears to me that the object of section 52 is fairly obvious. The harbour master is the person who controls the movements of the particular vessels when they are within the port on the occasion when they are within the port; and generally speaking, I have not the least doubt at all that his powers are given to him for the purpose of giving specific directions to specific ships for specific movements. Those are powers that must be exercised in the circumstances sometimes at once, or on an emergency in respect of which the procedure as to

1. *The Excelsior* (1868) L.R. 2 A. & E. 268.
2. *The Guelder Rose* (1927) 136 L.T. 226.

by-laws would be quite unreasonable and useless. The harbour master and his assistants are given equal powers. I am far from saying that there might not be good occasions on which the harbour master might give a direction which is to operate for more than the event of the particular voyage. For instance, Mr Nesbitt made the suggestion of a case where there was an obstruction in the harbour, which it was not contemplated would remain permanently within the harbour, and in respect of which I think it is very probable that the harbour master might give a general direction that as long as the obstruction remained vessels were to leave it either on the starboard or on the port side, or were to approach it in a particular way and at a particular tide. That seems to me to be something quite different from the general directions which were given in this case.

6.8 The decision in *The Guelder Rose* case was applied in the case of *Pearn v. Sargent*[3] where it was held that a direction at Looe Harbour that during specified hours (when a regatta would be in progress not in the whole harbour but in the 800 yards nearest the sea) no vessel should move within the harbour except with the express permission of the harbour master was *ultra vires* section 52. In the course of his judgment Lord Widgery, C.J., said:

The function of the harbour master under section 52 is to regulate the traffic; after all it is a public harbour where the public have a right to be there, and it is not the harbour master's function, as such, to keep them out. His function is to control and regulate them rather like a traffic policeman regulating traffic. Of course there will be cases when he has to go beyond these simple functions; of course there may be cases where necessity arises and he has to impose wider prohibitions for a particular time, but when that happens it is for consideration whether the directions he has given are reasonable for the emergency or circumstances which prompted them.

6.9 Following the case of *The Guelder Rose*,[4] section 52 of the Harbours, Docks and Piers Clauses Act 1847 as incorporated with the special legislation of particular harbour authorities is frequently modified by a declaration that the section, as incorporated:

(a) shall extend to empower the harbour master to give directions prohibiting the mooring of vessels in any particular part or parts of the harbour; and

(b) shall not be construed to require the harbour master in emergency to give particular directions in the case of every vessel in respect of which it is desired to exercise any of the powers of that section, but in pursuance of that section for all or any of the purposes thereof the harbour master shall be entitled in emergency to give general directions applicable to all vessels or to particular classes of vessels.

6.10 The wide powers of a harbour master under section 52 of the 1847 Act and similar provisions in local harbour legislation to regulate the position of ships within his harbour in the interests of safety may not be without qualification (leaving aside the powers of the the Secretary of State to give directions

---

3. *Pearn v. Sargent* [1973] 2 Lloyd's Rep. 141.
4. (1927) 136 L.T. 226.

to a harbour master under the Dangerous Vessels Act 1985 and section 137 of the Merchant Shipping Act 1995 (paragraphs 6.23 and 9.25 *post*). In the recent Scottish case of *Ullapool Harbour Trustees v. Secretary of State for Transport*,[5] it was held that an officer of the Marine Safety Agency, in exercising his power under section 30A of the Merchant Shipping Act 1988 as inserted by the Merchant Shipping (Registration etc.) Act 1993 (now section 95 of the Merchant Shipping Act 1995) to detain an unsafe ship as defined in that section and prohibit it from "going to sea" was entitled to prohibit the ship from proceeding seaward of a line within the statutory limits of a harbour determined by the officer having regard to the Merchant Shipping (Categorisation of Waters) Regulations 1992 (the waters downstream from the line concerned being "sea" within the meaning of those regulations) and that the harbour master was not entitled under section 52 to direct the ship to move to a position within the harbour seaward of the line concerned even although in his opinion (contrary to that of the officer of the Marine Safety Agency) this would be in the interests of safety. As stated by Lord Milligan in his judgment, both parties in this case accepted that there was a lacuna in the relevant legislation, in particular section 30A of the 1988 Act (now section 95 of the Merchant Shipping Act 1995) did not define "sea", which should be clarified by legislation.

6.11 Section 95(3) of the 1995 Act has been amended by section 9 of, and paragraph 2(4) of Schedule 1 to, the Merchant Shipping and Maritime Security Act 1997 to the effect that a detention notice under section 95, instead of simply prohibiting the ship from going to sea, requires it to comply with the terms of the detention notice. This appears to dispose of the question mentioned in the preceding paragraph.

General and special directions to vessels

6.12 Although the harbour master's powers under section 52 of the Harbours, Docks and Piers Clauses Act 1847 have proved effective there seemed to be a case for harbour authorities for major harbours to have somewhat wider powers—powers which would, in particular, enable the harbour authority to lay down general and long term rules to regulate the movement etc. of ships by a simpler and more flexible method than the by-law procedure.

6.13 Most harbour authorities for major harbours and several others have now obtained, by means of private Act of Parliament or harbour revision order, wider and up-to-date powers to regulate the movement and berthing of ships. An example of such powers are those contained in sections 20 and 21 of the Medway Ports Authority Act 1973 which are set out in Appendix G. These sections are in the form which has been adopted, with slight variations, by all the harbour authorities which have obtained such powers. Section 20 enables

5. *Ullapool Harbour Trustees v. Secretary of State for Transport* (1995) G.W.D. 11–627; The Times 13 April 1995 (OH).

the harbour authority to lay down general rules for the regulation of vessels navigating in the harbour. Rules for this purpose could also be included in by-laws but in modern conditions the by-law procedure may take too long in relation to such matters as the designation of routes and channels. Section 21 empowers the harbour master to enforce these rules and generally to direct the movement, etc., of individual ships (his powers in this respect being similar to those under section 52 of the Harbours, Docks and Piers Clauses Act but in rather more flexible terms). Sections 23 to 27, also set out in Appendix G, contain the related procedural and enforcement provisions.

6.14 Some harbour authorities have also obtained general powers to regulate vessels at docks and section 22 of the Medway Ports Authority Act 1973, also included in Appendix G, is an example in the usual form. This again is a more flexible and convenient alternative to by-laws.

6.15 Under powers of the kind referred to in paragraph 146 the harbour authority are normally required to consult the General Council of British Shipping before giving, or before revoking or amending, a general direction relating to the navigation of vessels in the harbour. The Port of London Authority are required to obtain the actual agreement of this body before giving, revoking or amending such a direction.

6.16 It appears from the case of *Pearn* v. *Sargent* referred to in paragraph 6.8 *ante* that the harbour master's power to regulate the movement, etc., of vessels under section 52 of the Harbours, Docks and Piers Clauses Act 1847 does not include power to prohibit a ship from entering harbour although the power to regulate the time of entry no doubt enables a harbour master, where appropriate, to postpone entry for a considerable period. The principle appears to be that a power to regulate does not include power to prohibit. With regard to provisions of the kind referred to in paragraph 6.13 *ante*, in some cases these include power for the harbour authority to give a direction for prohibiting entry into the harbour of a vessel which for any reason would be, or be likely to become, a danger to other vessels in the harbour. Section 20(1)(c)(ii) of the Medway Ports Authority Act 1973 is an example of this. It is in the usual form for such a provision and, under section 20(2)(a), may apply to all vessels or to a class of vessels designated, or the designation of which is provided for, in the direction. It is not therefore a very flexible provision and it is believed that few, if any, directions have been given under provisions of this kind.

Dangerous Vessels Act 1985

6.17 It was considered that given the highly dangerous nature of some modern cargos, and the catastrophe which could result if, say, a ship with defective steering collided with a gas carrier, there ought to be a clear power for a harbour master to prohibit a ship from entering, or to require a ship to leave, a harbour where, in his opinion, this was necessary to avoid the danger of a serious accident. This was the genesis of the Dangerous Vessels Act 1985.

6.18 Section 1 of the Dangerous Vessels Act enables a harbour master to give directions prohibiting the entry into, or requiring the removal from, the harbour of any vessel if, in his opinion, the condition of that vessel, or the nature or condition of anything it contains, is such that its presence in the harbour might involve:

(a) grave and imminent danger to the safety of any person or property; or

(b) grave and imminent risk that the vessel may, by sinking or foundering in the harbour, prevent or seriously prejudice the use of the harbour by other vessels.

6.19 The purpose of the Act is to enable the harbour master to take action to avoid a catastrophic accident. It does not give him *carte blanche* to exclude ships from harbour. It does not entitle a harbour master to exclude a ship simply because, in his view, oil from the ship may pollute the harbour—although, if he has reason to believe that a ship which proposes to enter the harbour does not comply with the requirements of the Merchant Shipping (Prevention of Oil Pollution) Regulations 1996, he may, and indeed must, under regulation 35 of those regulations, report the matter to the Secretary of State, who may deny the ship entry to port if he is satisfied that it presents an unreasonable threat of harm to the marine environment (see paragraph 9.19 *post*).

6.20 Directions by a harbour master under section 1 of the Dangerous Vessels Act may be given:

(a) to the owner of the vessel or to any person in possession of the vessel;

(b) to the master of the vessel (no doubt the usual case); or

(c) to any salvor in possession of the vessel, or to any person who is the servant or agent of any salvor in possession of the vessel and who is in charge of the salvage operation.

Such directions may be given in any reasonable manner as the harbour master thinks fit and, at the time when he gives directions to any person, the harbour master must inform that person of the grounds for giving them.

6.21 In deciding whether to give directions under section 1 in any particular case, a harbour master must have regard to all the circumstances of that case and, in particular, to the safety of any person or vessel, whether in or outside the harbour, and including the vessel which would be the subject of his directions.

6.22 Section 2 of the Dangerous Vessels Act makes clear that the right of a harbour authority under section 191 of the Merchant Shipping Act 1995 to limit their liability for loss or damage to vessels and goods, etc., on board a vessel (see paragraph 3.20 *ante*) extends to liability for any loss or damage occurring outside the harbour in consequence of directions given by a harbour master in purported exercise of his powers under section 1 of the Act.

6.23 Section 3 of the Dangerous Vessels Act contains a power for the Secretary of State to override action taken by a harbour master under section 1. Where a harbour master has given directions under section 1 as respects any vessel, the Secretary of State may, for the purpose of securing the safety of any person or vessel (including the vessel to which the harbour master's directions relate), give directions to the harbour master requiring him to permit the vessel in question to enter and remain, or (as the case may be) to remain, in the harbour, and to take any action which he may specify in the directions for the purpose of enabling the vessel to do so or for any connected purpose.

6.24 If the Secretary of State gives directions under section 3 to a harbour master, the latter's directions under section 1 cease to have effect. A harbour master to whom directions are given under section 3 must give notice of those directions to the person to whom his directions under section 1 were given or, failing that, to any of the other persons to whom those directions might have been given, in such reasonable manner as he may think fit. It is the duty of the harbour master to take any action in relation to the vessel in question specified in the Secretary of State's directions, and of the harbour master and the harbour authority to take all such further action as may be reasonably necessary to enable the vessel to enter and remain, or to remain, in the harbour.

6.25 Section 5 of the Dangerous Vessels Act provides that a person who, without reasonable excuse, contravenes or fails to comply with any directions under section 1 shall be guilty of an offence and shall be liable on summary conviction to a fine not exceeding £25,000 and, on conviction on indictment, to a fine.

6.26 These penalties are very much higher than those which may be incurred for failing to comply with directions by a harbour master under section 52 of the Harbours, Docks and Piers Clauses Act 1847 or under any provision of a local harbour Act or order. It is a defence for a person charged under section 5 to show that he took all reasonable precautions and exercised all due diligence to avoid the commission of the offence.

6.27 By virtue of section 6 of the Dangerous Vessels Act, directions under section 1 cannot be given in relation to:

(a) any vessel belonging to Her Majesty or employed in the service of the Crown for any purpose, including any such vessel in the possession of a salvor; or

(b) any vessel which is a pleasure boat of 24 metres or less in length.

6.28 Powers for a harbour master (*inter alia*) to prohibit the entry into a harbour in certain circumstances, and to regulate the movements, of a vessel carrying a dangerous substance are contained in the Dangerous Substances in Harbour Areas Regulations 1987 which are discussed in Chapter 8 *post*.

Power to remove unfit vessels from harbour

6.29 Under section 57 of the Harbours, Docks and Piers Clauses Act 1847 a harbour master may cause a vessel which has been "laid by or neglected as unfit for sea service" to be removed from the harbour at the expense of the owner of the vessel and "laid on any part of the strand or sea shore, or other place where the same may, without injury to any person, be placed". It was held in a Scottish case, the *Trustees of the Harbours of Peterhead* v. *Thomas Chalmers (The Clupea*[6]*)* that in disposing of a vessel after removing her from the harbour under the terms of section 57 the harbour master was not entitled to destroy her (which seems consistent with *The Crystal* referred to in paragraph 5.17 *ante* although that case was not cited) and that after the harbour master had removed the vessel from the harbour and laid her on the shore the control and possession of the vessel reverted to the owner.

The Merchant Shipping (Reporting Requirements for Ships Carrying Dangerous or Polluting Goods) Regulations 1995

6.30 These Regulations implement (*inter alia*) Council Directive 93/75/EEC concerning minimum requirements for vessels bound for or leaving Community ports and carrying dangerous or polluting goods. They also include provisions for the safety of ships under sections 21 and 22 of the Merchant Shipping Act 1979 (now replaced by sections 85 and 86 of the Merchant Shipping Act 1995). They apply to United Kingdom ships, as defined in regulation 2(2), wherever they may be and to other ships while they are within the United Kingdom or United Kingdom territorial waters. Regulations 9 to 11, which deal with the reporting of incidents, also apply, in the circumstances mentioned in paragraph 6.33 *post*, to a ship which is not a United Kingdom ship and is outside the United Kingdom or its territorial waters.

    6.31 Regulations 5 and 6 contain provisions requiring the owner, manager, charterer or agent of a ship carrying dangerous or polluting goods to give specified information to the competent authority for the state in which a port which the ship is leaving is situated (ferries on short sea voyages may be exempted from this requirement) and, where the ship is departing from a port outside the European Community and bound for a community port, to furnish such information to the competent authority for the member State where the latter port is situated. Regulation 4 designates the Coastguard Agency of the Department of Transport as the competent authority for the United Kingdom.

---

    6. *Trustees of the Harbours of Peterhead* v. *Thomas Chalmers (The Clupea)*, Ct. of Sess., 20 January 1982.

6.32 Regulation 7 requires the master of a ship entering or leaving a port in the United Kingdom to make use of any Vessel Traffic Services provided in that port. It is not limited to ships carrying dangerous or polluting goods and nor, it appears, are the subsequent provisions of the Regulations referred to below.

6.33 Regulations 9 to 11 contain detailed provisions about the reporting of incidents. In particular, in relation to the subject-matter of this book, the master of a ship, whether or not a United Kingdom ship and wherever situated, which is involved in an incident or circumstances at sea involving a threat of damage to the coastline or related interests of the United Kingdom, must report the particulars of the incident without delay and to the fullest possible extent, by means of the fastest telecommunications channels available and with the highest possible priority, to a maritime rescue centre of the Coastguard Agency.

6.34 Regulation 12 provides that the master of a ship before navigating in a port in the United Kingdom must complete a check list giving details of the ship, its equipment, crew and survey certificates. The master must make the completed check list available to any pilot boarding the ship to pilot it within the port and, if it so requests, to the competent authority (the Coastguard Agency) and to any other person (such as the port authority) specified by that authority. (The regulation imposes a similar duty on the master of a United Kingdom ship before navigating in a port in another member State of the European Union.)

6.35 Under regulation 13, if a pilot engaged in berthing, unberthing or manœuvring a ship in United Kingdom waters learns that there are deficiencies in the ship which may prejudice its safe navigation he must immediately inform the port authority (the harbour authority within the meaning of the Harbours Act 1964 or if there is no such authority the person having control of the operation of the port) who must immediately inform the Coastguard Agency.

6.36 Regulation 14(1) provides that if any pilot boards a ship to which the Regulations apply in order to pilot it into or out of a port, and knows or believes that there are defects which may prejudice the safe navigation of the ship which have not been notified to the port authority in accordance with regulation 12 or 13 referred to above, he shall notify the master of the defects. If the pilot knows or believes that the master, after having been notified, has failed to notify the port authority of the defects in question, the pilot must himself forthwith notify the port authority of the defects. Regulation 14(2) requires a pilot, to whom the master of a ship to which the Regulations apply has failed to make a checklist available in accordance with regulation 12 referred to above, forthwith to notify the port authority. (Regulation 14 appears to apply to United Kingdom ships in the ports of other member States of the Community as well as to ships in United Kingdom ports.)

6.37 Regulation 15 provides for failure to comply with requirements of the Regulations, or the deliberate making of false statements in purported compliance, to be offences and prescribes the maximum penalties on conviction.

The Collision Regulations

6.38 Under sections 85 and 86 of the Merchant Shipping Act 1995 the Secretary of State has powers to make regulations with regard (*inter alia*) to the prevention of collisions at sea.

6.39 The Merchant Shipping (Distress Signals and Prevention of Collisions) Regulations 1996, made under the enabling powers referred to above, give effect in relation to United Kingdom vessels and other vessels while they are within the United Kingdom or the territorial   waters of the United Kingdom to the current International Regulations for Preventing Collisions at Sea. These regulations apply to all vessels upon the high seas and in all waters connected therewith navigable by sea-going vessels. They therefore generally apply in harbours but not to land-locked artificial channels such as the Manchester Ship Canal: *The Hare*.[7] Rule 1(*b*) of the International Regulations states that:

"nothing in these Rules shall interfere with the operation of special rules made by an appropriate authority for roadsteads, harbours, rivers, lakes or inland waterways connected with the high seas and navigable by sea-going ships. Such special rules shall conform as closely as possible to these Rules".

It therefore appears that a by-law made by a harbour authority, if inconsistent with the Collision Regulations, will prevail but that strong reasons are necessary to justify the making of such a by-law. It was held in the case of *The Carlotta*[8] that a harbour by-law which deals with the same subject-matter as a provision of the Collision Regulations will exclude the application of that provision.

6.40 The Collision Regulations comprise steering and sailing rules, rules prescribing the lights and shapes which vessels are to exhibit in various circumstances, and rules for sound and light signals including distress signals. Regulation 6(1) of the Merchant Shipping (Distress Signals and Prevention of Collisions) Regulations 1996 provides that where any of the Collision Regulations is contravened, the owner of the vessel, the master and any person for the time being responsible for the conduct of the vessel is guilty of an offence punishable as provided in the regulation. Under regulation 6(2) it is, however,

---

7. *The Hare* [1904] P. 331.
8. *The Carlotta* [1899] P. 223.

a defence for any person charged under the regulations to show that he took all reasonable precautions to avoid the commission of the offence.[9]

Some Provisions of Part 1 of the Merchant Shipping (Port State Control) Regulations 1995

6.41 Part 1 of the above regulations applies to a sea-going ship which is not a British ship (as defined in section 1(1) of the Merchant Shipping Act 1995) calling at, or anchored off, a United Kingdom port or offshore installation. It does not apply to fishing vessels, ships of war, naval auxiliaries, wooden ships of a primitive build, government ships used for non-commercial purposes or pleasure yachts not engaged in trade.

6.42 Regulation 13(5) of the above regulations prohibits ships to which the paragraph applies from entering United Kingdom ports except, in certain circumstances, with the permission of the Secretary of State. The paragraph applies to a ship to which Part 1 applies, detained in a port in a member State of the European Community, after inspection has revealed deficiencies which are clearly hazardous to safety, health or the environment and which has been allowed by the competent authority for the State concerned to proceed to the nearest repair yard; but the ship has proceeded to sea without complying with the conditions determined by the competent authority of the member State in the port of inspection or failed to comply with the applicable requirements of the relevant Conventions by not calling into the indicated repair yard. The prohibition against entering United Kingdom ports is lifted if the owner of the ship provides evidence to the satisfaction of the competent authority of the member State where the ship was found defective that the ship fully complies with all applicable requirements of the relevant Conventions. Under regulation 18(2)(b), where a ship enters a port in contravention of regulation 13(5), the owner and master are each guilty of an offence and liable on summary conviction to a fine not exceeding the statutory maximum, or on conviction on indictment to imprisonment not exceeding two years, or a fine or both.

6.43 Under regulation 15(3) of the above regulations if a port authority (a harbour authority as defined in the Harbours Act 1964) when exercising their normal duties learn that a ship within their port to which Part 1 applies has deficiencies which may prejudice the safety of the ship or pose an unreasonable threat of harm to the marine environment, the authority must immediately inform the Marine Safety Agency.

6.44 Under regulation 15(1) a pilot, authorized pursuant to the Pilotage Act 1987 (see paragraphs 20.31 *et seq.*, *post*) and engaged in the berthing or unberthing of a ship to which Part 1 applies in the United Kingdom or

---

9. For a detailed description of, and commentary on, the Collision Regulations, reference may be made to *The Collision Regulations*, R.H.B. Sturt, 3rd ed., Lloyd's of London Press Ltd., 1991.

engaged on such a ship bound for a port within a member State of the European Community, who learns in the course of his normal duties that there are deficiencies which may prejudice the safe navigation of the ship or which may pose a threat of harm to the marine environment, must immediately inform the port authority who authorized him who, in turn, must immediately inform the Coastguard Agency for onward transmission to the Marine Safety Agency. In similar circumstances a pilot, other than one authorized under the Pilotage Act 1987, must immediately inform the Coastguard Agency for onward transmission to the Marine Safety Agency or the competent authority for another Member State.

6.45 A port authority or pilot failing to comply with regulation 15(1) or (3) is guilty of an offence and liable on summary conviction to a fine not exceeding level 3 on the standard scale.

Temporary exclusion zones

6.46 Sections 100A and B of the Merchant Shipping Act 1995, inserted in the Act by section 1 of the Merchant Shipping and Maritime Security Act 1997, enable the Secretary of State to establish temporary exclusion zones around stricken vessels. The purpose of this provision is to enable rescue or salvage operations or operations to prevent or clean up pollution, to proceed without interference from other vessels entering the area. Although such a zone could be established within the limits of a statutory harbour authority this seems unlikely given the regulatory powers of the harbour master. These provisions are not therefore discussed in detail here.

Secretary of State's power to require ships to be moved

6.47 Sections 100C, D and E of the Merchant Shipping Act 1995, inserted in that Act by section 10 of the Merchant Shipping and Maritime Security Act 1997, enable the Secretary of State for any one or more of the purposes mentioned below, to require ships in United Kingdom waters (other than a "qualifying foreign ship" as defined in section 313A of the 1995 Act which is exercising the right of innocent passage or the right of transit passage through straits used for international navigation) to move, or to be removed from a specified area or locality or from United Kingdom waters or alternatively not to be moved to a specified place or area within United Kingdom waters or over a specified route within such waters. But a United Kingdom ship cannot be required to be removed from United Kingdom waters.

6.48 The purposes for which this power may be used are the purpose of securing the safety of the ship or of other ships, of persons on the ship or other ships, or of any other persons or property, or of preventing or reducing any risk to such safety, and the purpose of preventing or reducing pollution in the United Kingdom, in United Kingdom waters or in a part of the sea specified under section 129(2)(b) of the 1995 Act (as an area of sea above an area designated under the Continental Shelf Act 1964), or of preventing or reducing any risk of such pollution.

6.49 The Secretary of State may exercise his powers under section 100C by giving directions to the owner of the ship concerned, or any person in possession of it, or to the master. If, in the Secretary of State's opinion, his power to give directions is inadequate for the purposes mentioned above he may himself take any such action as he has power to require to be taken by directions. The Secretary of State's power to take action himself is to be exercised by such persons as he may authorize for the purpose.

6.50 Section 100D makes it an offence for a person to fail to comply with a direction under section 100C or intentionally to obstruct any person who is taking action under that section or acting in compliance with a direction thereunder. A person guilty of such an offence is liable on summary conviction to a fine not exceeding £50,000 or on conviction on indictment to an (unlimited) fine. Section 100E contains provisions about the service of notices under section 100C.

6.51 Again, although this power to require ships to be moved could be exercised within the limits of a statutory harbour authority this would probably be unusual. Although a harbour authority could not usually require a ship to leave harbour, unless the harbour master's powers under the Dangerous Vessels Act 1985 (see paragraph 6.18 *ante*) or the Dangerous Substances in Harbour Areas Regulations 1987 (see Chapter 8 *post*) were relevant, they could impose heavy charges on a ship which anchored there indefinitely, subject to the owner's right to object to the Secretary of State under section 31 of the Harbours Act 1964 (see paragraphs 10.16 to 10.20 *post*). The harbour master could also require the ship to be moved to a place within the harbour where it would cause the least inconvenience or potential danger.

CHAPTER 7

HARBOUR AND COASTAL BY-LAWS

Harbour by-laws

7.1 By-laws are a harbour authority's main tool for the detailed management of their harbour. They fall between, on the one hand, the basic powers of the authority under general harbour legislation and their local Acts and, on the other, the executive powers of the harbour master, particularly his power to give directions to ships under section 52 of the Harbours, Docks and Piers Clauses Act 1847 (see paragraph 6.2 *ante*) and similar provisions.

7.2 By-laws are not perhaps quite so important as they once were. The power which some harbour authorities now have to give general directions for the regulation of shipping (see paragraph 6.13 *ante*), which was introduced partly because by-laws could not be made or modified quickly enough for the purpose, is a substantial encroachment on the matters dealt with by by-laws. So are the provisions in the Dangerous Substances in Harbour Areas Regulations 1987 requiring certain ships to give notice, and furnish specified information, before they enter port (see paragraphs 8.12 to 8.16 *post*), and some health and safety regulations made under the Health and Safety at Work etc. Act 1974 deal with matters, such as safe access to vessels, which used to be dealt with in by-laws. Nevertheless harbour by-laws are still an essential element in the management of harbours, particularly perhaps small ports.

By-laws must be within enabling powers

7.3 By-laws, like all subordinate legislation, must be within the terms of the enabling power, contained in the case of harbour authority by-laws in a local Act of Parliament, Scottish provisional order, or harbour revision or empowerment order, under which they are made.

Other requirements for validity of by-laws

7.4 In addition, however, by-laws, as distinct from, say, regulations made by a Minister of the Crown, may be declared invalid by the Courts if they are uncertain in their terms, if they are repugnant to any Act of Parliament or to the general principles of the common law, or if they are unreasonable.

7.5 As to what unreasonable means in this context, in the case of *Kruse* v. *Johnson*[1] Lord Russell, C.J., said:

Unreasonable in what sense? If, for instance, they (the by-laws) were found to be partial and unequal in their operation as between different classes; if they were manifestly unjust; if they disclosed bad faith; if they involved such oppressive or gratuitous interference with the rights of those subject to them as could find no justification in the minds of reasonable men, the court might well say "Parliament never intended to give authority to make such rules; they are unreasonable and *ultra vires*". But it is in this sense, and in this sense only, as I conceive, that the question of unreasonableness can properly be regarded. A by-law is not unreasonable merely because particular judges may think that it goes further than is prudent or necessary or convenient or because it is not accompanied by a qualification or an exception which some judges may think ought to be there.

7.6 There does not appear to have been any case of a harbour authority by-law being held to be unreasonable. In the case of *Parker* v. *Bournemouth Corporation*[2] it was held that it was unreasonable for the defendant Corporation to seek to regulate the selling or hawking of any article on their beach or foreshore by a by-law which provided that no person should sell etc. any article except in part or parts of the beach and foreshore as the Corporation should, by notice, from time to time appoint, and that the by-law was bad since it gave the Corporation power to make any agreement they chose without regard to the question of reasonableness or otherwise and because it reserved to the Corporation a right to refuse to give a licence to any particular person.

Powers to make by-laws

7.7 Powers to make harbour by-laws go back a long way. Eighteenth century harbour Acts often included powers to make by-laws. But the by-law making power which until quite recent years applied at nearly all harbours is section 83 of the Harbours, Docks and Piers Clauses Act 1847 as incorporated with a harbour authority's local Acts and orders. Section 83 authorizes by-laws for, among other things, regulating the use of the harbour, dock or pier, regulating the admission of vessels into or near the harbour, dock or pier and their removal into or near the harbour, dock or pier and their removal out of and from the same and for the good order and government of such vessels whilst within the harbour or dock or at or near the pier, for regulating the use of cranes etc. and for preventing damage or injury to any vessel or goods within the harbour or dock or at or near the pier or on the premises of the harbour undertakers. This section is set out in Part I of Appendix H.

7.8 A number of harbour authorities have now adopted more modern by-law making powers. These are usually more detailed than section 83 of the 1847 Act although not, in most cases, substantially much wider. The form of

1. *Kruse* v. *Johnson* [1898] 2 Q.B. 91.
2. *Parker* v. *Bournemouth Corporation* (1902) 86 L.T. 449.

these powers varies but section 78 of the Medway Ports Authority Act 1973 set out in Part II of Appendix H is a typical example of a modern power to make general harbour by-laws.

7.9 In addition to these powers to make general by-laws many harbour authorities have a separate power to make by-laws for prescribing lights, signals and steering and sailing rules. The Dangerous Substances in Harbour Areas Regulations 1987 include a power for harbour authorities to make by-laws as respects dangerous substances and this is discussed in Chapter 8 *post*. Paragraph 18.30 *post* refers to the potential powers of a harbour authority to make by-laws for certain environmental purposes.

Suggested model by-laws

7.10 A suggested set of model general harbour by-laws is set out in Part III of Appendix H, but the substance and form of harbour by-laws must always depend on local circumstances and some of the suggested model by-laws may not be appropriate in all cases.

General issues arising on by-laws

7.11 There are several general issues which arise from time to time on harbour by-laws.

7.12 One of them is whether a by-law can empower the harbour master to prohibit a ship from entering port or order it to leave. The answer of course depends on the terms of the enabling power but this nearly always authorizes by-laws to *regulate* ships entering or using the harbour. Regulation does not include prohibition. In the case of *Dick and Another* v. *Badart Freres*[3] it was held that a by-law made by a dock company which purported to exclude lumpers from working within the dock premises was *ultra vires* section 83 of the Harbours, Docks and Piers Clauses Act 1847. So a by-law which purports to prohibit, or enable the harbour master to prohibit, a ship entering port or provides for the removal of ships from the port is probably *ultra vires*. However, attention is drawn to the case referred to in paragraph 7.14 *post* where a by-law which prohibited tugs operating in the harbour without the prior permission of the harbour master was upheld as being within the powers of section 83 to make by-laws to regulate the use of the harbour.

7.13 Another general question is how far a harbour by-law can confer a discretion on the harbour authority or the harbour master. By-laws of course are delegated legislation made under a power conferred by Parliament, or indeed if the enabling power is contained in a harbour or empowerment revision order, under a power which is itself delegated legislation. Delegated legislation cannot, generally, itself delegate a power to legislate to anyone else

3. *Dick and Another* v. *Badart Freres* (1883) 10 Q.B. 387.

unless this is expressly authorized by the power under which the delegated legislation is made. There are in fact a few cases where a by-law making power does authorize by-laws which confer a discretion of this kind for a specific purpose, e.g., to authorize by-laws which enable the harbour authority to make schemes for the regulation of moorings. But, in general, by-law making powers do not authorize sub-delegation.

7.14 However, by-laws do in practice confer a discretion in various contexts on the harbour authority and, more particularly, on the harbour master. By-laws usually provide for a number of things which can only be done with the consent of the harbour master or in accordance with his directions. It would be very inconvenient if that were not permissible. In holding that a by-law which provided that a person should not without the prior permission of the harbour master use or cause to be used any vessel for the purposes of towing any vessel other than a small craft within the harbour was within the powers of section 83 of the Harbours, Docks and Piers Clauses Act 1847, Lord Penrose said "it is in my opinion inevitable that by-laws must confer upon the harbour master as the authority's officer a degree of discretion to enforce regulations as circumstances require".[4]

7.15 The principle appears to be that, in the absence of an express provision for the purpose in the enabling power, a by-law cannot confer a legislative discretion, such as a power to make regulations, but can confer an administrative or executive discretion, such as a power for the harbour master to give directions to the master of a vessel unloading cargo to prevent the cargo falling into harbour waters or a provision which prohibits the laying down of moorings except with the written consent of the harbour authority and in accordance with such conditions as they may impose. In practice the distinction between a legislative and an administrative discretion may no doubt be a fine one.

7.16 Another issue is whether by-laws should apply the Collision Regulations (see paragraphs 6.38 to 6.40 *ante*). It is submitted that unless the harbour concerned is a land-locked artificial channel such as the Manchester Ship Canal where the Collision Regulations do not apply of themselves—see *The Hare*[5]—they should not. The steering and sailing rules comprised in the Collision Regulations apply to all vessels upon the high seas and in all waters connected therewith navigable by sea-going vessels. They therefore apply of themselves in a harbour which is not a land-locked artificial channel but subject to any special rules made by an appropriate authority for, *inter alia*, harbours. Such special rules would of course include harbour by-laws. It was held in the case of *The Carlotta*[6] that a harbour by-law which deals with the

---

4. *Peterhead Towage Services Ltd. v. Peterhead Bay Authority* 1992 S.L.T. 593.
5. *The Hare* [1904] P. 331.
6. *The Carlotta* [1899] P. 223.

same subject-matter as a provision of the Collision Regulations will exclude the application of that provision.

7.17 If harbour by-laws for a harbour where the Collision Regulations apply of themselves, in terms incorporate or apply the regulations, that may have one of two results. The Courts might hold that the purported application had no effect. The Collision Regulations apply anyway. They might take the view that the purported application of the Regulations was *ultra vires*. On the other hand the Courts might take the view that the application of the Collision Regulations by the by-laws meant that the rules contained in the regulations have effect as part of the by-laws to the exclusion of the Collision Regulations themselves. If the latter view were taken then the maximum penalty for breach of the rules would be the maximum fine under the by-laws, probably level 3 on the standard scale, instead of the substantially higher penalties which apply for breach of the Collision Regulations themselves.

Procedure for making by-laws

7.18 The appropriate procedure for the making and confirmation of harbour by-laws (apart from the case of by-laws under the Dangerous Substances in Harbour Areas Regulations which is discussed in Chapter 8 *post*) depends on the special legislation of the harbour authority in question. Section 85 of the Harbours, Docks and Piers Clauses Act 1847 specifies the procedure for the confirmation of by-laws made under section 83 of that Act but where section 83 is still incorporated in a harbour authority's special legislation the special Act nearly always prescribes that by-laws shall be subject to confirmation by the Secretary of State for Transport. The provisions of section 85 for confirmation by a judicial authority now therefore hardly ever apply. The special legislation of nearly all harbour authorities now applies the provisions for the making and confirmation of by-laws contained in section 236 of the Local Government Act 1972 or, in Scotland, section 202 of the Local Government (Scotland) Act 1973, with appropriate modifications. These modifications always provide for by-laws to be confirmed by the Secretary of State for Transport. In the case of harbour authorities in England and Wales these modifications often enable the Secretary of State to modify a harbour by-law submitted to him for confirmation (in Scotland the local government procedure includes a power for the Secretary of State to modify).

7.19 The applied local government procedure provides that after by-laws have been made by the harbour authority they must publish notice of their intention to apply for confirmation of the by-laws and make copies available for inspection by, and sale to, the public. The procedure under the Local Government (Scotland) Act expressly provides that persons aggrieved by the proposed by-laws may object to the confirming authority, who must take his objection into consideration. The procedure under the Act for England and Wales does not expressly provide for this but it appears to be implicit.

7.20 The Local Government (Scotland) Act 1973 provides that, before confirming by-laws, the confirming authority may hold a local inquiry if they consider this to be necessary or desirable. The Act for England and Wales does not.

Penalties for contravention of by-laws

7.21 Until recently there were problems about the maximum fines which harbour by-laws could provide for contravention of the by-laws. This depended in each case on the harbour authority's local statutes and was sometimes absurdly low. The original maximum fine under the Harbours, Docks and Piers Clauses Act 1847 was £5 which may have been an adequate sum in 1847 but, although this maximum was sometimes increased in local Harbour Acts, it was not increased generally, to £50, until 1967. This and other general increases in penalties under Criminal Law and Criminal Justice Acts were usually inadequate and their operation depended on particular provisions of local Harbour Acts including sometimes the date when the 1847 Act had been incorporated and whether it had been modified.

7.22 These problems have been swept away by section 57 of the Criminal Justice Act 1988 which provides generally that harbour authority by-laws may impose a maximum fine of up to level 4 on the standard scale. In practice, however, the Department of Transport on the advice of the Home Office, will seldom confirm a by-law which provides for a maximum fine of more than level 3.

Local authority coastal by-laws

England and Wales

7.23 Local authorities in England and Wales which are bounded by the sea have various powers to make by-laws to regulate activities in the coastal area. Generally, the area of such an authority extends to low water mark but, where a local authority's area includes the bank of an estuary, it may be arguable, according to the circumstances, that the estuary is *intra fauces terrae* and that the authority's area extends to the middle of the estuary (or to the whole of it if the banks on both sides are in the area of the authority). The powers of a district council in England and (since the coming into force of the Local Government (Wales) Act 1994) the council of a principal area in Wales under section 235 of the Local Government Act 1972, to make by-laws for good rule and government and the suppression of nuisances is not specific to coastal areas but can be used in such areas, for example to prohibit activities on the seashore or, where applicable, in the waters of an estuary, which constitute a nuisance. But under section 235(3) this power cannot be used for any purpose as respects any area, if provision for that purpose as respects that area is made by, or is or may be made under, any other enactment—for example, if there is a more specific power to make by-laws for the purpose in question.

7.24 Perhaps the most important of the powers for local authorities to make coastal by-laws are those contained in sections 82 and 83 of the Public Health Acts Amendment Act 1907. Section 82 enables a district council in England or the council of a principal area in Wales which has adopted this section (as to which see paragraph 7.27 *post*), for the purpose of preventing danger, obstruction or annoyance to persons using the seashore, to make by-laws to:

(1) regulate the erection or placing on the seashore, or on such part or parts thereof as may be prescribed by such by-law, of any booths, tents, sheds, stands and stalls (whether fixed or moveable), or vehicles for the sale or exposure of any article or thing, or any shows, exhibitions, performances, swings, roundabouts or other erections, vans, photographic carts or other vehicles, however propelled, and the playing of any games on the seashore and generally regulate the user of the seashore for such purposes as shall be prescribed by such by-laws;

(2) regulate the user of the seashore for riding and driving;

(3) provide for the preservation of good order and conduct among persons using the seashore.

7.25 A by-law under section 82 which affects the foreshore below high water requires the consent of the Secretary of State for Transport before coming into operation. Section 82 was repealed by the Public Health Act 1936 so far as regards matters with respect to which by-laws can be made under Part VIII of that Act—in particular under section 231 of the 1936 Act which is described in paragraph 7.28 *post*.

7.26 Section 83 of the Public Health Acts Amendment Act 1907 enables such a council as is mentioned in paragraph 7.24 *ante* which has adopted the section, for the purpose of preventing danger, obstruction or annoyance to persons using the esplanades or promenades within the district, to make by-laws prescribing the nature of the traffic for which they may be used, regulating the selling and hawking of any article, commodity or thing thereon and for the preservation of order and good conduct among the persons using the same.

7.27 Sections 82 and 83 of the 1907 Act are adoptive provisions, originally under section 3 of that Act. By virtue of paragraph 24 of Schedule 14 to the Local Government Act 1972, sections 82 and 83 were excepted from the general application of public health adoptive provisions provided for by paragraph 23 of Schedule 14. Under paragraph 25 of Schedule 14 to the 1972 Act sections 82 and 83 of the 1907 Act can still be adopted by, in England, a district council and, in Wales, the council of a principal area by resolution of the council after giving the requisite notice. Formerly, such a council could by resolution disapply these sections but this power ceased on 1 April 1975.

7.28 Section 231 of the Public Health Act 1936 authorizes a local authority to make by-laws with respect to public bathing. Unlike the other local authority by-law making powers referred to in this chapter, section 231 applies to all local authorities within the meaning of the Local Government Act 1972—paragraph 18 of Schedule 14 to that Act. The authorities which may make by-laws under section 231 include, in England, county councils and parish councils as well as district councils, and in Wales community councils as well as councils for principal areas (both county and county borough councils). By-laws under section 231 may be made to:

(1) regulate the areas in which, and the hours during which, public bathing shall be permitted;

(2) prohibit or restrict public bathing at times when and places as respects which warning is given, by the display of flags or other means specified in the by-laws, that bathing is dangerous;

(3) fix the places at which bathing machines may be stationed or bathing huts or tents may be erected;

(4) regulate the manner in which bathing machines, huts or tents may be used, and the charges which may be made for the use thereof;

(5) regulate, as far as decency requires, the costumes to be worn by bathers;

(6) require persons providing accommodation for bathing to provide and maintain life saving appliances, or other means of protecting bathers from danger; and

(7) regulate, for preventing danger to bathers, the navigation of vessels used for pleasure purposes within any area allotted for public bathing during the hours allowed for bathing.

Section 231(2) provides that if a by-law under section 231 is inconsistent with a by-law made by dock undertakers (who would generally be a harbour authority within the meaning of the Harbours Act 1964) the latter prevails. The power to make by-laws regulating the navigation of vessels used for pleasure purposes may be of limited application having regard to the decision by Mr Justice Sheen in *Steadman* v. *Schofield and Another*[7] that "navigation" is not synonymous with movement on water and means planned or ordered movement from one place to another. However, the meaning of this expression may depend on the context and it may be arguable that, in the context of this by-law-making power, "navigation" does mean movement on water. In that case it was also held that a jet-ski was not a vessel within the meaning of the Merchant Shipping Act 1894.

7.29 The area with respect to which a local authority may make by-laws under section 231 of the Public Health Act 1936 is often extended by section 17 of the Local Government (Miscellaneous Provisions) Act 1976. That

---

7. *Steadman v. Schofield and Another* [1992] 2 Lloyd's Rep 163.

section provides that where any part of the area of a local authority having power to make by-laws under both section 231 of the Public Health Act 1936 and section 76 of the Public Health Act 1961 (as to which see paragraph 7.30 *post*) is bounded by, or is to seaward of, the low water mark, the authority may exercise that power as respects any area of sea which is outside the area of the authority and within 1000 metres to seaward of any place where the mark is within or on the boundary of the authority. However, since a county council or parish council in England and a community council in Wales do not have power to make by-laws under section 76 of the Public Health Act 1961, it would seem that the extension does not apply in their cases.

7.30 Section 76 of the Public Heath Act 1961 authorizes a district council in England and the council for a principal area in Wales to make by-laws for the prevention of danger, obstruction or annoyance by pleasure boats to persons bathing in the sea or using the seashore. Such by-laws may:

(1) regulate the speed of pleasure boats;
(2) regulate the use of pleasure boats so as to prevent their navigation in a dangerous manner or without due care or attention or without reasonable consideration for other persons;
(3) require the use of effectual silencers on pleasure boats propelled by internal combustion engines.

Section 76(4) provides that a by-law under section 76 shall be of no effect if and in so far as it is inconsistent with any by-law made by dock undertakers or a person authorized by any enactment or statutory order to construct or operate a pier.

7.31 As mentioned in paragraph 7.29 *ante*, the area as respects which by-laws under section 76 may be made is extended by section 17 of the Local Government (Miscellaneous Provisions) Act 1976. Again, the judgment in *Steadman* v. *Schofield and Another*, referred to above, may limit the application of this by-law making power in relation to certain water craft.

7.32 Section 185 of the Local Government Planning and Land Act 1980 authorizes a district council and the council of a Welsh county or county borough (a principal area) to make by-laws for:

(1) regulating the numbering and naming of pleasure boats and vessels which are let on hire to the public, and the mooring places for such boats and vessels; and
(2) fixing the qualifications of the boatmen or other persons in charge of such boats and vessels, and
(3) securing their good and orderly conduct while in charge.

Section 185(2) precludes the making of by-laws under section 185 in relation to pleasure boats or vessels operating on any water owned or managed by the British Waterways Board, on any inland waters in respect of which the Environment Agency may make by-laws, on any canal or other inland navigation which a navigation authority are required to manage or maintain under any enactment (unless the local authority are themselves required or empowered to manage or maintain the canal or inland navigation in question) or on any harbour maintained or managed by a harbour authority within the meaning of the Harbours Act 1964.

7.33 The procedure for making the by-laws referred to in paragraphs 7.23 to 7.32 *ante* is contained in section 236 of the Local Government Act 1972 and is summarized in paragraph 7.19 *ante* (in relation to harbour by-laws). The confirming authority is the Secretary of State. Under transfer of functions orders currently in force, this power is exercised by the Home Secretary.

7.34 Under section 237 of the Local Government Act 1972, read with section 31(2)(a) of the Criminal Law Act 1977 and section 46 of the Criminal Justice Act 1982, the maximum fine which may be imposed by by-laws made under any of the provisions referred to in paragraphs 7.23 to 7.32 *ante*, except for section 76 of the Public Health Act 1961, is level 2 on the standard scale. In the case of by-laws under section 76 the maximum is level 3 (in consequence of the maximum penalty specified in section 31(4) of the Criminal Law Act 1977). By-laws under any of these provisions may also provide, in the case of a continuing offence, for a further fine not exceeding £5 for each day during which the offence continues after conviction.

Scotland

7.35 Local authorities in Scotland (since 1 April 1996, under the Local Government (Scotland etc.) Act 1994, unitary councils and islands councils) have, under section 201 of the Local Government (Scotland) Act 1973, a similar general by-law making power to that referred to in paragraph 7.23 *ante* in the case of district councils in England and councils of principal areas in Wales. As mentioned in paragraph 7.23 it may sometimes be appropriate to use this power in respect of coastal areas.

7.36 The most important powers for Scottish local authorities to make coastal by-laws are those contained in section 121 of the Civic Government (Scotland) Act 1982. The section contains two by-law making powers. Section 121(1) authorizes by-laws relating to the "seashore" and section 121(3) authorizes by-laws relating to "adjacent waters". "Seashore" is defined in section 123(1) of the Act as the land between the low water mark and the high water mark of ordinary spring tides and every cliff, bank, barrier, dune, beach, flat, esplanade or other land above the said high water mark, adjacent to the shore, and to which the public have right of access. "Adjacent waters" are defined in section 123(1) as waters within a distance from low water mark of ordinary spring tides not exceeding 1000 metres or, where the width of the waters separating the area of one local authority from that of another is less than 2000 metres, measured by the shortest distance between the respective low water marks in these areas, the waters within the median line between those respective low water marks.

7.37 By-laws under section 121(1) may, insofar as it is necessary to do so for the purpose of preventing any nuisance or danger at, or preserving or improving the amenity of, or conserving the natural beauty (within the meaning of section 78(2) of the Countryside (Scotland) Act 1967) of, the seashore:

(a) regulate or prohibit any activity by way of trade or business with, or in expectation of personal reward from, members of the public on the seashore;

(b) regulate the use of vehicles on the seashore;

(c) regulate the exercise of sporting and recreational activities on the seashore.

7.38 Section 121(2) provides that by-laws under section 121(1) may confine the exercise of any activity (including the use of vehicles or kinds of vehicles) specified in the by-laws to a part of the seashore specified in the by-laws and prohibit the exercise in that part of the seashore of any other activity (including such use) so specified. (A power to regulate an activity would not, in itself, include power to prohibit the activity).

7.39 Under section 121(3) a Scottish local authority may make by-laws relating to adjacent waters for the purpose of:

(a) regulating the speed of pleasure boats in these waters;

(b) regulating the use of pleasure boats in these waters so as to prevent their navigation in a dangerous manner or without due care and attention or without reasonable consideration for other persons;

(c) requiring the use of effective silencers on pleasure boats in these waters;

(d) regulating the activities in these waters of divers, surfers, water skiers and persons engaged in similar recreational pursuits.

Having regard to the case of *Steadman* v. *Schofield and Another*, referred to in paragraph 7.28 *ante* (of persuasive authority only in Scotland), there may be doubt whether the references to pleasure boats include jet-skis. Perhaps their use would fall under head (d) above. There may also be some doubt about the meaning of "navigation".

7.40 Under section 121(5) and (6) a local authority, before making by-laws under section 121, must give public notice of their proposal to make the by-laws in a newspaper circulating in the area where the by-laws are to have effect. The authority must also make such other inquiries as may be reasonably necessary to ascertain the existence and identity of each person having an interest as proprietor or lessee which may be affected by the by-laws, in the case of proposed by-laws under section 121(1), in the seashore, or, in the case of proposed by-laws under section 121(3), the adjacent waters in question, and in either case in any salmon fishings and give notice in writing of their proposal to make by-laws to each person having such an interest.

7.41 After taking the steps mentioned in paragraph 7.40 *ante*, the local authority may, under section 121(7), not earlier than one month after the date of the newspaper advertisement, or, if there were more than one such advertisement, the latest, proceed to make the by-laws.

7.42 Under section 121(8) read with section 46 of the Criminal Justice Act 1982, by-laws under section 121 may provide that persons contravening the by-laws shall be liable, on summary conviction, to a fine not exceeding level 2 on the standard scale. The procedure for confirmation of by-laws under section 121 is that contained in section 202 of the Local Government (Scotland) Act 1973 which is summarized in paragraphs 7.19 and 7.20 *ante*. The confirming authority is the Secretary of State for Scotland.

7.43 In addition to the powers to make by-laws, section 121 authorizes a Scottish local authority to place notices or other indications on the seashore or in or on adjacent waters advising the public as to any danger or health hazard connected with the seashore or those waters (section 121(9)) and to provide staff for life saving and any boats or equipment which are appropriate for life saving (section 121(10)). Under section 121(11) a Scottish local authority, when exercising their powers under section 121, must have regard to the need to protect and maintain any public rights under the guardianship of the Crown to use the foreshore or adjacent waters.

By-laws by Environment Agency affecting the coast

7.44 The by-law-making powers of the Environment Agency include, under paragraph 4 of Schedule 25 to the Water Resources Act 1991, a power to make by-laws to control certain forms of pollution in controlled waters as defined in section 104 of the Act. Controlled waters as so defined include, *inter alia*, the waters which extend seaward for three miles from the baselines from which the breadth of the territorial sea adjacent to England and Wales is measured, and any waters which are within the area which extends landwards from those baselines as far as the limit of the highest tide and, in the case of the waters of any river or watercourse (not being a public sewer or a sewer or drain which drains into a public sewer), the fresh-water limit of the river or watercourse together with the waters of any enclosed dock which adjoins waters within that area. Under section 104(4) the Secretary of State may by order provide that any area of the territorial sea adjacent to England and Wales shall be treated as controlled waters.

7.45 By-laws made under this power may make such provision as the Environment Agency considers appropriate:

  (a) for prohibiting or regulating the washing or cleaning in any controlled waters of things of a description specified in the by-laws;

(b) for prohibiting or regulating the keeping or use on any controlled waters of vessels of a description specified in the by-laws which are provided with water closets or any other appliance which, not being a sink, bath or shower-bath, is designed to permit polluting matter to pass into the water where the vessel is situated and which is prescribed for the purposes of this by-law-making power by regulations made by the Secretary of State or the Minister of Agriculture, Fisheries and Food.

7.46 The procedure relating to by-laws made by the Environment Agency is contained in Schedule 26 to the Water Resources Act 1991. No by-law made by the Agency has effect until confirmed by the relevant Minister which, in the case of a by-law made under paragraph 4 of Schedule 25, means the Secretary of State. Before applying for confirmation of any by-law, the Agency must publish, and serve copies of, notice of its intention to make the application in accordance with paragraph 1(2) of Schedule 26. Paragraphs 1(3) and (4) provide for a copy of a proposed by-law to be deposited and reasonable facilities to be provided for its inspection. Under paragraph 1(5) a person is entitled to be furnished free of charge with a printed copy of a deposited by-law.

7.47 The Secretary of State may refuse to confirm a by-law submitted to him by the Agency or may confirm the by-law either without or, if the Agency consents, with modifications. If directed by the Secretary of State the Agency must cause notice of any proposed modification to be given in accordance with his direction. Before confirming a by-law submitted to him by the Agency, the Secretary of State must hold a local inquiry except in the circumstances mentioned in paragraph 2(3), which include the absence of any written objection. The Secretary of State may fix the date on which a by-law confirmed under Schedule 26 comes into force. If no date is fixed it comes into force at the end of a period of one month beginning with the date of confirmation.

By-laws made by Scottish Environmental Protection Agency

7.48 Under section 33(1) of the Control of Pollution Act 1974 as amended by paragraph 29(8) of Schedule 22 to the Environment Act 1995 the Scottish Environmental Protection Agency has a similar power to make by-laws for prohibiting the keeping or use on controlled waters (as defined in section 30A of the Act of 1974 which encompasses certain coastal and territorial waters) of vessels of a kind specified in the by-laws which are provided with sanitary appliances. By virtue of section 29 of the Environment Act 1995, the procedure relating to by-laws made by the Scottish Environmental Protection Agency is the same as for by-laws made by Scottish local authorities under the Local Government (Scotland) Act 1973 (which is briefly described in paragraphs 7.19 and 7.20 *ante*) with the additional provision that the Agency must send a copy of any by-laws made by it to the proper officer of the local authority for any area to the whole or part of which the by-laws will apply.

Other coastal by-laws

7.49 Certain by-law making powers related to coastal protection and defence against flooding are discussed in Chapter 17 *post*. Such powers related to conservation, including Special Areas of Conservation and Special Protection Areas are discussed in Chapter 18 *post*.

CHAPTER 8

DANGEROUS SUBSTANCES

The Dangerous Substances in Harbour Areas Regulations 1987

8.1 Since 1 June 1987 the carriage, loading, unloading and storage of dangerous substances at harbours have been governed, mainly but not exclusively, by the Dangerous Substances in Harbour Areas Regulations 1987. These regulations, made by the Secretary of State for Transport under enabling powers contained in the Health and Safety at Work, etc. Act 1974, replaced former provisions for the regulation of dangerous substances in harbours contained in by-laws made under the Explosives Act 1875 and the Petroleum (Consolidation) Act 1928. They also replaced the Conveyance in Harbours of Military Explosives Regulations 1977, and certain sections of the Explosives Act 1875, the Explosives Act 1923, the Petroleum (Consolidation) Act 1928 and a number of provisions contained in local Acts and orders and by-laws made thereunder. As indicated below, however, some local Act provisions have been retained.

8.2 To a large extent the regulations cover substantially the same ground as the controls which they replaced. The most important of the substantive changes are—

    (a) the express powers for harbour authorities, through powers vested in their harbour masters, to control the entry into their dock estates of dangerous substances brought from inland;

    (b) the establishment of a licensing system to control the handling, etc., of explosives; and

    (c) the requirement for harbour authorities to prepare emergency plans and for emergency arrangements to be made at berths.

Dangerous substances for purposes of the regulations

8.3 Regulation 3 describes what is a dangerous substance for the purpose of the regulations. Any substance (including any preparation or other mixture) which by reason of its "characteristic properties" creates a risk to the health and safety of any person when the substance is in a "harbour or harbour area" is a dangerous substance for this purpose. The "characteristic properties" are

71

specified in column 1 of Part I of Schedule 1 to the regulations and include explosive, flammable and toxic properties. In addition, any substance or article which is within the definition of "dangerous goods" in regulation 1(3) of the Merchant Shipping (Dangerous Goods and Marine Pollutants) Regulations 1990 is a dangerous substance for the purpose of the Dangerous Substances in Harbour Areas Regulations (except that nothing in the regulations of 1990 is to be construed as defining a marine pollutant in Class 9 of the 1990 consolidated edition of the International Maritime Dangerous Goods Code under UN number 3077 or 3082 or any substance otherwise included in Class 9 of the 1990 consolidated edition of the IMDG Code solely by reason of its being a marine pollutant, as a dangerous substance for the purposes of the Dangerous Substances in Harbour Areas Regulations). Regulation 3 contains a number of detailed exceptions and qualifications. Perhaps the most important of these is that under paragraph (2) of the regulation a substance or article which is brought into a harbour area from inland and which is not to be loaded onto a vessel as cargo is not to be treated as a dangerous substance for the purpose of the regulations except in the circumstances specified in regulation 3(2).

Meaning of "harbour" and "harbour area" for purposes of the regulations

8.4 Under regulation 5(1) the Dangerous Substances in Harbour Areas Regulations apply in every "harbour" and "harbour area" (and also, as indicated below, under regulation 33 the explosives licensing provisions of the regulations may apply outside a "harbour" or "harbour area"). "Harbour", as defined in regulation 2, is a harbour which is *not* managed under statutory powers. In practice, it is rare for dangerous substances to be loaded or unloaded at a harbour managed otherwise than under statutory powers.

8.5 Most areas to which the regulations will apply will be within the definition of "harbour area" contained in regulation 2. That is to say, they will be areas of water within the statutory jurisdiction of a "statutory harbour authority" defined in regulation 2 as a harbour authority within the meaning of section 57 of the Harbours Act 1964. Such a harbour authority is a person (in practice, a port trust, a company, a local authority, or Associated British Ports) in whom powers or duties of improving, maintaining or managing a harbour are vested by or under statute. "Harbour area" also includes any berth abutting on such a water area where the loading or unloading of any dangerous substances takes place whether or not that berth is for other purposes under the statutory jurisdiction of the harbour authority. Berth is defined in regulation 2 as any dock, pier, jetty, quay, wharf or similar structure at which a vessel may tie up and includes any plant or premises used for purposes ancillary or incidental to the loading or unloading of a dangerous substance *within the curtilage of that berth.*

8.6 "Harbour area" also includes any land within the statutory jurisdiction of the statutory harbour authority which is used in connection with the loading or unloading of vessels. It also includes a monobuoy connected to storage facilities in the harbour area and its monobuoy area.

8.7 Paragraph (*b*) of the definition of "harbour area" deals with the case where the limits of jurisdiction of statutory harbour authorities overlap, as happens in several cases. For the purpose of the regulations, the area where the limits of the two authorities concerned overlap falls within the harbour area comprising the harbour limits, berths or land which are used by vessels navigating in the area of overlap to a greater extent than they use berths or land within the other overlapping limits. For example, the limits of the Harwich Conservancy Board overlap with those of the Felixstowe Dock and Railway Company. Most of the ships which navigate in the overlapping area use berths at Felixstowe and therefore that area is included in the harbour area comprising Felixstowe's limits.

8.8 Another qualification relates to wharves and jetties managed under statutory powers by oil or other companies for the purposes of their own traffic. These are usually called "own account" undertakings and are described in the latter part of the definition of "statutory harbour authority" in regulation 2. Where such an own account undertaking, which usually includes a relatively small water area around the wharf or jetty, is within the limits of jurisdiction of another statutory harbour authority, as is usually the case, then the company concerned is not a statutory harbour authority for the purposes of the regulations and it follows, of course, that the wharf or jetty and the surrounding area within the jurisdiction of the company are included as part of the harbour area which comprises the statutory limits of jurisdiction within which the own account undertaking is situated. An example of this are the oil jetties at Milford Haven which were constructed by oil companies under statutory powers. For the purpose of these regulations they are within the harbour area which comprises the limits of jurisdiction of the Milford Haven Port Authority.

Applications of the regulations within harbours and harbour areas

8.9 Within "harbours" and "harbour areas" the regulations apply essentially to the loading and unloading of dangerous substances onto and from ships and the storage and movement of dangerous substances related to such loading and unloading. They do not, for example, apply to a dangerous substance which is brought into a "harbour" or "harbour area" from inland to be stored or used in a factory there unless it is to be loaded on board a ship in the "harbour" or "harbour area". A number of cases where the regulations do not apply are specified in paragraph (2) of regulation 5.

8.10 The Dangerous Substances in Harbour Areas Regulations are a detailed and comprehensive code. The following paragraphs deal with the aspects of the regulations which seem most likely to give rise to legal questions. They do not cover the whole content of the regulations, much of which consists of practical rules.

Meaning of "harbour master" for purposes of the regulations

8.11 A feature of the Dangerous Substances in Harbour Areas Regulations is the discretionary powers which in a number of contexts are vested in the harbour master. "Harbour master" is defined in regulation 2 as the "harbour master, dock or other officer duly appointed by the harbour authority to act in such capacity or any person having authority so to act". Generally, no doubt, the harbour master for the purpose of the regulations will be the harbour master in the ordinary sense. But if the exercise of any of the discretions conferred on the harbour master by the regulations appears to a harbour authority to require technical or scientific knowledge which the harbour master would be unlikely to possess it would be possible for the harbour authority to appoint someone else to act as harbour master for the purpose of exercising that particular discretion.

Powers of harbour master under the regulations

8.12 Perhaps the most important powers conferred on a harbour master by the Dangerous Substances in Harbour Areas Regulations are those contained in regulations 6 and 7. Regulation 6 provides for prior notice to be given of the entry of a dangerous substance into a "harbour" or "harbour area" in the case of a vessel by the master or agent and in the case of any other mode of transport (usually a lorry from inland) by the "operator" as defined in regulation 4. Notice must be given to the harbour master and, if the substance is to be brought to a berth, the berth operator. The notice may be given up to six months in advance. It must be in writing or in such other form as the harbour master may agree and contain such information as is adequate to evaluate the risk created by the substance to the health and safety of any person. In the case of a vessel the notice must also contain the information about the vessel specified in regulation 6(3).

8.13 Like the provisions of regulation 7, referred to below, which confers powers of prohibition, removal and regulation on the harbour master, so far as the entry from the sea is concerned regulation 6 overlaps substantially with existing powers, in particular with requirements for notice of entry contained in harbour authority general by-laws (see Chapter 7 *ante*). Again, like regulation 7, regulation 6 is an important extension of a harbour master's jurisdiction at most harbours in that it applies not only to entry to a "harbour" or "harbour area", as defined in the regulations, from the sea but also to entry from inland.

8.14 Regulation 6 confers quite wide discretions on harbour masters as to the length of notice. Normally, at least 24 hours' notice must be given or such longer time, not exceeding 14 days, as the harbour master may for operational reasons require. If, however, it is not reasonably practicable to give 24 hours' notice, the period of notice may be such shorter time as the harbour master and berth operator may together agree. Regulation 6 also authorizes a harbour master to grant exceptions from the notice requirements where it appears to him that this is necessary for securing the health and safety of any person.

8.15 Regulation 7 authorizes a harbour master to give directions to—

(a) regulate or prohibit the entry into;

(b) require the removal from; or

(c) regulate the handling movement or position within the "harbour" or "harbour area" of:–

  (i) any dangerous substance, if in his opinion its condition is such as to create a risk to the health and safety of any person; or

  (ii) any freight container, portable tank or receptacle containing a dangerous substance or any vehicle or vessel carrying a dangerous substance, if in his opinion the condition of the container, tank or receptacle, vehicle or vessel is such as to create a risk to the health and safety of any person from the substance which it contains or carries.

8.16 To enable a harbour master to give directions under regulation 7 there must therefore be, in his opinion, a risk to health and safety *from a dangerous substance* which may be caused either by the condition of the dangerous substance itself or by the condition of the container, tank or receptacle which contains the substance or of the vehicle or vessel which carries it. In deciding whether to give such directions a harbour master must have regard to all the circumstances of the case and in particular to the safety of any person, whether that person is within or outside the "harbour" or "harbour area". Paragraph (4) of regulation 7 enables the Secretary of State to require a harbour master to substitute different directions for those the harbour master has given, which corresponds to the similar provision of section 3 of the Dangerous Vessels Act 1985. This power for the Secretary of State to override the harbour master may be exercised only for the purpose of securing the safety of any person.

8.17 As indicated above, the powers conferred on a harbour master by regulation 7 in relation to ships overlap existing powers of harbour masters both under local legislation, including section 52 of the Harbours, Docks and Piers Clauses Act 1847 as incorporated in local Acts and orders, and the Dangerous Vessels Act 1985 (see paragraphs 6.2 to 6.27 *ante*). It does not, however, completely duplicate them, in particular because the regulation does not apply to a ship which is not carrying a dangerous substance. The Dangerous Vessels Act is intended to deal with acute emergencies and it would seem that the powers of that Act should generally be used where a harbour master considers that there is a grave and imminent risk of a major disaster.

8.18 Other important discretions conferred on a harbour master by the Dangerous Substances in Harbour Areas Regulations relate to the anchoring and mooring of a vessel carrying, or about to be loaded with, a dangerous substance (regulation 14) and to various operations by vessels in connection with the carriage, loading, unloading or transfer of liquid dangerous substances in bulk (regulations 19–22). Where the vessel is at a berth, the berth operator is also involved in these decisions.

Statutory harbour authorities required to prepare emergency plans

8.19 Regulation 26 of the Dangerous Substances in Harbour Areas Regulations imposed an important new duty on harbour authorities. Before dangerous substances are handled in their "harbour area" a harbour authority must prepare an effective emergency plan for dealing with emergencies which involve, affect, or could affect, dangerous substances that are brought into or are handled in the "harbour area". A harbour authority are required to keep the plan up to date and to consult the emergency services and any other body which appears to them to be appropriate about the preparation of the plan and keeping it up to date. Port users and berth operators are required to cooperate with a harbour authority in preparing the plan if so requested by the authority. A harbour authority must notify the contents of their plan to those responsible for putting it into effect.

Provisions of the regulations relating to explosives

8.20 Part IX of the Dangerous Substances in Harbour Areas Regulations deals with explosives. It introduces a new system for licensing the handling of explosives and this applies not only in "harbours" and "harbour areas" but also under regulation 33(1) to the loading on board or unloading from a vessel of any explosive on any part of the coast of Great Britain or in any tidal water or within territorial waters to which sections 1–59 and 80–82 of the Health and Safety at Work, etc. Act 1974 are applied by article 7 of the Health and Safety at Work, etc. Act 1974 (Application outside Great Britain) Order 1977 (i.e., areas designated under the Continental Shelf Act 1964). Regulation 33(2) specifies cases where a licence is not required. These include the case of explosives of less than one tonne in quantity intended for immediate use in connection with harbour works or for wreck dispersal in a "harbour" or "harbour area" if the consent in writing of the harbour master has been obtained and the explosives are carried and used in accordance with any conditions attached to that consent.

8.21 Under regulation 34(1) a person must not—

(a) bring any explosive into a "harbour" or "harbour area";

(b) carry or handle any explosive within a "harbour" or "harbour area"; or

(c) load or unload any explosive outside a "harbour" or "harbour area" where the licensing system applies by virtue of regulation 33(1),

unless there is in existence an explosives licence permitting that activity and the conditions attached to the licence are complied with.

8.22 The explosives licensing system is administered by the Health and Safety Executive. An application for a licence, where the explosive is being, or is to be, handled within a "harbour" or "harbour area" must be made to the Executive by the harbour authority or by the operator of the berth in question (if the latter he must inform the harbour authority of his intention). Where the explosive is to be loaded or unloaded outside a "harbour" or "harbour area" the application must be made by a person interested in such loading or unloading. The procedure for explosives licence applications is contained in Schedule 7 to the regulations. On receipt of an application the Health and Safety Executive may prepare a draft licence and may require the applicant to publish, in a form approved by the Executive, a notice giving such particulars of the draft licence as the Executive may require. Such notice must state that any comments or objections to the application must be sent to the Executive within one month of the publication of the notice. Within that time, the applicant must give to any interested person such additional information about the application as the Executive may determine.

8.23 In considering an application for an explosives licence or for any alteration in the terms of an existing licence the Health and Safety Executive must take into account any comments or objections received pursuant to the publication of the notice and may reject the application or may grant the licence or amending licence subject to such conditions as the Executive thinks fit. An explosives licence may be with or without limit of time and may be varied or revoked in writing by the Executive at any time. The Health and Safety Executive may grant a provisional explosives licence in cases of urgency which may have effect for a period of up to six months.

Repeal of certain legislation by the regulations

8.24 As indicated above, the Dangerous Substances in Harbour Areas Regulations supersede, and to a considerable extent substantially reproduce, the pre-existing regime for handling, etc., dangerous goods in harbours. The repeal provisions of the regulations are contained in regulation 47 and Schedule 8. With regard to the enabling powers for these repeal provisions, under section 15(3)(*a*) of the Health and Safety at Work, etc. Act 1974, health and safety regulations (a category which includes the Dangerous Substances in

Harbour Areas Regulations) may repeal or modify any of the "existing statutory provisions". The existing statutory provisions are defined in section 53 of, and Schedule 1 to, the 1974 Act as meaning, broadly, provisions of specified general statutes relating to health and safety at work and subordinate legislation made thereunder. The provisions in question include most of the Explosives Act 1875, the Explosives Act 1923 and the Petroleum (Consolidation) Act 1928. Under section 80 of the 1974 Act, which is cited among the enabling powers for the Dangerous Substances in Harbour Areas Regulations, the regulations may also repeal any other provision contained in an Act of Parliament or subordinate legislation which was passed or made before the passing of the 1974 Act on 31 July 1974 if it appears to the Secretary of State that the repeal is expedient in consequence of or in connection with any provision of the regulations.

8.25 The Dangerous Substances in Harbour Areas Regulations repealed on the one hand the existing explosives and petroleum by-laws made by harbour authorities under the Explosives Act 1875 and the Petroleum (Consolidation) Act 1928 and also the Conveyance in Harbours of Military Explosives Regulations which were made under the 1875 Act and, on the other hand, local harbour Acts and harbour by-laws passed or made before 31 July 1974 which in the Secretary of State's opinion duplicated or were inconsistent with, or otherwise did not fit in with, the regulations.

8.26 The regulations repealed certain of these provisions when the regulations came into force on 1 June 1987 and other provisions on 31 December 1989. Certain sections of the Explosives Acts, including the by-law making powers, and all by-laws made thereunder and the Military Explosives Regulations were repealed when the regulations came into force. The by-law making powers under the Petroleum (Consolidation) Act 1928 were repealed when the regulations came into force and most of the harbour petroleum by-laws made thereunder ceased to have effect on that date. But under paragraph (3) of regulation 47 the petroleum by-laws specified in Part I of Schedule 8 continued in force until 31 December 1989. The local Acts and by-laws specified in Part II of Schedule 8, all of which were passed or made before 31 July 1974, were repealed when the regulations came into force. The by-laws specified in Part III of Schedule 8, again being by-laws made before 31 July 1974, were repealed on 31 December 1989. However, the repeal of these pre-1974 local Acts and by-laws is expressed to be limited to the extent to which they applied within harbour areas in relation to dangerous substances. Insofar as they had a wider application they therefore continued in force.

8.27 The reason why the repeal of some of these provisions was postponed until the end of 1989 was that the provisions concerned related to particular local circumstances which could not adequately be catered for by the general provisions of the regulations. It was envisaged that before the end of 1989 by-laws would be made under regulation 43 (see paragraph 8.28 *post*) to deal with these local situations.

Power for statutory harbour authorities to make by-laws under the regulations

8.28 Regulation 43 of the Dangerous Substances in Harbour Areas Regulations authorizes a statutory harbour authority to make by-laws in respect of their "harbour area" prohibiting the entry or regulating the entry, carriage, handling and storage of dangerous substances. This is a wide power and was not intended merely to fill the gaps which were left when the provisions repealed by the regulations at the end of 1989 ceased to have effect. The by-law making power is intended to deal with any local circumstances which are not adequately covered by the general provisions of the regulations, but they must not of course conflict with those provisions. In particular, by-laws under regulation 43 may prohibit or regulate the entry of a particular dangerous substance which a statutory harbour authority consider would in itself, and not because of its condition (which is what the harbour master's powers under regulation 7 depend on—see paragraph 8.15 *ante*), create a danger to health and safety in the circumstances of their harbour.

8.29 Schedule 6 specifies the procedure for making by-laws and bringing them into force. Subject to one unusual provision which is mentioned below, the procedure is broadly similar to that which currently applies in the case of most harbour authority by-laws. The Secretary of State may confirm by-laws submitted to him by a statutory harbour authority with or without modification or may refuse to confirm them, but before reaching a decision he is required to consult the Health and Safety Commission. Where the Secretary of State proposes to confirm a by-law with a modification which appears to him to be substantial he must inform the statutory harbour authority and require them to take any steps he considers necessary for informing persons likely to be concerned with the modification and must not proceed to confirm the by-law until the statutory harbour authority and other persons concerned have had a reasonable opportunity to comment on the proposed modification.

8.30 The by-law procedure in Schedule 6 to the regulations includes one unique provision. Under paragraph 2 by-laws generally do not have effect until they are confirmed by the Secretary of State, which is of course the usual state of affairs. But under the proviso to that paragraph a by-law which prohibits or regulates the entry of a dangerous substance into a harbour area and which has been made after consultation with any berth operator who appears to the statutory harbour authority to be affected by the proposed by-law comes into force when application is made for its confirmation. However, as one would expect, such a by-law ceases to have effect if the Secretary of State subsequently refuses to confirm it. If he confirms it with modifications, then the by-law thereafter has effect as so modified. The purpose of this unusual provision is to enable a harbour authority to take action at short notice to prohibit or regulate the entry of a (new) dangerous substance into their harbour.

Enforcement of the regulations and penalties for contravention

8.31 Under regulation 44 of the Dangerous Substances in Harbour Areas Regulations a statutory harbour authority are responsible for enforcing Part II of the regulations (entry of dangerous substances into harbour areas), Part III (marking and navigation of vessels), regulation 19 (fitness of vessels for carrying, loading or unloading liquid dangerous substances in bulk), regulation 20 (permission for transfer between vessels of liquid dangerous substances in bulk), regulation 32(2) (parking of road vehicles carrying dangerous substances) and regulation 38 (vessels and vehicles loaded with explosives to be taken out of harbour areas) in their harbour area against persons other than themselves. Otherwise, the Health and Safety Executive are responsible for enforcing the Dangerous Substances in Harbour Areas Regulations.

8.32 The penalty provisions for failing to comply with the requirements of the Dangerous Substances in Harbour Areas Regulations are contained in the Health and Safety at Work, etc. Act 1974. Under section 33(1)(c) of that Act it is an offence for a person to contravene any health and safety regulations. It is also an offence to contravene any requirement or prohibition imposed under any such regulations and this would appear to include by-laws under regulation 43 of the Dangerous Substances in Harbour Areas Regulations. The maximum penalty which may be imposed for such an offence is a fine of £5,000 on summary conviction or, on conviction on indictment, an unlimited fine. In a few cases, including handling explosives without a licence under Part IX of the regulations, the maximum penalty on indictment may be, or include, imprisonment for a term not exceeding two years.

8.33 Regulation 45, however, provides that it is a defence for a person charged with a contravention of the regulations or of by-laws made under regulation 43, to prove that he took all reasonable precautions and exercised all due diligence to avoid the commission of the offence. Regulation 45 excepts proceedings for an offence under regulations 16, 31(a) or 32(1) from the defence which it provides but that is because each of those regulations requires something to be done so far as reasonably practicable or to take all reasonably practicable steps for a specified purpose so that, in effect, the same defence is built into them.

8.34 Under section 38 of the Health and Safety at Work, etc. Act 1974 proceedings for a contravention of the regulations in England and Wales can only be brought by an inspector appointed by an enforcing authority under section 19 of the Act or by or with the consent of the Director of Public Prosecutions (in Scotland such proceedings will be brought by the Procurator Fiscal).

Exemptions from provisions of the regulations

8.35 Under regulation 46 of the Dangerous Substances in Harbour Areas Regulations the Health and Safety Executive may grant exemption from the provisions of the regulations. The Executive must not grant such an exemption unless it is satisfied that neither the health or safety of any person nor the security of any explosive likely to be affected by the exemption will be prejudiced. The Secretary of State for Defence may also grant exemptions from the provisions of the regulations in the interests of national security.

Local legislation relating to dangerous substances

8.36 Apart from the Dangerous Substances in Harbour Areas Regulations, the special legislation of some harbour authorities includes provisions to control the entry of dangerous goods, including powers to prohibit the entry of such goods, on lines exemplified by sections 67 and 68 of the Forth Ports Authority Order Confirmation Act 1969 which are set out in Appendix I. Provisions of this kind are not repealed by the Dangerous Substances in Harbour Areas Regulations. The Dover Harbour Board, under the Dover Harbour Revision Order 1978, have considerably wider powers for regulating the entry of dangerous goods into their harbour and adjoining land owned or occupied by them which are also not affected by the Dangerous Substances in Harbour Areas Regulations.

The Planning (Hazardous Substances) Act 1990

8.37 There are other statutory controls in relation to dangerous substances which apply both at harbours and elsewhere. Reference should perhaps be made to the Planning (Hazardous Substances) Act 1990 (as amended by the Environmental Protection Act 1990) which, in England and Wales, requires the consent of the hazardous substances authority, usually the district council, for the presence on, over or under land of a hazardous substance specified in the Planning (Hazardous Substances) Regulations 1992 in the quantity prescribed by those regulations as the controlled quantity.

8.38 It is of importance to harbour authorities that section 4(3) of the Planning (Hazardous Substances) Act 1990 provides that the temporary presence of a hazardous substance while it is being transported from one place to another is not to be taken into account unless it is unloaded (neither "temporary" nor "unloaded" is defined by the Act). It is also important that under regulation 4(1) of the regulations mentioned in paragraph 8.37 *ante* a hazardous substances consent is not required for the temporary presence of a hazardous substance during the period when it is being unloaded from one means of transport and loaded on to another while it is being transported from one place to another. Regulation 4(4) provides that a hazardous substances consent is not required for the presence of a hazardous substance which has been unloaded from a ship or other sea-going craft in an emergency until the expiry of the period of 14 days beginning with the day on which it was so unloaded and specifies certain circumstances in which for this purpose a craft is to be treated as having been unloaded in an emergency.

8.39 In Scotland the Town and Country Planning (Hazardous Substances) (Scotland) Regulations 1993, made under the Town and Country Planning (Scotland) Act 1972 and section 38 of the Housing and Planning Act 1986, contain similar provisions. An application for a hazardous substances consent under these Regulations is to be made to the planning authority within the meaning of section 172 of the Local Government (Scotland) Act 1973.

CHAPTER 9

PREVENTION OF POLLUTION, ETC.

The Merchant Shipping (Prevention of Oil Pollution) Regulations 1996

9.1 Seaward of the baseline for measuring the breadth of the United Kingdom's territorial sea, the discharge of oil from ships into the sea is regulated by Part III of the Merchant Shipping (Prevention of Oil Pollution) Regulations 1996. These Regulations were made by the Secretary of State under powers conferred by the Merchant Shipping (Prevention of Oil Pollution) Order 1983 and the Merchant Shipping (Prevention of Pollution) (Law of the Sea Convention) Order 1996, Orders in Council made, or having effect as if made, under Part VI of the Merchant Shipping Act 1995. These Regulations give effect to the International Convention for the Prevention of Pollution from Ships 1973, including Annex I to the Convention which relates to pollution by oil, but not the other Annexes to the Convention, as amended by the Protocol of 1978. (The 1973 Convention, as amended by the Protocol of 1978, is usually called, and is hereafter referred to as, "MARPOL".) Regulation 12 regulates the discharge of oil into the sea from ships other than oil tankers and as respects oil tankers regulates such discharges from their machinery space bilges. Regulation 13 regulates other discharges of oil into the sea from oil tankers. The regulations define "sea" as including any estuary or arm of the sea.

9.2 Regulations 12 and 13 also prohibit the discharge into the sea of chemicals or other substances in quantities or concentrations which are hazardous to the marine environment and discharges containing chemicals or other substances introduced for the purposes of circumventing the conditions of discharge prescribed by regulations 12 and 13 respectively. These prohibitions apply landward as well as seaward of the baseline for measuring the breadth of the territorial waters of the United Kingdom (under section 1(1)(b) of the Territorial Sea Act 1987 this baseline is established by Her Majesty by Order in Council—it is currently prescribed by the Territorial Waters Order in Council 1964 and the Territorial Waters (Amendment) Order in Council 1979 which, although made before the passing of the Territorial Sea Act 1987, have effect as if made under it). Under regulation 36(2) of the Merchant

Shipping (Prevention of Oil Pollution) Regulations 1996, if a ship fails to comply with regulation 12 or 13, the owner and master are each guilty of an offence and section 131(3) of the Merchant Shipping Act 1995 applies as it applies to an offence under that section so that each of the owner and master is liable on summary conviction to a fine not exceeding £50,000 and on conviction on indictment to an (unlimited) fine. Section 131(3) of the 1995 Act is described in paragraph 9.6 *post*. Section 7(5) of the Merchant Shipping and Maritime Security Act 1997 makes clear that the amendment of section 131(3) of the 1995 Act by section 7(1) of the 1997 Act has not increased the maximum penalty on summary conviction under regulation 36(2) which therefore remains at £50,000. (It may well be that in future this will be increased to £250,000 by amending regulations. Such an amendment is authorized by section 7(6) and (7) of the 1997 Act.)

Provisions of Merchant Shipping Act 1995 relating to pollution by ships

9.3 The discharge of oil from ships into United Kingdom national waters (defined in section 313 of the Merchant Shipping Act 1995 as "United Kingdom waters landward of the baselines for measuring the breadth of its territorial sea") which are navigable by sea-going ships is dealt with in section 131 of the Merchant Shipping Act 1995. The waters within the jurisdiction of harbour authorities are in most cases wholly, and in other cases mainly, within United Kingdom national waters. Generally therefore the relevant provisions for controlling the discharge of oil from ships in harbour are those contained in section 131 and the subsequent related provisions of the Merchant Shipping Act 1995 although regulations 12 and 13 of the Merchant Shipping (Prevention of Oil Pollution) Regulations 1996 are the relevant provisions in relation to such discharges into the outer limits of some harbour authorities.

9.4 Section 131(1) of the Merchant Shipping Act 1995 provides that if any oil or mixture containing oil is discharged from a ship into United Kingdom national waters which are navigable by sea-going ships then, subject to the qualifications referred to below, the owner or master of the ship shall be guilty of an offence. If the discharge is from a ship but takes place in the course of a transfer of oil to or from another ship or a place on land and is caused by the act or omission of any person in charge of any apparatus in that other ship or that place, the owner or master of that other ship or, as the case may be, the occupier of that place, is guilty of an offence.

9.5 Section 131(2) of the Merchant Shipping Act 1995 provides that section 131(1) shall not apply to any discharge which is made into the sea and is of a kind or is made in circumstances for the time being prescribed by regulations made by the Secretary of State. The purpose of this provision is to enable the Secretary of State to exempt from prosecution under the 1995 Act certain discharges which would be permitted under regulations 12 and 13 of the Merchant Shipping (Prevention of Oil Pollution) Regulations 1996 if they applied to the waters in question. These discharges are, in particular, those which contain only very small proportions of oil.

9.6 Section 131(3) as amended by section 7(1) of the Merchant Shipping and Maritime Security Act 1997 provides that a person guilty of an offence under section 131 shall be liable on summary conviction to a fine not exceeding £250,000[1] and on conviction on indictment to an (unlimited) fine. Under section 146(2) of the Merchant Shipping Act 1995 the court may order the whole or any part of such fine to be applied towards defraying the expenses of removing the pollution attributable to the offence.

9.7 Subsections (4), (5) and (6) of section 131 of the Merchant Shipping Act 1995 provide, respectively, that, for the purposes of the section, "sea" includes any estuary or arm of the sea, "place on land" includes anything resting on the bed or shore of the sea or of any other waters included in United Kingdom national waters and also includes anything afloat (other than a ship) if it is anchored or attached to the bed or shore of the sea or any such waters and that "occupier" in relation to any such thing, if it has no occupier, means the owner thereof.

9.8 The Merchant Shipping Act 1995 provides for certain defences for a person charged with an offence under section 131 of the Act. Under section 132(1) it is a defence for the owner or master of a ship charged with such an offence to prove that the oil or mixture was discharged for the purpose of securing the safety of any ship or of preventing damage to any ship or cargo or of saving life, unless the court is satisfied that the discharge of the oil or mixture was not necessary for that purpose or was not a reasonable step to take in the circumstances.

9.9 Under section 131(2) it is also a defence for the owner or master of a ship charged with such an offence to prove that the oil or mixture escaped in consequence of damage to the ship and that, as soon as practicable after the damage occurred, all reasonable steps were taken for preventing, or (if it could not be prevented) for stopping or reducing the escape of the oil or mixture, or if the oil or mixture escaped by reason of leakage, that neither the leakage nor any delay in discovering it was due to any want of reasonable care, and that as soon as practicable after the escape was discovered all reasonable steps were taken for stopping or reducing it. Section 134 of the Act also provides that where any oil or mixture containing oil is discharged in consequence of the exercise of certain powers by a harbour authority, the authority or person acting on their behalf shall not be convicted of an offence under section 131 unless it is shown that they or he failed to take such steps (if any) as were reasonable in the circumstances for preventing, stopping or reducing the discharge.

---

1. In the case of fines imposed on summary conviction in respect of offences committed before section 7 of the 1997 Act came into force, the previous maximum of £50,000 applies.

9.10 Section 133 provides that where a person is charged, in respect of the escape of any oil or mixture, with an offence under section 131 as the occupier of a place on land it shall be a defence to prove that neither the escape nor any delay in discovering it was due to any want of reasonable care and that as soon as practicable after it was discovered all reasonable steps were taken for stopping or reducing it.

9.11 Under section 143 of the 1995 Act, proceedings for an offence under section 131 of the Act which consists of the discharge of oil, or a mixture containing oil, into the waters of a harbour in the United Kingdom can, in England and Wales, only be brought by the harbour authority or by or with the consent of the Attorney-General or by the Secretary of State or a person authorized by the Secretary of State (in Scotland all such proceedings are brought by the Procurator Fiscal). This also applies in respect of the offences under sections 135 and 136 of the 1995 Act referred to in paragraph 9.20 *post* except that, in those cases, proceedings may not be instituted by, or by a person authorized by, the Secretary of State.

9.12 In Chapter II of Part VI of the Merchant Shipping Act 1995 (which relates to oil pollution):

"harbour authority" means a person or body of persons empowered by an enactment to make charges in respect of ships entering a harbour in the United Kingdom or using facilities therein;

"harbour in the United Kingdom" means a port, estuary, haven, dock or other place the waters of which are within United Kingdom national waters and, in respect of entry into or the use of which by ships, a person or body is empowered by an enactment (including a local enactment) to make any charges other than charges in respect of navigational aids or pilotage.

9.13 Section 143(6) of the Merchant Shipping Act 1995 provides that any document required or authorized, by virtue of any statutory provision, to be served on a foreign company for the purposes of the institution of, or otherwise in connection with, proceedings for an offence under section 131 of the Act of 1995 alleged to have been committed by the company as the owner of a ship, shall be treated as duly served on that company if the document is served on the master of the ship. For this purpose "foreign company" means a company or body which is not one to which any of the provisions of sections 695 and 724 of the Companies Act 1985 (or the corresponding provisions of the Companies (Northern Ireland) Order 1986) apply—that is to say (in the case of Great Britain), an overseas company which does not have a place of business in Great Britain and which has not made arrangements for the service of documents in accordance with section 695. This provision corresponds to an amendment introduced into the Prevention of Oil Pollution Act 1971 by the Environmental Protection Act 1990 to secure that, where an oil pollution offence was committed by a foreign ship, the owner, who was usually outside British jurisdiction, could be prosecuted. Previously, in practice only the master of a foreign ship could be prosecuted. This resulted in the fines imposed for serious oil pollution offences by foreign ships often being lower than in the cases of similar offences by British ships where the owner was prosecuted. This was because, where proceedings are brought against the master of a ship and he is convicted, the court will take his personal financial resources into account in assessing the amount of the fine (the principles to be considered in fixing the amount of the fine where a person is convicted of an offence under (now) section 131 of the Merchant Shipping Act 1995 were discussed by His Honour Judge Forrester-Paton Q.C. in his judgment given on 8 September 1980 in the Teesside Crown Court in the case of *Vladyslav Paderewski* v. *Tees and Hartlepool Port Authority*). Section 18(3) of the Criminal Justice Act 1991 (as substituted by section 65 of the Criminal Justice Act 1993) requires a court, in fixing the amount of any fine (which therefore includes a fine for an offence under section 131), to take into account the circumstances of the case, including among other things the financial circumstances of the offender so far as they are known or appear to the court (whether this has the effect of increasing or reducing the amount of the fine—section 18(5)).

9.14 Section 144 of the Merchant Shipping Act 1995 authorizes a harbour master (including the Queen's harbour master in the case of a dockyard port) to detain a ship where he has reason to believe that the master or owner has committed an offence under section 131 of the Act by the discharge from the ship of oil, or a mixture containing oil, into the waters of the harbour. The section applies with appropriate modifications the provisions of the 1995 Act for enforcing the detention of ships and provides that where a harbour master detains a foreign ship he must immediately notify the Secretary of State who is then required to inform the consul or diplomatic representative of the State whose flag the ship is entitled to fly or the appropriate maritime authorities of that State.

9.15 A harbour master who detains a ship under this power must immediately release it:

    (a) if no proceedings for the offence in question are instituted within the period of seven days beginning with the day when the ship is detained (the section describes the circumstances in which proceedings are instituted);

    (b) if such proceedings, having been instituted within that period, are concluded without the master or owner being convicted (the section describes the circumstances in which this is the case);

(c) if either:
  (i) the sum of £255,000[2] is paid to the harbour authority by way of security (i.e., for any fine which the court may impose together with costs), or
  (ii) security which, in the opinion of the harbour authority, is satisfactory and is for an amount not less than £255,000[3] is given to the harbour authority, by or on behalf of the master or owner; or

(d) where the master or owner is convicted of the offence, if any costs or expenses ordered to be paid by him, and any fine imposed on him, have been paid.

9.16 The harbour authority must repay any sum paid by way of security, or release any security given, as mentioned above:

  (a) if no proceedings for the offence in question are instituted within the period of seven days beginning with the day on which the sum is paid; or
  (b) if such proceedings, having been instituted within that period, are concluded without the master or owner being convicted.

9.17 Where a sum has been paid by way of security, or security has been given, as mentioned above and the master or owner is convicted of the offence in question, the amount paid or the amount made available under the security must be applied first in payment of any costs or expenses ordered by the court to be paid by the master or owner and next in payment of any fine imposed by the court. Any balance is to be repaid to the person—the master or owner as the case may be—by, or on whose behalf, the sum was paid or the security given.

9.18 Regulation 37(1) to (8) of the Merchant Shipping (Prevention of Oil Pollution) Regulations 1996 contains provisions corresponding to those described in paragraphs 9.13 to 9.17 *ante* in relation to offences under regulation 12, 13 or 16 of those regulations. However, the relevant sum for the purpose of regulation 37(1) to (8) remains at £55,000 unless and until it is increased by amending regulations. Such an amendment is authorized by section 7(6) and (7) of the Merchant Shipping and Maritime Security Act 1997.

Powers of Secretary of State in relation to ships which present threat to marine environment

9.19 Regulation 34 of the Merchant Shipping (Prevention of Oil Pollution) Regulations 1996 contains powers for persons appointed by the Secretary of

---

2. This figure was increased from £55,000 to £255,000 by section 7(3) of the Merchant Shipping and Maritime Security Act 1997. The increase does not apply to ships detained before section 7 came into force.
3. *Ibid.*

State to inspect ships at United Kingdom ports and terminals. Such inspection is normally to be limited to verifying that there is on board a valid International Oil Pollution Prevention Certificate in the form prescribed by MARPOL or a valid United Kingdom Oil Pollution Prevention Certificate in the form prescribed by the regulations. If, however, there are clear grounds for believing that the condition of the ship or her equipment does not correspond substantially with the particulars of the certificate or if there is no valid certificate on board, the inspector must take such steps as he may consider necessary to ensure that the ship shall not sail until she can proceed to sea without presenting an unreasonable threat of harm to the marine environment. In such a case the Secretary of State may permit the ship to leave port for the purpose of proceeding to the nearest appropriate repair yard. Under regulation 34 the inspector may also investigate any operation regulated by the 1996 Regulations if there are clear grounds for believing that the master or crew are not familiar with essential ship board procedures for preventing pollution by oil. If his inspection reveals deficiencies, the inspector must take steps to ensure that the ship will not sail until the situation has been brought to order in accordance with the requirements of the 1996 Regulations. Regulation 35(1) of the 1996 Regulations provides that, if a harbour master has reason to believe that a ship which he believes proposes to enter the harbour in question does not comply with the requirements of the regulations (i.e., as respects the condition of the ship or her equipment) he must immediately report the matter to the Secretary of State who, if he is satisfied that the ship presents an unreasonable threat of harm to the marine environment, may deny the entry of such ship to United Kingdom ports or off-shore terminals. Regulation 35(2) enables the Secretary of State to detain a ship which is suspected of contravening the requirements of the 1996 Regulations. Where he does so, or where a ship is detained in connection with steps taken by an inspector under regulation 34, the provisions of section 284 of the Merchant Shipping Act 1995, which relate to the detention of a ship, apply with appropriate modifications.

Notice to be given to harbour master before oil is transferred in harbour or of discharge of oil into harbour

9.20 Section 135 of the Merchant Shipping Act 1995 requires notice to be given to the harbour master (or if there is no harbour master to the harbour authority) before oil is transferred between sunset and sunrise to or from a ship in any harbour. Section 136 provides that if any oil or mixture containing oil is discharged from a ship into the waters of a harbour in the United Kingdom, or is found to be escaping or to have escaped from a ship into any such waters, the owner or master of the ship must forthwith report the occurrence to the harbour master, or to the harbour authority if there is no harbour master, stating whether the occurrence is a discharge or an escape as mentioned above. Failure to comply with section 135 is punishable on summary conviction by a fine not exceeding level 3 on the standard scale and failure to comply with section 136 by a fine not exceeding level 5 on the standard scale.

Powers of harbour master to board and inspect vessels for purpose of investigating oil pollution

9.21 Under section 259(6) of the Merchant Shipping Act 1995, the harbour master for a harbour, for the purpose of ascertaining the circumstances relating to an alleged discharge of oil, or a mixture containing oil, from a ship into the harbour, may board the ship and make such examination and investigation as he considers necessary. He may also require the production of, inspect and take copies of, relevant documents.

Clearing up of oil spills etc.

9.22 Turning to the clearing up of oil spills, harbour authorities do not generally have specific powers for this purpose. However, it seems that the terms in which the general duties of a harbour authority are now commonly expressed (see, for example, the general duties of the Port of London Authority set out in Part II of Appendix C) are probably wide enough to cover this. Alternatively, the clearing up of oil spills would appear to be reasonably incidental to the express powers of a harbour authority.

9.23 The functions of harbour authorities in connection with the clearing up of oil spills overlap with those of local authorities and the Secretary of State. Under section 293 of the Merchant Shipping Act 1995 the Secretary of State continues to have the functions of taking, or co-ordinating measures to prevent, reduce and minimize the effects of marine pollution. Under section 293(2)(za), inserted by paragraph 13B of Schedule 6 to the Merchant Shipping and Maritime Security Act 1997, these functions include the preparation, review and implementation of a national plan setting out arrangements for responding to incidents which cause, or may cause, marine pollution with a view to preventing such pollution or reducing or minimizing its effects. The Secretary of State's functions under section 293 are now generally exercised via the Marine Pollution Control Unit. Where, pursuant to section 293, the Secretary of State agrees that another person shall take any measures to prevent, reduce or minimize the effects of marine pollution, he may agree to indemnify that other person in respect of liabilities incurred by that person in connection with the taking of the measures—subsection (4A) of section 293 inserted by section 6 of the Merchant Shipping and Maritime Security Act 1997.

9.24 Local authorities have traditionally taken a voluntary role to clean up beaches which have been affected by maritime oil spills. By virtue of subsection (3A) of section 128 of the Merchant Shipping Act 1995, inserted in that section by section 12 of the Merchant Shipping and Maritime Security Act 1997, an Order in Council under section 128(1)(d) (to give effect to provisions of the International Convention on Oil Pollution Preparedness, Response and Co-operation 1990), or regulations made thereunder, could impose duties on local authorities in relation to the preparation, review and implementation of any plans required by the Convention. It appears that duties for these purposes could also be imposed on harbour authorities by an Order under section 128(1)(d) of the 1995 Act or regulations made under such an Order.

9.25 Under section 137 of the 1995 Act as amended by the Merchant Shipping and Maritime Security Act 1997, the Secretary of State has wide powers to deal with shipping casualties (including those which occur in harbours) where, in his opinion, oil from the ship will or may cause significant pollution. The Secretary of State may exercise these powers where an accident has occurred to a ship and in his opinion oil from the ship will or may cause such pollution as is mentioned above and where also in his opinion the use of these powers is urgently needed. "Accident" for this purpose means a collision of ships, stranding or other incident of navigation or other occurrence on board a ship or external to it, resulting in material damage or imminent threat of material damage to a ship or cargo. Section 137(2) provides that, for the purpose of preventing or reducing oil pollution or the risk of oil pollution, the Secretary of State may give directions as respects the ship or its cargo to the owner, or to any person in possession of the ship, to the master of the ship, to any pilot of the ship (defined, in line with the Pilotage Act 1987, as any person not belonging to the ship who has the conduct of the ship) or to any salvor in possession of the ship or to any servant or agent of such salvor who is in charge of the salvage operations. Where the ship in question is within waters which are regulated or managed by a harbour authority, the Secretary of State may, for the purposes mentioned above, give directions to the harbour master or the harbour authority. The definition of "harbour authority" mentioned in paragraph 9.12 *ante* appears to apply for this purpose. "Harbour master" is defined for this purpose in section 151(1) of the 1995 Act as including a dock master or pier master and any person specially appointed by a harbour authority for the purpose of enforcing the provisions of Chapter II of Part VI of the 1995 Act. By virtue of section 137(3) directions under section 137(2) may require the person to whom they are given to take or refrain from taking any action of any kind whatsoever. Without prejudice to that generality section 137(3) specifies certain things which a direction under section 137(2) may require which include that the ship is to be moved to a specified place (which could be a particular harbour). Section 137(4) provides that if, in the Secretary of State's opinion, his powers under section 137(2) are, or have proved to be, inadequate he may, for the purpose of preventing or reducing pollution, take, as respects the ship or its cargo, any action of any kind whatsoever. Section 137(4) specifies, without prejudice to that generality, certain measures which the Secretary of State may take which include any such action as he has power to require to be taken by a direction under section 137(2) and the undertaking of operations which involve taking over control of the ship. Under section 137(5) the powers of the Secretary of State under section 137(4) are also exercisable by such persons as he may authorize for the purpose.

9.26 Section 138A of the 1995 Act, inserted by section 3 of the Merchant Shipping and Maritime Security Act 1997, provides that any reference to oil pollution in section 137 (and in section 138 which enables a person who suffers unreasonable loss or damage as a result of action taken under section 137 to recover compensation) includes a reference to pollution by any other substance which is prescribed by the Secretary of State by order for the purposes of the section or which, although not so prescribed, is liable to create hazards to human health, to harm living resources and marine life, to damage amenities or to interfere with other legitimate uses of the sea. Accordingly, the Secretary of State's wide powers to intervene where a shipping casualty causes, or threatens, significant pollution, apply in relation to pollution by virtually any substance. The 1997 Act revoked provisions of the Merchant Shipping (Prevention of Pollution) (Intervention) Order 1980 which covered substantially the same ground.

9.27 Where a harbour authority incur expenditure in clearing up a major oil spill they will generally be able to recover the cost from the owner of the ship concerned even in the absence of negligence on the part of the master or crew. Under section 153 of the Merchant Shipping Act 1995 the owner of a ship constructed or adapted for carrying oil in bulk as cargo is absolutely liable for (*inter alia*) the cost of any measures reasonably taken to prevent or minimize damage caused by contamination resulting from the discharge or escape of oil from the ship and under section 154 the owner of any other ship is similarly liable, unless, in either case, the contamination:

(a) resulted from an act of war, hostilities, civil war, insurrection or an exceptional, inevitable and irresistible natural phenomenon; or

(b) was due wholly to anything done or omitted to be done by another person, not being a servant or agent of the owner, with intent to do damage; or

(c) was due wholly to the negligence or wrongful act of a government or other authority in exercising its function of maintaining lights or other navigational aids for the maintenance of which it was responsible.

The owner of a ship constructed or adapted to carry oil in bulk as cargo will, however, be entitled to limit his liability in accordance with the provisions of section 157 of the Merchant Shipping Act 1995 unless it is proved that the discharge or escape, or (as the case may be) the relevant threat of contamination, resulted from anything done or omitted to be done by the owner, either with intent to cause the damage or cost in question or recklessly and in the knowledge that such damage or cost would probably result.

9.28 Where a harbour authority cannot recover, or recover in full, the cost of clearing up an oil spill from the owner of a ship constructed or adapted to carry oil in bulk as cargo because the discharge or escape occurred in circumstances in which, under the Merchant Shipping Act 1995, the owner is not liable (other than war, hostilities, civil war or insurrection) or because the owner cannot meet his obligations in full or because the cost incurred exceeds the statutory limitation on the owner's liability, the harbour authority will usually be entitled, under section 175 of the Merchant Shipping Act 1995, to claim from the Fund referred to in Chapter IV of Part VI of that Act (which was established pursuant to an international Convention and funded by contributions from the oil industry).

Discharge of oil into sea from places on land

9.29 Under section 2(1) of the Prevention of Oil Pollution Act 1971 the discharge of oil, or a mixture containing oil, from a place on land into waters to which section 2 applies is an offence on the part of the occupier of the place in question unless he proves that the discharge was caused by a person who is in that place without his permission, in which case that person is guilty of the offence.

9.30 The waters to which section 2 of the 1971 Act applies are defined in section 2(2) as:

(a) the whole of the sea within the seaward limits of the territorial waters of the United Kingdom; and

(b) all other waters (including inland waters) which are within those limits and are navigable by sea-going ships.

9.31 For the purposes of the Act of 1971 "place on land" includes anything resting on the bed or shore of the sea, or of any other waters to which section 2 applies and also includes anything afloat (other than a vessel) if it is anchored or attached to the bed or shore of the sea or of any such waters and "occupier", in relation to any such thing, if it has no occupier, means the owner of the thing and, in relation to a railway wagon or road vehicle, means the person in charge of the wagon or vehicle and not the occupier of the land on which the wagon or vehicle stands—section 2(3).

9.32 Under section 2(4) of the 1971 Act a person guilty of an offence under section 2 is liable on summary conviction to a fine not exceeding £50,000 and on conviction on indictment to an (unlimited) fine. By virtue of section 19 of the 1971 Act, where the offence consists of the discharge of oil, or a mixture containing oil, into the waters of a harbour, then proceedings for the offence may, in England and Wales, be brought only by the harbour authority or by or with the consent of the Attorney General or by the Secretary of State or a person authorized by the Secretary of State (in Scotland proceedings would be brought by the Procurator Fiscal).

9.33 Section 6(2) of the 1971 Act provides that where a person is charged with an offence under section 2 it shall be a defence to prove—

(a) that the oil was contained in an effluent produced by operations for the refining of oil;

(b) that it was not reasonably practicable to dispose of the effluent otherwise than by discharging it into waters to which section 2 applies; and

(c) that all reasonably practicable steps had been taken to eliminate oil from the effluent.

However, under section 6(3) this defence is not available if it is proved that, at the time to which the charge relates, the surface of the waters, into which the mixture was discharged from the place on land, or land adjacent to those waters, was fouled by oil unless the court is satisfied that the fouling was not caused, or contributed to, by oil contained in any effluent discharged at or before that time from that place.

9.34 Under section 11 of the 1971 Act if any oil or mixture containing oil is found to be escaping, or to have escaped, into the waters of a harbour in the United Kingdom from a place on land, the occupier of that place must forthwith report the occurrence to the harbour master or, if the harbour has no harbour master, to the harbour authority. If a person required to make such a report fails to do so he is liable on summary conviction to a fine not exceeding level 5 on the standard scale.

Landing and disposal of ships' wastes

9.35 Regulation 12 of Annex I and regulation 7 of Annex II of MARPOL require the provision at ports and terminals of reception facilities for the discharge from vessels of residues and mixtures which contain, respectively, oil or "noxious liquid substances" as specified in Appendix II to Annex II. The Prevention of Pollution (Reception Facilities) Order 1984 is an Order in Council originally made under enabling powers contained in section 20 of the Merchant Shipping Act 1979 and now having effect as if made under section 128 of the Merchant Shipping Act 1995 to give effect to these requirements. It is hereafter referred to as "the Reception Facilities Order".

9.36 Section 5 of the Merchant Shipping and Maritime Security Act 1997 inserts a new Chapter IA in Part VI of the Merchant Shipping Act 1995 dealing with waste reception facilities. This new Chapter, which is set out in Appendix J, includes a wide and flexible power for the Secretary of State to

make regulations. Regulations under this power may require a harbour authority to prepare a waste management plan and submit it to the Secretary of State
for approval. Such regulations may also include a wide range of provisions
relating to charges for the use of reception facilities and may require the master
of a ship to deposit waste carried by the ship in waste reception facilities
provided at harbours in the United Kingdom. As this book goes to press, no
regulations under the new Chapter IA of Part VI of the 1995 Act have been
made, but the Department of Transport have requested that, as an interim
measure, each port and harbour authority, marine and terminal operator
develop a waste management plan in accordance with guidelines specified in
a Merchant Shipping Notice.

9.37 The Reception Facilities Order applies to any "harbour authority" or
"terminal operator" whose harbour or terminal in the United Kingdom is
used by oil tankers, chemical tankers or other vessels, any of which are
carrying residues or mixtures which contain oil or noxious liquid substances.
"Harbour" is defined in the Order as a:

"harbour, port, estuary, haven, dock or other place which contains waters which are
within—
   (a) the sea within the seaward limits of the territorial waters of the United
       Kingdom; and
   (b) all other waters (including inland waters) which are within those limits and are
       navigable by sea-going ships
but does not include a terminal within the harbour managed by a person other than the
harbour authority for the harbour."

9.38 The Reception Facilities Order defines "harbour authority" as "a
person or body of persons having for the time being the management of a
harbour in the United Kingdom" so it does not appear to be limited to
harbour authorities managing harbours under statutory powers. "Terminal" is
defined as a "terminal, jetty, pier or mono-buoy" and "terminal operator" as
"a person or body or persons having for the time being the management of a
terminal in the United Kingdom". "Noxious liquid substance" is defined
as:

"any substance which may be specified by the Secretary of State in regulations made
under this Order and any other liquid substance which, when discharged into the sea
from tank cleaning or deballasting operations, presents a risk of harm to human health,
marine resources or other legitimate uses of the sea equivalent to that presented by any
substance so specified."

9.39 The Reception Facilities Order provides that the powers exercisable by
a harbour authority in respect of any harbour shall include power to provide
reception facilities for the discharge from vessels using the harbour of residues
and mixtures which contain oil or noxious liquid substances and that any such
powers shall include power to join with any other person in providing such
facilities. Such a provision in relation to terminal operators was presumably

not thought to be necessary because a terminal operator will usually be a company formed under the Companies Act and not therefore subject to the same limitations of legal power as a statutory corporation.

9.40 The Reception Facilities Order requires each harbour authority in respect of their harbour and each terminal operator in respect of its terminal to ensure that:

(a) if the harbour or terminal has reception facilities for the discharge from vessels of residues or mixtures containing oil or noxious liquid substances, those facilities are adequate to comply with the requirements of regulation 12 of Annex I or regulation 7 of Annex II, as the case may be, of MARPOL;

(b) if the harbour or terminal has no such facilities, such facilities are provided,

for vessels which may be expected to use the harbour for "a primary purpose other than utilizing reception facilities". This means that reception facilities must be provided for vessels which, for example, load or unload cargo at the harbour or terminal or are repaired or broken up there, but not for vessels which do not come to the harbour or terminal for a purpose other than discharging mixtures or residues to which the Order relates.

9.41 The Reception Facilities Order empowers the Secretary of State, after consultation with any organization appearing to him to be representative of owners of vessels registered in the United Kingdom, the harbour authority and, where appropriate, the terminal operator, to direct a harbour authority or terminal operator to provide or arrange for the provision of such reception facilities as he may specify if it appears to him either that a harbour or terminal has no reception facilities and that such facilities should be provided there, or that any existing reception facilities at the harbour or terminal are inadequate in order to comply, for vessels which in his opinion may be expected "to use the harbour or terminal for a primary purpose other than utilizing the reception facilities", with regulation 12 of Annex I or regulation 7 of Annex II of MARPOL.

9.42 The Reception Facilities Order authorizes a harbour authority or terminal operator providing reception facilities or a person providing such facilities by arrangement with a harbour authority to make reasonable charges for their use and to impose reasonable conditions in respect of their use. Any reception facilities provided by, or by arrangement with, a harbour authority or by a terminal operator must be open to all vessels which in the opinion of the harbour authority or terminal operator "are using the harbour or terminal for a primary purpose other than utilizing the reception facilities" on payment of any charges and subject to compliance with any conditions. The master of a vessel proposing to discharge a residue or mixture containing oil or a noxious liquid substance into a reception facility must first inform in writing the person providing the facility of the quantity and content of the substances to be discharged.

9.43 The Reception Facilities Order provides that it shall be an offence punishable only on summary conviction for a harbour authority or terminal operator to fail to comply with a direction by the Secretary of State under powers conferred on him by the Order, or for the master of a vessel to provide information about the quantity or content of a proposed discharge to reception facilities which he knows to be false in a material particular, or recklessly to provide such information which is false in a material particular, and prescribes maximum penalties for these offences.

9.44 With regard to the application of the statutory procedures for the disposal of waste in relation to residues and mixtures containing oil or noxious liquid substances discharged by vessels into reception facilities provided in accordance with the Reception Facilities Order, the Controlled Waste Regulations 1992 provide that tank washings landed in Great Britain are to be treated as industrial waste, and therefore controlled waste, for the purposes of Part II of the Environmental Protection Act 1990—regulation 5(1) of, and paragraph 18 of Schedule 3 to, the 1992 Regulations. By virtue of regulation 24 of the Special Waste Regulations 1996 and paragraph 36 of Schedule 3 to the Waste Management Licensing Regulations 1994 "tank washings" in this context means waste residue from the tanks (other than fuel tanks) or holds of a ship, or waste arising from the cleaning of such tanks or holds.

9.45 This means that, subject to 9.47, persons operating facilities for the receipt and storage of tank washings must hold a licence under Part II of the Environmental Protection Act 1990. However, by virtue of regulation 17 of, and paragraph 36(12) of Schedule 3 to, the Waste Management Licensing Regulations 1994 such a licence is not required for the temporary storage of waste consisting of tank washings, including any such waste which is special waste (as to which see 9.47 below) at reception facilities provided in accordance with the Reception Facilities Order which are within a harbour area (as defined in the Dangerous Substances in Harbour Areas Regulations 1987) where such storage is incidental to the collection or transport of the waste and so long as:

(a) the amount of tank washings consisting of dirty ballast so stored within a harbour area at any time does not exceed 30% of the total deadweight of the ships from which such washings have been landed;

(b) the amount of tank washings consisting of waste mixtures containing oil so stored within a harbour area at any time does not exceed 1% of the total deadweight of the ships from which such washings have been landed.

9.46 The exception provided for by regulation 17 of the 1994 Regulations applies as respects section 33(1)(a) and (b) of the Environmental Protection

Act 1990 but not as respects section 33(1)(c) of that Act. A licence will therefore always be required where it is proposed to keep, treat or dispose of tank washings in a manner likely to cause pollution of the environment or harm to human health.

9.47 Residues and mixtures discharged by vessels into reception facilities provided in accordance with the Reception Facilities Order will often be "special waste" as defined in regulation 2 of the Special Waste Regulations 1996. These regulations provide for a consignment note system in which all those involved with the disposal of the special waste participate. The standard procedure is set out in regulation 5 and the form of consignment note is specified in Schedule 1.

9.48 However, regulation 9 provides for a modified procedure where special waste is removed from a ship in a harbour area (as defined in the Dangerous Substances in Harbour Areas Regulation 1987) to:

   (a) reception facilities provided within that harbour area or;
   (b) by pipeline to any such facilities provided outside a harbour area.

("Reception facilities" are not defined for this purpose but they would no doubt usually be facilities provided under the Reception Facilities Order or under the Garbage Regulations mentioned below.)

9.49 Where regulation 9 applies, before the waste is removed from the ship, three copies of the consignment note must be prepared and Parts A and B of the note which, respectively, specify details of the consignment and describe the waste must be completed. The operator of the reception facilities must complete Part C which certifies certain matters which are certified by the "carrier" in the normal case. The master of the ship must ensure that Part D—the Consignor's Certificate which certifies, *inter alia*, that information specified in Parts B and C of the note are correct—is completed on each of the three copies of the consignment note, retain one copy himself and give the other two copies to the operator of the facilities. On receiving a consignment of special waste, the operator must complete Part E, the Consignee's Certificate, on each of the two copies of the note which have been given to him, retain one copy himself and forthwith furnish the other copy to the Environment Agency or the Scottish Environmental Protection Agency according to whether the place where the facilities are situated is in England or Wales or in Scotland.

9.50 In addition to the special provision made by regulation 9 for the case where ships' waste is removed to reception facilities, regulations 6(1)(d) and 7 of the Special Waste Regulations also make appropriate modifications of the consignment note procedure in relation to the case where a consignment of special waste is removed from a ship in a harbour area (as defined in the Dangerous Substances in Harbour Areas Regulations 1987) for transportation to a place outside that area.

9.51 Regulation 7 of Annex V of MARPOL requires the provision at ports and terminals of facilities for the reception of garbage from ships. The Merchant Shipping (Reception Facilities for Garbage) Regulations 1988, made under enabling powers contained in the Merchant Shipping (Prevention of Pollution by Garbage) Order 1988, an Order in Council originally made under section 20 of the Merchant Shipping Act 1979 and now having effect as if made under section 128 of the Merchant Shipping Act 1995, give effect to this requirement. They are hereafter referred to as "the Garbage Regulations".

9.52 The Garbage Regulations require each harbour authority in respect of their harbour and each terminal operator in respect of its terminal to ensure that:

(i) if the harbour or terminal has reception facilities for garbage from ships, those facilities are adequate, or

(ii) if the harbour or terminal has no such facilities, adequate facilities are provided.

9.53 The Garbage Regulations define:

"harbour authority" as a person or body of persons having for the time being the management of a harbour in the United Kingdom;

"harbour" as a harbour, port, estuary, haven, dock or other place used by ships;

"terminal" as a terminal, jetty, pier, wharf or mono-buoy used by ships which is either not within a harbour or, if it is within a harbour, is not managed by the harbour authority for that harbour;

"terminal operator" as a person or body of persons having for the time being the management of a terminal in the United Kingdom; and

"garbage" as all kinds of victual, domestic and operational waste excluding fresh fish and parts thereof generated during the normal operation of the ship and liable to be disposed of periodically except sewage originating from ships.

9.54 The Garbage Regulations enable the Secretary of State if it appears to him, after consultation with a harbour authority or terminal operator that:

(a) if the harbour or terminal has reception facilities for garbage from ships, those facilities are inadequate; or

(b) if the harbour or terminal has no such facilities, such facilities should be provided,

to direct the harbour authority or terminal operator to provide, or arrange for the provision of, such reception facilities as may be specified in the direction. Failure to comply with such a direction is an offence punishable on summary conviction by a fine not exceeding the amount specified in the regulations.

9.55 A harbour authority or terminal operator providing reception facilities for garbage from ships or a person providing such facilities by arrangement with a harbour authority or terminal operator may make reasonable charges for the use of the facilities and impose reasonable conditions in respect of such use. Reception facilities for garbage from ships provided by, or by arrangement with, a harbour authority or terminal operator are to be open to all ships which in the opinion of the harbour authority or terminal operator are using the harbour or terminal for a primary purpose other than utilizing the reception facilities. Therefore, as in the case of reception facilities for oily and noxious wastes, a ship is not entitled to use a harbour authority's reception facilities if it has no other business in the harbour.

9.56 The statutory procedures for the disposal of garbage discharged into facilities provided under the Garbage Regulations are similar to those described above in relation to residues and mixtures discharged into facilities provided under the Reception Facilities Order. The Controlled Waste Regulations 1992 provide that "garbage" as defined in the Garbage Regulations is to be treated as industrial waste, and therefore controlled waste, for the purposes of Part II of the Environmental Protection Act 1990—regulation 5(1) of, and paragraph 18 of Schedule 3 to, the 1992 Regulations. However, under regulation 17 of, and paragraph 36(1) of Schedule 3 to, the Waste Management Licensing Regulations 1994, a licence under Part II of the 1990 Act is not required for the temporary storage of waste consisting of garbage (as defined in the Garbage Regulations), including any waste which is special waste, at reception facilities provided within a harbour area (as defined in the Dangerous Substances in Harbour Areas Regulations 1987) in accordance with the Garbage Regulations where such storage is incidental to the collection and transport of the waste and so long as:

(a) the amount of garbage so stored within a harbour area at any time does not exceed 20 cubic metres for each ship from which garbage has been landed; and

(b) no garbage is so stored for more than seven days.

As in the case of tank washings, this exemption does not apply where it is proposed to keep, treat or dispose of garbage in a manner likely to cause pollution of the environment or harm to human health.

9.57 The provisions of the Special Waste Regulations described in paragraphs 9.47 to 9.50 *ante*, in relation to residues and mixtures discharged into facilities provided under the Reception Facilities Order which are special waste apply similarly to any garbage discharged into facilities provided under the Garbage Regulations which is special waste. It would, however, be unusual for garbage to fall within this category.

CHAPTER 10

HARBOUR AUTHORITY FINANCES

Charges

10.1 Leaving aside a few special cases, charges made by harbour authorities are essentially of two kinds. There are dues, which pay for the enjoyment of the basic or essential harbour or port works, and there are further charges, which pay for the enjoyment, usually optional, of ancillary services. Dues are, to some extent, in the nature of a tax, the amount payable by a user not necessarily being directly related to the service received by that user. However, as indicated below, the distinction between dues and other charges is now often blurred by the levying of combined charges which comprise elements both of dues and other charges. The practice of levying combined charges, which formerly raised some difficult legal questions, was expressly authorized by the Transport Act 1981.

10.2 The Harbours Act 1964 made important changes in the law relating to harbour charges but without departing drastically from basic concepts which had long been embodied in harbour legislation. The scheme of the Act was that, as regards dues, a harbour authority might impose such charges as they thought fit, subject to a right of appeal by users originally to the National Ports Council and, since the abolition of that body pursuant to the Transport Act 1981, to the Secretary of State, but as regards other matters (with immaterial exceptions) they might make only reasonable charges. The greater commercial freedom and flexibility in relation to charges provided by the 1964 Act was emphasized by section 38(1)(*c*) of the Act which repealed any statutory provision applying to a harbour authority insofar as it prohibited the authority from discriminating in the matter of charges against any person in favour of another.

10.3 The expression "ship, passenger and goods dues" is defined in section 57(1) of the Harbours Act 1964 as comprising three meanings, clearly corresponding to ship dues, passenger dues and goods dues. This definition is as follows—

"ship, passenger and goods dues" means, in relation to a harbour, charges (other than any exigible by virtue of section 29 of this Act) of any of the following kinds, namely,—

    (a) charges in respect of any ship for entering, using or leaving the harbour, including charges made on the ship in respect of marking or lighting the harbour;

    (b) charges for any passengers embarking or disembarking at the harbour (but not including charges in respect of any services rendered or facilities provided for them); and

    (c) charges in respect of goods brought into, taken out of, or carried through the harbour by ship (but not including charges in respect of work performed, services rendered or facilities provided in respect of goods so brought, taken or carried).

(The reference to charges under section 29 of the Act is to charges by a local lighthouse authority who are not a harbour authority—such charges are now made under section 210(2) of the Merchant Shipping Act 1995.)

10.4 Section 26 of the Harbours Act 1964 removed the limitations (usually in the form of prescribed maxima) which previously applied to harbour authorities' powers under their special legislation to levy ship, passenger and goods dues. The section did not, however, repeal statutory exemptions from dues or provisions which otherwise prohibited the levying of dues. Such provisions therefore remain in force. (Section 26 did not apply to the nationalized harbour authorities—neither did section 27 of the Harbours Act—but, as indicated below, the Harbours Act achieved substantially the same result so far as those authorities were concerned.)

10.5 Section 26(2) confers on harbour authorities the power to demand, take and recover such ship, passenger and goods dues as they think fit subject to the provisions for objections to dues contained in section 31 of the Harbours Act (the provisions of section 31 are discussed below), and subject also to any express exemptions from, or other prohibitions on levying, dues contained in their special legislation. Section 26 did not repeal powers to levy dues in harbour authorities' special legislation and it therefore appears that a harbour authority may levy dues either under section 26(2) or under their special legislation as amended by section 26. It seems, however, immaterial which of these powers a harbour authority rely on. In practice ship, passenger and goods dues are generally levied under section 26(2). Under section 26(3) of the Harbours Act references in special legislation, including incorporated provisions of the Harbours, Docks and Piers Clauses Act 1847, to charges made under that legislation include references to dues levied under section 26. Section 30 of the Harbours Act requires a harbour authority to keep available at their offices for inspection, and for sale, a list of the ship, passenger and goods dues exigible at their harbour under section 26 (or under section 43 of the Transport Act 1962 paragraph 10.11 in the case of a nationalized harbour authority). Under section 30(3) a harbour authority's power to levy dues is conditional on their complying with this requirement. The special legislation of many harbour authorities makes clear that charges reduced by compounding arrangements or rebates need not be included in the harbour authority's list of dues.

10.6 The 1964 Act did not originally contain any power for harbour authorities to levy charges other than ship, passenger or goods dues. Except in the case of the nationalized and formerly nationalized harbour authorities charges other than dues, for example charges for cargo handling and warehousing and mooring charges, are generally levied under provisions contained in the harbour authority's special legislation. It seems that, in the absence of any statutory power for the purpose, a harbour authority would have implied powers to charge for services which they are authorized to provide. In fact, however, virtually all harbour authorities have express statutory powers to make charges other than dues. The justification for this may be that the statutory power is a peg on which to hang the requirement mentioned below that charges (other than dues) must be reasonable.

10.7 Under section 27 of the 1964 Act where a charge which a harbour authority were authorized to make (other than ship, passenger and goods dues and a few special kinds of charges) was, by virtue of a provision contained in the harbour authority's special legislation, subject to a limitation (other than an express exemption from, or other prohibition on the making of, the charge or a requirement that the charge should be reasonable) that limitation was replaced by a requirement that the charge should be reasonable. This section therefore applied the test of reasonableness to most harbour charges, other than dues, which were not already subject to it. It does not of course apply in relation to charging powers contained in subsequent legislation but in practice these are nearly always in terms that the charges in question—usually charges for services and facilities provided by the authority—shall be such reasonable charges as the harbour authority may determine. The one common exception to this is a power to make charges for floating plant, which is not a ship as defined in the Harbours Act 1964, entering or leaving the harbour. Provisions for this purpose in the special legislation of harbour authorities effectively equate such charges to ship dues, giving the harbour authority power to levy such charges as they think fit subject to a right of objection to the Secretary of State. Where a charge is subject to a statutory requirement that it shall be reasonable any question of whether or not it is being levied at a reasonable level is for the courts to decide. The authors are not however aware of any case where the reasonableness of a harbour charge has been the subject of judicial consideration.

10.8 Section 18(1) of the Transport Act 1981 inserted in the Harbours Act 1964 a new power to make combined charges—section 27A of the 1964 Act as set out in paragraph 8(1) of Schedule 6 to the Transport Act 1981. This power applies where a harbour authority have power to levy ship, passenger and goods dues or equivalent dues ("equivalent dues" are defined as dues exigible in respect of things other than ships for entering, using or leaving a harbour including charges for marking or lighting the harbour) and to make other charges. In such a case section 27A authorizes the harbour authority to make a combined charge referable in part to matters for which ship, passenger and goods dues or equivalent dues may be levied and in part to matters for which other charges may be made. However, section 27A provides that a harbour authority may not make a combined charge where the person who would be liable to pay the charge objects to paying a combined charge or, where a number of persons would be jointly and severally liable to pay the charge, any of them objects to paying a combined charge. This limitation on a harbour authority's power to make combined charges means that the power cannot be used to deprive the user of his right to object to the Secretary of State under section 31 to ship, passenger and goods dues. If a combined charge comprises, say, a goods due element and a cargo handling element and the customer wishes to object to the former he may object to paying the combined charge and the harbour authority will then have to levy a separate goods due, to which the customer can object under section 31, and make a separate charge for cargo handling which, under the relevant charging power, will in virtually all cases be required to be reasonable. But a customer may not object to paying a combined charge after he has incurred the charge by taking advantage of the service to which it relates or if he has already agreed with the harbour authority to pay it.

10.9 The Transport Act 1981 amends sections 30 and 31 of the Harbours Act 1964 so as to make clear that a combined charge under section 27A does not have to be included in the list of dues which a harbour authority is required to keep under section 30 (see paragraph 10.5 *ante*) and is not open to objection under section 31.

10.10 Prior to the Transport Act 1981 the practice of making combined charges, particularly combined wharfage and cargo handling charges at container terminals, had become fairly common. It was not clear however that harbour authorities had power to make such charges. Also, they sometimes raised difficult problems in relation to objections under section 31. These difficulties were removed by section 27A.

10.11 As mentioned above, sections 26 and 27 of the Harbours Act 1964 did not apply to the nationalized harbour authorities. The powers of those authorities to levy harbour charges, both dues and other charges, stemmed from section 43(3) of the Transport Act 1962 under which, as amended by the Transport Act 1968, they had power to demand, take and recover or waive such charges for their services and facilities as they saw fit. (It seems that the reference to "services and facilities" in the context of this provision should be widely construed in contrast to the references to "services rendered or facilities provided" in the definition of "ship, passenger and goods dues" in section 57(1) of the Harbours Act which, in the context, appear to refer to ancillary matters. This is discussed in paragraphs 10.23 to 10.29 *post* in connection with the question of whether a wharfage charge is a goods due.)

10.12 The powers of the nationalized harbour authorities to charge under section 43(3) of the Transport Act 1962 were, by virtue of section 43(2), subject to any express exemption from, or other prohibitions on the making of, any charge contained in special legislation relating to any of their harbours. By virtue of section 50 of the Transport Act 1962 these powers were also subject to the provisions of the Ninth Schedule to that Act as regards the harbours specified in that Schedule.

10.13 Schedule 9 to the Transport Act 1962 was amended by section 39(3) of the Harbours Act 1964 and much of it was repealed by section 63 of that Act (which also repealed sections 50(3) and 51 of the Transport Act 1962 which related to harbour charges). The result was that, as respects harbour charges, the nationalized harbour authorities were in substantially the same position as other harbour authorities. At the harbours specified in Schedule 9 to the Transport Act 1962 ship, passenger and goods dues were subject to a right of objection under section 31 of the 1964 Act. Other charges at these harbours were required to be reasonable. Section 36(*a*) of the 1964 Act provided that sections 31 and 32 of that Act should not apply to charges imposed by the nationalized harbour authorities at harbours not specified in Schedule 9 to the Transport Act 1962. However, so far as the BTDB and the BRB were concerned, there were no such harbours.

10.14 Now that the BTDB has been reconstituted under Part II of the Transport Act 1981 as Associated British Ports the charging provisions of the Transport Act 1962 no longer apply to them (see paragraphs 2.5 and 2.6 *ante*). Associated British Ports have power to levy dues under section 26 of the Harbours Act 1964, and paragraph 1(2) of Schedule 4 to the Transport Act 1981 makes clear that sections 26, 27, 30, 31 and 40 of the 1964 Act apply to them (as also does section 27A). Paragraph 20(1) of Schedule 3 to the Transport Act 1981 confers on Associated British Ports a power to make such reasonable charges (other than ship, passenger and goods dues) as they think fit for services and facilities provided by them or their subsidiaries.

10.15 When Sealink ceased to be a subsidiary of BRB the charging powers of the Transport Act 1962 also ceased to apply at the harbours managed by Sealink Harbours Limited who, like Associated British Ports, therefore relied on the same general charging provisions as other harbour authorities and, in particular, levied ship, passenger and goods dues under section 26 of the Harbours Act 1964. Paragraph 3(1) of Schedule 1 to the Transport Act 1981 authorized Sealink Harbours Limited to make such reasonable charges as it saw fit for its services and facilities at the harbours which it managed. As mentioned in paragraph 2.11 *ante* most of these harbours have now been transferred to other companies. These of course have power to levy dues under section 26 of the Harbours Act and in each case the harbour revision order which effected the transfer contained a power to charge for services and facilities similar to paragraph 3(1) of Schedule 1 to the Transport Act 1981. The charging powers of nationalized harbour authorities described above now therefore only apply at the few small harbours for which the BWB are the harbour authority.

10.16 Section 31 of the Harbours Act 1964 enables written objections to be made to the Secretary of State as respects ship, passenger and goods dues imposed by a harbour authority at their harbour. An objector must be a person appearing to the Secretary of State to have a substantial interest (i.e., in the charge in question) or a body representative of persons so appearing and an objection may be made on all or any of the following grounds—

(a) that the charge ought not to be imposed at all;

(b) that the charge ought to be imposed at a rate lower than that at which it is imposed;

(c) that, according to the circumstances of the case, ships, passengers or goods of a class specified in the objection ought to be excluded from the scope of the charge either generally or in circumstances so specified;

(d) that, according to the circumstances of the case, the charge ought to be imposed, either generally or in circumstances specified in the objection, on ships, passengers or goods of a class so specified at a rate lower than that at which it is imposed on others.

10.17 The procedure for making, and dealing with, objections under section 31 is complicated. In each case there can only be one objector (or joint objectors) but other persons, or bodies representative of persons, having a substantial interest may make written representations to the Secretary of State within the period (which cannot be less than 42 days) specified in the notice of the objection which is required to be published. Such representations may be in favour of the charge concerned but usually they are, in effect, additional objections but not necessarily made on the same grounds as the originating objection. The procedure therefore provides an opportunity for all issues relating to a particular charge to be considered and dealt with at the same time.

10.18 Where there is an outstanding objection or representations under section 31 the Secretary of State is required to hold an inquiry unless he is satisfied that he can properly proceed to a decision in the matter without holding an inquiry. In practice an inquiry is always held. The Harbours Act does not lay down any specific considerations to which the Secretary of State is to have regard in determining objections under section 31. The considerations which are taken into account depend on the circumstances of particular cases but usually include the costs of the harbour authority in providing the service to which the charge in question relates, the importance to the harbour authority of the revenue from that charge and the burden which the charge imposes on the objector.

10.19 The Secretary of State may determine a case under section 31 in either of two ways. He may—

(a) approve the charge in question but set a limit (not being later than 12 months from the date on which he approves it) to the period during which the approval is to be of effect, or

(b) give the harbour authority such direction with respect to the charge as would meet objection thereto made on any of the grounds mentioned in paragraphs 10.16 *ante* (whether or not that was the ground, or was included among the grounds, on which the originating objection was made). Such a direction must specify a date for its coming into operation and the period from that date (not exceeding 12 months) during which it is to have effect. The harbour authority are required to comply with such a direction and are liable, on summary conviction, to a fine not exceeding level 4 on the standard scale if they fail to do so.

It seems clear from the terms of section 31 that the Secretary of State does not have power under that section to decide questions of law. However, for the purpose of his functions under section 31 it is sometimes necessary for him to form an opinion on a question of law, most commonly on whether he has jurisdiction under the section, i.e., whether or not the charge in question is a ship, passenger or goods due. Insofar as a determination by the Secretary of State under section 31 is based on the view that he has taken of a legal question it is open to challenge in the courts. And where the Secretary of State has declined to determine a case under section 31 because he has decided that the charge in question is not a ship, passenger or goods due it seems that the decision may also be challenged in the courts. Except on the grounds that the Secretary of State has taken a mistaken view of the law there is no right of appeal against a determination by the Secretary of State under section 31.

10.20 Where the Secretary of State has determined a case under the section by approving the charge in question no new proceedings may be initiated under section 31 as respects that charge during the period when the approval has effect. There is, however, nothing to prevent the harbour authority from increasing an approved charge during the period when the approval has effect but if they do the increased charge is open to objection under section 31. Similarly, where the Secretary of State has given a direction, a charge made by a harbour authority in accordance with the direction is immune from challenge under section 31 for so long as the direction has effect.

10.21 A question which has arisen is whether a direction given by the Secretary of State under section 31 can be retrospective. Section 31(7) provides that a direction under section 31(6)(*b*) must specify a date for its coming into operation and the period from that date (not exceeding 12 months) during which it is to have effect. This seems to have a prospective, rather than a retrospective, flavour but it might perhaps be argued that the fact that this provision does not require the period to run from the date when the Secretary of State gave the direction, in contrast to the requirement under section 31(6)(*a*) that the period during which an approval has effect runs from the date of the approval, indicates that the date to be specified under section 31(7) may be in the past. However, the latter part of section 31(10), which provides, in effect, that where a direction has been given under section 31(6)(*b*) a further objection to the charge in question cannot be lodged during the period when the direction has effect, seems to imply that the period envisaged is wholly in the future. Furthermore, to construe section 31(6)(*b*) as authorizing a retrospective direction could lead to absurd results. For example, if the same charge had been imposed by a harbour authority for three years and it was then objected to, it would, on this basis, seem arguable that a direction by the Secretary of State could go back to the beginning of the three-year period and have effect in respect of the dues paid or payable during the first of those years and that further objections could then be lodged in respect of each of the two subsequent past years. The better view therefore seems to be that a direction by the Secretary of State under section 31 cannot be retrospective.

10.22 In proceedings under section 31 of the Harbours Act 1964 questions sometimes arise of whether a particular charge is a ship, passenger or goods due and therefore whether the Secretary of State has jurisdiction under that section. One kind of charge which has been considered from this point of view is a "wharfage charge"—a charge in respect of goods which are placed on a wharf either for loading on, or after unloading from, a ship.

10.23 This question appears to turn upon the meaning of "facilities" in paragraph (c) of the definition of "ship, passenger and goods dues" mentioned above. *Prima facie* the word "facilities" is wide enough to embrace the provision of a wharf or quay for the receipt of goods, and has been so used by the legislature in the past. For example, by section 2(1)(*b*) of the Transport Act 1947, the whole of the British Transport Commission's powers as regards ports and harbours were described as the provision of "port facilities", a term defined in section 125(1) of that Act in the widest possible terms.

10.24 The wide meaning, however, cannot necessarily be applied to the word where used in the definition under consideration. One must look at other provisions of the Harbours Act 1964 and, if need be, to the general circumstances under Parliament's consideration in order to see what meaning must be attached to "facilities" and there are clear indications in the 1964 Act that the meaning is a narrower one. Thus, under subsection (8) of section 32 (repealed by the Transport Act 1981) charges fixed under that section, if at a port specified in Schedule 9 to the Transport Act 1962, were deemed to have been imposed under section 43 of that Act. This was a reference to section 43(3) which empowered *inter alia* the BTDB to make charges "for their services and facilities". Therefore the services and facilities of the Transport Act must have a wider meaning than the work, services and facilities, a charge for which is not a goods due within the definition in section 57(1) of the Harbours Act.

10.25 Parliament clearly envisaged that goods dues were payable in respect of some consideration and that some other payment might be exigible for the work, services or facilities performed or afforded in respect of the goods. The question resolves itself into an inquiry where the line is drawn and on which side of it wharfage comes. The distinction, long recognized in harbour legislation, that the dues pay for the enjoyment of the basic or essential harbour or port works and further charges pay for the enjoyment, usually optional, of ancillary services has already been referred to. The distinction was very clearly drawn in the BTC (Harbours) Charges Scheme 1948, where the Commission were empowered to levy maximum dues in respect of goods shipped and unshipped, and reasonable charges in respect of the "services and facilities" listed in the Second Schedule to the Scheme. In such a context provision of a wharf or quay is part of the consideration for the dues and is not an ancillary service or facility.

10.26 Did Parliament intend to move this dividing line so that under the Harbours Act wharfage fell on the other side, among the facilities? At first sight there appear to be indications that it did. The customary reference to "shipping and unshipping" is omitted, and the goods are described as those "brought into, taken out of, or carried through the harbour by ship". The definition, however, makes no mention of the consideration, and the words quoted are words defining what goods are chargeable and give no hint as to what are the harbour works, the enjoyment of which is the reason for the charge. A clue to the strangeness of this phraseology is to be found in the definition of "harbour". In the past there was often in practice a distinction between a harbour authority, who were conservators, and a dock authority, who provided the transhipment facilities. Both are embraced in the definition of "harbour authority" in section 57(1) by virtue of "harbour" being defined as including a dock and a wharf. The draughtsman had the task of defining goods dues in a way which would cover the dues imposed by a variety of authorities, from a large conservancy to the statutory operator of a single wharf. This explains part of his phraseology but does not explain the absence of reference to shipping and unshipping, and the absence of that or a similar phrase may point, though not very strongly, towards wharfage being excluded from goods dues.

10.27 On the other hand, the wording appears to contemplate a well-defined point of demarcation between the goods dues (to be subject to sections 26 and 31) and ancillary charges (to be subject to section 27 and to the jurisdiction of the courts as to reasonableness). Here the practice as existing at the time of the passing of the 1964 Act is relevant. At the majority of ports there was a tonnage rate on goods expressed to cover shipping or unshipping and to remunerate the authority for the maintenance of the port, and there were ancillary charges for such services as cranage. It would be surprising if the definition of goods dues was intended by Parliament to disturb this practice.

10.28 Moreover, the practice of goods dues including the use of the wharf corresponds to the legal right of access under section 33 of the Harbours,

Docks and Piers Clauses Act 1847: "upon payment of the rates made payable by this and the special Act, . . . the harbour dock and pier shall be open to all persons for the shipping and unshipping of goods . . . ". The rates (or dues) entitle the public to the use of the fixed installation of the port. The shipper may provide his own transport and do his own stevedoring—*LNER* v. *British Trawlers Federation*[1] referred to in paragraph 4.4 *ante*. If he pays the authority to do the work he is paying for an ancillary service, but he is entitled to the use of the wharf subject to the payment of dues.

10.29 These arguments appear to outweigh that derived from the absence of any reference to shipping and unshipping in the definition. Weight is lent to this view by the consideration that the words "facilities provided" should be construed *ejusdem generis* with "work performed" and "services rendered", both of which point to some process ancillary to the basic provision of the essential works of the port. The better view therefore appears to be that a wharfage charge is a goods due.

10.30 Another question which has arisen is whether a mooring charge is a ship due. The question of whether a particular "mooring charge" is within paragraph (a) of the definition of "ship, passenger and goods dues" must always be considered in relation to the facts of the particular case. However, it seems true to say that nearly all "mooring charges" are either—

(a) a charge made by a harbour authority for the use of a mooring provided by the authority in the harbour, or

(b) a charge made by a harbour authority for the grant to a person of a licence for that person to lay and maintain his own mooring in the harbour. Such a charge is sometimes made, where the authority own the bed or shores of the harbour, by virtue of that ownership but more often by virtue of a provision in the authority's local enactments—see, for example, sections 16(2)(a) and 24(2) of the Salcombe Harbour Order 1954.

10.31 It seems that charges of the kind mentioned in (b) of paragraph 10.30 *ante* are clearly not within paragraph (a) of the definition of ship, passenger and goods dues. A charge made in consideration of a grant to a person of a right for that person to lay, maintain and use a mooring is not a charge "in respect of any ship entering, using or leaving the harbour".

10.32 In the case of charges made by a harbour authority for the use of their own moorings the position may not be quite so clear. The question appears to turn on whether such a charge is "in respect of any ship for . . . using the harbour". The definition of "harbour" in section 57(1) of the Harbours Act includes wharves, quays and piers in addition to the water area. It does not, however, appear to include a mooring in the ordinary sense of the word.

---

1. [1934] A.C. 279.

10.33 It might possibly be argued that a mooring is a facility provided in connection with the harbour; that charges in respect of facilities are expressly excluded in paragraphs (b) and (c) of the definition of "ship, passenger and goods dues" but not in paragraph (a) of that definition, and that this implies that paragraph (a) does include charges for facilities. The answer to this seems to be that the charges described in paragraph (a) of the definition are expressed to be charges "in respect of . . . using the harbour" and that, having regard to the definition of "harbour" in section 57(1), this could not include charges in respect of facilities in the sense mentioned above. There was therefore no need expressly to exclude charges in respect of ancillary matters as there was in paragraphs (b) and (c) where the words "charges for any passengers embarking or disembarking at the harbour" and "charges in respect of goods brought into, taken out of or carried through the harbour" might each, in the absence of the express exclusion, have included charges for ancillary matters.

10.34 It therefore appears that a charge made by a harbour authority for the use of their own moorings will not usually be a charge in respect of "using . . . the harbour" within the meaning of paragraph (a) of the definition of "ship, passenger and goods dues" because (in general at any rate) a mooring is not part of the essential harbour works—the infrastructure of the port—and not within the definition of "harbour" in section 57(1) of the Harbours Act.

10.35 Another question about harbour dues which has arisen on several occasions is whether, or to what extent, a harbour authority can enter into a contract with a user which limits the authority's power under section 26 of the Harbours Act "to demand, take and recover such ship, passenger and goods dues as they think fit". There is a long line of authorities on the general issue of whether a body with a statutory discretion can fetter the exercise of that discretion by contract, beginning with the Scottish cases of *Paterson* v. *Provost of St. Andrews*[2] and *Ayr Harbour Trustees* v. *Oswald*.[3] They establish the general principle that a body entrusted with statutory powers cannot by contract fetter the exercise of those powers but some cases indicate that the courts will not press this principle to unreasonable lengths. However, the cases do not lay down precise rules about how far the contractual fettering of the statutory discretion may be permissible. It has been suggested that the test is whether the body concerned is renouncing its "statutory birthright" but the judgments in *British Transport Commission* v. *Westmoreland County Council*[4] indicate that a pragmatic criterion should be applied.

10.36 As to whether a contract by a harbour authority fixing the dues they may charge over a long period is enforceable, the case most clearly in point is

---

2. *Paterson* v. *Provost of St. Andrews* (1881) 6 App. Cas. 883.
3. *Ayr Harbour Trustees* v. *Oswald* (1883) 8 App. Cas. 623.
4. *British Transport Commission* v. *Westmoreland County Council* [1958] A.C. 126.

York Corporation v. *Henry Leetham & Sons Ltd.*[5] In that case the plaintiffs were entrusted by statute with the control of navigation in parts of the rivers Ouse and Fosse with power to charge such tolls as the Corporation deemed necessary to carry on the navigation in which the public had an interest. The Corporation made two contracts with the defendants under which they agreed to accept, in consideration of the right to navigate the Ouse, a regular payment of £600 in place of the authorized tolls. The contract with regard to the navigation of the Fosse was on similar lines. It was held by Russell, J., that the contracts were *ultra vires* and void because under them the Corporation had disabled themselves, whatever emergency might arise, from exercising their statutory powers to increase tolls as from time to time might be necessary. The judge based his decision on the incapacity of a body charged with statutory powers for public purposes to divest itself of such powers or to fetter itself in the use of such powers.

10.37 Russell, J.'s decision was criticized by the House of Lords (and previously by the Court of Appeal) in *Southport Corporation* v. *Birkdale District Electric Supply Co. Ltd.*[6] in which it was held that a contract on the part of the electricity company not to charge higher prices than those charged in the borough of Southport was not *ultra vires*. (The contract had been made with the local authority and not with the company's customers, this being one of the grounds, although not perhaps a very satisfactory one, on which the case was distinguished from *York Corporation* v. *Leetham*.) It was pointed out that the body executing the statutory duties in question was a trading corporation and that the discharge of such duties would be facilitated rather than fettered by a reasonable latitude of discretion in fixing prices (i.e., by contract). However, *York Corporation* v. *Leetham* was distinguished and not overruled. The facts in the *Southport* case were very different and the judgments appear to have turned to some extent on the fact that the undertakers concerned in that case were a limited company rather than a statutory corporation (which may be a relevant consideration where, as is now the case at several important harbours, the harbour authority is a company formed under the Companies Act 1985). *York Corporation* v. *Leetham* appears to have been treated as good law by the Court of Appeal in *William Cory & Sons Ltd.* v. *London Corporation*[7] in which it was held that the Corporation could not by contract fetter their statutory duty to make certain by-laws.

10.38 The courts might now be disposed to adopt a more commercial approach. Contracts purporting to fix the level of dues for a particular customer are not uncommon but, in view of the authorities, it seems that a contract by a harbour authority which purported to fetter their discretion under section 26 over a long period would still probably be held to be *ultra*

5. *York Corporation v. Henry Leetham & Sons Ltd.* [1924] 1 Ch. 557.
6. *Southport Corporation v. Birkdale District Electric Supply Co. Ltd.* [1926] A.C. 355.
7. *William Cory & Sons Ltd v. London Corporation* [1951] 2 K.B. 476.

vires. In this connection, section 32 of the Harbours, Docks and Piers Clauses Act 1847, where it is incorporated, authorizes the harbour authority to compound for dues by the year or other shorter period but it seems doubtful whether this extends to the long term fettering of a harbour authority's discretion under section 26. Nor, indeed, does any express power to compound for dues now seem to be necessary since this would appear to be covered by the terms of section 26(2). (It seems, incidentally, that the proviso to section 32, which provides that if the harbour authority agree to dues being compounded in respect of any user all other users are entitled to be treated in the same way, has ceased to have effect by virtue of section 38(1)(c) of the Harbours Act 1964.)

10.39 With regard to the recovery of charges by a harbour authority, the authority's special legislation nearly always include a provision to the effect that, in addition to any other remedy under the special legislation or provisions of the Harbours, Docks and Piers Clauses Act 1847 incorporated therewith, the authority may recover any charges payable to them in any court of competent jurisdiction.

10.40 Under section 44 of the Harbours, Docks and Piers Clauses Act 1847, which is incorporated in the special legislation of most harbour authorities, the authority may recover any rates payable to them in respect of a ship by distraint and sale of the ship and its tackle. By virtue of section 26(3) of the Harbours Act 1964 the rates referred to in section 44 include ship dues levied under section 26.

10.41 Under section 45 of the 1847 Act, which again is incorporated in the special legislation of most harbour authorities, a harbour authority may recover rates payable to them in respect of any goods (again, by virtue of section 26(3) of the Harbours Act 1964 these include goods dues levied under section 26) by distraint and sale of the goods concerned or, if these have been removed from the port premises without payment of the dues, by distraint and sale of other goods on those premises belonging to the person liable for payment of the dues.

10.42 Where sections 44 and 45 of the 1847 Act are not incorporated in a harbour authority's special legislation, such legislation virtually always includes substantive provisions to the same effect. It has been held that a harbour authority may exercise a statutory right to detain a vessel until rates are paid notwithstanding the prior existence of a maritime lien in favour of the master and crew: *The Emilie Millon.*[8]

10.43 Section 43 of the Harbours, Docks and Piers Clauses Act 1847 provides that if the master of any ship or the owner of any goods evades the payment of the rates payable to the harbour authority in respect of the ship or goods (these, again, by virtue of section 26(3) of the Harbours Act 1964 including ship dues or goods dues levied under section 26) he must pay the

8. *The Emilie Millon* [1905] 2 K.B. 817.

authority three times the amount of the rates evaded. Section 43 is not usually incorporated in modern local harbour legislation but a substantive provision to the same effect has sometimes been included in recent local harbour Acts and orders.

Council Regulation (EC) No. 2978/94

10.44 The purpose of the above EC Regulation, which came into force on 1 January 1996 and is directly applicable in all Member States of the Community, is to prescribe differential charges in favour of tankers with segregated ballast tanks. So far as harbour and pilotage charges in the United Kingdom are concerned, it is unique in imposing on harbour authorities a duty to levy differential charges (leaving aside directions by the Secretary of State following objections under section 31 of the Harbours Act 1964 or under that section as applied by section 10 of the Pilotage Act 1987—see paragraphs 10.16 to 10.20 *ante* and paragraphs 20.77 and 20.78 *post*).

10.45 Under Article 2 of the Regulation it applies to oil tankers which:

1. can carry segregated ballast in specially appointed tanks;
2. are designed, built, adapted, equipped and operated as segregated ballast oil tankers including double hull oil tankers and tankers of an alternative design;
3. meet the requirements of the International Convention on Tonnage Measurement of Ships 1969; and
4. hold the International Tonnage Certificate (1969).

10.46 Article 3 defines (*inter alia*) "segregated ballast oil tanker", and terms used in that definition are also defined in Article 3. That Article defines "port and harbour authority" as "a public or private person which charges fees to ships for providing facilities and services to shipping" and "pilotage authority" as "a public or private person entitled to render pilotage services to shipping".

10.47 Article 4 provides that the International Tonnage Certificate (1969) issued for a segregated ballast oil tanker which has been measured in accordance with the rules of the International Convention on Tonnage Measurement of Ships 1969 shall include a statement specifying:

(i) the tonnage of the segregated ballast tanks of the ship calculated in accordance with the formula specified in paragraph 4 of Annex 1 to the Regulation; and

(ii) the reduced gross tonnage arrived at by deducting the tonnage of the segregated ballast tanks from the total tonnage of the ship.

10.48 Article 5 specifies three systems for securing differential charges in favour of oil tankers to which the Regulation applies. Under paragraph 1 of the

Article, when fees for oil tankers are based fully or partly on gross tonnage, a port and harbour authority or a pilotage authority must calculate the fee for a tanker to which the Regulation applies on the basis of the reduced gross tonnage indicated in the statement referred to above in the ship's International Tonnage Certificate (1969). Alternatively, under paragraph 2, when fees for oil tankers are based fully or partly on gross tonnage, a port and harbour authority or a pilotage authority may prescribe a flat rate differential of at least 17% in favour of tankers to which the Regulation applies (where on 13 June 1994 a flat rate differential of less than 17% in favour of such tankers was already in force, the authority concerned were required to increase the differential to at least 17% not later than 1 January 1997). Under paragraph 3, where the fees for oil tankers are assessed otherwise than on the basis of gross tonnage, the port and harbour authority or pilotage authority concerned, must ensure that tankers to which the Regulation applies are, as respects the fees in question, treated no less favourably than they would have been if the fees had been based on gross tonnage and the differential had been calculated in accordance with paragraph 1 or paragraph 2 of the Article. Paragraph 4 of the Article provides that port and harbour authorities and pilotage authorities shall apply, for all segregated ballast tankers, only one of the systems mentioned in paragraphs 1, 2 and 3.

10.49 The Regulation, which is rather loosely drafted by British standards, raises some questions. In the first place to what "fees" does it apply? It may be arguable that the wide terms of the definition of "port and harbour authority" imply that the Regulation bites on charges for all services which are provided as an integral part of a ship entering or leaving port including towing and mooring charges. It seems doubtful, however, whether this definition governs the nature of the fees in question. It appears from Article 5 that the Regulation is concerned with charges which are usually or commonly, although not invariably, assessed on the basis of gross tonnage, for example, in the British context, ship dues. This view is supported by references in the recitals to the Regulation. The seventh recital refers to Resolution A747(18) of the IMO Assembly which invited governments to advise port and harbour authorities to apply its recommendation in relation to the assessment of fees based on gross tonnage. The eleventh recital refers to the charging of dues and the fourteenth to the charging of levies, both of which expressions seem more apt to refer to charges on ships of the kinds which are normally assessed on a tonnage basis than to charges for specific services such as towage and mooring charges which are not usually so assessed. The seventeenth recital refers to an alternative (to the basis mentioned in IMO Resolution A747(18)) scheme for tonnage-based fees. It goes on to refer to cases where fees are not calculated on the basis of gross tonnage but the implication appears to be that the fees in question are of a kind which are usually calculated on that basis. It would probably give rise to difficulties and anomalies if the Regulation were held to apply to charges of kinds which are not normally assessed on a tonnage basis.

10.50 With regard to paragraph 4 of Article 5, it seems that, in the British context, a harbour authority as defined in the Harbours Act 1964 who are also a competent harbour authority within the meaning of the Pilotage Act 1987 would not be precluded by the paragraph from basing differentials in favour of segregated ballast oil tankers on different systems (being in each case one of those mentioned in paragraphs 1, 2 and 3 of the article) as between charges which they levy in their capacity as a port and harbour authority as defined in the Regulation and those which they levy in their capacity as a pilotage authority as so defined.

10.51 Paragraph 1 of Article 5 might perhaps give rise to anomalies in some cases where fees are based only partly on gross tonnage as are some pilotage dues.

10.52 The Regulation is an important and unique qualification to the power of harbour authorities in Great Britain to levy such dues as they see fit under section 26 of the Harbours Act 1964 (and the powers of competent harbour authorities to levy pilotage charges under section 10 of the Pilotage Act 1987) subject only to the right of objection under section 31 of the 1964 Act. By virtue of the European Communities Act 1972, under which community law takes precedence over British law, the exercise of the Secretary of State's jurisdiction under section 31 is subject to the provisions of the Regulation as respects the differentials prescribed in favour of segregated ballast oil tankers.

Borrowing by harbour authorities

10.53 Virtually all harbour authorities which are statutory corporations have powers under their special legislation to borrow both for capital purposes and for temporary purposes. The form of port trusts' capital borrowing powers as in force prior to the commencement of section 3 of the Ports (Finance) Act 1985 (whose provisions are described below) varied considerably. In a few cases this was a simple power to borrow with the Secretary of State's consent. In most cases, however, the port trust had power to borrow such sums of money as they thought necessary for capital purposes not exceeding in the aggregate a specified sum and this was usually, although not always, coupled with a provision that the port trust might with the consent of the Secretary of State borrow such further sums of money as they might require. Specified limits on the amount to be borrowed usually applied to the total amount borrowed without regard to repayments (but excluding, in some cases, borrowings for the repayment of amounts previously borrowed). In a few cases the limit was expressed to apply to the amount outstanding from time to time (the limit thus being "ever green").

10.54 The usual power for a port trust to borrow temporarily by way of overdraft or otherwise for meeting or discharging their statutory obligations or functions was usually subject to a specified limit which applied to the total amount borrowed.

10.55 The borrowing powers of statutory harbour companies were usually expressed as a power to borrow up to a specified limit applying to the total amount borrowed. In no case was the Secretary of State's consent required to borrowing by a statutory harbour company.

10.56 These borrowing powers were substantially affected by the provisions of section 3 of the Ports (Finance) Act 1985, which came into force on 1 January 1986. This section applied in relation to any borrowing power contained in an "existing local provision" of a "relevant harbour authority". A "relevant harbour authority" is defined in section 5(1) of the Act as a harbour authority constituted by or under an "existing local provision" for the purpose of managing a harbour. An "existing local provision" is defined in section 5(1) as a provision of a local Act of Parliament, including an Act comprising a provisional order, or a provision of an instrument made under a local Act or of an instrument in the nature of a local enactment made under any other Act, being a provision in force on the date on which section 5 comes into force (1 January 1986). "An instrument in the nature of a local enactment made under any other Act" appears to include a harbour revision or empowerment order or harbour reorganization scheme made under the Harbours Act 1964.

10.57 Section 3 therefore applied in relation to the borrowing powers of port trusts and statutory harbour companies. It did not affect local authorities. Nor did it affect Associated British Ports, the British Waterways Board or a company formed under the Companies Act 1985 (at that time the only important harbour authority which was such a company was Sealink Harbours Ltd.).

10.58 Subsection (1) of section 3 abolished the need for any consent or approval of a Minister of the Crown under the borrowing powers to which section 3 applied.

10.59 Subsection (2) fixed limits to the amounts which may be borrowed under borrowing powers to which section 3 applied where the consent or approval of a Minister of the Crown had been required. Where the borrowing power specified a limit, that limit was increased by 20 per cent. Where no limit was specified in the borrowing power, then the limit on the amount which might be borrowed thereunder became an amount equal to the aggregate of the sums specified in the Ministerial consents or approvals given under the provision in question increased by 20 per cent.

10.60 Subsection (3) provided that, where a relevant harbour authority might, by virtue of an existing local provision, borrow any amount without the consent or approval of a Minister of the Crown and, by virtue of that or another such provision, might borrow a further amount with such consent or approval, the amount which might be borrowed without such consent or approval should be increased by 20 per cent.

10.61 Subsection (4) provided that the limit specified in any borrowing power to which section 3 applied should bite on the amount for the time being outstanding in respect of money borrowed under the power in question (instead of, as was formerly the position in most cases, on the total amount borrowed) thus making the limit "ever green".

10.62 The effect of section 3 on the usual forms of borrowing powers to which it applied seems to be as follows—

(a) If the borrowing power specified a limit to the amount which might be borrowed without any power to borrow further with the consent of a Minister of the Crown, then section 3 did not affect the amount of the limit but the limit became "ever green" if it was not so already.

(b) If the power was simply to borrow with the consent of a Minister of the Crown, the requirement to obtain such consent disappeared but borrowing became subject to an "ever green" limit equal to the aggregate of all the sums the borrowing of which the Minister had consented to before section 3 came into force increased by 20 per cent.

(c) If the power was to borrow with the consent of a Minister of the Crown up to a specified limit, then the requirement to obtain such consent disappeared but borrowing became subject to the former limit increased by 20 per cent which also became "ever green" if it was not so already.

(d) In the most common case, where a port trust had power to borrow up to a specified limit without the consent of a Minister of the Crown and above that with such consent, the requirement to obtain the Minster's consent disappeared and the limit on borrowing became the aggregate of the former limit increased by 20 per cent and any additional amounts to the borrowing of which the Minister had consented before section 3 came into force also increased by 20 per cent, the new limit being, of course, "ever green".

10.63 Since the Ports (Finance) Act 1985 new harbour authority capital borrowing powers have authorized borrowing up to a specified limit on the amount outstanding at any time in respect of borrowed money.

10.64 There is some variation in harbour authority borrowing powers as to the security on which the authority may borrow for capital purposes. In the most recent provisions the security is described in wide terms, e.g., "all or any of the revenues and property of the authority", which would appear to enable the authority to secure a loan on particular property although it is no doubt usually appropriate for borrowings to be charged on the authority's undertaking or revenues as a whole. In some cases the borrowing power describes the authorized security in more limited terms, e.g., "on the security of the revenues of the undertaking".

10.65 With regard to methods of borrowing for capital purposes, modern harbour authority borrowing powers usually authorize the authority to borrow by any method or methods they see fit. Older borrowing powers tend to be more specific, sometimes containing detailed provisions for the issue of bonds or debentures.

10.66 Local authorities have powers to borrow under local government legislation but local authorities which are harbour authorities often have in addition powers under their special harbour legislation to borrow for harbour purposes sometimes without the Ministerial sanction required under local government legislation. The provisions relating to local authority borrowings contained in general legislation usually apply to borrowings under these special powers which are therefore normally charged on all the revenues of the authority concerned.

10.67 In order to avoid possible difficulties arising from the limited terms in which the borrowing powers of some harbour authorities were expressed, section 39 of the Docks and Harbours Act 1966 provided that the purposes for which a harbour authority (other than a nationalized harbour authority) might borrow money should include "meeting any expenses properly chargeable to capital, being expenses incurred in connection with the provision or improvement of assets in connection with any activity in which the authority has power to engage". This section also enabled any harbour authority (other than a nationalized harbour authority) to borrow for the purpose of acquiring a harbour business or shares in a harbour business under the powers for those purposes conferred by the Docks and Harbours Act 1966.

10.68 The borrowing powers of Associated British Ports are contained in paragraph 21 of Schedule 3 to the Transport Act 1981. These powers are wide and flexible. They include powers to issue debentures and to mortgage or charge by way of security all or any part of the undertaking, revenues, property or assets (present or future) of Associated British Ports. However, the aggregate amount outstanding at any time of the money borrowed by Associated British Ports and their subsidiaries (and of guarantees given by Associated British Ports and their subsidiaries) must not exceed the limit for the time being set by Associated British Ports Holdings plc.

10.69 Harbour authorities (other than the British Waterways Board who, as the only remaining nationalized harbour authority, may, under the Transport Act 1962, borrow only from the Secretary of State for capital purposes and may borrow temporarily only from the Secretary of State or from someone else with his consent), may borrow from whom they please. Under section 11 of the Harbours Act 1964, as extended by section 40(5) of the Docks and Harbours Act 1966, the Secretary of State with the approval of the Treasury may make loans to a harbour authority in respect of expenses (which he is satisfied are such as ought properly to be regarded as being of a capital nature) incurred by them in respect of a harbour for which they are the harbour authority—

(a) in executing works for the improvement, maintenance or management of an existing harbour or for the construction of a new harbour;

(b) in acquiring plant or equipment required for the carrying out of harbour operations at an existing harbour or at a harbour which the harbour authority are constructing or proposing to construct;

(c) in acquiring land required for the purposes of an existing harbour or an extension thereof or for the construction of a new harbour.

A loan under section 11 may also be made to enable a harbour authority to repay principal or pay interest on a loan previously made to them under that section but not in respect of any part of the principal which does not fall due for repayment until more than five years from the date on which the loan was made nor in respect of interest for any period beginning more than five years from that date.

10.70 A further power for the Secretary of State to make loans to harbour authorities is conferred by the Harbours (Loans) Act 1972. Under that Act the Secretary of State, where it appears to him that a harbour authority are, or are likely to be, unable to pay off a debt when it falls due, and it also appears to him "that the financial prospects of the authority justify making them a loan for the purpose of enabling them to make the payment or repayment", may, with the approval of the Treasury, make the harbour authority concerned a loan to pay off the debt in question which may be either a capital debt or a temporary loan or overdraft. The purpose of this provision is to enable a harbour authority whose financial position is basically sound to be tided over a difficult period.

10.71 Section 43 of the Harbours Act 1964, which is also applied by the Harbours (Loans) Act 1972 for the purposes of that Act, provides that loans which the Secretary of State makes to harbour authorities shall be repaid to him at such times and by such methods, and interest thereon shall be paid to him at such rates and at such times as he may, with the approval of the Treasury, from time to time direct. This seems to mean that the terms of the relevant mortgage deeds could, in theory, subsequently be varied from time to time but it is believed that in practice this has never happened.

10.72 Under section 4 of the Harbours (Loans) Act 1972 the aggregate amount of loans made after the passing of that Act under that Act and under section 11 of the Harbours Act 1964 is not to exceed £200 million or, if the House of Commons so resolve, £300 million. This limit does not take account of loan repayments. In recent years few loans to harbour authorities have been made under the Harbours Act 1964 and none under the Harbours (Loans) Act 1972.

10.73 Where a harbour authority is a company formed under the Companies Act 1985 (of which, following the transfer of the undertakings of several port trusts to such companies under the Ports Act 1991, there are now some important examples) the company will borrow money for harbour purposes under powers for that purpose contained in its memorandum of association. Schemes under Part I of the Ports Act 1991 have in practice always repealed the borrowing powers of the former port trust.

10.74 What are the remedies of the secured creditors of a harbour authority if the authority should default in making payments to them or their security should be in jeopardy? As indicated in paragraphs 3.8 to 3.10 *ante*, it seems probable that in general a harbour authority cannot be wound up except by means of an Act of Parliament. With regard to the remedies of a secured creditor of a port trust in England and Wales, it may often be doubtful whether the powers of a mortgagee under section 101 of the Law of Property Act 1925, where the mortgage is made by deed, are available. This is because, according to the terms of the harbour authority's special legislation, the creditors' security may be created by statute rather than by mortgage deed. But in any case, it appears from the old cases of *Gardner* v. *London, Chatham and Dover Railway Company*[9] and *Blaker* v. *Herts and Essex Waterworks Co.*[10] that where, as is usually the case with port trusts, security holders have a charge on the revenue and/or the undertaking of statutory undertakers section 101 of the Law of Property Act 1925 will not apply so as to enable the security holders to sell assets (and therefore, presumably, the right to appoint a receiver under section 101 will not arise). This is because a charge of this nature is essentially a charge on "the fruit of the fruit bearing tree" represented by the complete undertaking. In the course of his judgment in the former case Lord Cairns said:

Whatever may be the liability to which any of the property or effects connected with [the Railway Company's undertaking] may be subjected through the legal operations and consequences of a judgment recovered against it, the undertaking, so far as these contracts of mortgage are concerned, is, in my opinion, made over as a thing complete or to be completed; as a going concern, with internal and Parliamentary powers of management not to be interfered with; as a fruit-bearing tree, the produce of which is the fund dedicated by the contract to secure and to pay the debt. The living and going concern thus created by the Legislature must not, under a contract pledging it as security, be destroyed, broken up or annihilated. The tolls and sums of money *ejusdem generis*—that is to say, the earnings of the undertaking—must be made available to satisfy the mortgage; but in my opinion the mortgagees cannot, under their mortgages, or as mortgagees—by seizing, or calling on this Court to seize, the capital, or the lands, or the proceeds of sales of land, or the stock of the undertaking—either prevent its completion, or reduce it into its original elements when it has been completed.

10.75 A secured creditor of a port trust in England and Wales may commence proceedings and obtain judgment for unpaid principal or interest due to him and could then levy execution on the assets of the port trust. However,

---

9. *Gardner* v. *London, Chatham and Dover Railway Company* (1867) L.R. 2 Ch. App. 201.
10. *Blaker* v. *Herts and Essex Waterworks Co.* (1889) L.R. 41 Ch. 399.

it seems that assets necessary for the carrying on of the port trust's under-taking could not be taken in execution. There does not appear to be direct authority for this proposition but it seems to follow from the established principle that a body on which Parliament has imposed duties may not dispose of assets necessary for carrying out those statutory duties: *Re Woking Urban District Council (Basingstoke Canal) Act 1911.*[11]

10.76 The secured creditors of such a port trust might also apply to the court for the appointment of a receiver on the grounds either that payments of principal or interest were in arrear or that their security was in jeopardy. It appears from *Gardner* v. *London, Chatham and Dover Railway* that such a receiver could not be appointed also as manager. In the course of his judgment Lord Cairns said:

> When Parliament, acting for the public interest, authorizes the construction and maintenance of a railway . . . it confers powers and imposes duties and responsibilities of the largest and most important kind, and it confers and imposes them upon the company which Parliament has before it, and upon no other body or person. These powers must be executed and those duties discharged by the company. They cannot be delegated or transferred.

However, the Port of London Authority (Borrowing Powers) Revision Order 1971 contains provisions for the appointment by the court on the application of security holders of a receiver and manager of the PLA's undertaking if that authority are in default as mentioned in that order.

10.77 With regard to the remedies of secured loan creditors of harbour authorities in England and Wales which are statutory companies, the relevant principles are substantially the same as in the case of port trusts but incorpor-ated provisions of the Companies Clauses Consolidation Act 1845 may be relevant. In the case of the Mersey Docks and Harbour Company, the Mersey Docks and Harbour Act 1971 contains special provisions for the appointment of a receiver and manager by the court on the application of secured creditors in the circumstances specified in that Act.

10.78 In the case of a harbour authority which is a company formed under the Companies Act 1985, it would appear that the remedies of a secured creditor will be the same as in the case of any other such company except that, for the reasons mentioned in paragraph 3.8 *ante*, where the *Salisbury Railway and Market House* case is referred to, it seems doubtful whether the Courts would allow a winding up of the company under the Companies Act 1985 which prejudiced the carrying out of its statutory duties as a harbour authority. In addition, for the reasons mentioned in paragraph 10.75 *ante* in relation to port trusts, it seems doubtful whether assets necessary for the carrying out of those duties could be taken in execution.

10.79 Paragraphs 10.74 to 10.78 *ante* refer to the law in England and Wales. The remedies of secured loan creditors of harbour authorities in

---

11. *Re Woking Urban District Council (Basingstoke Canal) Act 1911* [1914] 1 Ch. 300.

Scotland are a matter of Scottish law and the author is not qualified to deal with them.

Other financial assistance to harbour authorities

10.80 Under section 2 of the Fisheries Act 1955 the Minister of Agriculture, Fisheries and Food has power to make grants or loans to (*inter alia*) a harbour authority towards expenses incurred by the authority for the provision of fishery harbour works. Since the section describes the bodies to which financial assistance may be given thereunder as "not trading for profit" it would seem that a loan or grant under the section could probably not be made to a harbour authority with share capital.

Accounts of harbour authorities

10.81 Under section 42 of the Harbours Act 1964, as substituted for the original section by the Transport Act 1981 and set out in paragraph 10 of Schedule 6 to that Act, the legal requirements as respects the accounts of harbour authorities are closely assimilated to those which apply to companies under the Companies Act 1985.

10.82 Section 42 requires every harbour authority (with a few exceptions referred to below) to prepare an annual statement of accounts relating to "harbour activities" and to any "associated activities" carried on by them. "Harbour activities" are defined as activities involved in carrying on a statutory harbour undertaking or in carrying out harbour operations (as to which see paragraph 1.19 *ante*). "Associated activities" in relation to any harbour activities mean such activities as may be prescribed by regulations made by the Secretary of State. The Statutory Harbour Undertakings (Accounts, etc.) Regulations 1983 made by the Secretary of State under powers conferred by section 42 provide that, in relation to harbour authorities other than local authorities and natural persons, all activities other than harbour activities and the activities of a pilotage authority[12] are associated activities. The accounts prepared by a port trust or a harbour company will therefore relate to all the activities carried on by that body. With regard to the inclusion of pilotage revenue and expenditure in a harbour authority's statement of accounts see paragraphs 20.79 and 20.80 *post*.

10.83 The "associated activities", as defined in the 1983 regulations, of a port trust or statutory harbour company will nearly always be port related activities. That is not, however, necessarily the case in relation to a harbour authority which is a company formed under the Companies Act 1985, which may well be authorized by its memorandum of association to carry out a wide

---

12. As indicated in Chapter 20 *post*, pilotage authorities have now been abolished and pilotage has become a function of harbour authorities.

range of diverse activities, some of which have nothing to do with its harbour. When the 1983 regulations came into force Sealink Harbours Ltd. was the only significant example of such a harbour authority but, following the Ports Act 1991, several important harbour authorities are companies formed under the Companies Act. The current definition of associated activities in the Statutory Harbour Undertakings (Accounts, etc.) Regulations 1983 seems inappropriate in relation to such authorities.

10.84 Where a harbour authority have subsidiaries, for example subsidiary companies carrying out cargo handling activities, section 42 requires that, in addition to the statement of accounts mentioned above relating to their own activities, the harbour authority must prepare an annual statement of accounts relating to the harbour activities and associated activities carried on by them and their subsidiaries.

10.85 The requirements mentioned above are not satisfied by the preparation of a statement of accounts which relates to other matters in addition to harbour activities and associated activities. It also seems that a harbour authority which is a company formed under the Companies Act 1985 will be required to prepare accounts under section 42 as well as under the Companies Act although, having regard to the provisions referred to in paragraph 10.88 *post* and the current definition of associated activities in the 1983 regulations (see paragraph 10.83 *ante*), the form of the two sets of accounts would be similar and the range of activities covered would be the same. However, the two sets of accounts would differ if only because of the additional requirement as respects section 42 accounts referred to in paragraph 10.91 *post*.

10.86 Any provision for the auditing of a harbour authority's accounts applies to a statement of accounts prepared by that authority under section 42.

10.87 A harbour authority by whom a statement of accounts is prepared pursuant to section 42 is required to send a copy of the statement, together with a copy of the auditor's report on it, to the Secretary of State. They must also prepare and send to the Secretary of State a report on the state of affairs disclosed by the statement. This corresponds to a directors' report under the Companies Act 1985.

10.88 Section 42(6) provides that, subject to any regulations made by the Secretary of State under section 42—

(a) the provisions of the Companies Act 1985 relating to company accounts shall apply to a harbour authority's annual statement of accounts relating to the harbour activities and any associated activities carried on by them;

(b) the provisions of those Acts relating to group accounts shall apply to an annual statement of accounts relating to the harbour activities and associated activities carried on by a harbour authority and its subsidiaries; and

(c) the provisions of those Acts relating to the directors' report required to be attached to a company's balance sheet shall apply to the report which a harbour authority is required to prepare and send to the Secretary of State on the state of affairs disclosed by their statement or statements of accounts.

10.89 The Secretary of State may by regulations prescribe cases in which the provisions of the Companies Act 1985 referred to above are not to apply. The Statutory Harbour Undertakings (Accounts, etc.) Regulations 1983 provide that those provisions shall not apply in the case of a person who carries on a statutory harbour undertaking where the annual turnover is less than £250,000. The regulations define the circumstances in which the annual turnover of a statutory harbour undertaking is to be treated as being less than that amount.

10.90 The Secretary of State may also by regulations modify the relevant provisions of the Companies Act in their application to harbour authority accounts. The regulations mentioned above provide that provisions of the Companies Act 1985 that small or medium-sized companies shall be entitled to the benefit of certain exemptions in relation to accounts shall not apply in relation to the accounts and reports required to be prepared under section 42.

10.91 The Secretary of State may also prescribe by regulations requirements additional to those imposed by the provisions of the Companies Act. The regulations mentioned above provide that, where an annual statement of accounts prepared under section 42 relates to associated activities, then, in addition to complying with the requirements of the Companies Act 1985, the statement of accounts must include a statement of the gross revenue for the period in question in relation to those associated activities.

10.92 Section 42 does not apply to harbour authorities for nationalized harbours. Their accounts are governed by the provisions of section 24 of the Transport Act 1962 which requires that their accounts must be in such form, contain such particulars and be compiled in such manner, as the Secretary of State may from time to time direct. As mentioned above the only remaining nationalized harbour authority is the British Waterways Board.

10.93 Section 42 also does not apply to a statutory harbour undertaker of a class exempted from the section by regulations made by the Secretary of State. The Statutory Harbour Undertakings (Accounts, etc.) Regulations 1983 provide that section 42 shall not apply to a statutory harbour undertaker in respect of any undertaking carried on by him which is used wholly or mainly for ships resorting to the harbour in question wholly or mainly for the purpose of bringing or receiving goods which have been manufactured or produced by the statutory harbour undertaker or which are to be used by him for the manufacture or production of goods or electricity. For this purpose the activities of manufacture or production carried on by a holding company or subsidiary of the statutory harbour undertaker, or by members of a consortium who between them own more than half the issued share capital of the statutory undertaker, are to be treated as carried on by the statutory harbour undertaker in question.

Auditors of harbour authority accounts

10.94 Virtually all harbour authorities which are port trusts or statutory companies have provisions in their local Acts and orders for the appointment of auditors. The form of these varied somewhat but section 4 of the Ports (Finance) Act 1985 provided that any requirement of an "existing local provision" (see paragraph 10.56 *ante*) that the auditor of a "relevant harbour authority" (see paragraph 10.56 *ante*) should be appointed, or that his appointment must be approved, by a Minister of the Crown should cease to have effect, any former Ministerial power of appointment being exercisable instead by the harbour authority. Section 4 also provided that notwithstanding anything to the contrary in any existing local provision a person should be qualified for appointment as auditor of a relevant harbour authority only if he would be qualified for the appointment under section 389 of the Companies Act 1985 if the authority were a company to which that section (other than subsection (2) which related to unquoted companies) applied. This meant that the auditor of a port trust or a statutory harbour company must be a member of—

(a) the Institute of Chartered Accountants in England and Wales,
(b) the Institute of Chartered Accountants of Scotland,
(c) the Chartered Association of Certified Accountants, or
(d) the Institute of Chartered Accountants in Ireland,

(or be authorized by the Secretary of State as mentioned in section 389(1)(*b*) of the Companies Act 1985).

10.95 Section 389 of the Companies Act 1985 was repealed by the Companies Act 1989 and replaced by the more complicated provisions about eligibility for appointment as auditor contained in Part II of the 1989 Act. However, under those provisions, a person who is a member of one of the bodies mentioned in paragraph 10.94 *ante* continues to be eligible for appointment as a company auditor and therefore as the auditor of a port trust or statutory harbour company. Under section 25(2) of the Companies Act 1989 either an individual or a firm may be appointed as auditor.

CHAPTER 11

SUBORDINATE LEGISLATION UNDER THE HARBOURS ACT 1964

11.1 The Harbours Act 1964 includes important provisions for three different kinds of subordinate legislation—harbour revision orders, harbour empowerment orders and harbour reorganization schemes. The purpose of each of these powers for subordinate legislation and the related procedures are described below. The provisions of the Harbour Act 1964 containing the enabling powers, and the procedure for harbour revision and empowerment orders as currently in force are set out in Appendix K. Several harbour reorganization schemes were made to implement the amalgamation of harbours in estuaries as recommended in the Rochdale Report but no such scheme has been made in recent years.

11.2 These provisions for subordinate legislation were intended to be a simpler and cheaper alternative to private Bills so far as harbour legislation was concerned. However, section 62 of the Harbours Act 1964 provided that a private Bill (or in Scotland a provisional order under the Private Legislation Procedure (Scotland) Act 1936) might nevertheless be used to achieve objects which might be achieved by a harbour revision or empowerment order or a harbour reorganization scheme. As mentioned in paragraph 1.27 *ante*, section 62 was repealed by the Transport and Works Act 1992 which also extended the *vires* of harbour revision and empowerment orders and made some amendments in the procedure for such orders.

Harbour revision orders

11.3 Under section 14 of the Harbours Act 1964 a harbour authority may apply to the Secretary of State for Transport for a harbour revision order for the purpose of achieving in relation to their harbour all or any of the objects specified in Schedule 2 to the Harbours Act or in subsection (2A) of section 14. This subsection which was inserted by the Transport Act 1981 enables a harbour revision order to be used to consolidate statutory provisions of local application affecting a harbour or to repeal such provisions which are obsolete or otherwise unnecessary. In addition to the harbour authority for a harbour any other person who appears to the Secretary of State to have a substantial interest in a harbour, or a body representative of such persons, may apply for a harbour revision order in relation to the harbour in question. And, as mentioned below, in certain circumstances the Secretary of State may promote a harbour revision order himself.

11.4 The objects specified in Schedule 2 to the Harbours Act for which a harbour revision order may be made cover a wide field and have been clarified, and extended, by the Transport and Works Act 1992. They include, in particular, reconstituting a harbour authority, establishing a new harbour authority (either an existing body or one constituted for the purpose) for a harbour in place of the existing one, varying the powers of a harbour authority for managing or operating their harbour or for regulating the activities there of other persons (the latter purpose having been clarified by the amendment made by paragraph 9(2) of Schedule 3 to the 1992 Act) and conferring new powers for these purposes on a harbour authority, altering a harbour authority's limits of jurisdiction, authorizing a harbour authority to purchase land compulsorily and empowering a harbour authority to borrow money.

11.5 New purposes added to Schedule 2 by the Transport and Works Act 1992 are—

(1) Extinguishing or diverting public rights of way over footpaths or bridleways for the purposes of works described in the order or works ancillary to such works. "bridleway", in relation to England and Wales, has the same meaning as in the Highways Act 1980 and, in relation to Scotland, has the same meaning as in Part III of the Countryside (Scotland) Act 1967. "footpath", in relation to England and Wales, has the same meaning as in the Highways Act 1980 and, in relation to Scotland, has the same meaning as in the Roads (Scotland) Act 1984. Where a harbour revision order includes provision for extinguishing or diverting a public right of way over a footpath or bridleway, there must be annexed to the order a map of a scale not less than 1:2,500 on which the path or way concerned and, in the case of a diversion, the new path or way, are plainly delineated.

(2) Extinguishing public rights of navigation for the purposes of works described in the order or works ancillary to such works, or permitting interference with the enjoyment of such rights for the purposes of such works or for the purposes of works carried out by a person authorized by the authority to carry them out. While the view had been taken that a power in a harbour revision order for a harbour authority to execute works below high water mark implied a power to extinguish or interfere with public rights of navigation in so far as this was a necessary consequence of the works it was by no means clear that a power for a harbour authority to license other persons to carry out works below high water mark in the harbour "notwithstanding interference with public rights of navigation" (see paragraph 16.16

post) could be conferred by a harbour revision order. This new purpose added to Schedule 2 removed all doubt on this point.

(3) Enabling the harbour authority to close part of the harbour or to reduce the facilities available at the harbour.

(4) Empowering the authority (alone or with others) to develop land not required for the purposes of the harbour with a view to disposing of the land or of interests in it, and to acquire land by agreement for the purpose of developing it together with such land.

(5) Empowering the authority to delegate the performance of any of the functions of the authority except—

   (a) a duty imposed on the authority by or under any enactment;
   (b) the making of by-laws;
   (c) the levying of ship, passenger and goods dues;
   (d) the appointment of harbour, dock and pier masters;
   (e) the nomination of persons to act as constables;
   (f) functions relating to the laying down of buoys, the erection of lighthouses and the exhibition of lights, beacons and sea-marks, so far as these functions are exercisable for the purposes of the safety of navigation.

It is a constitutional principle that a body on whom functions are conferred by Parliament or by an instrument made under a power enacted by Parliament cannot delegate those functions to another person in the absence of express statutory authority. This new purpose enables a harbour authority to be authorized to delegate functions but not their basic functions as a harbour authority. It is likely that such delegation will usually be to a company formed by the authority under section 37 of the Docks and Harbours Act 1966—see paragraph 1.18 *ante*.

(6) Imposing or conferring on the authority duties or powers (including powers to make by-laws) for the conservation of the natural beauty of all or any part of the harbour or of any fauna, flora or geological or physiographical features in the harbour and all other natural features.

11.6 At the end of Schedule 2 there is a "sweeping up" provision under which a harbour revision order may be made for any object which, though not falling within any of the foregoing paragraphs, appears to the Secretary of State to be one the achievement of which will conduce to the efficient functioning of the harbour.

11.7 In addition to these main objects for which a harbour revision order may be made such an order may also, by virtue of section 14(3) of the Harbours Act 1964 (as extended by the Transport Act 1981 and the Transport and Works Act 1992) include all such provisions as appear to the Secretary of

State to be requisite or expedient for rendering of full effect any other provision of the order and any supplementary, consequential or incidental provisions appearing to him to be requisite or expedient for the purposes of, or in connection with, the order, including, but without prejudice to the generality of the foregoing words, penal provisions and provisions incorporating, with or without modifications, any provisions of the Lands Clauses Acts or any other enactment and provisions for excluding or modifying any provision of any Act or of any instrument made under any Act (including the Harbours Act 1964) and for repealing any statutory provisions of local application affecting the harbour to which the order relates.

11.8 The power to include provisions for excluding or modifying any provision of any Act or any instrument made under an Act and therefore to exclude or modify the application of general legislation if this appears to the Secretary of State to be requisite or expedient for rendering of full effect any other provision of the order or to be a supplementary, consequential or incidental provision which is requisite or expedient for the purpose of, or in connection with, the order, was introduced by the Transport and Works Act 1992. It appeared that, in the absence of express statutory authority, a harbour revision order could not affect the application of general legislation (partly on grounds of constitutional principle and also because the express powers in section 14(3) of, and paragraph 3 of Schedule 2 to, the Harbours Act for a harbour revision order to repeal or amend a statutory provision of local application seemed to exclude by implication power to affect general legislation). However, the power in section 14(3) to incorporate, with or without modifications, "any provision of . . . any . . . enactment" appears to apply to general legislation, and it is not unusual for harbour revision orders to include provisions which supplement those of statutory provisions of general application such as the common provisions which supplement the powers of a harbour authority to deal with wrecks under section 252 of the Merchant Shipping Act 1995. Section 43(3) of the Docks and Harbours Act 1966 authorizes a harbour revision order to repeal or amend general legislation for the purpose of securing the welfare of the officers or servants of the harbour authority and empowering that authority to provide, or secure the provision, for or in respect of their officers and servants, of pensions, gratuities and other like benefits (this being the purpose specified in paragraph 15 of Schedule 2 to the Harbours Act 1964).

11.9 Section 14(3) of the Harbours Act also prescribes the maximum penalties which may be provided for by a penal provision contained in a harbour revision order. On a person being convicted of an offence under such a penal provision no penalty may be inflicted on him other than a fine. In the case of an offence triable only summarily the maximum fine which may be imposed on conviction is level 4 on the standard scale or, in the case of a continuing offence, a daily fine of £50 for each day on which the offence continues after conviction. In the case of an offence triable either summarily or on indictment the maximum fine which may be imposed on summary conviction is the prescribed sum. On conviction on indictment there is no limitation to the amount of the fine which may be imposed.

11.10 Under the terms of section 14(2)(*b*) of the Harbours Act the Secretary of State cannot in most cases make a harbour revision order unless he is satisfied that this is desirable in the interests of securing the improvement, maintenance or management of the harbour in an efficient and economical manner or of facilitating the efficient and economic transport of goods or passengers by sea or in the interests of the recreational use of sea-going ships. The reference to recreational use was introduced by the Transport and Works Act 1992 and makes clear that a harbour revision order may be used to legislate in relation to a mainly recreational harbour. Subsection (2A) of section 14 provides that the conditions precedent for the making of an order specified in section 14(2)(*b*) do not apply where the objects of the order are the repeal of obsolete or otherwise unnecessary statutory provisions of local application affecting the harbour or of consolidating any statutory provisions of local application affecting the harbour. And subsection (2B) of section 14 inserted by the Transport and Works Act 1992 provides that nothing in section 14(2)(*b*) shall prevent the making of an order for facilitating—

(a) the closing of part of the harbour,
(b) a reduction in the facilities available in the harbour, or
(c) the disposal of property not required for the purposes of the harbour,

if the Secretary of State is satisfied that the making of the order is desirable on grounds other than those specified in section 14(2)(*b*).

11.11 The Transport and Works Act 1992 inserted in section 14 a new subsection (4A) which provides that, where two or more harbours have the same harbour authority or where the harbour authorities for those harbours are members of the same group, a harbour revision order may relate to more than one of those harbours. For this purpose two authorities are members of the same group if one is a subsidiary (within the meaning of the Companies Act 1985) of the other or both are subsidiaries of another company (within the meaning of that Act). This provision seems to imply that these are the only circumstances in which a harbour revision order may relate to more than one harbour.

11.12 Section 15 of the Harbours Act enables the Secretary of State to promote a harbour revision order himself if he is satisfied that a harbour revision order ought to be made to reconstitute a harbour authority or alter their constitution and/or to regulate (in whole or to a less extent) the procedure of, or of any committee of, the authority and to fix the quorum at a meeting of, or of any committee of, the authority. Before making an order under this section the Secretary of State must be satisfied as mentioned in section 14(2)(*b*) of the Act referred to in paragraph 11.10 *ante*.

Harbour empowerment orders

11.13 The second kind of subordinate legislation provided for in the Harbours Act, originally as an alternative to private Bills, is authorized by section 16 of the Act and enables the Secretary of State for Transport to make "harbour empowerment orders" to authorize the construction and/or improvement, maintenance or management of harbours (including docks and wharves) where no sufficient powers for the purpose already exist. Such an order can be made only on the application of a person desirous of securing the achievement of any of the objects specified in section 16(1). The application may ask for the requisite powers to be conferred on the applicant or a designated person other than the applicant or a body to be constituted for the purpose by the order.

11.14 A harbour empowerment order may include all such powers, including power to acquire land compulsorily and to levy charges other than ship, passenger and goods dues (if the order comes into force the new harbour authority will have power to levy such dues by virtue of section 26 of the Harbours Act) as are requisite for enabling the object of the order—the construction of an artificial harbour or a dock or wharf and its subsequent improvement, maintenance or management or, as the case may be, the improvement, maintenance or management of an existing harbour, whether natural or artificial—to be achieved. Under section 16(6) a harbour empowerment order may include such ancillary provisions as appear to the Secretary of State to be requisite or expedient. This subsection is in similar terms to section 14(3), which authorizes the inclusion of such provisions in harbour revision orders, including, following the Transport and Works Act 1992, a power to exclude or modify any provision of any Act or of any instrument made under any Act (including the Harbours Act 1964) (see paragraph 11.8 *ante*). It does not, however, refer to provisions for repealing or amending statutory provisions of local application (presumably because, *ex hypothesi*, there are no such provisions relating to a harbour which is the subject of a harbour empowerment order). A new subsection (7A) inserted in section 16 by the Transport and Works Act 1992, contains the same requirements for a map to be annexed to the order if it provides for extinguishing a public right of way over a footpath or bridleway as in the case of a harbour revision order (see paragraph 11.5 *ante*). This presumably implies power to include such a provision in a harbour empowerment order. The position as respects the penalties which may be provided for by a harbour empowerment order is the same as in the case of a harbour revision order.

11.15 Before making a harbour empowerment order the Secretary of State must be satisfied that the making of an order is desirable in the interests of facilitating the efficient and economic transport of goods or passengers by sea or in the interests of the recreational use of sea-going ships. As in the case of the conditions precedent for the making of a harbour revision order (see paragraph 11.10 *ante*) the reference to recreational use was introduced by the Transport and Works Act 1992. A harbour empowerment order can therefore now be used to authorize the construction, or provide for the management etc., of a recreational harbour such as a yacht marina. Formerly, it had appeared from the terms of section 16(5), which were narrower than those of section 14(2)(*b*), that a harbour empowerment order could not be used to establish, or secure the regulation of, a recreational harbour.

Harbour reorganization schemes

11.16 In addition to harbour revision and empowerment orders the Harbours Act also contains, in section 18, powers for the grouping together of harbours by means of "harbour reorganization schemes". Section 18 provides that "with a view to securing the efficient and economical development of a group of harbours each of which is being improved, maintained or managed by a harbour authority in the exercise and performance of statutory powers and duties" a harbour reorganization scheme with respect to the group may be submitted to the Secretary of State by all or any of the harbour authorities for the harbours in question. Section 18, as amended by the Transport Act 1981, further provides that if the Secretary of State is of opinion that, with a view to securing the efficient and economical development of a group of harbours each of which is being improved, maintained or managed by a harbour authority in the exercise and performance of statutory powers and duties, a harbour reorganization scheme ought to be made, he may by order make such a scheme.

11.17 What is a group of harbours for this purpose? It seems that section 18 envisages two or more harbours in close geographical proximity although not necessarily contiguous to each other. Perhaps the typical group are the harbours in an estuary. The five harbour reorganization schemes which have been made each amalgamated the harbours in a major estuary—the Forth, Tyne, Medway, Humber and Southampton. It seems probable however that a scheme under section 18 could amalgamate harbours on the coast within, say, 15 or 20 miles of each other—but probably not harbours 50 miles apart and certainly not an arbitrary group of harbours scattered around the coastline.

11.18 A harbour reorganization scheme may provide for the transfer either to one of the harbour authorities concerned or to a new body constituted by the scheme (whichever is to be the harbour authority for the amalgamated group of harbours) of powers and duties conferred by statutory provisions of local application on the harbour authority for any of the harbours in question for the purposes of that harbour together with that authority's interests in property related to such powers and duties.

11.19 A scheme may also provide for appropriate transfers of other powers and duties under statutory provisions of local application and interests in property. In particular, a harbour reorganization scheme may provide for the transfer of the statutory powers and duties and the interests in property of a local lighthouse authority (not being a harbour authority) relating to any of the harbours in the group and of interests in property used by a person other than one of the harbour authorities concerned for carrying out harbour operations at any of those harbours (if a scheme does provide for the transfer of interests in property used for the purposes last mentioned it must also provide for the payment of compensation in respect of the transfer).

11.20 A harbour reorganization scheme may also provide for transferring staff and preserving or otherwise securing pension rights (and by virtue of section 43(3) of the Docks and Harbours Act 1966 may for the latter purpose repeal or amend general legislation) and may include such ancillary provisions as appear to the Secretary of State to be necessary or expedient, including provisions repealing or amending any statutory provision of local application affecting all or any of the harbours concerned. By virtue of section 42 of the Docks and Harbours Act 1966 a harbour reorganization scheme may include provision for most of the purposes for which provision may be made by a harbour revision order.

Procedure for making harbour revision and empowerment orders

11.21 The procedure for making harbour revision and empowerment orders is prescribed by section 17 of, and Schedule 3 to, the Harbours Act 1964, which, as currently in force, are among the provisions set out in Appendix K. The main features of this procedure are as follows—

(a) If the proposed order would authorize the execution of works, the person intending to apply must give the Secretary of State prior notice of the application and may not proceed with it until the Secretary of State has responded as mentioned below—paragraph A2(1) inserted in Schedule 3 by the Harbour Works (Assessment of Environmental Effects) (Amendment) Regulations 1996. If it appears to the Secretary of State that the proposed application relates to a project which falls within Annex I to the European Communities Directive on Environmental Assessment (the construction of a trading port which permits the passage of vessels of over 1,350 tonnes) or Annex II to that Directive (the construction of any other harbour or the modification of a project included in Annex I) and, in the latter case, that the characteristics of the project require that an environmental assessment should be made, he must direct the applicant to supply him with relevant information in accordance with paragraph A2(3) inserted in the Schedule by the 1996 Regulations. Where the Secretary of State does not consider that the proposed application relates to such a project as is mentioned above, he must forthwith notify the proposed applicant accordingly.

(b) Such fees as may be determined by the Secretary of State are payable on the making of an application for an order and the application must be accompanied by not less than six copies of any map or maps which, if the order is made in the form of the draft, will be required to be annexed to it.

(c) The applicant is required, as a condition precedent to the Secretary of State taking further steps in the matter, to publish and serve notices in accordance with paragraph 3 of Schedule 3 and to comply with the requirements of paragraph A2(3) if they are applicable. The Secretary of State must furnish such bodies appearing to him to have environmental responsibilities as he thinks fit with any information supplied to him under paragraph A2 and must consult such bodies. In the case of an order which the Secretary of State proposes to make of his own motion the Secretary of State must publish and serve notice in accordance with paragraph 7 of Schedule 3. In either case there is a right to object to the Secretary of State within the period of 42 days from the date of the first publication of the advertisement or of the service of the notice as the case may be.

(d) If an objection is made and not withdrawn, the Secretary of State, unless he decides that the application or proposal shall not proceed further, is required to cause an inquiry to be held unless he considers that it is frivolous or too trivial to warrant the holding of an inquiry. If an objection relates only to a provision authorizing the compulsory acquisition of land the Secretary of State may, instead of causing an inquiry to be held, give the objector an opportunity of appearing before, and being heard by, a person appointed by the Secretary of State (affording the like opportunities to the applicant for the order and any other person to whom he considers it expedient to do so). The Secretary of State may disregard an objection to an application for, or proposal to make, a harbour revision or empowerment order unless it states the grounds on which it is made and may also disregard an objection so far as regards the inclusion in the draft order of a provision authorizing the compulsory acquisition of land if he is satisfied that it relates exclusively to matters which can be dealt with by the tribunal by whom compensation in respect of the acquisition will fall to be assessed in default of agreement.

(e) After considering the objections (if any) made and not withdrawn, any information supplied under paragraph A2(3)(b), the result of any consultation with bodies appearing to him to have environmental responsibilities and the report of any person who held an inquiry and of any person appointed to hear an objector, the Secretary of State, unless he decides not to make the order, may make it in the form proposed or applied for or subject to such modification as he thinks fit. If he proposes to make an order with modifications which appear to him substantially to affect the character of the order he is required to take such steps as appear to him to be reasonably practicable for informing persons likely to be concerned (and, in particular, if the order has been applied for, the applicant) and must not make the order until such period for consideration of, and comment upon, the proposed modifications as he thinks reasonable has elapsed. The Secretary of State is precluded from modifying an order so as to authorize the compulsory acquisition of land that was not described in the draft submitted to him unless all persons interested consent.

(f) Where it appears to the Secretary of State that the application relates to a project which falls within Annex I to the European Communities Directive on Environmental Assessment or to a project which falls within Annex II to the Directive, the characteristics of which require that it should be subject to environmental assessment, he must publish, in such manner as he thinks fit, his decision whether or not to make an order and the reasons and considerations upon which his decision was based, including a statement that the matters mentioned above, which he is required to consider before reaching a decision on an application, have been taken into consideration.

(g) When a harbour revision or empowerment order has been made the applicant or, in the case of an order made by the Secretary of State of his own motion, the Secretary of State, is required to publish and serve notice stating that the order has been made, and, unless it is subject to special parliamentary procedure, the date on which it came, or will come, into operation. The notice must name a place where a copy of the order may be inspected at all reasonable hours. Following the Transport and Works Act 1992 a harbour revision or empowerment order will be subject to special parliamentary procedure if, and only if, it authorizes the compulsory acquisition of certain special categories of land. In the case of an order relating to a harbour in England or Wales this is land of the kind referred to in section 18 or 19 of the Acquisition of Land Act 1981 (National Trust land, commons etc.). In the case of an order relating to a harbour in Scotland it is land of the kind referred to in section 1(2)(b) of the Acquisition of Land (Authorisation Procedure) (Scotland) Act 1947 (land forming part of a common or open space or held inalienably by the National Trust for Scotland). It would be unusual for a harbour order to authorize the compulsory acquisition of such land and, in the result, it seems that, in practice, future harbour revision and empowerment orders will hardly ever be subject to special parliamentary procedure. If works authorized by a harbour revision order have been the subject of an environmental assessment the Secretary of

State must, as soon as may be after the order has been made, publish in any such manner as he thinks fit his decision whether or not to make the order.

Procedure for making harbour reorganization schemes

11.22 The procedure for the submission or making, and confirmation of, harbour reorganization schemes is prescribed by Schedule 4 to the Harbours Act 1964 as amended by section 42(2) and (3) of the Docks and Harbours Act 1966 and paragraph 6(6) and (7) of Schedule 6 to the Transport Act 1981. The main features of this procedure are as follows—

(a) In the case of a scheme submitted to the Secretary of State by a harbour authority or authorities the first step after the submission of the scheme is for the Secretary of State to decide whether or not it should proceed. If he decides that the scheme should proceed he is required to publish and serve notices in accordance with paragraph 2 of Schedule 4 as he is also required to do where he proposes to make a scheme of his own motion.

(b) The provisions as respects objections, inquiries and hearings are substantially the same as those contained in Schedule 3 in relation to harbour revision and empowerment orders. The Secretary of State may disregard an objection so far as regards the inclusion in the scheme of a provision transferring interests in property if he is satisfied that the objection relates exclusively to matters in respect of which compensation falls to be provided under the scheme and the scheme is so framed as to enable those matters to be properly dealt with.

(c) The Secretary of State, after considering any outstanding objections and the report of any person who held an inquiry, may, if he then decides to make, or as the case may be, confirm, the scheme, make or confirm it by order either without modifications or with such modifications as he sees fit. If the Secretary of State proposes to make or confirm the scheme with modifications which appear to him substantially to affect the character of the scheme, similar provisions apply as in a case where he proposes to make a harbour revision or empowerment order with modifications which appear to him substantially to affect its character. The Secretary of State cannot make or confirm a scheme subject to a modification which provides for the transfer of an interest of a person in property which was not described in the scheme as proposed to be made or submitted as being property in which interests of that person were subject to be transferred unless the person in question gives his consent.

(d) As soon as may be after a harbour reorganization scheme has been confirmed or made by the Secretary of State, he must publish notice that it has been confirmed or made naming a place where a copy of the scheme as confirmed or made may be inspected at all reasonable hours and must serve a copy of the scheme as confirmed or made on each harbour authority on whom a copy of the scheme as submitted to, or proposed to be made by, the Secretary of State was served under paragraph 2 of Schedule 4.

Inquiries

11.23 Provisions relating to inquiries contained in section 250 of the Local Government Act 1972 or, in the case of Scotland, section 210 of the Local Government (Scotland) Act 1973 are applied, with some modification, by section 47 of the Harbours Act 1964 to inquiries required to be held by Schedule 3 to the Harbours Act 1964 in relation to harbour revision and empowerment orders and also to inquiries required to be held by Schedule 4 in relation to harbour reorganization schemes. The Transport and Works Act 1992 has extended the power to make orders as to costs or expenses under these provisions to enable such an order to be made not only where the inquiry or hearing takes place but also where arrangements are made for it but it does not take place.

11.24 In relation to harbour reorganization schemes dealing with harbours in Scotland (and any harbour revision or empowerment order relating to a harbour in Scotland which is subject to special parliamentary procedure although, as indicated in paragraph 11.21 *ante*, these will be rare), the Secretary of State, under section 47(3) of the Harbours Act, may direct that any inquiry which may be required under Schedule 3 or Schedule 4 to the Harbours Act, as the case may be, shall be held by Commissioners under the Private Legislation Procedure (Scotland) Act 1936. Section 2 as read with section 10 of the Statutory Orders (Special Procedure) Act 1945 requires such an inquiry to be held in any case if there are outstanding objections. So unless the Secretary of State gives a direction under section 47(3) in relation to a Scottish harbour revision or empowerment order (in a case where the order is subject to special parliamentary procedure) or harbour reorganization scheme to which there are outstanding objections, it seems that two inquiries would have to be held. In practice, such a direction has always been given. If the Secretary of State is not prepared to accept recommendations made by Commissioners who hold an inquiry into objections to a Scottish harbour revision or empowerment order or harbour reorganization scheme that the order or scheme should not be made or confirmed or should be modified, he may present to Parliament a Bill for the confirmation of the order or scheme. The procedure on such a Bill is the same as that provided by section 9 of the Private

Legislation Procedure (Scotland) Act 1936 in relation to the Confirmation Bills referred to in that Act.

Special parliamentary procedure

11.25 It seems that special parliamentary procedure will seldom occur in future in relation to subordinate legislation under the Harbours Act 1964. For the reasons mentioned above, harbour revision and empowerment orders will hardly ever in future be subject to it and, although harbour reorganization schemes are still subject to this procedure, it is doubtful whether many such schemes will be made in future. However, the summary of special parliamentary procedure included in previous editions of this book is set out in paragraphs 11.26 to 11.35 *post*.

11.26 Special parliamentary procedure is prescribed by the Statutory Orders (Special Procedure) Acts 1945 and 1965. The first step in this procedure is for the Secretary of State to lay before Parliament the order as made by him, after publishing the requisite notice of his intention to do so. Within the period of 21 days beginning with the day on which the order is laid before Parliament petitions may be presented against it and these stand referred to the Lord Chairman of Committees and the Chairman of Ways and Means ("the Chairmen"). Such a petition may pray for particular amendments to be made in the order ("a petition for amendment") or may be a prayer against the order generally ("a petition of general objection").

11.27 As soon as practicable after the expiration of the period of 21 days during which petitions may be presented the Chairmen consider all petitions and, if they are satisfied with respect to any petition that the provisions of the Statutory Orders (Special Procedure) Acts and of the Standing Orders of each House have been complied with, they are required to certify that the petition is proper to be received and is a petition for amendment or a petition of general objection as the case may be.

11.28 The next step is for the Chairmen to report to Parliament whether any petitions have been presented against the order and, if so, which of them have been certified as proper to be received and as petitions for amendment and petitions of general objection respectively. Their report is required to be laid before both Houses of Parliament.

11.29 If either House, within the period of 21 days beginning with the date on which the Chairmen's report is laid before it ("the resolution period"), resolves that the order be annulled it thereupon becomes void. If within the resolution period no such resolution is passed then (subject to what is said below about Scottish orders) any petitions which have been certified as proper to be received stand referred to a joint committee of both Houses, except that either House may resolve within the resolution period that a petition of general objection shall not be so referred. If neither House resolves that the order be annulled and no petitions stand referred to a joint committee as mentioned above, the order comes into operation at the expiration of the resolution period or on such later date, if any, as may be specified in the order.

11.30 In the case of a Scottish order a petition certified as proper to be received does not stand referred to a joint committee of both Houses unless either House orders that it shall be so referred. This provision has regard to the fact that the order will already have been considered by a panel of Commissioners consisting wholly or mainly of Members of Parliament.

11.31 Where a petition against an order stands referred to a joint committee of both Houses the order in question also stands so referred for the purpose of the consideration of the petition. The committee may report the order either without amendment or with such amendments as they think expedient to give effect, either in whole or in part, to the petition and with such consequential amendments as they think proper. Where the petition is a petition of general objection the committee may nevertheless report the order with amendments if they think it right to do so, but if in their opinion the order ought not to take effect they must report that it be not approved.

11.32 The report of the joint committee is laid before both Houses of Parliament. If the order is reported without amendment it comes into effect on the date on which it is so laid or on such later date if any as may be specified in the order.

11.33 If the order is reported with amendments it comes into effect on such date as the Secretary of State may by notice determine unless he considers it inexpedient for the order to take effect as amended by the committee. In that event he may either withdraw the order or may present to Parliament a Bill for the confirmation of the order.

11.34 If the joint committee report that the order be not approved it is also open to the Secretary of State to present to Parliament a Bill for the confirmation of the order.

11.35 The procedure on the Bills referred to in paragraphs 11.33 and 11.34 *ante* is of a special character and is prescribed by section 6(4) and (5) respectively of the Statutory Orders (Special Procedure) Act 1945.

Powers of court in relation to orders and schemes under Harbours Act 1964

11.36 Under section 44 of the Harbours Act 1964 as amended by section 44 of the Docks and Harbours Act 1966 and set out in Schedule 2 to that Act (and as further amended by the Transport Act 1981), a harbour revision or empowerment order or a harbour reorganization scheme, unless confirmed by Act of Parliament under the provisions of the Statutory Orders (Special Procedure) Act, may, within six weeks from the date when the order or scheme becomes operative, be challenged in, as the case may be, the High Court or the Court of Session on the ground that there was no power to make the order or confirm the scheme, or that a requirement of the Harbours Act 1964 (which is deemed to include Part III of the Docks and Harbours Act 1966) was not complied with in relation to the order or scheme. The court may suspend the operation of the order or scheme or of any provision thereof either generally or so far as may be necessary for the protection of the interests of the applicant until the final determination of the proceedings and, if satisfied that there was no power to make the order or confirm the scheme or that the interests of the applicant have been substantially prejudiced by a failure to comply with a requirement of the Harbours Act, may quash the order or scheme or any provision thereof either generally or so far as may be necessary to protect the applicant's interests. Section 44 provides the only method for challenging the legality of a harbour revision or empowerment order or harbour reorganization scheme. The section states that, except as therein provided, such an order or scheme shall not, either before or after it is made or confirmed, be challenged in any legal proceedings whatever. It appears from the case of *Smith* v. *East Elloe RDC*,[1] in which the effect of the similar provisions limiting the right to question compulsory purchase orders was considered, that this means that an order or scheme cannot even be challenged on the ground of bad faith at any rate after the six weeks period has expired.

Powers of Secretary of State to abolish or change certain powers to appoint members of port trusts

11.37 The Transport Act 1981 conferred a new power on the Secretary of State to make orders about appointments to the boards of port trusts. Section 15A of the Harbours Act 1964, inserted in that Act by section 18 of, and paragraph 5 of Schedule 6 to, the Transport Act 1981, authorizes the Secretary of State by order, where he is required to appoint a member or members of a port trust, to abolish any such power of appointment, except where this is a power to appoint the chairman of the harbour authority in question, or provide for the power of appointment to be exercised by someone else. An order under section 15A may not, however, be made with respect to the constitution of a port trust where all the members, apart from *ex officio* and co-opted members, are appointed by the Secretary of State. This power to reduce Ministerial appointments does not, therefore, in practice apply in relation to major port trusts. Before making an order under section 15A of the Harbours Act the Secretary of State must consult the harbour authority concerned and such other persons affected, or bodies representative of such persons, as he thinks fit. The Transport Act 1981 extends to orders under section 15A of the Harbours Act the provisions of section 44 of that Act limiting the right to challenge orders, etc., in legal proceedings and applies to such orders the provisions of section 54(2) of the Harbours Act so that they are subject to annulment by either House of Parliament.

1. *Smith* v. *East Elloe RDC* [1956] A.C. 736.

CHAPTER 12

PRIVATIZATION OF PORT TRUSTS UNDER PORTS ACT 1991

12.1 Part I of the above Act deals with the privatization of port trusts other than the Port of London Authority (PLA) and Part II with the privatization of the PLA's undertaking at Tilbury.

Privatization of port trusts other than PLA

12.2 Section 1 confers power on any "relevant port authority" to form under the Companies Act 1985 a company limited by shares whose objects (under the company's memorandum of association) include the acquisition of the port authority's property, rights and liabilities and the assumption of its functions under any local statutory provision. "Local statutory provision" is defined in section 40(1) of the Act as a provision contained in, or in a document made or issued under, any local Act (including an Act confirming a provisional order) or a provision of any other instrument which is in the nature of a local enactment. This contrasts with the use of the undefined expression "statutory provision of local application" in the Harbours Act 1964. The reference to any other instrument which is in the nature of a local enactment would appear to include harbour revision and empowerment orders and harbour reorganization schemes under the 1964 Act. "Relevant port authority" means a harbour authority as defined in the Harbours Act 1964 (see paragraph 1.5 *ante*) other than the bodies specified in section 1(4)—companies, local authorities, the British Waterways Board, Associated British Ports and the PLA. In short, it means any port trust (within the usual meaning of that expression (see paragraph 2.14 *ante*) except the PLA.

12.3 Under sections 2 and 9 a relevant port authority may submit to "the appropriate Minister" a scheme which specifies a company formed under section 1 which is a wholly owned subsidiary of the authority to be the authority's successor company.[1] "The appropriate Minister" is defined in

---

1. Schemes have so far been submitted by the Tees and Hartlepool Port Authority, the Medway Ports Authority, the Clyde Port Authority, the Forth Ports Authority and the Dundee Port Authority. All these schemes were confirmed by the Secretary of State and the undertakings of the port trusts concerned have been transferred to their respective successor companies—Tees and Hartlepool Port Authority Ltd., Medway Ports Ltd., Clydeport Ltd., Forth Ports PLC and Port of Dundee Ltd. Medway Ports Ltd. has been re-named Port of Sheerness Ltd.

section 20 in terms which include the cases of, as well as fishery harbours in England (where the appropriate Minister would be the Minister of Agriculture, Fisheries and Food), such harbours in Wales (where the appropriate Minister would be the Secretary of State for Wales) and marine works in Scotland (where the appropriate Minister would be the Secretary of State for Scotland). However, it seems unlikely that any port trust which is the harbour authority for a harbour which is, wholly or partly, a fishery harbour (as defined in the Sea Fish Industry Act 1951) in England or Wales, or a marine work in Scotland would be a serious candidate for privatization, so, for practical purposes, the appropriate Minister will probably always be the Secretary of State for Transport.

12.4 Under section 2 where a scheme which specifies a company formed under section 1 which is the wholly owned subsidiary of a relevant port authority as the port authority's successor company (and also makes the necessary "supplementary provisions" referred to below) is made, then, by virtue of section 2, when the scheme comes into force, all property, rights and liabilities of the authority (except securities of the successor company held by the authority and rights or liabilities of the authority in respect of such securities held by a nominee of the authority) and all the authority's functions under any local statutory provision, are transferred to the successor company.

12.5 Part I of Schedule 1 contains provisions which apply to all schemes under Part I of the Act. Most of these provisions are well precedented and relate to the consequential adaptation of contracts, statutory provisions and other documents and of powers to enforce legal rights. Paragraph 5 applies the Transfer of Undertakings (Protection of Employment) Regulations 1981 to the transfer of a relevant port authority's undertaking to a successor company under section 2 (including any part of the undertaking which is not in the nature of a commercial venture) with the result that the contract of any person employed by the authority in the undertaking will have effect after the transfer as if made between that person and the successor company. But it seems that the regulations as extended by section 33(2) of the Trade Union Reform and Employment Rights Act 1993 (which removed the restriction in the regulations to undertakings which are not of a commercial nature) would now apply directly to such a transfer and that the provision in paragraph 5 is therefore no longer of significance.

12.6 Part II of Schedule 1 contains supplementary provisions which may be included in schemes under Part I of the Act (and under sections 2(1)(b) and 6 such a scheme must include the supplementary provisions for the purposes of the transfer provided for under section 2). Which of these provisions should be included in a particular scheme will depend on the circumstances of the case. Most of the specific provisions relate to accounts and audit. There is also power to include provisions altering the constitution of the authority and such supplementary, incidental or consequential provisions as appear to the relevant port authority in question (or where the scheme is made by the Secretary of State as mentioned below, to the Secretary of State) to be necessary or expedient for the purposes of, or in consequence of, or in connection with, the operation of any provision of Part I of the Act or of the scheme. Such supplementary, incidental or consequential provisions may include provisions for repealing or amending any local statutory provision affecting the relevant port authority or any harbour for which that authority are the harbour authority.

12.7 When a relevant port authority submit a scheme to the appropriate Minister under section 9 they must also submit to him a copy of the memorandum and articles of association of the successor company. Section 9 provides for the subsequent procedure. This includes the publication and service on specified persons (including every employee of the authority) of notice of the scheme (containing the particulars specified in section 9(4)) and a right for any person within the specified period to make representations to the Minister with respect to the proposed transfer under section 2 or any provisions of the scheme or the successor company's memorandum or articles. The Minister must decide whether or not to confirm the scheme after considering any representations duly made to him and if he decides to confirm it may do so either without modifications or with such modifications as he thinks fit after consulting the authority. Also, he may first if he thinks fit direct the authority to secure that such alterations are made to the successor company's memorandum and articles as are specified in his direction.

12.8 The procedure prescribed by section 9 does not include a local inquiry. Under section 9(7) confirmation of a scheme is given by an order made by the appropriate Minister and a scheme so confirmed takes effect on the date on which the order confirming it comes into force or on such date as may be specified in that order. Where a scheme under Part I is initiated by a relevant port authority the order confirming it is a statutory instrument but is not subject to any Parliamentary control.

12.9 Sections 3 to 6 provide for the disposal of the ownership of a successor company. After a relevant port authority's undertaking has been transferred to their successor company under section 2, on the scheme under that section taking effect the authority may direct the successor company to issue such of its securities as the authority may from time to time direct to the authority or to any person entitled to require the issue of the securities following their initial allotment to the authority. The authority's power to direct the successor company to issue securities ceases when the company ceases to be their wholly owned subsidiary.

12.10 Subsequently, the authority must provide for the disposal of their holding in the successor company which is to be regarded as—

(a) the shares subscribed for by the authority or by any nominee of the authority on the formation of the successor company; and

(b) all securities of the successor company issued, or rights to require the issue of such securities initially allotted to the authority, in pursuance of a direction by them as mentioned above.

The authority must pay to the successor company a sum equal to 32.5 per cent of the consideration received on the disposal of any such securities or rights within the period of 60 days beginning with the date of the disposal.

12.11 The authority's power to direct the successor company to issue securities and to provide for the subsequent disposal of such securities is under the firm control of the appropriate Minister. The authority must not exercise these functions without his consent and the Minister has power to give directions to the authority. In exercising these powers the Minister is required to have particular regard to the desirability of encouraging the disposal of the whole or a substantial part of the equity share capital of the company to employees of the company or another company the whole or a substantial part of whose equity share capital is owned by such employees.

12.12 Under section 6 the authority may do anything they consider neces-sary or desirable for the purpose of carrying out their functions of directing the successor company to issue securities and disposing of their holding in the successor company. The company is required, if it is reasonably able to do so, to make premises and other facilities available for the use of the authority for the purposes of carrying out their functions under Part I and, if directed by the authority, to meet any expenses incurred by the authority in carrying out those functions.

12.13 Section 7 provides for the dissolution of a relevant port authority. When the appropriate Minister is satisfied that the authority have disposed of the whole of their holding in the successor company, that nothing further remains to be done under any provision of the scheme and that the authority have met all expenses and liabilities incurred in carrying out their functions under Part I (including liabilities in respect of the levy referred to below on the initial disposal of securities of the successor company or corporation tax on chargeable gains) other than any expenses met by the company under section 6 or any liabilities which he does not consider should be transferred to the successor company, he may, after consulting the authority, by order dissolve the authority on a day specified in the order. On such dissolution any property, rights and liabilities to which the authority are then entitled or subject (includ-ing the proceeds of the sale of the successor company after payment of the levy on the initial disposal of securities and any corporation tax on chargeable gains) are transferred to the successor company.

12.14 Sections 10 to 12 contain powers for the Secretary of State to take steps on his own initiative to secure the privatization of a port trust.[2] After the end of the period of two years beginning with the date when the Act was passed (25 July 1991) the Secretary of State, under section 10 may direct a relevant port authority who meet the annual turnover requirement referred to below to form a company under section 1 before such date as may be specified in the direction and, where a relevant port authority who meet the annual turnover requirement have already formed such a company or have been directed to do so as mentioned above, may also direct them to submit to him a scheme for the purposes of section 2. In preparing that scheme the authority must take into account any advice about the provisions of the scheme given by the Secretary of State. The Secretary of State must consult the relevant port authority concerned before giving any direction under section 10. If, following such consultation, he decides not to give a direction he must notify the authority in writing of that decision and in that event the Secretary of State cannot again exercise his powers under section 10 in relation to the authority in question until after the end of the period of five years beginning with the date when the notification was given. The procedure prescribed by section 9 applies in relation to a scheme submitted in compliance with a direction under section 10 except that "the appropriate Minister" in such a case is the Secretary of State (as indicated above, it seems virtually certain that, in practice, the Minister would always be the Secretary of State for Transport). Also, whereas a scheme initiated by a relevant harbour authority is not subject to Parliamentary control, where the scheme was submitted pursuant to a direction by the Secretary of State the order confirming it cannot be made unless a draft of the instrument containing it has been laid before, and approved by, each House of Parliament—section 37(3) and (4) of the Ports Act 1991.

12.15 The annual turnover requirement is prescribed by section 11. To calculate whether a relevant port authority meet the requirement on the date when the Secretary of State gives them a direction under section 10 one takes the aggregate of all sums received by the port authority in question (excluding grants from any public authority or any capital receipts or loans) as shown in the authority's accounts under section 42(1) of the Harbours Act 1964 (see paragraphs 10.81 to 10.93 *ante*), or under section 42(2) if they have subsidiaries, for each of the authority's three accounting years ending before the date when the direction is given. If in at least two of those accounting years, the aggregate of the sums received as mentioned above exceeds "the turnover limit" for "the reference year" in which the accounting year ends the authority concerned meet the turnover requirement for the purpose of section 10. The

---

2. The Secretary of State has taken steps under these provisions to secure the privatization of the undertakings of the Dover Harbour Board, the Ipswich Port Authority and the Port of Tyne Authority. In the case of Dover, the procedure has been discontinued. The undertaking of the Port of Ipswich Authority has been privatized. In the case of the Tyne, the Secretary of State has made a scheme under section 12 (see paragraph 12.16 *post*) and the order confirming the scheme has been approved by each House of Parliament. However, at the time of writing, the procedure for privatizing the port has not been completed.

reference years are the year ending immediately before the date on which the Act was passed ("the base date"), the year beginning with that date and each succeeding year beginning with an anniversary of that date. To calculate the turnover limit for each reference year one takes the sum of £5 million and, if the retail price index for the month in which that year begins shows a percentage increase over that for the month in which the base date falls, increase that sum by a percentage equal to that percentage increase and round the result to the nearest £100,000.

12.16 If the Secretary of State is dissatisfied with a scheme submitted to him by a relevant port authority pursuant to a direction under section 10, section 12 provides that he may make a scheme himself to secure the transfer under section 2 of the undertaking of the authority to the company specified in the authority's scheme. Before preparing the scheme the Secretary of State must consult the authority concerned and before making it publish notice of the scheme, containing the particulars specified in section 11(3) and stating that any person who wishes to make representations to him with respect to the proposed transfer or any provision of the proposed scheme or of the memorandum or articles of association of the company should do so in writing within the period of 42 days beginning with the date when the notice is first published. He must also serve the relevant port authority with a copy of the scheme and with a notice directing the authority to take such steps as are reasonably practicable to give such information as may be specified in the notice in such manner as may be so specified to the persons on whom the authority would have been required to serve notice of a scheme submitted by them under section 9. The Secretary of State's power, after considering any representations, to make the scheme, with or without modifications, and to direct the authority to secure that alterations are made in the company's memorandum or articles is the same, *mutatis mutandis*, as his power to confirm a scheme submitted under section 9. However, as in the case of a scheme submitted to comply with a direction by the Secretary of State, the order making the scheme cannot be made unless a draft of the instrument containing it has been laid before, and approved by, each House of Parliament.

12.17 Sections 13 to 16 provide for a levy on the initial disposals of securities of successor companies by relevant port authorities. A relevant port authority who dispose of such securities must pay levy at the rate of 50 per cent on the proceeds of sale but may deduct from the amount on which levy would otherwise be payable certain expenditure wholly and exclusively incurred for the purposes of the disposal. The Secretary of State may, with the consent of the Treasury, substitute for the rate of 50 per cent such other percentage as may be specified in the order. Such an order must not be made unless a draft has been laid before, and approved by a resolution of, the House of Commons. Levy chargeable on a disposal must be paid to the appropriate Minister by the relevant port authority. The amount is assessed by the appropriate Minister who serves a notice of assessment on the authority. The amount assessed is payable within the period of three months beginning with the date on which the disposal was made or within the period of 30 days beginning with the date of issue of the notice of assessment if that period ends later. Interest is payable if a payment of levy is not made within the period during which it is payable, as mentioned above. Under section 15A mentioned below, if it appears to the Minister that there are reasonable grounds for believing that the amount of the assessment may be excessive he may direct that these provisions shall not apply to the whole amount of the assessment but only to such lesser amount as he may specify. Also under section 15A, if a further amount is payable by the authority following a final determination of the amount of the assessment, these provisions apply to that further payment as if the date of the determination were substituted for the date when the notice of assessment was issued. Section 15A (inserted by section 159(1) of the Finance Act 1995) contains supplementary provisions about the notice of assessment under which a former relevant port authority may, within the period of three months or 30 days, as the case may be, mentioned above, request the appropriate Minister to reconsider the amount of the assessment (an appeal lies to the High Court or, in Scotland, the Court of Session, against the decision of the Minister on such a request) and the appropriate Minister may in any other case, if he thinks fit, confirm or reduce the amount of the assessment. There are provisions for a payment made under an assessment to be adjusted when the amount of the assessment is finally determined. A notice of assessment is not to be questioned in any legal proceedings whatsoever except as provided by section 15A (see subsection (6)). Thus the correctness of such a notice may not be challenged by application for judicial review, or by way of defence to legal proceedings brought to recover unpaid levy. Section 15 requires information for the purposes of the levy to be given to the appropriate Minister. Section 16 contains consequential and supplementary provisions relating to the levy.

12.18 Section 17 provides that where property, rights liabilities and functions of a relevant port authority are transferred under section 2 to a successor company then a levy must be paid by the company to the appropriate Minister in respect of any gain accruing to the company on a chargeable disposal of—

(a) relevant land (as defined in section 17(2)(a)); or
(b) a relevant interest in land (as defined in section 17(2)(b)),

made within the period of 10 years beginning with the date on which the company ceased to be a wholly owned subsidiary of the relevant port authority in question ("the levy period"). The levy is charged at the rate of 25 per cent on the amount of the gain in the case of a disposal within the first five years of the levy period, at the rate of 20 per cent on the amount of the gain in the case of a disposal within the sixth or seventh years of that period and at the rate of 10 per cent on the amount of the gain in the case of a disposal made during the remainder of that period. Different percentages for this purpose may be substituted by an order made by the Secretary of State with the consent of the Treasury—section 18(1). Such an order cannot be made unless a draft of the instrument containing it has been laid before, and approved by a resolution of, the House of Commons.

12.19 Section 17, and the Ports Act 1991 (Levy on Disposals of Land etc.) Order 1991 made by the Secretary of State under the enabling power contained in section 17, contain detailed and extremely complex provisions for determining relevant matters including what is treated as a disposal of land for the purposes of the section, when a disposal is chargeable and the amount of any gain. Section 18 contains supplementary and consequential provisions with regard to the allowability of levy as a deduction in the computation under the Capital Gains Tax Act 1979 of gains accruing on the disposal. The Capital Gains Tax Act 1979 has been repealed and replaced by the Taxation of Chargeable Gains Act 1992.

12.20 Section 19 of the Ports Act 1991 enables a relevant port authority who propose to form, or have formed, a company under section 1 or a body which were such an authority before their property, rights, liabilities and functions were transferred to a successor company under section 2, to provide financial assistance to persons who are employees of the authority (before the transfer) or employees of the company (after the transfer). Such persons must have formulated a proposal for maximizing participation by employees of the company in ownership of its equity share capital which appears to the relevant port authority, or former relevant port authority, to have a reasonable prospect of success. Such assistance may be given by indemnifying the persons concerned in respect of the whole or any part of any expenditure incurred wholly and exclusively for the purposes of the proposal or by discharging on behalf of those persons the whole or any part of any liability incurred wholly and exclusively for those purposes.

Privatization of Port of Tilbury

12.21 As indicated in paragraph 12.32 *post*, Part II of the Act has already been implemented. Section 21 authorized the PLA to form a company limited by shares under the Companies Act 1985 for the purpose of operating the PLA's docks and landing places at Tilbury ("the port of Tilbury").

12.22 Where the PLA had formed a company under section 21 they could, under section 22, submit a scheme to provide for the transfer to the company of any of the PLA's property, rights and liabilities which it appeared to them to be appropriate to transfer to the company. In preparing the scheme the PLA were required to take into account any advice given by the Secretary of State. When submitting a scheme under section 22 the PLA were also required to submit to the Secretary of State a copy of the memorandum and articles of the company. The PLA were not required to publish, or serve copies of a notice of a scheme under section 22 (as relevant port authorities are required to do when submitting a scheme under Part I of the Act). The reason for this difference in procedure was presumably that, by enacting Part II, which refers specifically and exclusively to the Port of Tilbury, Parliament had endorsed in principle a scheme under that Part.

12.23 The scheme required confirmation by the Secretary of State and, if he decided to confirm it, he might do so with or without modifications. If it appeared to him that a scheme did not accord with any advice he had given he might, after consulting the PLA, make a scheme himself. Before confirming a scheme or making a scheme himself the Secretary of State might, if he thought fit, give the PLA a direction requiring them, before a specified date, to secure that such alterations were made to the memorandum and articles of the company as might be specified in the direction.

12.24 Unlike a scheme under section 2, a scheme under section 22 provided itself for the transfer and vesting of the property, rights and liabilities in question but, under section 22(8)(*b*), related functions of the PLA under any local statutory provision were transferred to and vested in the company by virtue of that section.

12.25 The company is therefore a harbour authority as defined in the Harbours Act 1964 with powers, *inter alia*, to levy dues under section 26 of that Act and carry out harbour operations under section 38(2) of the Docks and Harbours Act 1966.

12.26 Schedule 2 contained general supplementary provisions in relation to a transfer of property, rights, liabilities and functions to the company. These provided, among other things, for the division and apportionment of property etc. between the PLA and the company. Section 23 also authorized the inclusion in a scheme under section 22 of certain other supplementary provisions. These included excepting specified statutory functions from the transfer of such functions under section 22(8)(*b*) and repealing or amending certain statutory provisions. Provision could be made with respect to the consideration to be provided by the company for any transfer under the scheme.

12.27 Section 24 required the scheme under section 22 to include detailed provisions for the protection of the pension rights of persons who were transferred by the scheme from the employment of the PLA to that of the company, who immediately before the date of transfer were members of the Port of London Authority Pension Fund and who ceased to be members of that fund by virtue of the transfer. It also required the scheme to protect the pension rights of certain persons who acquire pension rights on the death of a person within the category mentioned above.

12.28 Section 22(9) and (10) provided for a scheme under section 22 to be confirmed or made by order of the Secretary of State and to come into force on such date as might be specified in the order.

12.29 Section 25 provided that where any property transferred to the company by the scheme under section 22 is of a nature requiring a works licence from the PLA under the Port of London Act 1968 to maintain it such a licence shall be deemed to have been granted.

12.30 Section 26 provided that following the transfer to the company of property, rights, liabilities and functions, the PLA might provide for the disposal of securities of the company in such manner, at such time or times and on such terms as they thought fit. But the exercise of this power required the consent of the Secretary of State and, while the company remained a subsidiary of the PLA, the PLA could not without his consent permit—

(a) any disposal by the company of any securities of a subsidiary of the company; or

(b) any disposal by the company of any part of its undertaking or of any assets of the company (other than securities of a subsidiary of the company) which appeared to the PLA to affect materially the structure of the company's business.

While the company remained a wholly owned subsidiary of the PLA the Secretary of State might give the PLA directions requiring them to secure the issue by the company of such securities as might be specified or to exercise their power to provide for the disposal of securities of the company in a specified manner. In exercising these powers the Secretary of State was required, as in the case of his control over the disposal of securities of a successor company by a relevant port authority (see paragraph 12.11 *ante*), to have particular regard to the desirability of encouraging the disposal of the whole or a substantial part of the equity share capital of the company to employees of the company.

12.31 Section 28 contained provisions to enable the PLA to provide financial assistance for proposals to maximize employee participation in the equity of the company on the lines of those contained in section 19 in the case of relevant port authorities (see paragraph 12.20 *ante*).

12.32 The PLA submitted a scheme under section 22 within a few months after the passing of the Act which has been confirmed by the Secretary of State. The scheme transferred the Port of Tilbury to Port of Tilbury London Limited.

CHAPTER 13

HARBOUR AUTHORITIES' POWERS TO FORM AND ACQUIRE COMPANIES

13.1 It seems that a corporation created by statute does not have power to acquire securities (except perhaps as an investment) or form companies in the absence of express statutory provision. Most harbour authorities are still statutory corporations although a significant minority are now companies formed under the Companies Act 1985 who will not normally be inhibited in acquiring securities or forming companies.

13.2 However, there is the further point that any harbour authority, whether a statutory corporation or a Companies Act company, on whom discretionary powers have been conferred by or under statute cannot transfer those powers to a company formed or acquired by that authority in the absence of an express or implied statutory power for that purpose. It makes no difference that the company concerned is a subsidiary of the harbour authority—it is still a separate legal entity.

13.3 There are a number of examples of express powers for harbour authorities to acquire securities in, or form, companies and (whether expressly or by implication) to arrange for such companies to perform functions of the harbour authority.

13.4 Section 14(4) of the Transport Act 1962 provided that each of the Boards (which included the then British Transport Docks Board, the British Railways Board and the British Waterways Board) should have power, with the consent of the Secretary of State and for the purposes of their business, to subscribe for or acquire any securities of a body corporate.

13.5 Section 50(8) of the Transport Act 1968 provided that without prejudice to their powers apart from that subsection (presumably a reference to section 14(4) of the 1962 Act) each of the Boards (again including the British Transport Docks Board, the British Railways Board and the British Waterways Board) should have power to form, promote and assist, or join with any other person in forming, promoting and assisting, a company for carrying on any activities which that Board had power to carry on.

13.6 Among harbour authorities, the British Waterways Board can still use these Transport Act powers in relation to the few small harbours which it owns and corresponding provisions (but without the requirement for Ministerial consent) are included among the powers of Associated British Ports contained in Schedule 3 to the Transport Act 1981.

13.7 For harbour authorities generally (apart from "the Boards"), section 37(2) of the Docks and Harbours Act 1966 provided that a harbour authority might subscribe for or acquire any securities of a body corporate which was wholly or mainly engaged, or which it was proposed should become wholly or mainly engaged, in carrying out harbour operations (or in providing, maintaining or operating an inland clearance depot). "Harbour operations" meant the operations defined as such in section 57(1) of the Harbour Acts 1964 which included, in particular, cargo handling operations and warehousing.

13.8 Doubt has been expressed about whether the power contained in section 37(2) of the 1966 Act to subscribe for securities implies power to form a company. This is partly because, presentationally, section 37 seems to emphasize the acquisition of a harbour business or shares in a harbour business rather than the formation of a company. The marginal note to section 37 gives this impression (Upjohn L.J. said in *Stephens* v. *Cuckfield RDC*,[1] "Whilst the marginal note to a section cannot control the language used in the section it is at least permissible to approach a consideration of its general purpose and the mischief at which it is aimed with the note in mind"). However, a more important point is that, as indicated above, in spite of the power to subscribe for securities, contained in section 14(2) of the Transport Act 1962, it was thought appropriate to include in section 50(8) of the Transport Act 1968 a further express power for the bodies concerned to form companies as distinct from acquiring their securities.

13.9 Probably the better view is that section 37(2) of the 1966 Act does confer on harbour authorities power to form companies as well as acquire their securities but it is perhaps a pity that in the Transport and Works Act 1992 the opportunity was not taken to put the matter beyond any possible doubt.

13.10 Several harbour authorities have obtained, by local Act of Parliament or harbour revision order under section 14 of the Harbours Act 1964, powers to acquire securities in, or form, companies for wider purposes than those originally referred to in section 37(2) of the 1966 Act. For example, section 43(1) of the Great Yarmouth Outer Harbour Act 1986 authorizes the Great Yarmouth Port and Haven Commissioners to form and promote, or join with other persons in forming and promoting, a company for the purpose of:

(a) carrying on any activities which the Commissioners have power to carry on;

(b) carrying goods which have been unshipped or which are to be shipped at the Port (of Great Yarmouth);

(c) developing land or providing facilities in the vicinity of the Port for the purposes of any trade or business associated with the Port.

---

1. *Stephens* v. *Cuckfield RDC* [1960] 2 Q.B. 373.

13.11 Section 43(2) authorises the Commissioners to subscribe for or acquire any securities of a company which is wholly or mainly engaged, or which it is proposed should become wholly or mainly engaged, in carrying out any of the activities specified in section 43(1).

13.12 Section 5(1) of the Port of Tyne Act 1989 authorized the Port of Tyne Authority to form and promote a wholly-owned subsidiary for carrying on any activities which the Authority had power to carry on. Section 5(2) required the Authority to secure that any company formed under section 5(1) should remain a wholly-owned subsidiary of the Authority. Section 4(1) of the Port of Tyne Act 1989 authorized the Port of Tyne Authority to form and promote, or join with any other person in forming and promoting, a company for using or developing for any purpose, or carrying on any business on, any land within or formerly within the Port of Tyne not being an activity which might be carried on by a company formed under section 5 mentioned above. Under section 4(2), except as otherwise provided by any enactment or rule of law, the powers of a company formed under section 4(1) might include power to do anything necessary or expedient for the purposes of the objects mentioned in section 4(1) or for purposes incidental to those purposes, notwithstanding that the Port of Tyne Authority would not themselves have the power to do that thing.

13.13 The Shoreham Port Authority Harbour Revision Order 1988 authorizes the Shoreham Port Authority to (*inter alia*):

"subscribe for or acquire any shares, stock, debentures, debenture stock or any other security of a like nature of a body corporate which is wholly or mainly engaged, or which it is proposed should become wholly or mainly engaged, in the provision, maintenance or operation of a harbour or in providing services or facilities which the Authority themselves are authorised to provide; form and promote, or join with any other person in forming and promoting, a company for carrying on any function of the Authority."

13.14 However, the order provides that this power to form and promote companies does not enable a company to be formed to exercise the Authority's basic harbour powers which are specified as its powers under the Harbours Docks and Piers Clauses Act 1847 and the Harbours Act 1964 and powers to make by-laws.

13.15 These provisions of the Shoreham Port Authority Harbour Revision Order 1988 have been followed, substantially, in several subsequent harbour revision orders. Although they have not been challenged, it may be arguable that they strain the *vires* of section 14 of the Harbours Act 1964.

13.16 Following the Transport and Works Act 1992, local provisions of the kind mentioned above should no longer be necessary, assuming that section 37(2) of the 1966 Act authorizes a harbour authority to form a company as well as acquire securities in a company (these local provisions appear to envisage that a power to subscribe for securities may not suffice for this purpose, probably because of the provisions of the Transport Acts referred to above).

13.17 Section 63(2)(b) of the Transport and Works Act 1992 amends section 37(2) of the 1966 Act by substituting for the references to harbour operations references to "activities relating to harbours".

13.18 The powers of a harbour authority to form and acquire companies under section 37(2) are now therefore very wide indeed. They would appear to include power for a harbour authority (which is a statutory corporation) to form, or acquire securities in, a company which carries out, or which it is proposed should carry out, activities relating to harbours which go beyond the statutory powers of the authority itself. Nor does it seem that the activities relating to harbours must be limited to the harbour managed by the harbour authority which forms, or acquires securities in, the company. "Activities relating to harbours" seems to encompass a great variety of matters which might perhaps include, according to circumstances, the provision of a hotel and running a ferry service (but a harbour authority cannot of course claim that an activity relates to a harbour simply because it undertakes it—the activity must genuinely relate to a harbour). It might even be argued that the extended powers under section 37(2) of the 1966 Act enable a port trust to take over a privatized harbour authority! Certainly it seems to make privatization under the Ports Act 1991 a less attractive option.

13.19 These extended powers should greatly facilitate joint ventures between harbour authorities and other bodies concerned with harbour activities.

13.20 The extended power under section 37(2) is, however, qualified by the new subsection (2A) inserted in section 37 of the 1966 Act by the Transport and Works Act 1992. This provides that nothing in section 37(2) is to be construed as authorizing a harbour authority to delegate to another body any function that it could not delegate apart from that subsection.

13.21 Following the Transport and Works Act 1992, a harbour authority may apply for a harbour revision order to empower it to delegate the performance of any of its functions except:

  (a) a duty imposed on the authority by or under any enactment;
  (b) the making of by-laws;
  (c) the levying of ship, passenger and goods dues;
  (d) the appointment of harbour, dock and pier masters;
  (e) the nomination of persons to act as constables;
  (f) functions relating to the laying down of buoys, the erection of light-houses and the exhibition of lights, beacons and sea-marks so far as those functions are exercisable for the purposes of the safety of navigation. (See paragraph 9B inserted in Schedule 2 to the Harbours Act 1964 by paragraph 9(5) of Schedule 3 to the Transport and Works Act 1992).

13.22 A harbour authority cannot therefore delegate any of these basic harbour functions to a company which it has formed, or whose securities it has acquired, under section 37(2) of the 1966 Act. If it wishes to transfer any of its other functions to such a company, it will have to obtain a harbour revision order to authorize it to do so.

CHAPTER 14

CARGO HANDLING, ETC.

Powers of harbour authorities to carry out cargo handling etc.

14.1 As indicated in paragraph 1.18 *ante*, the Docks and Harbours Act 1966 authorizes a harbour authority (within the meaning of the Harbours Act 1964) to carry out harbour operations as defined in section 57(1) of the 1964 Act (section 38(2) of the Act of 1966). These include:

(a) the warehousing, sorting, weighing or handling of goods on harbour land (defined in section 57(1) of the Harbours Act 1964 as land adjacent to a harbour and occupied wholly or mainly for the purposes of activities there carried on) or at a wharf (defined in section 57(1) as any wharf, quay, pier, jetty or other place at which sea-going ships can ship or unship goods or embark or disembark passengers);

(b) the movement of goods or passengers within the limits within which the harbour authority have jurisdiction or on harbour land;

(c) in relation to a harbour other than a wharf (i.e. the water area)—

    (i) the loading or unloading of goods, or the embarking or disembarking of passengers, in or from a ship which is in the harbour or the approaches thereto, and

    (ii) the lighterage or handling of goods in the harbour;

(d) in relation to a wharf, the loading or unloading of goods, or the embarking or disembarking of passengers, at the wharf in or from a ship.

14.2 Many harbour authorities already possessed powers for these purposes under their special legislation before the commencement of the Docks and Harbours Act 1966. Cargo handling activities, and particularly the loading and unloading of goods at wharves, became a much more important activity of harbour authorities partly as a result of the Dock Workers Employment Scheme 1967 and the provisions for the licensing of port employers contained in Part I of the Docks and Harbours Act 1966. The Dock Workers Employment Scheme was abolished and Part I of the 1966 Act repealed by the Dock Work Act 1989 following which the number of private port employers may again be increasing.

Powers for harbour authorities to acquire or set up cargo-handling companies

14.3 These powers are discussed in chapter 13 *ante*. In recent years a number of harbour authorities have acquired all or most of the share capital in cargo-handling companies and many such companies, particularly at major harbours, are now therefore subsidiaries of the harbour authority.

Liability of harbour authorities for goods stored on their premises

14.4 Most harbour authorities provide some warehousing or storage facilities. In carrying out this activity a harbour authority have the same common law duty as any other bailee for reward to exercise reasonable care in respect of the goods and the burden of proof that they have complied with this duty rests on them. This common law duty may be modified by contract and most harbour authorities make their acceptance of goods for storage subject to terms and conditions. However, under the Unfair Contract Terms Act 1977, any such terms and conditions must be fair and reasonable within the meaning of that Act.[1] Also any such terms and conditions are subject to the provisions of the Unfair Terms in Consumer Contracts etc. Regulations 1994.

14.5 The special legislation of many harbour authorities provides that the authority shall not be responsible for the safety of any goods deposited in any part of their docks or land adjoining the harbour which is not specifically set apart by the authority for the purpose of warehousing. Such a provision would exclude liability as bailee on the part of the harbour authority but it seems doubtful whether it would exclude liability for damage to goods caused by the negligence of the harbour authority's employees (although the onus would then of course be on the owners of the goods to prove negligence).

Safety of cargo handling

14.6 With regard to the safety of cargo handling, the Docks Regulations have been the principal legislation by which health and safety in ports and harbours in Great Britain, particularly in relation to cargo handling, has been regulated for the greater part of this century.

14.7 In 1899 two factory inspectors surveyed conditions in the nation's docks and wharves and their report led to the adoption of the first set of Docks Regulations in 1904. Made under the Factory and Workshop Act 1901, they were almost certainly the first such provisions adopted anywhere in the world.

14.8 The regulations of 1904 were superseded by the Docks Regulations 1925 which had a wider scope and included first-aid provisions.

1. For a case in which a harbour authority's conditions for bailment of goods were discussed see the *Singer Company (UK) Limited and Singer do Brazil Industria E. Commercia Ltda.* v. *Tees and Hartlepool Port Authority* [1988] 2 Lloyd's Rep. 164.

14.9 Dock safety was one of the first matters considered by the International Labour Organization (ILO) which was established to deal with international matters concerned with employment. Convention 32, which was adopted in 1932, was concerned with the protection of dockers against accidents and it was quickly ratified by the United Kingdom Government and reflected in a further set of Docks Regulations which were made in 1934.

14.10 Like their predecessors, the new regulations applied to Great Britain and in 1936 were reflected in a similar set of regulations covering Northern Ireland (no such provisions have been made in respect of the Channel Islands or the Isle of Man).

14.11 Each of the sets of regulations was principally a set of work rules covering cargo handling and the lifting machinery then in use, both on the ship and on shore. The nature of such work was based to a large extent on manual operations and had changed very little over the years. Thus, the legal provisions equally had changed only in the light of experience.

14.12 However, the rapid mechanization and extensive changes in cargo packaging and handling which took place from the 1960s onward resulted in a revolution in port operations which had the effect of rendering the old laws obsolete, more because of what was not covered rather than because the actual provisions had become obsolete.

14.13 This situation was recognized by ILO, who adopted a new Convention, Number 152, in 1979. This Convention, "Health and Safety in Dockwork", not only reflected the new conditions and methods, but, in recognition of the fact that change was continuing, was drafted in more general terms, thus making it more flexible for the future.

14.14 With regard to the implementation of this Convention in Great Britain, it was decided that, contrary to what had been the position before, the new legislation would be split between a new set of Docks Regulations dealing with activities on the shore and use of equipment on the ship and Merchant Shipping Regulations which would cover the provision of safety equipment, plant, etc., on the ship.

14.15 The main new shoreside provisions, the Docks Regulations 1988, were made under the Health and Safety at Work, etc. Act 1974 and deal comprehensively with modern-day port operations. They are drafted with the future as well as present operations in mind, and cover such facets as planning, lighting, access by land and by water, rescue and emergency arrangements, hatches, training, fitness and competence of drivers, maintenance and use of vehicles, testing, examination, marking and use of lifting plant, records, confined spaces and protective equipment. These regulations are health and safety regulations within the meaning of the Health and Safety at Work, etc. Act 1974 and are enforceable as such under the provisions of that Act.

14.16 In accordance with section 16 of the 1974 Act, an approved code of practice and a guidance note were also published at the same time to make the intentions clear and to detail how the regulatory requirements can be applied in the complex circumstances of a modern port. With a few exceptions, the Docks Regulations 1988 came into force on 1 January 1989, replacing the 1934 Regulations (except for Part I of those Regulations mentioned in the next paragraph).

14.17 Also made and coming into force at the same time, the Loading and Unloading of Fishing Vessels Regulations 1988 deal with the landing of wet fish across quays and the fuelling, provisioning and icing of vessels. They replace the previous provisions of Part I of the 1934 Regulations.

14.18 The Docks Regulations 1988 are complemented by regulations under the Merchant Shipping Act 1979 (and having effect as if made under the Merchant Shipping Act 1995) dealing with the provision of safe equipment and working conditions on board ship.

New law to keep dangerous ships out of harbours

By JOHN PETTY Shipping Correspondent

DANGEROUS ships will be banned from British harbours from July 23 as a result of a Private Member's Bill promoted in the Lords by Lord Walston and sponsored in the Commons by Mr Roger Moate, Conservative M P for Faversham.

The British Ports Association has welcomed the law as "plugging a gap in the powers of harbour authorities to deal with serious emergencies."

At present, only a few ports have local legislation enabling them forbid a dangerous ship from entering a harbour or to require a ship to depart.

"Having regard to the highly dangerous nature of some cargoes which ships carry these days, the extension of the powers of harbour masters contained in the Act seemed essential," said Mr N. H. Finney, director of the association.

Harbour masters will be able to ban any ship under two categories.

The first is one that might present "grave and imminent danger to the safety of any person or property."

The second is one that presents a grave or imminent risk that, by sinking or foundering the harbour.

A fine of £25,000 is provided on summary conviction for disobeying an order.

CONCORDE BOOM

CUNARD is getting such a flood of transatlantic holiday bookings that its £36 million contract to hire aircraft from British Airways this year is being extended so that Concorde will fly from Manchester, Birmingham and Bristol airports as well as from London.

The attraction is that travellers pay less than the normal single fare by Concorde in a package that gives them a one-way crossing by supersonic airliner, a stay at the Waldorf Astoria Hotel in New York, and five days on the Atlantic in the 67,000-ton liner Queen Elizabeth 2.

Depending on season, the package starts at between £1,200 and £1,300 per person.

There is also a cheaper package, known as Dollar Pounders, which starts at £625 and includes the QE2, a stay at a first-class hotel in Manhattan and return by subsonic airliner.

CHAPTER 15

PORT SECURITY

Aviation and Maritime Security Act 1990, Part III as amended by the Merchant Shipping and Maritime Security Act 1997

15.1 Part III of the Aviation and Maritime Security Act 1990 contains provisions for the protection of ships and harbour areas against acts of violence. The purposes of Part III are, in section 18(1) of the Act, expressed to be the protection against acts of violence—

    (a) of ships and of persons and property on board ships;

    (b) of harbour areas, of such persons as are at any time present in a harbour area and of such property as forms part of a harbour area or is at any time (whether permanently or temporarily) in any part of a harbour area.

15.2 For the purposes of Part III "act of violence" is defined in section 18(2) as any act (whether actual or potential, and whether done or to be done in the United Kingdom or elsewhere) which either—

    (a) being an act done in Great Britain, constitutes, or

    (b) if done in Great Britain would constitute,

the offence of murder, attempted murder, manslaughter, culpable homicide or assault or an offence under section 18, 20, 21, 22, 23, 24, 28, or 29 of the Offences against the Person Act 1861, under section 2 of the Explosive Substances Act 1883 or under section 1 of the Criminal Damage Act 1971 or, in Scotland, the offence of malicious damage.

15.3 "Harbour area" is defined by section 18(3) for the purposes of Part III as the aggregate of:—

    (i) any harbour in the United Kingdom in respect of which there is a harbour authority within the meaning of the Merchant Shipping Act 1995 (see paragraph 1.7 *ante*), and

    (ii) any land which is adjacent to such a harbour and which is either land occupied by the harbour authority or land in respect of which the harbour authority has functions of improvement, maintenance or management (thus including, in the case of a harbour managed under statutory powers, berths abutting on the harbour owned by other persons where dangerous goods are loaded or unloaded and the authority therefore have jurisdiction under the Dangerous Substances in Harbour Areas Regulations 1987—see paragraph 8.5 *ante*).

The definition of "harbour area" also includes any hoverport within the meaning of the Hovercraft Act 1968 which does not form part of any area which falls within (i) or (ii) above.

15.4 The basic provisions of Part III of the Aviation and Maritime Security Act 1990 consist of powers for the Secretary of State to give directions to harbour authorities and others in the interests of the purposes of Part III mentioned above and for the enforcement of those provisions. Part III is a complex and detailed piece of legislation. It is set out in Appendix L. The following paragraphs summarize the basic provisions and draw attention to important points in their application to harbour areas.

Power of Secretary of State to require information

15.5 Section 19 confers on the Secretary of State wide powers to require (*inter alia*) a harbour authority, a person who carries on harbour operations in a harbour area or a person who is permitted to have access to the "restricted zone" of a harbour area (designated as mentioned below) for the purpose of exercising his business activities there to furnish him with such information as he may require to enable him to determine whether to give a direction under one of the broad enabling powers described below or to ascertain whether any such direction is being or has been complied with. "Harbour operations" are defined in section 46(1) as:

(a) the marking or lighting of a harbour or any part of it;
(b) the berthing or dry docking of a ship or the towing or moving of a ship into or out of or within the harbour area;
(c) the transportation, handling or warehousing of goods within the harbour area;
(d) the embarking, disembarking or movement of passengers within the harbour area.

15.6 The maximum penalty for failing to provide the required information or for knowingly making a false statement or recklessly making a statement which is false in a material particular, in the course of furnishing such information is, on summary conviction, a fine not exceeding "the statutory maximum" or on conviction on indictment to an (unlimited) fine or to imprisonment for a term not exceeding two years or to both.

15.7 Section 20 provides for the designation of "restricted zones" for the purposes of Part III. A harbour authority may, and must if requested by the

Secretary of State, apply to the Secretary of State for the designation of the whole or any part of the harbour area as a restricted zone. Also, a "harbour operator", that is, a person who carries on harbour operations in a harbour area and is designated for the purposes of Part III by an order made by the Secretary of State (which may be revoked by a subsequent order), may, and must if so requested by the Secretary of State, apply to him for the designation of the whole or any part of so much of the harbour area as is under his control ("the operating area") as a restricted zone. If the Secretary of State approves such an application with or without modification he is required to designate the restricted zone accordingly. Before approving an application with modifications the Secretary of State must consult the applicant who, as indicated above, may be the harbour authority or a harbour operator. If an applicant, after having been requested by the Secretary of State to submit an application for a restricted zone, fails to do so within a specified period, the Secretary of State may designate such a zone on his own initiative. An area may be designated as a restricted zone for specified days or times of day only and the designation may be revoked at any time by the Secretary of State.

Unauthorized presence in restricted zone

15.8 Section 39 makes it an offence for a person to enter any part of a restricted zone except with the permission of "the competent authority" (who, in the case of a zone designated on the application of a harbour authority, is that authority and, in the case of a zone designated on the application of a harbour operator, is that operator) or a person acting on behalf of the competent authority and in accordance with any conditions subject to which that permission may have been given. The penalty on summary conviction for this offence is a fine not exceeding level 5 on the standard scale. A constable or any person acting on behalf of the competent authority may use reasonable force to remove from a restricted zone a person remaining in it in contravention of section 39.

Powers of Secretary of State

15.9 The enabling powers of the Secretary of State referred to above are contained in sections 21, 22, 23 and 24.

   15.10 Under Section 21 the Secretary of State may give directions to (*inter alia*) a harbour authority requiring them—

   (a) not to cause or permit persons or property to go or to be taken on board any ship to which the direction relates or to come or be brought into proximity to any such ship unless such searches of those persons or that property as are specified in the direction have been carried out by constables or by other persons of a description specified in the direction, or

(b) not to cause or permit any such ship to go to sea unless such searches of the ship as are specified in the direction have been carried out by constables or by other persons of a description specified in the direction.

Any direction under this section not to cause or permit anything to be done is to be construed as requiring the harbour authority (or as the case may be) to take all such steps as in any particular circumstances are practicable and necessary to prevent that thing from being done.

15.11 Under Section 22 the Secretary of State may give directions to a harbour authority or to a harbour operator, requiring the person to whom the direction is given to use his best endeavours to secure that such searches of the harbour area or any part of it, or, as the case may be, of the operating area or any part of it, or of any ship in the area in question or of persons and property (other than ships) in that area, as are specified in the direction, are carried out by constables or by other persons of a description specified in the direction. The section contains a wide power of entry etc. for constables or other persons specified in the direction to carry out searches for firearms, imitation firearms, explosives or imitation explosive articles and other articles made or adapted for use for causing injury, incapacitating a person or destroying or damaging property. These powers may however only be exercised in the case of premises used only as a private dwelling house under the authority of a warrant issued by a justice of the peace (who may issue such a warrant if satisfied on an application made by a constable that there are reasonable grounds for suspecting that there is a firearm or such other article as mentioned above in the premises) and by a constable who is a member of a force maintained by a police authority, or by an authority who has entered into an agreement with the Police Complaints Authority or, in Northern Ireland, with the Independent Commission for Police Complaints for Northern Ireland.

15.12 Section 23 enables the Secretary of State to direct a person who carries on harbour operations in a harbour area to use his best endeavours to secure that searches of any land which he occupies within the harbour area and of persons and property which may at any time be on that land are carried out by persons of a description specified in the direction. The section also enables the Secretary of State to direct a person who is permitted to have access to a restricted zone of a harbour area for the purposes of his business activities to secure that searches by such persons as mentioned above are carried out on any land which he occupies outside the harbour area and of persons and property which may at any time be on that land. A direction may not be given under this section to a harbour authority or a harbour operator.

15.13 Section 24 contains a more general power for the Secretary of State to give directions. Under it he may give directions to a harbour authority requiring them in respect of their harbour area to take such measures as are specified in the direction for the purposes of Part III of the Act. The section refers specifically to the provisions of persons charged with the duty of guarding the harbour area or persons or property (including ships) in any part of that area, against acts of violence. The Secretary of State may also give such directions to a person carrying on harbour operations in a harbour area (e.g., to the operator of a terminal) in respect of the harbour operations which he carries on there or to a person who is permitted to have access to a restricted zone for the purpose of his business activities in respect of such of those activities in the zone as are specified in the direction.

15.14 Failure to comply with a direction under section 21, 22, 23 or 24 is an offence which carries a maximum penalty, on summary conviction, of a fine of the statutory maximum and, on conviction on indictment, to an unlimited fine or to imprisonment for a term not exceeding two years or both. Continued failure to comply following such conviction constitutes a further offence for which the maximum penalty is a daily fine while the offence continues of one-tenth of level 5 on the standard scale.

Supplemental provisions with respect to directions

15.15 Section 25 prescribes matters which may be included in directions under sections 21 to 24. These include the minimum number of persons to be employed for the purpose of complying with a direction and the qualifications, including training and experience, which such persons are to have. Where a direction requires searches to be carried out, or other measures to be taken, by constables, the direction may require the person to whom it is given to inform the chief officer of police for the area that the Secretary of State considers it appropriate that constables should be duly authorized to carry, and should carry, firearms where carrying out the search or taking the measures in question.

15.16 Section 26 imposes certain limitations on the scope of directions under sections 21 to 24. Except as mentioned in paragraph 15.15 *ante*, or to the extent necessary for the purpose of removing any firearm found pursuant to a search under section 22 from the restricted zone and delivering it to a person authorized to carry it, a direction must not require or authorize any person to carry a firearm. A direction (except in so far as it requires any building or other work to be constructed, executed, altered, demolished or removed) is not to be construed as requiring or authorizing the person to whom the direction was given, or any person acting as his employee or agent, to do anything which, apart from the direction, would constitute an act of violence but this provision does not restrict the use of reasonable force in exercising powers of search and entry in compliance with a direction under section 22. A direction given under section 24 to a harbour authority, another person who carries on harbour operations in a harbour area or any person permitted to have access to a restricted zone of a harbour area, which requires a building or other work to be constructed, executed, altered or demolished on land outside the harbour area, or requires any other measures to be taken on such land, does not confer on the person to whom the direction is given any rights, as against a person who has an interest in that land or has a right to occupy it or a right restrictive of its use.

15.17 By virtue of section 28 a person to whom a direction is given under section 24 which requires him to take measures consisting of or including the construction, execution, alteration, demolition or removal of a building or other works may object to the Secretary of State on the grounds that the measures are unnecessary and should be dispensed with or are excessively onerous or inconvenient and should be modified. The Secretary of State is required to consider such an objection and may confirm, modify or withdraw the direction.

15.18 Sections 29 to 33 contain provisions for the enforcement by persons authorized in writing by the Secretary of State for the purposes of Part III of the Act of directions given by the Secretary of State under sections 21 to 24. Under section 36 such an authorized person has a general power of entry and inspection for the purpose of enabling the Secretary of State to determine whether to give a direction under sections 21 to 24 or ascertaining whether such a direction has been complied with.

15.19 Where an authorized person considers that any person has failed to comply with a direction under section 21, 22, 23 or 24 he may serve on that person an enforcement notice—

(a) specifying those general requirements of the direction (i.e., requests which have been included in two or more directions given to different persons and are framed in general terms applicable to all persons to whom those directions were given) with which, in the opinion of the authorized person, he has failed to comply, and

(b) specifying the measures that ought to be taken to comply with those requirements but subject to the provisions about the contents of enforcement notices referred to below.

15.20 An enforcement notice may specify in greater detail means which are described in general terms in the provisions of the direction to which it relates which impose general requirements of the kind mentioned in the preceding paragraph but may not impose any requirement which could not have been imposed by a direction given by the Secretary of State under the provision under which the direction was given. Section 30 contains several other provisions about the contents of enforcement notices.

15.21 A person who without reasonable excuse fails to comply with an enforcement notice is guilty of an offence and liable on summary conviction to a fine not exceeding the statutory maximum and on conviction on indictment to an unlimited fine. If without reasonable excuse the failure in respect of which he was convicted continues after conviction he is guilty of a further offence and liable on summary conviction to a fine not exceeding one-tenth of level 5 on the standard scale for each day on which the failure continues. A person who intentionally interferes with any building or works constructed or executed on any land in compliance with an enforcement notice or with anything installed on, under, over or across any land in compliance with such a notice is also guilty of an offence and liable on summary conviction to a fine not exceeding the statutory maximum and on conviction on indictment to an unlimited fine.

15.22 Under Section 32 the person on whom an enforcement notice is served may object to the notice by serving a written notice of objection on the Secretary of State before the end of the period of seven days beginning with the date when the enforcement notice was served or, if that notice specified measures consisting of or including the construction, execution, alteration, or demolition of a building or other works, before the end of the period of 30 days beginning with that date. The notice of objection must state the grounds of objection and those may be—

(a) that the general requirements of the direction (i.e., requirements of the kind mentioned in paragraph 15.19 *ante*) have been complied with;

(b) that the enforcement notice purports to impose a requirement which could not have been imposed by a direction given under the provision under which the direction to which the notice relates was given, or

(c) that any requirement of the enforcement notice—
  (i) is unnecessary for complying with the general requirements specified as mentioned in (a) above and should be dispensed with, or
  (ii) having regard to the terms of those general requirements is excessively onerous or inconvenient and should be modified in a manner specified in the notice of objection.

15.23 Where an enforcement notice has been objected to as mentioned above the Secretary of State must consider the grounds of objection and, if required by the objector, must afford him an opportunity of appearing before, and being heard by, a person appointed by the Secretary of State. The Secretary of State must then serve on the objector a notice in writing either—

(a) confirming the enforcement notice as originally served, or

(b) confirming it subject to one or more modifications specified in the notice served by the Secretary of State, or

(c) cancelling the enforcement notice.

Section 32(5) provides for when an enforcement notice which is subject to objection has effect.

15.24 Section 34 contains provision about the operation of directions under sections 21 to 24 in relation to rights and duties under other laws. Section

34(2) provides that, in so far as a direction under section 21, 22, 23 or 24 requires anything to be done or not done in the United Kingdom the direction shall have effect notwithstanding anything contained in any contract or contained in or having effect by virtue of any other Act or any rule of law; and that accordingly no proceeding (whether civil or criminal) shall lie against any person in any United Kingdom court by reason of anything done or not done by him or on his behalf in compliance with a direction. This is a sweeping provision but the limitations on the scope of a direction contained in section 26 (see paragraph 15.16 *ante*) must be borne in mind.

Aviation and Maritime Security Act 1990, Part II

15.25 In addition to Part III of the Aviation and Maritime Security Act 1990, section 12(1) in Part II of the Act is of concern to harbour authorities. This makes it an offence, punishable by life imprisonment, for any person unlawfully and intentionally to destroy or damage, or seriously to interfere with the operation of, any property used for the provision of maritime navigation facilities, including any land, building or ship so used, and including any apparatus or equipment so used, whether it is on board a ship or elsewhere, where the destruction, damage or interference is likely to endanger the safe navigation of any ship. Such property used for the provision of navigation facilities would include property of harbour authorities including buoys, lights and other navigational aids, radar and radio installation and launches used by the harbour master and his assistants. Under section 13(2) it is also an offence, punishable by life imprisonment, if, in order to compel any other person to do or abstain from doing any act, a person threatens that he or some other person will do something which is an offence under section 12(1) if the threat is likely to endanger the safe navigation of any ship.

CHAPTER 16

CONTROL OF HARBOUR AND COASTAL DEVELOPMENT

16.1 This chapter examines the law in relation to the carrying out of development, below high-water mark, both inside and outside harbours. It also covers the powers of a harbour authority to carry out landside development within the limits of a statutory harbour.

Construction of works below high-water mark may be actionable nuisance

16.2 At common law the construction of works below high-water mark in navigable waters so as to interfere with the public right of navigation is an actionable nuisance. In the case of *Attorney-General* v. *Terry*[1] the owner of a wharf at the port of Sandwich who sought to extend his wharf about three feet into the River Stour was restrained from doing so in an action for nuisance brought by the Attorney-General on the relation of Sandwich Corporation who at that time were the harbour authority for the port. It was held both in the court of first instance and in the Court of Appeal that the wharf as extended would in fact obstruct navigation. It appeared from the judgment of Jessel, M.R., in the court of first instance, that even if obstruction to navigation had not been proved, the extension of the wharf would still be restrained because it might become an obstruction in the future. However, having regard to the judgments of the House of Lords in *Orr-Ewing* v. *Colquhoun*,[2] it seems doubtful whether that is good law. It appears that even if an erection below high-water mark obstructs navigation it may not be a nuisance if it results in a direct public benefit, to the same public as use the navigation, which outweighs the inconvenience caused to them by the obstruction—e.g. works to straighten the sides of a harbour of irregular shape might not be a nuisance even if they are to some extent an obstruction to navigation—per Jessel, M.R., in *Attorney-General* v. *Terry*. In *Iveagh* v. *Martin*,[3] Paull, J., said, in relation to the position where the owner of the foreshore erects thereon a permanent building such as a quay, that in a proper case the public "may have the right

1. *Attorney-General* v. *Terry* (1874) L.R. 9 Ch. 423.
2. *Orr-Ewing* v. *Colquhoun* (1877) 2 App. Cas. 839.
3. *Iveagh* v. *Martin* [1960] 1 Q.B. at p. 273.

in an action properly constituted to obtain a mandatory injunction ordering the owner of the quay to remove the quay on the grounds that it seriously interferes with their rights of navigation". (He added that he could see no evidence that such a cause of action existed in the particular case he was dealing with.)

Authorization of works interfering with navigation

16.3 Any significant structure below high-water mark, such as a quay, jetty or pier or land reclamation, is by its nature likely to interfere with the public's right of navigation to some extent and will therefore need to be authorized by or under a statute in order to be immune from actions for public nuisance. Such authorization may take one of several forms, depending upon the circumstances of the case. The forms described in this chapter are:

(1) private and hybrid Acts;
(2) harbour revision orders and harbour empowerment orders under the Harbours Act 1964;
(3) orders under section 3 of the Transport and Works Act 1992;
(4) works licences; and
(5) public general Acts.

Private and hybrid Acts

16.4 Until the Harbours Act 1964, promoters of schemes involving works below high-water mark sought statutory authorization for those works by means of a private Act of Parliament. Private Acts are particular, rather than general, in their effects. They confer specific powers or benefits on a person or body of persons, in excess of or in conflict with the general law. Bills for private Acts are not introduced by a member of the legislature, but are sought by the person or body promoting them, who must deposit a petition for the Bill in Parliament, together with a copy of the Bill itself. Thousands of harbour and pier works were constructed under powers conferred by private Act, and continue to owe their authorization to those statutes but, since the passing of the Harbours Act 1964 and, in particular, the Transport and Works Act 1992, the scope for using a private Act to confer authorization has been very greatly reduced (see *post*). The above also applies to Scottish provisional orders as to which see paragraph 1.12 *ante*. Works powers could be either specific or general.

16.5 A hybrid Act, as its name suggests, is a combination of a public and a private Act. It is public in that it raises questions of public policy; its private element derives from the fact that it treats a particular private interest in a different way from the interests of other persons or bodies in the same category or class. Hybrid Bills are introduced by the government, and proceed as government measures. Recent examples of hybrid Acts which conferred authorization for works below high-water mark are the Channel Tunnel Act

1987, the Severn Bridges Act 1992 and the Channel Tunnel Rail Link Act 1996.

Harbour revision orders and harbour empowerment orders under the Harbours Act 1964

16.6 Today, the most common form of specific statutory authorization for works below high-water mark is by means of an order under the Harbours Act 1964. In the case of an existing harbour regulated by a harbour authority, works may be authorized by means of a harbour revision order under section 14 of the Act. In most cases the applicants for the order will be the harbour authority themselves, although it is possible for a third party with a "substantial interest" (or a body representative of such parties) to apply for an order (section 14(2)—see Appendix K which sets out the enabling powers and procedural provisions contained in the Harbours Act 1964 for harbour revision and empowerment orders). Harbour revision orders are described in detail in chapter 11 (at paragraphs 11.3 to 11.12 *ante*). For present purposes it is, however, important to observe that the works which may be authorized by a harbour revision order are effectively limited by section 14(2)(b) of the Act, which provides that a harbour revision order shall not be made unless the appropriate Minister (who will be either the Secretary of State or the Minister of Agriculture, Fisheries and Food) is:

"satisfied that the making of the order is desirable in the interests of securing the improvement, maintenance or management of the harbour in an efficient and economical manner or of facilitating the efficient and economic transport of goods or passengers by sea or in the interests of the recreational use of sea-going ships".

Any works which cannot meet this requirement will, accordingly, have to be authorized in some other manner, most probably by an order under section 3 of the Transport and Works Act 1992 (see below). Where there is no existing harbour authority, or no authority having sufficient powers to (*inter alia*) construct an artificial harbour or dock, a person may apply under section 16 of the Harbours Act 1964 to become a statutory harbour authority. Such an order—known as a harbour empowerment order—can include power to carry out works, if the appropriate Minister is satisfied that the making of the order "is desirable in the interests of facilitating the efficient and economic transport of goods or passengers by sea or in the interests of the recreational use of sea-going ships" (section 16(5)—see Appendix K). The process for making harbour empowerment orders is also described in Chapter 11 (paragraphs 11.13 to 11.15 *ante*).

16.7 The most common method of authorizing works under harbour revision orders and harbour empowerment orders is for the order to describe specifically the nature of the works and their location (by reference to plans and sections), within specified limits of deviation. Such orders often go on to provide in more general terms for the carrying out of subsidiary works (within the same limits). Recent examples include the Bristol City Docks Harbour Revision Orders (Nos 1 and 2) 1995 and the Harwich Parkeston Quay Harbour Revision Order 1996.

16.8 As with private Acts, a harbour revision order or harbour empowerment order may sometimes confer upon a harbour authority a general power for that authority to construct works in their harbour. For example, under article 10 of the Sealink (Transfer of Newhaven Harbour) Harbour Revision Order 1991, Newhaven Port and Properties Limited have power to "execute, place, maintain and operate in and over the . . . harbour such works and equipment as are required for or in connection with the exercise by it of any of its functions and may alter, renew or extend any works so constructed or placed". The question whether works are constructed under "specific" or "general" powers is important in determining if specific planning permission must be obtained for their construction (see paragraph 16.31 *post*). Both types of power —whether found in a private Act or an order—are usually subject to provisions on the lines of sections 42 to 45 of the Medway Ports Authority Act 1973 set out in Appendix E. These are designed to prevent danger to navigation.

Orders under section 3 of the Transport and Works Act 1992

16.9 Where the works are such that neither form of harbour order just described would be appropriate, it may be possible to obtain the necessary statutory authority by means of an order under section 3 of the Transport and Works Act 1992. Section 3 enables the Secretary of State to make orders:

(a) which would authorize the construction or operation in England and Wales of inland waterways (defined as including both natural and artificial waterways, and waterways within parts of the sea within Great Britain, but not managed or maintained by a harbour authority); or

(b) which would authorize the carrying out of works which interfere with rights of navigation in waters within or adjacent to England and Wales, up to the seaward limits of the territorial sea.

16.10 The power in (b) above is subject to the qualification that the works must be of a description prescribed by order under section 4 of the 1992 Act.

16.11 Section 3(2) provides that the Secretary of State shall not make a section 3 order if, in his opinion, the primary object of the order could be achieved by means of an order under the Harbours Act 1964. The effect of this provision is to ensure that a harbour revision order or harbour empowerment order is used for the purpose of authorizing works below high-water mark, rather than a section 3 order, where the primary object of the scheme complies with the requirements of section 14(2)(b) of, and Schedule 2 to, the 1964 Act (in the case of a harbour revision order) or section 16(5) (in the case of a harbour empowerment order) (see above). If only a subsidiary aspect of the scheme falls within the scope of harbour order powers, it is possible to use a section 3 order to obtain the necessary statutory authorization.

16.12 Schedule 1 to the 1992 Act sets out the matters which are within section 1 (which deals with railways and other guided transport modes) and section 3. These matters include demolition, the carrying out of civil engineering or other works, the acquisition of land (whether compulsorily or by agreement), the payment of compensation, the making of by-laws and the transfer, leasing, discontinuance and revival of undertakings. Section 5 provides that an order under section 3 may apply, modify or exclude any statutory provision which relates to any matter as to which such an order could be made and that the order may make such amendments, repeals and revocations of statutory provisions of local application as appear to the Secretary of State to be necessary or expedient in consequence of any provision of the order or otherwise in connection with the order. A section 3 order may not extinguish any public right of way over land unless the Secretary of State is satisfied that an alternative right of way has been or will be provided or that the provision of an alternative right of way is not required.

16.13 The current prescribed descriptions of works under section 3 of the 1992 Act are contained in the Transport and Works (Descriptions of Works Interfering with Navigation) Order 1992. They comprise a barrage, bridge, cable, land reclamation, navigational aid, offshore installation, pier, pipeline, tunnel and utilities structure. Each of these works is specifically defined for the purposes of the Order. For example, a "barrage" includes a dam, weir, barrier, embankment or breakwater, whilst a "utilities structure" means a structure or plant, whether attached to dry land or otherwise and whether fixed or floating, used or intended to be used, or which has been used, for a transport, communications, electricity generation, water extraction (including desalination), waste disposal or similar purpose (article 3(1)). It should be noted that statutory authority for carrying out some of the works prescribed by the Order may be secured under other enactments. As has already been said, section 3(2) of the 1992 Act prevents the Secretary of State from making an order under that Act if the primary object of the order could be achieved by means of an order under the Harbours Act 1964. Accordingly, a pier or breakwater to be constructed by a harbour authority for the improvement of their harbour could not be authorized by an order under section 3 of the 1992 Act. Furthermore, section 13(2) of that Act provides that where an application for a Transport and Works Order has been made and the Secretary of State considers that any of the objects of the order could be achieved by other means, he may on that ground determine not to make the order. Even where the Harbours Act 1964 is not applicable, a potential developer must therefore check whether the proposed works could be authorized under another enactment. In the case of pipelines, for example, authorization may be granted under the Petroleum and Submarine Pipelines Act 1975 (see paragraph 16.21 *post*).

16.14 The procedure for applying for an order under section 3 of the 1992 Act is governed by section 6 and by the Transport and Works (Applications and Objections Procedure) Rules 1992. These rules prescribe the requirements as to such matters as the plans and sections of works which must accompany the application for the draft order, consultation with local planning authorities, the giving and publication of notices and the submission of environmental information. Objections made within 42 days of the application may cause a public inquiry or hearing to be held, following which the Secretary of State will decide whether to make the order. The Secretary of State will reach his decision as soon as possible after the expiry of the objection period. Once made, the validity of an order may be challenged in the High Court under the procedure laid down by section 22 of the 1992 Act, on the ground that the order is not within the powers of the Act or that any requirement imposed by or under the Act or the Tribunals and Inquiries Act 1992 has not been complied with. Such a challenge must be made within 42 days beginning with the day on which formal notice of the making of the order is published in the *London Gazette*. On an application under section 22 the court may (*inter alia*) quash the order in whole or in part if satisfied that the order (or any provision in it) is not within the powers of the Act or that the interests of the applicant have been substantially prejudiced by a failure to comply with any requirement imposed by or under the Tribunals and Inquiries Act 1992. Except as provided in section 22, an order under section 3 shall not be questioned in any legal proceedings whatever, either before or after it has been made (section 22(3)).

Licensing of works by harbour authorities

16.15 At many harbours (including nearly all important commercial harbours) the harbour authority's special legislation prohibits persons other than the harbour authority from constructing works below high-water mark without first obtaining a licence from the harbour authority. In recent years most harbour authorities for major harbours have adopted provisions for this purpose which follow a common pattern although with some variations.

16.16 Articles 18 to 22 of the Sealink (Transfer of Newhaven Harbour) Harbour Revision Order 1991, which are set out in Appendix D, are a recent example of the powers of a harbour authority to license works. It will be noted that under article 20(1) a person may be granted a licence to construct, etc., works below high-water mark "notwithstanding any interference with public rights of navigation or other public rights by such works . . . ". Although it may be arguable that a provision in this form merely enables the harbour authority to grant a licence for works which, when constructed, may interfere with public rights, it seems that the better view is that a licence granted under this provision authorizes the licensee to construct and maintain the works in question without being liable for nuisance on the grounds that the works interfere with the public rights of navigation or fishing (provided no doubt that the licensee is not guilty of negligence and that his use of the works is reasonable). If this view is correct, a licence granted under a provision of this kind removes the need there might otherwise be to obtain statutory powers to authorize the construction and maintenance of the works. This view appears to be endorsed by the judgment of Lord Templeman in the House of Lords in *Tate and Lyle Industries Ltd. and Another* v. *Greater London Council and Another*.[4] His Lordship referred to the cases of *Kearns* v. *The Cordwainers' Co.*[5] and *Attorney-General* v. *Thames Conservators*[6] as showing that no action would lie for an interference with the public right of navigation caused by works licensed by the PLA under section 243 of the Port of London (Consolidation) Act 1920 (that section, which has been replaced by section 66 of the Port of London Act 1968—a modern licensing power of the kind referred to above —did not refer expressly to the public right of navigation). However, where, as in some cases, a harbour authority's licensing powers do not provide for the construction and maintenance of the licensed works to override the public right of navigation, statutory authority for their construction and maintenance will usually be necessary.

16.17 What considerations can a harbour authority take into account in exercising their discretionary powers to license works by other persons? In some cases the form of the licensing powers in a harbour authority's special legislation indicate that safety of navigation is the only consideration (and, in a case where these powers do not provide for the construction and main-tenance of the licensed works to override the public right of navigation, there is thus an almost complete overlap with the control exercised by the Secretary of State under section 34 of the Coast Protection Act 1949 described in paragraphs 16.45 to 16.50 *post*) but where these powers are on the lines of those set out in Appendix D or otherwise do not provide expressly or by implication that the licensing power is geared exclusively to navigational considerations, it seems that the scope may be wider. In the case of *Rex* v. *Port of London Authority ex parte Kynoch*[7] it was held that, in considering whether to grant a licence for another person to construct works in the River Thames, the PLA were entitled to take into account that the proposed works would be used for purposes competitive with works which they had statutory powers to provide. It seems that the range of considerations which a harbour authority may take into account under licensing provisions of the kind set out in Appendix D depends on the range of the harbour authority's general powers and duties. A harbour authority whose functions are virtually limited to conservancy are probably only entitled to take navigational considerations into

---

4. *Tate and Lyle Industries Ltd. and Another* v. *Greater London Council and Another* [1983] 2 Lloyd's Rep. 117.
5. *Kearns* v. *The Cordwainers' Co.* (1859) 6 C.B. (N.S.) 388.
6. *Attorney-General* v. *Thames Conservators* (1862) 1 H. & M. 1.
7. *Rex* v. *Port of London Authority ex parte Kynoch* [1919] 1 K.B. 176.

account. But it appears that a harbour authority responsible for the full range of harbour authority functions are entitled also to take into account whether the proposed works are necessary or desirable for the trade of the port having regard to the works which both they and other persons have provided or may provide and the good planning and efficient management of the port generally.

16.18 It will be noted that the licensing powers set out in Appendix D provide for appeals to the Secretary of State against decisions of the harbour authority.

16.19 Section 37 of the Merchant Shipping Act 1988 requires all harbour authorities with works licensing powers, before an operation which they have licensed has been begun, to furnish the Hydrographer of the Navy with written particulars of the operation with a plan showing where it is to be carried out and, once the operation has been carried out, to furnish the Hydrographer with a notification of that fact and with such plans and additional information relating to the completed operation as he may require for the purpose of determining whether, and if so what, changes should be made to any chart or other publication produced under his superintendence.

Public general Acts

16.20 A number of public general Acts contain mechanisms and procedures whereby certain particular forms of works may be authorized to be carried out below high-water mark, without the need for *ad hoc* statutory authority by way of, for example, an order under section 3 of the Transport and Works Act 1992. Amongst the most commonly used provisions are the following:

Pipelines and cables

16.21 Onshore pipelines are authorized under the Pipelines Act 1962 and submarine pipelines by the Petroleum and Submarine Pipelines Act 1975. The dividing line between the two is usually low-water mark but in bays, estuaries and harbours it is the "bay closure line"—that is to say a straight line drawn across the opening of the bay, estuary or harbour—where that line is less than 24 miles long (Territorial Waters Order in Council 1964). Pipelines which, from low-water mark (or bay closure line) to the boundary fence of the terminal, are more than 10 miles long require authorization by the Secretary of State under section 1 of the 1962 Act. Otherwise, the pipeline is a "local pipeline" in respect of which notification to the Secretary of State is required under section 2 before the works in question are executed. Upon granting authorization for a "cross-country pipeline" under section 1 the Secretary of State is empowered by section 5 to provide that planning permission for the development shall be deemed to be granted. Unless the Secretary of State decides, under section 6, to direct that a local pipeline shall be treated as a cross-country pipeline, local pipelines will, therefore, be subject to local authority planning control. Certain gas pipelines are excluded from the 1962 Act but are dealt with under the Gas Act 1986. So much of a pipeline as lies below low-water mark requires to be authorized under section 21 of, and Schedule 4 to, the Petroleum and Submarine Pipelines Act 1975. The requirement extends to so much of any pipeline (defined by section 33) as is in, under or over "controlled waters", that is to say the territorial sea adjacent to the United Kingdom and the sea in any designated area within the meaning of the Continental Shelf Act 1964 (section 20(2)). Authorizations may be time-limited. The application and determination procedures in Schedule 4 to the 1975 Act are designed to ensure that those potentially affected (e.g. fisher-men) are notified of the application and that, in deciding the question, the Secretary of State may have regard, *inter alia*, to navigational, fishing and environmental issues.

16.22 The laying of telecommunications cables in tidal waters is governed by the telecommunications code contained in Schedule 2 to the Tele-communications Act 1984. Persons authorized by licence under section 7 to run a telecommunication system (and the Secretary of State if running such a system) are "operators" for the purposes of that code. Paragraph 11 of Schedule 2 provides that the operator shall have the right, for statutory purposes:

(a) to execute any works (including placing any buoy or seamark) on any tidal water or lands for or in connection with the installation, main-tenance, adjustment, repair or alteration of telecommunications apparatus;

(b) to keep telecommunications apparatus installed on, under or over tidal water or lands; and

(c) to enter any tidal water or lands to inspect any telecommunications apparatus so installed.

Such a right may not be exercised in relation to land in which the Crown has an interest except with the latter's agreement. An operator other than the Secretary of State must generally submit plans of any proposed works to the Secretary of State for his approval. The Secretary of State is required to consult interested persons and shall not approve the plan unless he is satisfied that adequate arrangements have been made for compensating any persons appearing to him to be owners of interests in the tidal waters or lands in question for any loss or damage sustained by those persons in consequence of the execution of the works. The Secretary of State may cause a survey to be carried out, at the operator's expense, of the site or proposed site of any works or apparatus (Schedule 11, paragraph 11(2) to (6) and (9)).

Anti-pollution and flood control works

16.23 The Environment Agency, established by the Environment Act 1995, carries out the functions formerly exercised by the National Rivers Authority,

Her Majesty's Inspectorate of Pollution and waste regulation authorities and waste disposal authorities. In connection with those functions, the Agency has various powers relating to works affecting tidal waters. Section 161 of the Water Resources Act 1991 enables the Agency to carry out the following works and operations:

(a) in a case where poisonous, noxious or polluting matter or solid waste matter appears likely to enter any controlled waters, works and operations for the purpose of preventing it from doing so; or

(b) in a case where the matter appears to be or have been present in any controlled waters, works and operations for the purpose:
  (i) of removing or disposing of the matter;
  (ii) of remedying or mitigating any pollution caused by its presence in the waters; or
  (iii) so far as it is reasonably practicable to do so, of restoring the waters, including any flora and fauna dependent on the aquatic environment of the waters, to their state immediately before the matter became present in the waters.

"Controlled waters" include territorial waters (up to the three-mile limit) and coastal waters landwards of the baselines for measuring territorial waters, up to the limit of the highest tide (section 104(1)). The Agency is, however, able to exercise its powers under section 161 only when the Agency considers that the works or operations are required forthwith, or no person can be found on whom a notice under section 161A can be served. Under section 161A (which has yet to come into force) the Agency may serve a "works notice" in the same circumstances as those described in section 161(1). The notice is to be served on the person who caused or knowingly permitted the poisonous etc. matter to be present in the controlled waters or in a place from which such entry is likely. Under section 162 of the 1991 Act, the Agency has additional powers on its own land (or over which it has the necessary rights) to construct and maintain drains, sewers etc. for intercepting, treating or disposing of foul water arising or flowing on that land or otherwise preventing pollution. In connection with flood defence and land drainage, section 165 of the 1991 Act empowers the Agency, *inter alia*, to construct works and machinery in connection with a main river within the meaning of Part IV of the Act.

16.24 In Scotland the Scottish Environmental Protection Agency ("SEPA"), which was also established by the Environment Act 1995, carries out similar (but somewhat narrower) functions to that of the Environment Agency, including the functions of the former river purification authorities. Under section 46 of the Control of Pollution Act 1974 SEPA can carry out anti-pollution works and operations, in the same terms as section 161 of the Water Resources Act 1991. As with the Agency, SEPA's powers under that section will be exercisable only when it considers that works or operations are required forthwith or where no person can be found on whom a new works notice can be served. The works notice system is introduced (prospectively) by new sections 46A to 46D, which correspond with sections 161A to 161D of the 1991 Act.

Coast protection works

16.25 The councils of districts any part of which adjoins the sea are coast protection authorities for their districts under section 1 of the Coast Protection Act 1949. As such, they have power under Part I of that Act to carry out coast protection works, which may involve works below high-water mark. These powers are described in detail in Chapter 17.

Seashore amenity works in Scotland

16.26 In Scotland, a local authority has power under section 122 of the Civic Government (Scotland) Act 1982 to execute works on any part of the seashore or in or on adjacent waters or the bed thereof, for the purpose of preserving, improving or restoring amenity. The consent of those with an interest in the shore or seabed is normally required. Adjacent waters are those normally within a distance of 1000 metres from low-water mark (1982 Act, section 123(1)).

Control of development under Town and Country Planning legislation

16.27 It is important to note that, in addition to statutory authorization (including authorization pursuant to a harbour authority's works licensing powers), works below high-water mark may require other authorizations and consents and that, conversely, those other authorizations and consents do not relieve the developer from the need to obtain such statutory authorization in a case where he would otherwise be potentially liable for an action in nuisance for interfering with public rights of navigation. The following paragraphs deal with these other authorizations and consents, beginning with the town and country planning legislation. Subject to what is said in the next paragraph about development below low-water mark, permission is required under the Town and Country Planning Act 1990, or, as the case may be, the Town and Country Planning (Scotland) Act 1972, for the construction of harbour works but, as mentioned below, development by harbour authorities is in some cases permitted by virtue of the Town and Country Planning (General Permitted Development) Order 1995 or its Scottish equivalent.

16.28 It appears that the jurisdiction of a local planning authority does not extend beyond low-water mark except possibly where the land in question is within the general administrative area of the local authority concerned, e.g., in a tidal estuary falling *intra fauces terrae*. In the Scottish case of *Argyll and Bute*

District Council v. *Secretary of State for Scotland*,[8] which seems to be the only authority directly in point, the Lord Justice-Clerk, Lord Wheatley, held that the jurisdiction of a planning authority in Scotland did not apply below low-water mark even where the site concerned was within the general jurisdiction of the local authority. In England and Wales, however, the authorities, although not directly in point, appear to indicate that planning control may apply to land below low-water mark which is within the general jurisdiction of the authority in question.

16.29 Under the Town and Country Planning (General Permitted Development) Order 1995 and the equivalent order in force in Scotland certain development by harbour authorities and their lessees is automatically given planning permission and does not, therefore, require to be sought from the local planning authority or the Secretary of State.

16.30 This authorized development is specified in Class B of Part 17 of Schedule 2 to the 1995 Order and consists, subject to certain exceptions and qualifications, of development by a harbour authority or their lessees of a harbour authority's operational land for the purpose of shipping or in connection with the embarking, disembarking, loading, discharging or transport of passengers, livestock or goods at a harbour. Section 263 of the Town and Country Planning Act 1990 defines "operational land" in relation to statutory undertakers (which include harbour authorities) as:

(a) land which is used for the purpose of carrying on their undertaking; and

(b) land in which an interest is held for that purpose,

not being land which, in respect of its nature and situation, is comparable rather with land in general than with land which is used, or in which interests are held, for the purpose of the carrying on of statutory undertakings.

Section 264 of the Town and Country Planning Act 1990 specifies certain circumstances in which land of statutory undertakers is to be treated as not being operational land. Basically, land acquired by a harbour authority on or after 6 December 1968 will not be operational land unless and until it is subject to a specific planning permission for development which, if carried out, would involve or have involved the use of the land for the purpose of the authority's undertaking. Thus, for example, land acquired by a harbour authority in 1970 will become operational land upon becoming subject to a planning consent from the local planning authority for its use for warehousing purposes. Thereafter, subject to what is said at paragraph 16.33 *post*, it may be used for other purposes of shipping etc., as described above, without any further application for planning permission. Except for some differences in relevant dates, the corresponding Scottish provisions are in substantially similar terms.

8. *Argyll and Bute District Council* v. *Secretary of State for Scotland* 1977 S.L.T. 33.

16.31 Another class of development authorized by the General Permitted Development Order which is relevant in relation to harbour authorities is that specified in Class A of Part 11 of Schedule 2 to that Order. This consists, subject to certain qualifications, of development authorized:

(i) by any local or private Act of Parliament; or

(ii) by any order approved by both Houses of Parliament; or

(iii) by any order made under section 14 or section 16 of the Harbours Act 1964 (i.e. harbour revision and empowerment orders);

which designates specifically both the nature of the authorized development and the land upon which it may be carried out. Again, the corresponding Scottish provisions are in similar terms. Works carried out under "general" works powers described in paragraph 16.8 *ante* or under a works licence (paragraphs 16.15 to 16.18 *ante*) are not covered by this concession and must be the subject of specific planning consent (to the extent that the works are within the jurisdiction of the local planning authority).

16.32 Under article 4 of the General Permitted Development Order, the Secretary of State or a local planning authority (subject in most cases to the Secretary of State's approval) may give directions restricting development permitted under the Order.

16.33 In England and Wales, the usefulness of the provisions granting planning permission for development on operational land is significantly restricted by article 3(10) of the Order, which in effect provides that development is not permitted by the Order (i.e. automatically) if—were a specific application for planning permission for that development to have been made to the local planning authority—an environmental assessment of the effects of the proposed development would have been required to be submitted in accordance with the Town and Country Planning (Assessment of Environmental Effects) Regulations 1988. Accordingly, any land-based development by harbour authorities which is likely to have significant effects upon the environment will require specific planning permission, whether or not the land in question is operational land. It should be observed, however, that development within Class A of Part 11 of Schedule 2 to the 1995 Order is not subject to this restriction. Any works which have been specifically authorized by an order under the Harbours Act 1964 will already have been subject to environmental scrutiny under the Harbour Works (Assessment of Environmental Effects) (Amendment) Regulations 1996 (see paragraphs 16.65 to 16.67 *post*).

16.34 Any planning permission granted by a general development order, wherever made, is subject to a condition that development which is likely to have a significant effect on a European site (such as a Special Protection Area under the EC Birds Directive), either alone or in combination with other plans or projects, and is not directly connected with or necessary to the management of the site, shall not be begun until the developer has received written notification of the approval of the local planning authority under regulation 62 of the

Conservation (Natural Habitats, etc.) Regulations 1994. These Regulations are discussed in Chapter 18.

16.35 Works authorized by orders under section 3 of the Transport and Works Act 1992 (see paragraphs 16.9 to 16.14 *ante*) do not fall within the General Permitted Development Order, since under section 90(2A) of the Town and Country Planning Act 1990, the Secretary of State—on making a section 3 order—may direct that planning permission for that development shall be deemed to be granted, subject to such conditions (if any) as may be specified in the direction. It is for the applicant for the order to decide whether and if so what amount of "deemed" planning permission to apply for, as part of the order application.

16.36 Works authorized under public general legislation will (to the extent that they are within the jurisdiction of the local planning authority) require specific planning permission, unless the developer is able to rely upon some provision of the General Permitted Development Order.

Planning policy guidance for the coast

16.37 In England and Wales, government guidance in relation to coastal planning is currently contained in a planning policy guidance note known as PPG20 (issued in September 1992). PPG20 deals with the coastal zone which, as we have seen, for planning purposes, generally does not extend seaward below low-water mark. The limits of the coastal zone will be determined by local planning authorities according to local circumstances and the key coast-related planning issues to be covered in their planning policies. The inland limit of the zone will depend on the extent of direct maritime influences and coast-related activities (paragraph 1.5). Special conservation policies will apply in the cases of specifically designated areas of high landscape value or of nature conservation or scientific interest. Certain of these areas, and the applicable policies, are considered in Chapter 18. PPG20 states that, in the coastal zone, development plan policies should normally not provide for development which does not require a coastal location (paragraph 2.9).

On the coast, development opportunities may be limited by such factors as the risk of flooding or erosion. Development for housing and employment should generally be made elsewhere in a district where the coastal zone represents only a small part of the area of the local planning authority.

Therefore whilst realistic provision should be made in development plans for the foreseeable development needs of an area, the coast, particularly the undeveloped parts, will seldom be the most appropriate location. Few developments require a coastal location. Given both the physical and policy constraints in most parts of the undeveloped coast, it should not be expected to accommodate new development that could be located inland or in existing developed areas (paragraph 2.10).

By contrast, the developed coast may provide opportunities for restructuring and regenerating existing urban areas, particularly in areas of significant architectural or historic interest or where there is derelict land. Accordingly, where new development requires a coastal location, the developed coast will usually be the best option. Regard must, however, be had to the possibility of erosion or flooding. New development should not generally be permitted in areas which would need expensive engineering works to forestall erosion or flooding. The local planning authority will need to evolve policies to control or restrict development in low-lying coastal areas or on land at risk of erosion (such as certain cliffs). Planning policies should take account of whether the coastal defence policy for an area is one of managed retreat from the advancing sea.

16.38 Amongst the uses and activities which may require a coastal location are tourism and recreation; developments, such as ports and marinas, that depend on access to the sea; and mineral extraction and energy generation. PPG20 considers each of these.

Tourism and recreation

16.39 In general, tourism developments should be guided to existing urban areas, particularly where they can assist in regeneration. The pressures which recreational activities may place on the coast are considerable. Management measures may be able to balance and reconcile recreational interests with the need to protect the natural beauty and landscape variety of the coast. Coastal management plans are considered in Chapter 18. Marinas and other facilities for boat mooring, parking and launching are a particular concern of PPG20. The increase in demand for such facilities which has been seen over the past 20 years is considered to be likely to continue for the foreseeable future. Accordingly, policies for development of further activities should be based on an assessment of the capacity of the local environment to accommodate further water-based recreation. Policies should encourage the imaginative re-use of disused commercial docks as part of the regeneration of such areas (paragraph 3.5 and 3.6). Especially, as respects the developed coast, the impact of on-shore facilities such as clubhouses, jetties and slipways requires careful consideration.

16.40 PPG20 states that public access to the coast (whether developed or undeveloped) should be a "basic principle" unless it can be demonstrated to be damaging to nature conservation or impractical. Wherever appropriate, new developments and regeneration schemes should seek to include provision securing such access, by means of planning agreements under section 106 of the Town and Country Planning Act 1990 (paragraph 3.9).

Major developments

16.41 Accordingly, PPG20 Developments such as ports and barrages, which are of national or regional importance, will normally be included in local authority structure plans prepared under the 1990 Act. Such proposals are subject to the general rule that all planning applications are to be determined in accordance with development plan policies, unless material considerations dictate otherwise (paragraph 3.10 and 1990 Act, section 54A).

Mineral extraction

16.42 As might be expected, PPG20 considers that the sensitivity of many coastal areas is such that exploration for, and exploitation of, minerals need to be undertaken with considerable care, although the planning issues raised by mineral extraction in the coastal zone will, it seems, generally be broadly similar to those inland.

Energy generation

16.43 Although traditional coal- and oil-fired power stations required water-side locations for cooling and (sometimes) the supply of fuel by water, whilst gas-fired and nuclear stations required water merely for cooling, the newer types of power station are less dependent on the need for coastal locations. The need for such stations on the coast will be balanced against the potential environmental impact.

16.44 PPG20 stresses the importance of local planning authorities ensuring that their planning policies for the coast (as expressed in their development plans) are consistent. Development on one part of the coast may have an impact on another, for example as a result of hydrological changes. Co-operation between authorities is therefore encouraged (paragraph 4.1 to 4.4).

Consent required under section 34 of Coast Protection Act 1949

16.45 Generally, perhaps the most important of the consents which (in addition to statutory authority and—where it applies—planning permission) have to be obtained before the construction of works below high-water mark can be undertaken is the consent required from the Secretary of State under section 34 of the Coast Protection Act 1949 for the purpose of securing safety of navigation. For the application of section 34 in the case of dredging, see paragraphs 16.60 and 16.64 *post.*

16.46 Under section 34(1) of the Coast Protection Act 1949, as amended by the Merchant Shipping Act 1988, the consent of the Secretary of State is required before any person may:

    (a) construct, alter or improve any works on, under or over any part of the seashore lying below the level of mean high-water springs;

    (b) deposit any object or any materials on any such part of the seashore as aforesaid; or

    (c) remove any object or any materials from any part of the seashore lying below the level of mean low-water springs, if the operation (whether while being carried out or subsequently) causes or is likely to result in obstruction or danger to navigation.

16.47 Section 35(1) of the Coast Protection Act excepts certain operations from the restriction imposed by section 34(1). By virtue of section 63(3) of the Transport and Works Act 1992 these operations include any operations authorized by a harbour revision order or a harbour empowerment order under section 14 or section 16 of the Harbours Act 1964. The exceptions also include any work carried out by, or in accordance with, a licence or permission granted by a harbour authority or navigation authority, in pursuance of any Act, where:

(i) the Act requires that if the approval of the Secretary of State is not previously obtained for the work, other conditions must be complied with; and

(ii) the said approval has been so obtained or the said conditions are complied with.

So far as works licensed by a harbour authority are concerned, it is believed that this exception applies only to works licensed by the Port of London Authority under section 66 of the Port of London Act 1968. Under section 76(1) of that Act, a work on the bed of the River Thames licensed by the Port of London Authority is not to be carried out unless it has been previously approved in writing by the Secretary of State or, if such approval has not been obtained, the licence imposes a condition that the work will be immediately removed if the Secretary of State requires it.

16.48 Section 34(3) of the Coast Protection Act requires the Secretary of State, if he is of the opinion that any operation for which an application is made to him under section 34 will cause or is likely to result in obstruction or danger to navigation, either to refuse consent or to give his consent subject to such conditions as he may think fit, having regard to the nature and extent of the obstruction or danger which it appears to him would otherwise be caused or be likely to result. Subsection (4A) inserted by the Merchant Shipping Act 1988 provides that conditions imposed by the Secretary of State under section 34:

(a) shall (subject to the Secretary of State's power to revoke them) either remain in force for a specified period or remain in force without limit of time;

(b) shall, in addition to binding the person to whom consent is given, bind, so far as is appropriate, any person who for the time being owns, occupies, or enjoys any use of the works in question;

(c) may, if the condition relates to the provision of any lights, signals or other aids to navigation or to the stationing of guard ships in the vicinity of the works in question or to the taking of any other measures for the purpose of controlling the movements of ships in the vicinity of those works, be varied by the Secretary of State in the interests of the safety of navigation; and

(d) may be revoked by the Secretary of State if he thinks fit to do so.

16.49 The scope of section 34 of the Coast Protection Act 1949 was considered in the case of *Harwich Harbour Conservancy Board* v. *Secretary of State for the Environment, East Suffolk Council and Stour River Estate.*[9] The question at issue was whether the Secretary of State, in considering whether to give his consent to the construction of a marina, was entitled to take into account not only whether the proposed works would, in themselves, constitute an obstruction or danger to navigation (either directly or by causing siltation) but also whether the additional vessels which would be likely to be attracted to the area by the works would obstruct or endanger navigation. It was held that section 34(1) did not enable the Secretary of State to refuse his consent to the construction of a work on the ground that the work might be used by vessels which he desired to exclude from the area (and accordingly, in the case under consideration, that the Secretary of State for the Environment had been wrong in refusing to deal with that issue under the Town and Country Planning Acts on the ground that it was a matter to be considered by the Secretary of State (for Trade, at that time) under the Coast Protection Act). (It was, however, indicated that possible obstruction by boats actively using the work—e.g., by a boat tied up at a jetty—could be taken into account.)

16.50 This limitation of the scope of the Secretary of State's jurisdiction under section 34 has now been removed by the new subsection (3A) inserted in the section by the Merchant Shipping Act 1988. This provides that, in the case of a proposal to construct, alter or improve any works on, under or over any part of the seashore lying below the level of mean high-water springs, references in subsection (1) or (3) of section 34 to an operation being likely to result in obstruction or danger to navigation shall be construed as including a reference to its being likely to have such a result by reason of any use intended to be made of the works in question when constructed, altered or improved. This clearly enables the Secretary of State to take into account the sort of consideration which was held in the *Harwich* case to be outside his jurisdiction under section 34.

16.51 There is a considerable overlap between the Secretary of State's jurisdiction under section 34 of the Coast Protection Act 1949 and the powers of harbour authorities to regulate the construction of works and dredging by other persons below high-water mark in their harbours (see paragraphs 16.15 to 16.18 *ante* and 16.62 *post*). With a view to reducing this overlap, section 37 of the Merchant Shipping Act 1988 contains an enabling power for the Secretary of State by regulations to disapply section 34 as respects any operations of a kind falling within the Secretary of State's jurisdiction under that

9. *Harwich Harbour Conservancy Board* v. *Secretary of State for the Environment, East Suffolk County Council and Stour River Estate* [1975] 1 Lloyd's Rep. 334.

section which a harbour authority have power to license or otherwise regulate under their local Acts and orders. This regulation-making power may be exercised either on the application of the harbour authority concerned or on the Secretary of State's own motion after consulting the harbour authority. Regulations to disapply section 34 at a harbour may supplement and adapt the harbour authority's existing works licensing powers. Section 37 of the 1988 Act provides that where section 34 of the 1949 Act has been disapplied as mentioned above, the Secretary of State may redetermine an application already determined by the harbour authority even in the absence of an appeal if he considers that it would be appropriate for him to do so in the interest of safe navigation. He must, however, initiate the procedure for this purpose within 30 days after the harbour authority's determination.

Licence required under Food and Environment Protection Act 1985

16.52 Part II of the Food and Environment Protection Act 1985 which provides for deposits in the sea to be licensed, and which replaced the Dumping at Sea Act 1974, sets up another hurdle to be surmounted before works may be constructed below high-water mark. The purpose of this licensing system is to protect the marine environment and the living resources which it supports. It seems that the prohibition imposed by section 5 of the Food and Environment Protection Act on the deposit of substances or articles in the sea, except in pursuance of a licence, applies to the construction of harbour works subject to the exceptions mentioned below. This might seem incongruous but when the point was taken at the Committee stage in the House of Lords of the Bill which became the Dumping at Sea Act 1974 it was stated that "it is important for those charged with the responsibility of safeguarding the marine environment to be in a position to maintain an effective oversight of operations which could conceivably introduce or release heavy metals or other persistent substances into the food chain via marine life". The Deposits in the Sea (Exemptions) Order 1985 provides that a licence under Part II of the Food and Environment Protection Act 1985 is not required for the operations specified in the Schedule to that Order. These include the deposit of any article in connection with the provision of moorings or aids to navigation by a harbour authority or lighthouse authority or by any other person if the consent of a harbour authority or lighthouse authority is required.

16.53 The licensing authority for the purposes of Part II of the Food and Environment Protection Act 1985 is the Minister of Agriculture, Fisheries and Food in England and Wales and the Secretary of State for Scotland in Scotland. The Act confers a right on the applicant for, or the holder of, a licence to make written representation relating to a decision of the licensing authority and requires such representations to be considered. Part II of the 1985 Act is also important to harbour authorities in relation to dredging, since the deposit at sea of dredged spoil needs to be licensed under Part II (see paragraph 16.61 *post*). The dumping at sea of industrial waste or power station ash is no longer permitted and the government have announced that the dumping at sea of sewage sludge will not be permitted after 1998.

16.54 Section 85 of the Water Resources Act 1991 creates offences relating to the pollution of controlled waters. Section 88 of the 1991 Act provides, however, that a person is not to be guilty of an offence under section 85 if the entry or discharge of the polluting etc. matter into controlled waters is made under and in accordance with, or as a result of, any act or omission under and in accordance with (*inter alia*) a licence to dump at sea issued by the Minister of Agriculture, Fisheries and Food under Part II of the 1985 Act.

Crown Estate Commissioners

16.55 As mentioned earlier, most land below high-water mark is vested in the Crown and, where it is proposed to construct harbour works below high-water mark, it is therefore usually necessary to purchase or lease the site from the Crown Estate Commissioners. Under section 3 of the Crown Estate Act 1961, the Crown Estate Commissioners are required (subject to section 4 of that Act), on the sale, lease or other disposal of any land of the Crown Estate, to obtain the best consideration in money or money's worth which in their opinion can reasonably be obtained, having regard to all the circumstances of the case but excluding any element of monopoly value attributable to the extent of the Crown's ownership of comparable land. Section 4(1) of the Act of 1961 provides as follows:

"for the development, improvement or general benefit of any land of the Crown Estate, the Commissioners with the consent of Her Majesty signified under the Royal Sign Manual may dispose of land or of a right or privilege over or in relation to land, without consideration or for such consideration as they think fit where the land is to be used and occupied, or the right or privilege is to be enjoyed—

    (a) for the purposes of any public or local authority, or for the purposes of any authority or person exercising powers conferred by or under any enactment for the supply of water; or

    (b) for the construction, enlargement, improvement or maintenance of any road, dock, sea-wall, embankment, drain, water-course or reservoir; or

    (c) for providing, enlarging or improving a place of religious worship, residence for a minister of religion, school, library or scientific institution, or any communal facilities for recreation, or the amenities of, or means of access to any land or building falling within this paragraph; or

    (d) for any other public or charitable purpose in connection with any land of the Crown Estate, or tending to the welfare of persons residing or employed on any such land."

16.56 It has been argued that the Crown Estate Commissioners have a discretion to sell or lease land for the construction of docks (and the other public purposes mentioned in section 4(1) of the Crown Estate Act 1961) at less than the full commercial price (excluding monopoly value, which incidentally has not proved easy to assess in the case of land under the sea). This argument turns on whether the words "for the development, improvement or general benefit of any land of the Crown Estate" at the beginning of section 4(1) include land which the Commissioners are disposing of as mentioned in the subsection. The legal advisers to the Crown Estate Commissioners take the view that the words at the beginning of section 4(1) refer only to land retained by the Commissioners. This construction (which may be supported by a comparison with section 55 of the Settled Land Act 1925 as read with section 107 of that Act) gives section 4(1) a very limited application and results in the Commissioners charging high purchase prices or (more usually) rents, for the sites of harbour works below high-water mark.

16.57 The Commissioners have a significant role in controlling the dredging of marine aggregates (see paragraph 16.63 *post*) and the establishing of salmon farms in marine waters (see paragraph 16.72 *post*).

Dredging

16.58 The subject of dredging, whilst closely related to works below high-water mark, requires separate consideration. Two forms of dredging will be examined:

(a) navigation dredging; and
(b) dredging for marine aggregates.

Navigation dredging

16.59 Although dredging activities may obstruct or impede navigation whilst they are taking place, unlike works they cause no permanent interference with navigation. Accordingly, many harbour authorities rely upon their general statutory powers of maintenance and improvement of the harbour in order to carry out navigation dredging within that harbour, although the legislation of some authorities confers a specific power to dredge (e.g., article 11 of the Sealink (Transfer of Newhaven Harbour) Harbour Revision Order 1991 and see paragraph 5.2 *ante*). Such specific dredging powers normally provide for materials (other than wreck within the meaning of the Merchant Shipping Act 1995) taken up or collected in the case of such operations to be the property of the harbour authority concerned and that they may be used, sold, deposited etc. as the authority think fit, save that such materials are not to be placed below the level of high-water except as the Secretary of State may approve and subject to such conditions and restrictions as he may impose.

16.60 Section 35(1) of the Coast Protection Act 1949 exempts from the requirement to obtain consent under section 34(1) (see paragraphs 16.45 to 16.50 *ante*) "the carrying out of any dredging operations (including the deposit of dredged materials) authorized by any local Act in accordance with the provisions thereof". Section 35(1) of the 1949 Act also exempts "any operations authorized by an order under section 14 or 16 of the Harbours Act 1964".

16.61 Deposit at sea of any dredged materials will require a licence from the Minister of Agriculture, Fisheries and Food under Part II of the Food and Environment Protection Act 1985 (see paragraphs 16.52 and 16.53 *ante*). Agitation dredging (such as "jet-sedding") does not involve deposit of gathered materials and, hence, does not require a licence under Part II (see further paragraph 16.74 *post*).

16.62 Many harbour authorities whose local legislation confers power to license third parties to construct works in the harbour also possess powers in that legislation to license dredging (see articles 18, 21 and 22 of the Sealink (Transfer of Newhaven Harbour) Harbour Revision Order 1991 contained in Appendix D). The analysis in paragraph 16.17 *ante* of the considerations which a harbour authority can take into account in exercising powers to license works also applies in the case of powers to license dredging.

Dredging of marine aggregates

16.63 Marine dredged sand and gravel is an important source of aggregates for the construction industry, in 1989 providing 18 per cent of the total consumption of sand and gravel in England and Wales. Where extraction occurs within the jurisdiction of the local planning authority (for example, in certain estuaries), the planning process will determine whether and, if so, under what conditions, extraction may be carried out. Most extraction will, however, take place outside the jurisdiction of the local planning authority. In these circumstances, the Government View procedure operated by the Department of the Environment (in England) and the Welsh Office (in Wales) will be followed where (as is usually the case) the Crown is the owner of the seabed from which the extraction is to take place. The Government View procedure concerns a wide range of considerations, including environmental factors. Permission will not be granted where the extraction would cause damage to sea fisheries or the marine environment, or if there is a risk that coastal erosion would result. The Government View may impose conditions to safeguard coastal, fishing and other interests.

16.64 Consent under section 34 of the Coast Protection Act 1949 will, in addition, be required where the operations may involve danger or obstruction to navigation (see paragraphs 16.45 to 16.50 *ante*). Although section 18 of the 1949 Act contains powers for coast protection authorities to take on responsibilities for licensing offshore removal of materials from the seabed, these are in practice rarely used.

European Community's Directive on Environmental Assessment

16.65 The European Community's Directive on Environmental Assessment (EEC/85/337) provides that for certain projects which may have an important impact on the environment, information about environmental effects must be provided by the developer and taken into account by the competent authority before deciding whether to give development consent to the project. Annex I to the Directive specifies classes of project for which an environmental assessment is always required. These include "trading ports and also inland waterways and ports for inland waterway traffic which permit the passage of vessels of over 1350 tonnes" (it appears that the creation of a new navigable water area is envisaged). Annex II to the Directive specifies classes of project which are to be made subject to an environmental assessment where the Member State considers that their characteristics so require. These include harbours, including fishing harbours and yacht marinas. They also include the modification of a project included in Annex I. The Directive does not apply to "projects the details of which are adopted by a specific act of national legislation". In the United Kingdom therefore it does not apply to a project which is specifically authorized by an Act of Parliament.

16.66 Since, as mentioned in paragraphs 1.12 and 1.27 *ante*, by virtue of the Transport and Works Act 1992, a private Bill cannot now be promoted to achieve objects which can be achieved by a harbour revision or empowerment order, harbour development of the kind which the Directive envisages as requiring environmental assessment will usually be specifically authorized by such an order. As mentioned in paragraph 11.21 *ante*, a harbour revision or empowerment order is not, except in rare cases, subject to Parliamentary control, and the Directive therefore applies in relation to development authorized by such an order. Such development will generally have the benefit of deemed planning permission as falling within Class A of Part 11 of Schedule 2 to the General Permitted Development Order 1995 (see paragraph 16.31 *ante*) and, where this is the case, the normal planning procedures by reference to which the Directive on Environmental Assessment is implemented in most cases do not apply.

16.67 It is also possible that harbour development of a kind requiring environmental assessment may consist of works below low-water mark constructed by a harbour authority under a general works power in their special legislation or by another person pursuant to a licence granted by the harbour authority (see paragraphs 16.15 to 16.18 *ante*) where the relevant power enables the licensed works to be constructed and maintained notwithstanding interference with the public right of navigation. Again, except possibly where the site of the proposed works below low-water mark (in England or Wales) is situated in an estuary *inter fauces terrae* (paragraph 16.28 *ante*) the normal planning consent procedures by reference to which the Directive is implemented do not apply.

16.68 Regulations have been made under section 2 of the European Communities Act 1972 to implement the Directive in cases of the kind referred to in paragraphs 16.66 and 16.67 *ante*. The procedure for making harbour revision and empowerment orders specified in Schedule 3 to the Harbours Act

1964 has been amended by the Harbour Works (Assessment of Environmental Effects) (Amendment) Regulations 1996 so as to provide for environmental assessments in appropriate cases (see paragraph 11.21 *ante* and Schedule 3 to the 1964 Act as amended, set out in Appendix K). As respects harbour works constructed below low-water mark under a general works power or pursuant to a licence, the Harbour Works (Assessment of Environmental Effects) (No. 2) Regulations 1989 apply to works below the low-water mark of medium tides, involved in the construction of a harbour (as widely defined in section 57 of the Harbours Act 1964—see paragraph 1.4 *ante*) or in the making of modifications to an existing harbour, being works which are:

(a) not subject to planning control pursuant to the Town and Country Planning Act 1990 or the Town and Country Planning (Scotland) Act 1972 or pursuant to orders made under either of those Acts; and

(b) not specifically described in or authorized to be carried out by a harbour revision or empowerment order or by a provisional order (as defined in section 57 of the Harbours Act 1964); and

(c) not specifically described in or authorized to be carried out by any enactment conferring powers to carry out works at a harbour.

16.69 The "No 2 Regulations" were amended by the Harbour Works (Assessment of Environmental Effects) (Amendment) Regulations 1996. They provide for any of the following applications or notices to trigger the consideration by the "appropriate Minister" (usually the Secretary of State) of whether the proposed works are harbour works to which the Regulations apply and, if so, whether they constitute a project within Annex I to the Directive or a project within Annex II to the Directive whose characteristics are such that it should be made subject to an environmental assessment:

(a) an application for coast protection consent under section 34 of the Coast Protection Act 1949 (see paragraphs 16.45 to 16.50 *ante*);

(b) a notice from a harbour authority pursuant to regulations under section 37 of the Merchant Shipping Act 1988 that application has been made for a licence to carry out operations (see paragraph 16.51 *ante*);

(c) an application for approval of operations pursuant to any other Act (see paragraph 16.47 *ante*);

(d) an application for approval required to be obtained in relation to any work (other than one specifically authorized by an enactment) under any provision of a local Act, harbour revision order or harbour empowerment order, where in any case consent under section 34 of the Coast Protection Act 1949 is not required.

16.70 The main case caught by (d) above (which was added by the 1996 Regulations) is that of dredging by a harbour authority under a local Act or order where, as is usual (see paragraph 5.2 *ante*), the general power to dredge prohibits the deposit of dredged material below the level of high water except in such position as the Secretary of State may approve and subject to such conditions and restrictions as he may impose. This would not apply in a case where the dredged material was not deposited below the level of high water, for example, in the case of agitation dredging.

16.71 Where it appears to the appropriate Minister that an environmental assessment is required in order to comply with the Directive, the proposed works must not be carried out without his consent under the regulations, and he must direct the person wishing to carry out the works ("the developer") to furnish him with the information necessary to enable him to carry out such an assessment. In that event, the developer is required by the regulations to publish notice of his proposals and to provide the public with an opportunity to inspect the information and other documentation supplied to the Secretary of State and to make representations to the Secretary of State. The Secretary of State must consult suitable bodies with environmental responsibilities about the proposals and may, if he thinks fit, hold an inquiry. Where an environmental assessment has been held in accordance with the regulations, the Secretary of State may consent to the carrying out of the proposed works either unconditionally, or subject to such conditions as he thinks fit, or may refuse consent, after considering all the relevant information, any representations received and the report of any inquiry held.

16.72 In the case of an application for an order under section 3 of the Transport and Works Act 1992 to construct etc. works interfering with rights of navigation (paragraphs 16.9 to 16.14 *ante*) the Transport and Works (Applications and Objections Procedure) Rules 1992 provide for an environmental statement to be submitted with the application unless (at the request of the applicant) the Secretary of State determines that such a statement (or part thereof) need not be so submitted (rule 6). In the case of pipelines below low-water mark, the Electricity and Pipeline Works (Assessment of Environmental Effects) Regulations 1990 contain similar provisions to those in the Harbour Works (Assessment of Environmental Effects) (Amendment) Regulations 1996 (paragraph 16.68 *ante*). In the case of salmon farming in marine waters which are outside the jurisdiction of the local planning authority, the Directive is implemented by the Environmental Assessment (Salmon Farming in Marine Waters) Regulations 1988. In this case the "trigger" is the making of an application to the Crown Estate Commissioners for consent for salmon farming.

16.73 Above low-water mark etc., where the town and country planning legislation operates (see paragraphs 16.27 and 16.28 *ante*), the Town and Country Planning (Assessment of Environmental Effects) Regulations 1988 (and their Scottish equivalent) provide a mechanism whereby (in the first instance) the local planning authority determines whether the development for which permission is sought requires an environmental assessment. As mentioned in paragraph 16.33 *ante*, permitted development rights for development on operational land of harbour authorities is, in effect, withdrawn by the Town and Country Planning (General Permitted Development) Order 1995, where the project is one which falls within Annex I to the Directive or within Annex II and the environmental effects are likely to be significant.

16.74 At paragraph 16.61 *ante*, it was mentioned that agitation dredging does not require a licence under Part II of the Food and Environment Protection Act 1985 because it does not involve the deposit of spoil. For the same reason, the requirement for the Secretary of State's consent under the usual form of general dredging power referred to in paragraph 16.70 *ante* will not usually apply to agitation dredging. Such dredging will not therefore usually require any ministerial consent which could "trigger" an assessment of the environmental effects of such dredging (it would do so if the relevant dredging power in a harbour revision order made dredging in itself, and not just the deposit of dredged material, subject to the Secretary of State's consent, but it is believed that at present there is no example of this). Although the creation of a licensing regime for such dredging has been mooted, no specific proposals have been produced.

Provision of warehouses etc.

16.75 In addition to works below high-water mark, harbour authorities commonly provide storage sheds and other facilities for harbour purposes on land adjoining the harbour (in which, of course, they must first have or acquire the necessary rights or interests). Section 21 of the Harbours, Docks and Piers Clauses Act 1847 contains express powers for this purpose but is seldom now incorporated in special harbour legislation. The special legislation of most harbour authorities for major harbours now contains general powers to provide, maintain and operate warehousing services and facilities, and services and facilities for the consignment of goods on routes which include the port premises, e.g., section 5 of the Port of London Act 1968 set out in Part II of Appendix C. Indeed, if a harbour authority have the capacity as a statutory corporation to manage a harbour (not solely from the conservancy angle), then the power to provide warehouses etc., on land in which they have a sufficient interest appears to be implicit.

CHAPTER 17

COASTAL PROTECTION

17.1 This chapter sets out the legal framework within which flood defence and coastal protection works and flood warning systems are carried out. Important policy issues are raised by the carrying out of such works which are particularly topical in view of the fact that the climatic changes predicted over the next few decades may involve a possible rise in sea levels and increased storminess which will increase vulnerability to coastal flooding and erosion. Already many areas in Great Britain are at risk from flooding and coastal erosion. According to government statistics, over 5% of the population of England and Wales live in areas below the five metre contour and many of these areas are protected by defences. Over 50% of Grade 1 agricultural land in England and Wales is also below this level. A number of coastal towns such as Blackpool are defended against flooding by sea and, without such defences, urban areas with key infrastructure, businesses, homes and agricultural and recreational land would be vulnerable to flooding and coastal erosion. In addition, a number of historic sites and buildings, some of which are protected by statute, and environmentally valuable areas such as sites of special scientific interest are at risk.

17.2 Since flood defence and coastal protection works are largely publicly financed and raise environmental issues, difficult decisions must be made which are influenced to a substantial extent by the Government through the provision—or withholding—of central grants for capital flood defence and coast protection works and flood warning systems. The current government policy, as set out in the "Code of Practice on Environmental Procedures for Flood Defence Operating Authorities" (December 1996) issued by the Ministry of Agriculture, Fisheries and Food and the Welsh Office, is that protection against flooding or erosion must strike a balance between costs and benefits to the nation as a whole: to attempt to protect every inch of coastline from change would not only be uneconomic but would work against the dynamic processes which determine the coastline and could have an adverse effect on defences elsewhere and on the natural environment. The Government has therefore stressed that flood and coastal defence work should be developed within a strategic framework which takes account of long-term sustainability and recognizes the significant impact on the form and long term development of river and coastal systems which such works can impose. Flood and coastal defence work should be environmentally acceptable as well as technically sound and economically viable. They should also be sustainable and based on an understanding of river and coastal processes.

17.3 The Crown has power to construct, or to order the construction of, sea walls or embankments as protection against the sea as part of the Crown's prerogative to defend the realm and to act for the general safety of the public.[1] Although this power is sometimes described as a duty, it does not confer upon a subject a right which is enforceable against the Crown itself[2] and has now largely been superseded by the statutory provision made by the Acts mentioned below.

17.4 The statutory powers to set up flood warning systems and to carry out flood defence and coast protection measures and drainage works are contained in the Coast Protection Act 1949, the Water Resources Act 1991, the Land Drainage Act 1991 and the Environment Act 1995. Those Acts empower coast protection authorities (which are local authorities), the Environment Agency and internal drainage boards ("IDBs") to undertake flood defence measures. While those four Acts confer on the relevant authorities powers to carry out flood defence and coast protection activities, they do not impose duties on them to do so. The relevant Ministers (in England, the Minister of Agriculture, Fisheries and Food, in Wales, the Secretary of State for Wales and, in Scotland, the Secretary of State for Scotland) are empowered to provide government grants for flood defence and coast protection works and flood warning systems but do not have direct powers to carry out the works themselves. The Coast Protection Act 1949 extends to Scotland but the Water Resources Act 1991 and the Land Drainage Act 1991 extend to England and Wales only.

17.5 Under section 40 of the Environment Act 1995, the relevant Minister may give directions to the Environment Agency in respect of its flood defence and land drainage functions. The relevant Minister may give a direction under section 61D of the Land Drainage Act 1991 to an IDB if he considers that destruction or serious damage to an environmental asset of national or international importance could result from any works, operations or activities which are being or are about to be carried out. In both cases, except in an emergency, those powers can be exercised only after consultation with the body concerned. Ministers may also issue or approve codes of practice (see paragraph 17.104 *post*).

17.6 The Environment Agency, through its regional and local flood defence committees, is empowered to undertake measures to reduce the risks of flooding from the sea. It also exercises general supervision over all matters

---

1. For the historical background to this power see *Coulson & Forbes on Waters and Land Drainage*, 6th Edn, S. R. Hobday, pp. 44–47.
2. *Hudson v. Tabor* (1877) 2 Q.B.D. 290; *AG v. Tomline* (1880) 14 Ch. D. 58.

relating to flood defence in England and Wales. About 240 internal drainage boards carry out measures in respect of inland flooding—and in some cases sea defence—in specified districts with special drainage needs. The Environment Agency may issue directions to IDBs in connection with drainage works as part of its supervisory role under the Land Drainage Act 1991. Local authorities are empowered to undertake flood and sea defence works by Part I of the Coast Protection Act 1949.

The Coast Protection Act 1949

Coast protection authorities

17.7 Under Part I of the Coast Protection Act 1949 the relevant Minister (the Minister of Agriculture, Fisheries and Food in relation to England and the Secretary of State in relation to Wales or Scotland) may make an order providing for the constitution of a coast protection board to be the coast protection authority for any area if it appears to him to be expedient to do so for the protection of land in that area. Where no such order has been made, the coast protection authority for each maritime district is the council for that district. The maritime district is defined as a district or a Welsh county or county borough any part of which adjoins the sea. To date, no order constituting a coast protection board has been made. The provisions of the 1949 Act, set out in paragraphs 17.8 to 17.43 *post*, apply to England, Wales and Scotland.

Execution of works by coast protection authorities

17.8 Under section 4 of the Coast Protection Act 1949 coast protection authorities are empowered to carry out such coast protection work, whether within or outside their area, as may appear to them to be necessary or expedient for the protection of any land in their area and may enter into agreements with other persons for the carrying out of such work. That general power does not, however, authorize any act or omission on the part of the authority which apart from section 4 is actionable at the suit of any person (see section 4(4)). "Coast protection work" is defined in section 49 as "any work of construction, alteration, improvement, repair, maintenance, demolition or removal for the purpose of the protection of any land, and includes the sowing or planting of vegetation for the said purpose". "Land" includes land covered by water. An authority may enter into agreements with another person for the carrying out by that person of any coast protection work which the authority have power to carry out under the 1949 Act.

17.9 The authorization of coastal protection works which affect landowners substantially because it is proposed to exercise compulsory purchase powers or to levy coast protection charges[3] are subject to special procedures under Part I of the 1949 Act. Those procedures are described in paragraphs 17.13 to 17.19 *post*. In other cases, where the coast protection authority proposes to carry out any coast protection work other than work of maintenance or repair, the authority must publish notice of the proposal under section 5 including an estimate of the cost of the work by advertising in one or more local newspapers circulating in the area, by serving notice on the Environment Agency or Scottish Environmental Protection Agency and on any IDB in whose district the work is to be carried out and in any other way directed by the Minister. Where the estimated costs of the work exceeds £50,000, notice must also be published in the *London Gazette*.

17.10 Written notice of objection may be made to the proposals within a period of 28 days stating the grounds of the objection.[4] If any objection is made to the proposal and the ground of the objection is that the proposed work would be detrimental to the protection of any land specified in the notice, or will interfere with the exercise by the objector of his functions under any enactment other than the 1949 Act, the Minister must either cause a local inquiry to he held or give the objector and all other persons appearing to him to be affected by the proposal, an opportunity of being heard by a person appointed by him for the purpose. The Minister then determines the objection after considering the report of the person appointed to hold the inquiry or to hear objections.

17.11 As soon as possible after the expiry of the objection period, the Minister must either approve the proposal or direct the authority not to carry out the proposed work or impose such modifications of the proposal or such conditions as to the carrying out of the work as he thinks fit, having regard to the determination of any objections.

17.12 The above procedures are not required if the coast protection authority considers that the works in question are urgently necessary for the protection of any land in their area. But, in such a case, notice must still be given to the Environment Agency (or, in Scotland, the Scottish Environmental Protection Agency) and any IDB in whose district the work is to be or has been carried out before, or as soon as possible after, the commencement of the work.

17.13 Where any coast protection work (other than work of maintenance or repair) is proposed to be carried out by a coast protection authority and it appears to the authority that the work cannot be carried out except in exercise of compulsory powers, the work must be authorized by a works scheme, promoted in accordance with sections 6 to 8 of the 1949 Act and confirmed by the Minister under section 8.

---

3. In practice, coast protection authorities do not exercise their powers to levy coast protection charges. See para 17.14 *post*.
4. Reg. 5 of the Coast Protection (Notices) Regulations 1950.

17.14 Section 7 of the 1949 Act enables coast protection authorities to include in works schemes provisions levying coast protection charges on landowners whose land would be benefited by the carrying out of the work provided by the scheme. However, although those powers have never been repealed, they have ceased to have any practical significance following a ministerial policy directive that compulsory contributions should not be recovered from householders and other private interests.[5] Works schemes are therefore now only made by coast protection authorities if it is necessary to obtain compulsory powers to carry out work on land which is not in ownership of the authority concerned.

17.15 A works scheme must indicate the nature of any work to be carried out by the authority on land vested in them or proposed to be acquired by them for the purposes of the scheme, specify the work (if any) to be carried out on land not so vested or proposed to be acquired, and specify the estimated cost of all work comprised in the scheme. The requirements as to publishing notice of the scheme are in some respects similar to those applying to pro-posals which do not require to be made by work schemes which are described in paragraph 17.9 *ante*. Notice of the works scheme must be published in one or more local newspapers circulating in the area of the authority and, if the estimated cost of the scheme exceeds £50,000, in the *London Gazette*. The notice must name a place at which a copy of the scheme may be seen at all reasonable hours and explain the right to object to the scheme. Copies of the scheme must be served on the owner and occupier of any land, other than land vested in and occupied by the authority, on which the work provided for by the scheme is to be carried out, the Environment Agency (or, in Scotland, the Scottish Environmental Protection Agency), on any IDB in whose district the work is to be carried out and such other authority or person as the Minister may prescribe in regulations or direct.

17.16 Persons who wish to object to the works scheme may do so by serving on the Minister and on the authority, by post within 28 days, written notice of objection to the scheme stating the grounds of the objection.[6] The Minister must cause a local inquiry to be held or give the objector and all other persons appearing to the Minister to be affected by the scheme an opportunity of being heard by a person appointed by him, if notice of objection has been served and not withdrawn and the ground of the objection is:

(a) that work provided for by the scheme, or any part of it, is unneces-sary;

(b) that the carrying out of the work in the manner provided by the scheme would cause hardship to the objector; or

(c) that the work provided for by the scheme would be detrimental to the protection of any land specified in the notice of objection, or would

5. See Ministry of Housing and Local Government Circular 41/62.
6. Reg. 5 of the Coast Protection (Notices) Regulations 1950.

interfere with the exercise by the objector of his functions under any enactment.

Where an inquiry or hearing is held, the Minister must determine the objection after considering the report of the person appointed to hold the inquiry or to hear objections.

17.17 The Minister must make an order either confirming the works scheme (with or without modifications) or quashing the scheme as soon as possible after the time for serving notices of objection has expired and having regard to the determination of any objections.

17.18 After an order confirming the works scheme has been made, the Minister must publish it in the *London Gazette* or in such other way as he considers is best suited for bringing the order to the notice of the persons affected. Under paragraph 7 of Part III of Schedule 1 to the 1949 Act, any person aggrieved by an order who desires to question its validity on the ground that it is not within the powers of the Act or that any requirement of the 1949 Act has not been complied with, may make an application to the High Court within six weeks after the date of the first publication of the notice. Paragraph 7 states that "except as aforesaid the order shall not at any time be questioned by prohibition or *certiorari* or in any proceedings whatsoever". Similar provisions are to be found in other enactments, for example section 44(3) of the Harbours Act 1964 and section 22 of the Transport and Works Act 1992. See paragraphs 11.36 and 16.14 *ante*. In *Webb* v. *Minister of Housing and Local Government*,[7] it was held that, notwithstanding that no application to quash the order confirming the works scheme in that case had been made within the time allowed by paragraph 7, the Minister's order confirming the related compulsory purchase order could be quashed although the quashing of that order entailed exposing the invalidity of the works scheme. In *R* v. *Cornwall County Council, ex parte Huntington*[8] the Court of Appeal held that a similar provision in paragraph 12 of Schedule 15 to the Wildlife and Countryside Act 1981 precluded the Court from entertaining any application to quash a decision to make an order until after the order had been confirmed.

17.19 Once a works scheme has been confirmed by the Minister, the authority has power to take all necessary steps for carrying out the work provided for by the scheme. However, under section 9 of the 1949 Act, where the scheme specifies work to be carried out on land which is neither vested in the authority nor proposed to be acquired by them, the owner of the land may, within six weeks from the confirmation of the scheme, serve a notice on the authority stating that he proposes to carry out the work himself. Where such a notice is served and not withdrawn, the authority may only carry out the work if the owner fails to do so and they have first given him notice that, unless

7. *Webb* v. *Minister of Housing and Local Government* [1965] 2 All E.R. 193.
8. *R* v. *Cornwall County Council, ex parte Huntington* [1994] 1 All E.R. 694.

he carries out the work within a specified time, they will carry out the work themselves.

Powers of coast protection authorities to maintain and repair works

17.20 Where it appears to a coast protection authority that for the protection of land in their area any works are in need of maintenance or repair, the authority may, under section 12 of the 1949 Act, serve on the owner and occupier of the land on which the works are situated a notice specifying the work of maintenance or repair which the authority considers to be necessary. The notice must give the owner and occupier a period of time within which to complete the work, failing which the authority may take all necessary steps for carrying out the work themselves. However, the authority may carry out works of repair immediately, without serving such a notice or waiting for the time to expire, if it appears to them that the work is urgently necessary for the protection of land in their area. The authority's power to carry out works of maintenance or repair under section 12 does not apply where the works in question are maintained under statutory powers by the British Railways Board, the British Waterways Board, Railtrack PLC or other bodies to whom the relevant statutory functions previously vested in the British Railways Board have been transferred.

17.21 A coast protection authority may recover the reasonable costs of carrying out any work of maintenance or repair under section 12 of the 1949 Act (not being works constructed, altered or improved under a works scheme) from the owner or occupier of the land on which the works are situated. This right is subject to the procedures set out in section 13 of the 1949 Act which require the authority to have included in the section 12 notice served on the owner or occupier concerned, a statement that 13 applies to the works in question, that the authority propose to exercise their right of recovery against the owner or occupier and a sufficient indication of the effect of section 13. The owner or occupier on which such a notice is served may, within 21 days, make a complaint in writing to the Magistrates' Court on any one or more of the following grounds:

(a) that having regard to all the circumstances of the case it is equitable that the right of recovery should be exercisable, as respects the whole or some part of the cost of carrying out the work, against whichever of the owner and occupier is not the complainant;

(b) that having regard to all the circumstances of the case it is equitable that the coast protection authority should bear the whole or some part of the cost of carrying out the work;

(c) that any of the work specified in the notice is not work of maintenance or repair;

or

(d) that having regard to all the circumstances of the case, and in particular to the amount of the cost or the probability that there will be a recurrent need for maintenance or repair, the cost ought to be provided for by a scheme under section 13.

A summons granted on such a complaint must be served on the coast protection authority and, if the complaint is made on the ground specified in paragraph (a), on whichever of the owner and the occupier is not the complainant. Where a complaint has been made, the court may make one or more of the following orders:

(a) that the right of recovery shall be exercisable, as respects the whole or such part as may be specified in the order of the cost of carrying out the work, against whichever of the owner and occupier is not the complainant;

(b) debarring the authority from recovering the cost of carrying out the work or so much of that cost as may be specified in the order;

(c) declaring that any of the work specified in the notice is not a work of maintenance or repair; or

(d) debarring the authority from recovering the cost but empowering them to make a scheme under section 13.

17.22 Where the court empowers a coast protection authority to make a scheme for the maintenance or repair of work under section 13, the authority can only recover the cost of carrying out the work in accordance with that scheme. The Act contains procedural requirements as respects the making of section 13 schemes which are a modified version of those relating to a works scheme made under section 7.

Ancillary powers of coast protection authorities

17.23 A coast protection authority may acquire, whether by way of purchase, feu, lease or exchange, any land, whether within or without their area, which is either required by them for the purpose of carrying out on the land any coast protection work which they have power to carry out under Part I of the 1949 Act or for the protection of which they propose to carry out any coast protection work (other than work of maintenance or repair). The Minister may authorise the compulsory acquisition of land (see paragraph 17.24 *post*). The power to acquire land can only be exercised for the purposes set out in section 4. That section was considered in *Webb v. Minister of Housing and Local Government*.[9] In that case, the coast protection authority, the Bognor Regis Urban District Council, were proposing to carry out a works scheme to construct a sea wall and had made a compulsory purchase order over a strip

---

9. *Webb v. Minister of Housing and Local Government* [1965] 2 All E.R. 193.

of land along the sea shore. The strip of land in dispute was required not for the construction of the sea wall itself but for the construction of a paved way which was to be used as a promenade and which, it was claimed by the Council, was also needed to provide access to the sea wall for maintenance purposes. The compulsory purchase order had been confirmed by the Minister. The Court of Appeal found that, although the coast protection works were urgently needed, the compulsory acquisition of the disputed land was not required for the purposes of coast protection since the landowners in question had been prepared to grant easements to the Council over their land to enable the sea wall to be maintained. Accordingly, the compulsory purchase order was quashed. Lord Justice Danckwerts said:

"So [section 4] is purely an empowering section, and the power can only be exercised 'subject to the following provisions of this Act' (the opening words of subsection (1)). Therefore, the authority is limited in the exercise of these powers to the purpose of coast protection, and the authority has to form the opinion that the coast protection work is necessary or expedient for the protection of land in their area, and they may only acquire land which is required by them for the purpose of carrying out thereon any coast protection works, which, of course, means properly required for that purpose."[10]

17.24 A coast protection authority may be authorized under section 14 of the 1949 Act by the Minister to acquire by compulsory purchase any land which they are authorized by section 4 of the 1949 Act to acquire by agreement and the Acquisition of Land Act 1981 applies to any such compulsory purchase. However, where they propose to acquire land for the protection of which they propose to carry out coast protection works, the land may only be acquired if it appears that the value of the land immediately after completion of the works will be greater than it would be if the work had not been carried out, assuming that the proposed coast protection works would be maintained without expense to any person entitled to an interest in the land. Any dispute as to value may be referred to the Lands Tribunal for arbitration and rules (2) to (4) of section 5 of the Land Compensation Act 1961 apply (see sections 14(2) and 24 of the 1949 Act).

17.25 Once land has been properly acquired for the purposes of coast protection works (see paragraph 17.23 *ante*), it may also be used for recreational or other public purposes such as restaurants, bandstands, concert halls and public conveniences provided that those purposes do not interfere with the use of land for the construction, maintenance or repair of the coast protection works in question (see section 22 of the 1949 Act). If the land ceases to be required for coast protection purposes it may be disposed of by the authority in question under the powers applicable to land held by them for other purposes.

10. [1965] 2 All E.R. 193, 203.

17.26 In addition to acquiring land for the construction of the coast protection works, the authority may under section 27 of the 1949 Act, by agreement or compulsorily, secure the creation of a right of passage over other land if that appears necessary to gain convenient access on the land on which the coastal protection work has been or is proposed to be carried out. The right of passage may include passage for persons, vehicles, plant and materials and a right to carry out work to facilitate their passage. The authority may also, by agreement or compulsorily, purchase land required by them to provide convenient access to land on which any coast protection work has been or is proposed to be carried out.

17.27 To enable them to carry out their functions, coast protection authorities may require information as to the ownership of land from any occupier of the land or any person who either directly or indirectly receives rent in respect of the land. Failure to provide such information or knowingly making a misstatement is a summary offence punishable with a fine not exceeding level 1 on the standard scale.[11]

17.28 In addition, coast protection authorities have powers of entry and inspection of land under section 25 of the 1949 Act. They may sell any materials severed from land in carrying out works which are not claimed by the owner within 14 days but must pay the proceeds of sale to the owner.

Effect of the Coast Protection Act 1949 on subsisting obligations to carry out coast protection work

17.29 Part I of the Coast Protection Act 1949 does not affect any obligation to which a person is subject to carry out coast protection work apart from the Act. Accordingly, the Act does not operate to release a person from any obligation to which he is subject by reason of tenure, custom, prescription or otherwise nor does such an obligation in itself render a person liable to maintain or repair any works which are works constructed, altered or improved under a works scheme or works for whose maintenance or repair provision is made by a scheme under section 13 of the 1949 Act. However, a coast protection authority is given power under section 15(4) to enforce such an obligation by serving notice on the person liable, requiring him to carry out the work within a specified period and, in default, carrying out the work themselves and recovering from him the expenses reasonably incurred in doing so. In addition, a coast protection authority may make representations to the Minister that any sea defence commissioners (defined as a body established by or under a local Act wholly or mainly for the purpose of carrying out coast protection work) have failed to carry out any coast protection work which the commissioners are authorized or required to carry out and which is necessary or expedient for the protection of land in the area of the authority.

11. Level 1 on the standard scale is currently £200.

The Minister may, after giving the commissioners an opportunity to make representations, make an order authorizing the coast protection authority to carry out the work and to recover from the commissioners the whole or part of any expenses reasonably incurred by the authority in doing so.

Control by coast protection authorities over works carried out by others

17.30 Under section 16 of the 1949 Act, the written consent of the coast protection authority is required for the carrying out of any coast protection work (other than work of maintenance or repair). Such a consent may be given subject to conditions. Before giving their consent, the authority must give notice of the application to any coast protection authority whose area adjoins their area, to the Environment Agency (or, in Scotland, the Scottish Environmental Protection Agency) and to any IDB whose district comprises the whole or any part of their area, and must consider any representations made by any of those bodies. Carrying out such work without consent or in contravention of any conditions subject to which the consent is granted is a summary offence carrying a maximum fine of level 3 on the standard scale.[12] In addition, the coast protection authority may serve notice on a person who has constructed, altered or improved any works without consent or in contravention of conditions, requiring him within a specified period of time of not less than 30 days to remove the works or to make specified alterations to them. In default, the authority may themselves remove or alter the works and recover the expense from the person on whom the notice was served.

17.31 The requirement to obtain a consent under section 16 to the carrying out of coast protection work does not apply to works carried out by a coast protection authority, a body or person upon whom any powers or duties relating to the protection of land have been conferred or imposed by or under any enactment, a highways authority, a harbour authority, the British Waterways Board, the British Railways Board or any body such as Railtrack PLC to whom relevant statutory functions of the British Railways Board have been transferred. Instead, provision is made in section 17 for the body in question to give the coast protection authority in whose area the work is to be carried out, and the other bodies specified in paragraph 17.30 *ante*, not less than 28 days notice of their intention to carry out the specified works. Provision is made for any person on whom such notice is served to object to the Minister, in which case the Minister determines whether or not the body in question may carry out the works and may make modifications to those works or may lay down conditions subject to which the works are to be carried out. The requirement to serve advance notice before undertaking works does not apply where it appears to the body in question that the works are urgently necessary for the protection of any land but, in such a case, the body must, before or as

12. Level 3 on the standard scale is currently £1,000.

soon as possible after the commencement of the work, give the coast protection authority in whose area the work is to be carried out, notice of the nature of the work.

17.32 Section 18 of the 1949 Act enables a coast protection authority to make an order applying the provisions of section 18 to a specified portion of the seashore within their area or of the seashore lying to seaward of their area but within three nautical miles of the baselines from which the breadth of the territorial sea adjacent to Great Britain is measured. A section 18 order renders it unlawful to excavate or remove any materials (other than materials more than 50 feet below the surface) on, under or forming part of any portion of the seashore to which the order relates without a licence granted by the authority. A licence may be granted subject to conditions and cannot render lawful anything which would be unlawful if section 18 had not been enacted. To excavate or remove any materials without a licence or in contravention of the conditions of a licence is a summary offence punishable with a maximum fine of level 3 on the standard scale.[13] The prohibition applies notwithstanding anything contained in any other enactment but does not affect the excavation or removal of any materials by the Minister in the exercise of the powers conferred by Part II of the 1949 Act or by any other person in compliance with a notice served under that Part.

17.33 An order under section 18 may apply the provisions of the section without qualification or may except from those provisions the carrying out of operations of any specified class, either unconditionally or subject to conditions specified in the order.

17.34 The procedure for the making of orders is contained in Schedule 2 to the Act, which provides for the publication of the draft order by newspaper advertisement and by service of notices and for the making of objections. If an objection is made:

    (a) by any person on the ground that the order would interfere with the exercise of his functions under any enactment other than the 1949 Act; or

    (b) by any person having an interest, right or privilege conferred on him by any local or private Act, on the ground that any such interest, right or privilege of his would be affected by the order;

and the objection is not withdrawn, the order is subject to special parliamentary procedure. (Special parliamentary procedure is briefly described, in relation to orders and schemes under the Harbours Act 1964, in paragraphs 11.25 to 11.35 *ante*.) In other cases where objections are made which are not withdrawn, the Minister must cause a local inquiry to be held or give the objector an opportunity of being heard by a person appointed by him at a

---

13. Level 3 on the standard scale is currently £1,000.

hearing at which the authority is given an opportunity to be heard too. In a case which is not subject to special parliamentary procedure, the Minister may confirm the order with or without modifications having regard to the determination of any objections and to the report of the person appointed to hold an inquiry or to hear objections.

17.35 Under paragraph 10 of Schedule 2, a person aggrieved by the order may question its validity on the ground that it is not within the powers of the Act, or that any requirement of the Act has not been complied with, by making an application to the High Court within six weeks after the date on which notice of the confirmation of the order is published or, where the order is subject to a special parliamentary procedure, on the date upon which it becomes operative. This provision, which does not apply to an order which is confirmed by an Act of Parliament under section 6 of the Statutory Orders (Special Procedure) Act 1945, is similar to that contained in paragraph 7 of Schedule 1 (see paragraph 17.18 *ante*).

17.36 There are special provisions under Part II of Schedule 3 to the 1949 Act for the making of interim orders where this appears to the authority to be urgently necessary for the protection of any land by reason of emergency.

17.37 The power to make a coast protection order under section 18 of the 1949 Act was considered in *British Dredging (Services) Ltd. v. Secretary of State for Wales and Monmouthshire*.[14] In that case, sand abstracting companies had for many years, with the permission of the freeholders of Margam Sands, extracted sand for sale in increasing quantities from the seashore. Observing that the clay sub-strata of the beach was gradually being eroded, the local coast protection authority made a coast protection order under section 18 making it unlawful for sand to be removed from the beach except under licence from them, so that they could control the rate at which the sand was extracted. The abstracting companies objected to the order and an inspector was appointed by the Minister to hold a public inquiry. The inspector reported to the Minister that the reason for the erosion of the clay sub-strata which underlay the beach was not properly understood but could be due wholly or in part to the sand extraction operations, or to storms, or to alterations in local tidal conditions brought about by the construction of a harbour. The inspector stated that before any long term conclusions could be reached, a detailed study of the foreshore and conditions of the seabed would have to be made over a period of at least three years, that there was a serious danger of overexploitation of the current beach regime and that it was important for the purpose of providing a bulwark against the sea that the quantity of sand removed from the beach should not exceed the amount replenishing the beach. He recommended that the coast protection order should be confirmed so that the long term management of the beach and its potential yield could be

14. *British Dredging (Services) Ltd. v. Secretary of State for Wales and Monmouthshire* [1975] 2 All E.R. 845.

controlled by the coast protection authority through a licensing system conducted on a scientifically conceived and properly monitored basis. The Minister confirmed the order. The sand extracting companies applied for the coast protection order to be quashed on the grounds that it was *ultra vires* the coast protection authority and the Minister, in that there was no evidence that the making of the order would serve the purposes for which the 1949 Act was passed (namely for the protection of the coast against erosion and encroachment by the sea). It was held that the coast protection order was not *ultra vires*. Although section 18 did not spell out the circumstances in which it would be permissible for the coast protection authority to make an order, its terms were sufficiently wide to enable a coast protection authority to make an order under section 18 not only where it could be shown that the extraction of materials from the seashore was causing erosion or encroachment by the sea but also where there was, by reason of the degree of erosion of the seashore, from whatever cause, reasonable apprehension of further erosion or encroachment and it appeared to the coast protection authority to be necessary or expedient or prudent to make such an order to enable them to discharge their statutory duty under the 1949 Act to protect the land.

Compensation

17.38 Under section 19 of the 1949 Act any person may make a claim for compensation on the basis that the value of an interest of his in land has been depreciated, or that he has suffered damage by being disturbed in his enjoyment of land, in consequence of the carrying out of coast protection work by a coast protection authority in the exercise of their powers under Part I of the Act, or that the value of his interest in land has been depreciated in consequence of the refusal of consent under section 16 of the Act, or in consequence of the granting of such consent subject to conditions. A claim must be made within 12 months of the completion of the works, the refusal of consent, or the imposition of conditions giving rise to the claim. Where a claim is made out, the coast protection authority must pay to the claimant compensation equal to the amount of the depreciation or damage, but no compensation is payable in respect of the carrying out of coast protection work unless the act or omission causing the depreciation or disturbance would have been actionable by the claimant if it had been done or omitted otherwise than in the exercise of statutory powers. Any dispute as to compensation may be referred to arbitration by the Lands Tribunal and rules (2) to (4) of section 5 of the Land Compensation Act 1961 apply.

Powers of the Minister

17.39 The Minister has power under section 28(1) to make an order authorizing a person, other than a coast protection authority, to carry out coast protection work in accordance with a works scheme or with a notice served under section 12 of the 1949 Act (see paragraphs 17.13 and 17.20 *ante*) if the work cannot be carried out without the order. This applies where the person's power to carry out the work is affected by a covenant or other restriction or by inability to obtain access to land on which the work is to be carried out or over which a right of passage is required. Similarly, a coast protection authority may apply for an order under section 28 where they wish to carry out coast protection work on land belonging to them under section 4 of the 1949 Act but are prevented from doing so by reason of any covenant or other restriction affecting the land. Provision is made for notice of an application for an order to be served on any person known to be entitled to enforce the covenant or restriction in question or whose land is to be affected. Such a person may serve notice of objection on the Minister within four weeks of service of the notice and, where an objection is served and not withdrawn, an opportunity must be given to the objector and the applicant of being heard by a person appointed by the Minister. The Minister, after considering the report of any person appointed by him to hear objections may make an order authorizing the applicant to carry out work or enter on the land concerned and such an order may be made subject to conditions and require the applicant to pay compensation to the person affected.

17.40 The Minister may cause a local inquiry to be held under section 29 of the 1949 Act if a complaint is made to him that a coast protection authority have failed to take sufficient measures for the protection of any land in their area or if he considers that an investigation should be made. If the Minister is satisfied, following the inquiry, that there has been a failure on the part of the coast protection authority, he may make an order declaring them to be in default and directing them to exercise powers under the 1949 Act specified in the order within a specified time.

Application to the Crown and protective provisions

17.41 The provisions of Part I of the 1949 Act bind the Crown and apply in relation to Crown land but the powers of compulsory purchase, powers to enter land, and powers to require the payment of coast protection charges, do not bind the Crown without consent. An order under section 18 which prohibits the excavation of materials in or under the seashore only binds the Crown if the order has been confirmed by the Minister (section 32 of the 1949 Act.).

17.42 Works may not be carried out under the powers of the 1949 Act which would affect works constructed or maintained by the Environment Agency or an IDB or on land on which the sowing or planting of vegetation is carried out or vegetation is maintained, by such a body unless the Environment Agency or the IDB consent.

17.43 Section 47 provides that the statutory powers in the 1949 Act do not authorize or require any person to carry out any work or do anything in contravention of the Ancient Monuments and Archaeological Areas Act 1979. The consent of the Secretary of State is required for the carrying out of any work of alteration, improvement, repair, maintenance, demolition or removal of any works constructed for the drainage of agricultural land in Scotland. There are also savings for the powers of the Admiralty under the Dockyard Ports Regulation Act 1865 and for the rights of an operator of a telecommunications code system under the telecommunications code.

The Water Resources Act 1991 and the Environment Act 1995

The Environment Agency and regional flood defence committees

17.44 Various functions under the Water Resources Act 1991 and the Land Drainage Act 1991 relating to flood defence which were previously exercisable by the National Rivers Authority were transferred to the Environment Agency ("the EA") by the Environment Act 1995. For the purposes of those Acts "flood defence" is defined as "the draining of land and the provision of flood warning systems" and "drainage" includes defence against water, including sea water. Under section 106 of the Water Resources Act 1991, the EA must arrange for those functions (described in paragraphs 17.51 to 17.56 *post*) to be carried out by regional flood defence committees. So the EA's functions are performed, in relation to the area of each regional flood defence committee, by the committee for that area and, in cases involving the areas of more than one regional flood defence committee, by such committees, or jointly by such committees, as may be determined in accordance with arrangements made by the EA. The committees do not, however, handle the EA's function of issuing levies or drainage charges. Under section 106(3), the EA may give a regional flood defence committee a direction of a general or specific character as to the carrying out of any function relating to flood defence (other than certain functions not relevant to coastal protection) so far as the carrying out of that function appears to the EA likely to affect materially the EA's management of water for purposes other than flood defence.

17.45 The regional flood defence committees are constituted under section 14 of the Environment Act 1995. There is a regional flood defence committee for each of the areas for which there was an old committee under the Water Resources Act 1991 immediately before the transfer of functions under the Environment Act 1995 to the EA, but where any function of the EA falls to be carried out at a place beyond the seaward boundaries of the committee's area, that place shall be assumed to be within the area of the committee whose area is adjacent to the area where that place is situated. The EA is required to maintain a principal office for each regional flood defence committee's area. Schedule 4 to the Environment Act 1995 makes provision for regional flood defence committee areas to be altered or amalgamated by ministerial order. Where orders are proposed, provision is made for advertisement, objections, consideration of objections by the relevant Minister and, in certain cases, the application of special parliamentary procedure.

17.46 Section 15 of the Environment Act 1995 provides for the composition of regional flood defence committees. Each committee consists of a chairman appointed by the relevant Minister, a number of other members appointed by the relevant Minister, two members appointed by the EA and a number of members appointed by or on behalf of the "constituent councils" (i.e. the local authorities for any part of a committee's area). None of the committee's members may be members of the EA. Normally a committee has not less than 11 and not more than 17 members.

17.47 Where constituent councils are to make joint appointments but cannot agree, the relevant Minister appoints the member or members concerned. The relevant Minister or constituent council (but not the EA) must, in making appointments, have regard to the desirability of appointing a person who has experience of, and has shown capacity in, some matter relevant to the functions of the committee. This may not necessarily be flood defence itself but could, for example, include agriculture or nature conservation. Section 16 of the Environment Act 1995 deals with changes in the composition of regional flood defence committees.

Local flood defence committees

17.48 Section 17 of the Environment Act 1995 provides for the creation, by local flood defence schemes, of local flood defence committees within the area of a regional flood defence committee. A scheme may provide for the creation of one or more local flood defence districts and for the constitution, membership, functions and procedure of the committee for each such district (a "local flood defence committee"). A regional flood defence committee may submit to the EA a local flood defence scheme for any part of its area where a scheme is not already in force or it may submit a scheme to vary or revoke an existing scheme or replace it with another scheme.

17.49 Before submitting a scheme to the EA, the regional flood defence committee must consult the local authorities for the area of the proposed scheme, as well as organizations representative of persons interested in flood defence. The EA must send any submitted scheme to the relevant Minister who may approve it with or without modifications and, if so, shall specify a date for its coming into force.

17.50 Section 18 of the Environment Act 1995 provides for the composition of local flood defence committees as established in local flood defence schemes made under section 17. Normally a committee has not less than 11 nor more than 15 members. The committee consists of a chairman appointed from among their own members by the regional flood defence committee, other members appointed by that committee, and members appointed by or on behalf of constituent councils in accordance with the scheme. The number of members appointed by or on behalf of constituent councils must be one more than the total appointed by the regional committee. The regional committee must have regard to the desirability of appointing persons who have experience of, and who have shown some capacity in, some matter relevant to the functions of the committee.

Functions of the Environment Agency

17.51 Under section 6(4) of the Environment Act 1995, the EA is under a duty to exercise a general supervision over all matters relating to flood defence in relation to England and Wales. That duty is, however, exercisable through committees (see paragraph 17.44 *ante*). The EA's flood defence functions extend to the territorial sea adjacent to England and Wales in so far as the area of any regional or flood defence committee includes any area of the territorial sea or in so far as section 165 of the Water Resources Act 1991 provides for the exercise of any power in the territorial sea (see paragraph 17.53 *post*). The EA has a duty under section 105 of the Water Resources Act 1991, for the purpose of carrying out its flood defence functions, from time to time to carry out surveys of the areas in relation to which it carries out those functions. In exercising its flood defence functions under the Water Resources Act 1991, the EA must have due regard to the interests of fisheries, including sea fisheries.

17.52 Under section 111 of the Water Resources Act 1991, the EA may, with the consent of the relevant Ministers, enter into an arrangement with a navigation or conservancy authority for the transfer to the EA of the whole or any part of the authority's undertaking or property or the alteration or improvement by the EA of any of the authority's works if the arrangements are made with a view to improving the drainage of any land. For this purpose a "navigation authority" is defined as being "any person who has a duty or power under any enactment to work, maintain, conserve, improve or control any canal or other inland navigation, navigable river, estuary, harbour or dock" and "conservancy authority" means "any person who has a duty or power under any enactment to conserve, maintain or improve the navigation of a tidal river and is not a navigation authority or harbour authority".

17.53 The EA's power to carry out flood defence and drainage works is conferred by section 165 of the Water Resources Act 1991. Under that section the EA has power to maintain, improve or construct drainage works for the purpose of defence against sea water or tidal water, and that power is exercisable both above and below the low-water mark. The EA may construct all such works and do all such things in the sea or in any estuary as may, in its opinion, be necessary to secure an adequate outfall for a main river. The EA may enter into agreements with any person to carry out, improve or maintain, at that person's expense, any drainage works which that person is entitled to carry out, improve or maintain. For this purpose the expense to be borne by that person shall not include the amount of any grant paid under section 149(3) of the Water Resources Act 1991 in respect of the works in question. The powers under section 165 are discretionary and, in the absence of any contractual obligation,[15] the EA is liable only for misfeasance and not for omitting to exercise its powers.[16]

17.54 Under section 166 of the Water Resources Act 1991, the EA has power to provide and operate flood warning systems, to provide, install and maintain apparatus required for the purposes of the systems and to carry out any engineering or building operations required for such systems. This provision is not to be construed as authorizing, on the part of the EA, any act or omission which, apart from that provision, would be actionable. Section 166 powers, like other functions under the 1991 Act, are exercisable through the relevant regional flood defence committee and, where the area of the relevant committee is adjacent to Scotland, its functions may be exercised in relation to Scotland subject to prior consultation with the Scottish local authority for the area concerned. A "flood warning system" is defined as:

"any system whereby, for the purpose of providing warning of any danger of flooding, information with respect to—
    (a) rainfall, as measured at a particular place within a particular period; or
    (b) the level or flow of any inland water, or part of an inland water, at a particular time; or
    (c) other matters appearing to the EA to be relevant for that purpose;
is obtained and transmitted, whether automatically or otherwise, with or without provision for carrying out calculations based on such information and for transmitting the results of those calculations".

"Inland water" is defined as—

"any of the following in any part of Great Britain:
    (a) any river, stream or other watercourse, whether natural or artificial and whether tidal or not;
    (b) any lake or pond, whether natural or artificial, and any reservoir or dock; and
    (c) any channel, creek, bay, estuary or arm of the sea."

17.55 The EA is given various ancillary powers to enable these works powers to be carried out, including power to acquire land under section 37 of the Environment Act 1995, power under section 167 of the Water Resources Act 1991 to dispose of spoil in connection with flood defence works, and

---

15. *Smith* v. *River Douglas Catchment Board* [1949] 2 All E.R. 179, C.A.
16. See *Smith* v. *Cawdle Fen, Ely (Cambridge) Commissioners* [1938] 4 All E.R. 64; *Gillette* v. *Kent Rivers Catchment Board* [1938] 4 All E.R. 810; *East Suffolk Rivers Catchment Board* v. *Kent* [1940] 4 All E.R. 527, H.L.

power under section 170 of that Act to enter premises to carry out surveys or tests.

17.56 In addition, the EA may apply to Ministers for a compulsory works order under section 168 of the Water Resources Act 1991 where it is proposed, for the purposes of, or in connection with, the carrying out of any of its functions, to carry out any engineering or building operations. A compulsory works order may confer such compulsory powers, and grant such authority, as the Minister considers necessary or expedient for the purpose of enabling any engineering or building operations to be carried out for the purposes of, or in connection with, the carrying out of the functions with respect to which the application was made. In particular, a compulsory works order may confer power to acquire land compulsorily, make any authority granted by the order subject to conditions, and amend or repeal any local or statutory provision. Provision is made by Schedule 19 to the Water Resources Act 1991 for advertising and giving notice of an application for a compulsory works order, making objections, consideration of objections by a local inquiry or hearing and compensation to be paid if the order is made. As well as the power to apply for a compulsory works order, the EA may be authorized by the relevant Minister to purchase land in England and Wales compulsorily under section 154 of the Water Resources Act 1991.

Protective provisions

17.57 Under paragraph 5 of Schedule 21 to the Water Resources Act 1991, the EA is liable to make full compensation to any person who has sustained injury by reason of the exercise by the EA of any powers under section 165(1) to (3). In case of dispute, the amount of the compensation is determined by the Lands Tribunal. Where injury is sustained by any person by reason of the exercise by the EA of its powers under section 167(1)(b), the EA may, if it thinks fit, pay to that person such compensation as it may determine but must do so if the injury could have been avoided if those powers had been exercised with reasonable care.

17.58 Schedule 22 to the Water Resources Act 1991 contains provisions for the protection of various statutory undertakers including any navigation authority, harbour authority or conservancy authority, any IDB, any railway company or any public utility undertaking carried on by a local authority. The EA may not, except with the consent of the person carrying on the protected undertaking, carry out any works under the Water Resources Act 1991 which, whether directly or indirectly, would interfere with works or property vested in or under the control of the undertaker or with the use of any such property or works so as to affect injuriously those works or that property or the carrying on of that undertaking. The undertakers' consent may be given subject to reasonable conditions but may not be unreasonably withheld. Provision is made for disputes to be referred to arbitration. The flood defence provisions of the 1991 Act do not confer on the EA power to do anything which prejudices the exercise of any statutory power, authority or jurisdiction from time to time vested in or exercisable by any person carrying on a protected undertaking. Nor do the flood defence provisions authorize any person to interfere with any railway bridge, or other work connected with a railway or the structure, use or maintenance of a railway or the traffic on it, without the consent of the railway company concerned. Again, such consent may be given subject to reasonable conditions but shall not be unreasonably withheld, and disputes are to be referred to arbitration.

17.59 Under section 179 of the 1991 Act, the powers in the Act may not be exercised so as to interfere with any sluices, floodgates, groynes, sea defences or other works used by any person for draining, preserving or improving any land under any local statutory provision without the consent of the person who uses them. Such consent may be given subject to reasonable conditions but shall not be unreasonably withheld and any dispute is to be referred to arbitration. Where the EA proposes, otherwise than in exercise of any compulsory powers, to construct or alter any inland waters in any internal drainage district or to construct or alter any works on or in any inland waters, the EA must consult the IDB for that district before doing so.

17.60 The flood defence provisions of the Water Resources Act 1991 do not authorize the construction of any work on, over or under, or the use for any purpose of, any tidal lands except with the consent of the owner of the land and of the Secretary of State and in accordance with approved plans and sections and subject to prescribed restrictions and conditions. However, this restriction on the power does not apply to work done in maintaining existing works on tidal lands. For this purpose "tidal lands" means lands below the high-water mark of ordinary spring tides but does not include any lands which are protected, by means of walls, embankments or otherwise, from the incursion of the tides (see section 74 of the Land Drainage Act 1991, as applied by section 181(4) of the Water Resources Act 1991).

17.61 The powers in the Water Resources Act 1991 do not override the need to obtain planning permission for carrying out coast protection works under the Act nor the need to obtain consents under the Ancient Monuments and Archaeological Areas Act 1979 or the Food and Environment Protection Act 1985 (see paragraphs 17.106 to 17.112 *post*).

17.62 The flood defence provisions of the Water Resources Act 1991 do not release any person from an obligation to which he is subject by reason of tenure, custom, prescription or otherwise, but the functions of the EA as respects the doing of any work under the flood defence provisions of the Act are not to be treated in any way as limited by the fact that some other person is under such an obligation to do that work (see section 185 of the Water Resources Act 1991).

The Land Drainage Act 1991

Internal drainage boards

17.63 Section 1 of the Land Drainage Act 1991 provides that, for the purposes of the drainage of land, there shall continue to be districts, known as internal drainage districts, which are such areas within the areas of the regional flood defence committees as will derive benefit, or avoid danger, as a result of drainage operations and for an internal drainage board ("IDB") to be established for each such district. These drainage districts and boards are statutory successors of the drainage districts and boards which were constituted under the Land Drainage Act 1930. An IDB exercises a general supervision over all matters relating to the drainage of land within their district and has the other functions conferred on them by the Land Drainage Act 1991. IDBs are constituted under Schedule 1 to the Land Drainage Act and consist both of members elected by persons occupying land in the relevant district which is subject to drainage levy and members appointed by the relevant charging authorities.

17.64 For the purposes of the Land Drainage Act 1991 "drainage" has the same meaning as in the Water Resources Act 1991 and is defined as including defence against water, including sea water (see paragraph 17.44 *ante*). The functions of IDBs, the EA and local authorities conferred by the Land Drainage Act 1991 are therefore complementary to, and substantially overlap with, the functions of the EA, exercisable through regional and local flood defence committees, under the Water Resources Act 1991, and those of coast protection authorities under the Coast Protection Act 1949.

17.65 The boundaries of inland drainage districts may be reviewed by the EA who may also, in accordance with procedures in Schedule 3 to the Land Drainage Act 1991, prepare schemes to alter or amalgamate inland drainage districts, to reconstitute IDBs or to alter their functions under local Acts. Any such scheme is submitted to the relevant Minister who, subject to the consideration of objections made and dealt with in accordance with the provisions of Schedule 3, may confirm the order. In some cases schemes are subject to special parliamentary procedure.

17.66 There are provisions in sections 3 and 4 of the Land Drainage Act 1991 for the relevant Minister to make an order, in accordance with the provisions of Schedule 3, constituting the EA the IDB for any internal drainage district.

Powers of internal drainage boards

17.67 The general powers of IDBs to undertake drainage works within their district is contained in section 14 of the Land Drainage Act 1991. These powers include powers to maintain existing works (including cleansing, repairing or otherwise maintaining in a due state of efficiency any existing drainage work), to improve any existing works (including raising, widening or otherwise improving any existing drainage work) and to construct new works (including making any new drainage work, erecting any machinery or doing any act required for the drainage of any land). Those powers may not be exercised in relation to a main river or the banks of a main river but, by virtue of the wide definition of "drainage" mentioned in paragraph 17.64 *ante*, include works to defend land against sea water. Section 14(5) provides that, where injury is sustained by any person by reason of the exercise of powers under section 14, the IDB shall be liable to make full compensation to the injured person which, if not agreed, is to be determined by the Lands Tribunal.

17.68 Ancillary powers are conferred on IDBs under Part V of the Land Drainage Act 1991 to enable them to perform their functions. These powers include powers to acquire land by agreement or, if authorized by the relevant Minister, compulsorily, to dispose of land subject to the safeguards in section 63 of the Land Drainage Act 1991 and powers to enter land. The Acquisition of Land Act 1981 applies in relation to the compulsory acquisition of land. Under section 15 of the Land Drainage Act, IDBs have powers as to the disposal of spoil removed in the course of the carrying out of any work for widening, deepening or dredging any ordinary watercourse.

17.69 Under section 19 of the Land Drainage Act 1991, an IDB, with a view to improving the drainage of any land situated in their district, may, with the approval of the relevant Ministers, enter into an arrangement with a navigation authority or conservancy authority for the transfer to the IDB of the whole or any part of the authority's undertaking or property or for the alteration or improvement by the IDB of any of the authority's works. This power is similar to that conferred on the EA by section 111 of the Water Resources Act 1991 (see paragraph 17.52 *ante*).

17.70 An IDB may, by agreement with any person and at that person's expense, carry out and maintain any drainage works which that person is entitled to carry out and maintain. This power is exercisable in relation to works outside, as well as inside, the IDB's district but is not exercisable in relation to drainage works in connection with a main river or the banks of such a river.

The supervision of drainage boards by the Environment Agency

17.71 The EA may, for the purpose of securing the efficient working and maintenance of existing drainage works and the construction of necessary new drainage works, give general or special directions under section 7 of the Land Drainage Act 1991 to IDBs with respect to the exercise and performance of their functions. IDBs require the consent of the EA to construct any drainage works or alter any existing drainage works if the construction or alteration will affect the working of any drainage works of another IDB or affect the interest of another IDB. The consent of the EA is also required where the work affects the discharge of water into a main river. Any such consent of the EA may be given subject to reasonable conditions but may not be unreasonably withheld. If an IDB acts in contravention of these provisions, the EA has power itself to carry out and maintain any works or do what is necessary to prevent or remedy any damage which may result, or has resulted, from the action of the IDB and to recover the costs of doing so from the IDB. Any dispute may be referred to the relevant Minister for decision.

17.72 Under section 9 of the Land Drainage Act 1991, the EA may exercise powers of an IDB where, in the opinion of the EA, any land is injured or likely to be injured by flooding or inadequate drainage that might be remedied wholly or partly by the exercise of drainage powers vested in the IDB which are not being exercised at all or not to the necessary extent. Before exercising these default powers, the EA must give the IDB not less than 30 days notice of its intention to do so and if the IDB objects within that period the EA may not exercise the powers except with the consent of the relevant Minister who may, if he thinks fit, cause a public local inquiry to be held to consider the objections. On the application of the council of any county, county borough, metropolitan district or London borough, the EA may direct that the default powers conferred on the EA under section 9 may be exercisable by that council as respects land in the council's area instead of by the EA. If the EA do not comply with the council's application, the council may appeal against the refusal to the relevant Minister who may, if he thinks fit, require the EA to comply with the application. Any direction given for the exercise of default powers by the council may be revoked by the EA subject to the consent of the relevant Minister and on giving the council concerned not less than six months notice.

Functions of local authorities

17.73 The Land Drainage Act 1991 confers on a local authority powers under the Act in relation to their area so far as may be necessary for the purpose of preventing flooding or mitigating any damage caused by flooding in their area (section 14(1)(b)). A local authority means the council of a county, county borough, a district or London borough or the Common Council of the City of London.

17.74 In addition, a scheme may be made under section 18 of the Land Drainage Act 1991 to enable a local authority (other than a district council) to enter on land and carry out drainage works. Such a scheme may be made in relation to land in the local authority's area if the authority is of the opinion that the land is capable of improvement by drainage works, but that the constitution for that purpose of an internal drainage district would not be practicable—for instance where the area of land concerned is small. The scheme must state the works proposed to be carried out, the area to be improved by the works, the estimated expenses of carrying out the works, the maximum amount to be recoverable by the local authority in respect of those expenses and the manner in which the expenses of carrying out and maintaining the works are to be apportioned among the lands comprised in the area concerned. The amount of the estimated expenses must not exceed £50 per acre (which limit may be varied by order) in the area to be improved unless a relevant Minister exempts the scheme from that limit on the grounds that the works proposed to be carried out are urgently required in the public interest. The scheme must be made in accordance with the procedures in Schedule 4 to the Land Drainage Act 1991 which provides for the making of objections by the owners and occupiers of the land concerned or other persons affected by the scheme, the dealing with those objections by a public local inquiry or by a hearing, and for proposed schemes to be subject to confirmation, with or without modification, by a relevant Minister. The EA has similar powers to make a scheme under section 18 for the carrying out of work by it.

17.75 Where a local authority considers it necessary for the purpose of preventing flooding or mitigating any damage caused by flooding in their area, or has power to carry out works in pursuance of a scheme under section 18 of the Land Drainage Act 1991, the local authority has the same powers as those conferred on IDBs by sections 14 and 15 and Part V of the Land Drainage Act 1991, which powers are described in paragraphs 17.67 and 17.68 *ante*. A scheme made under section 18 is a local land charge, registrable under the Local Land Charges Act 1975.

17.76 Where a non-metropolitan district council has the powers mentioned above but does not exercise them, those powers may be exercised by the county council either at the request of the district council or after not less than six weeks notice has been given to the district council in writing by the county council, subject to the district council's right to appeal to the Secretary of State. This does not apply in relation to power conferred on a Welsh county council or county borough council. Where powers are conferred by the Act on a metropolitan district council, a London borough council, a Welsh county council or county borough council or the Common Council of the City of London and are not exercised by that council, they may be exercised by the EA at the request of the council or after not less than six weeks notice has been given to the council in writing by the EA, subject to the council's right to appeal to the Secretary of State.

17.77 A local authority's powers under the Land Drainage Act 1991 are subject to section 17. That section requires the consent of the EA to be obtained to the carrying out or maintenance by a local authority of any drainage works in connection with a watercourse. Such consent may be given, subject to reasonable conditions, but may not be unreasonably withheld and, before giving any consent or imposing any condition with respect to any drainage works in connection with a watercourse under the control of an IDB, the EA must consult with the IDB. Any question as to whether a consent is unreasonably withheld or whether any condition imposed by the EA is un-reasonable may be referred to and determined by the Ministers.

Arrangements between drainage authorities

17.78 Section 11 of the Land Drainage Act 1991 enables agreements to be made between the EA and an IDB for the carrying out by the IDB of any work in connection with the main river which the EA is authorized to carry out. Conversely, the EA may, with the consent of an IDB, carry out and maintain in the IDB's district, any works which the IDB might carry out or maintain, or agree to contribute to the expense of carrying out or maintenance of any works by the IDB. Similarly, an IDB may, with the consent of the IDB for any other district, carry out and maintain in that other district any works which the IDB might carry out or maintain within their own district. An IDB may agree to contribute to the expense of the carrying out and maintenance of any works by the IDB of another district. Any agreements made under section 11 may contain terms as to the payment of the expenses of the carrying out or maintenance of the works concerned.

Interaction with private obligations or obligations under local enactments

17.79 Section 21 of the Land Drainage Act 1991 provides for the enforce-ment by an IDB or the EA of any obligation to which a person is liable by reason of tenure, custom, prescription or otherwise (other than an obligation under the Land Drainage Act 1991 or the Water Resources Act 1991) to do work in relation to any watercourse, bridge or drainage work (whether by way of repair, maintenance or otherwise). If a person who is liable to do work under such an obligation fails to do so and the works are in an internal drainage district, the IDB concerned may serve a notice on him requiring him to do the necessary work with all reasonable and proper despatch. If the person fails, within seven days, to comply with such a notice, the IDB may do the work themselves and recover from him the expenses reasonably incurred in doing so. Where the work concerned is not within an internal drainage district, the enforcement powers are exercisable by the EA. These powers are similar to those conferred on coast protection authorities by section 15(4) of the Coast Protection Act 1949 which are mentioned in paragraph 17.29 *ante*.

17.80 Under section 33 of the Land Drainage Act 1991, the EA or the IDB of any internal drainage district concerned may commute an obligation imposed on a person by reason of tenure, custom, prescription or otherwise, to do any work in connection with the drainage of land (whether by way of repairing banks or walls, maintaining watercourses, or otherwise). Where the EA or the IDB propose to commute any obligation under section 33, notice must be given to the appropriate Minister of the proposal, including the terms on which the obligation is to be commuted and the period within which objection to the proposal may be made. The person on whom the obligation is imposed may object to the proposal within one month of being given notice, in which case the question of whether the proposal shall proceed must be referred to the appropriate Minister whose decision is final. The financial consequences of computation are dealt with in section 34 of the Land Drainage Act 1991.

17.81 The powers in sections 21 and 33 of the Land Drainage Act 1991 are not exercisable by the IDB in relation to work affecting a main river or the banks of such a river. Instead, the powers are exercisable by the EA by virtue of section 107 of the Water Resources Act 1991.

17.82 The relevant Ministers are empowered under section 35 of the Land Drainage Act 1991, by order made by statutory instrument, to revoke, vary or amend the provisions of any local Act relating to navigation rights over any canal, river or navigable waters or to the powers and duties of a navigation authority with respect to any canal, river or navigable waters. Such an order may extinguish, vary or suspend, during such period as the Minister making the order may think proper, any specified rights, powers or duties. The power to make an order is exercisable only where it appears to the Minister that a navigation authority is not exercising at all, or not to the necessary extent, the powers vested in it, and it appears to the Minister desirable to make an order with a view to securing the better drainage of land. The order must be made on an application by the EA and (except where the application is made in connection with a main river) the IDB for every internal drainage district within which any of the waters to which the applications relates are situated. The power is exercisable only after consultation with the Secretary of State for the Environment and requires the consent of the Secretary of State for Transport if it is made in relation to any waters within the ebb and flow of the tide at ordinary spring tides. The provisions of Schedule 3 to the Land Drainage Act 1991 apply with respect to an order under section 35.

Protective provisions

17.83 Section 67 of, and Schedule 6 to, the Land Drainage Act 1991 contain protective provisions and savings. The provisions in Schedule 6 for the protection of statutory undertakers are broadly similar to those contained in Schedule 22 to the Water Resources Act 1991 described in paragraph 17.58 *ante*. Schedule 6 does not apply in relation to the carrying out of works under the Land Drainage Act by the EA, but instead the provisions of sections 179 and 183 of, and Schedule 22 to, the Water Resources Act 1991 (which are described in paragraphs 17.58, 17.59 and 17.61 *ante*) apply. Section 67(3) makes it clear that the powers in the Land Drainage Act 1991 do not preclude the need to obtain consent under the Ancient Monuments and Archaeological Areas Act 1979. Section 67(4) provides that in the exercise of the powers conferred by the Act, due regard shall be had to the interests of fisheries, including sea fisheries. An equivalent provision is contained in section 105(3) of the Water Resources Act 1991 (see paragraph 17.51 *ante*).

By-laws

17.84 The EA may make by-laws under paragraph 5 of Schedule 25 to the Water Resources Act 1991 in relation to any particular locality or localities if it considers it necessary to do so for securing the efficient working of any drainage system including the proper defence of any land against sea or tidal water. In particular, by-laws under paragraph 5 may be made for regulating the use and preventing the improper use of any watercourses, banks or works vested in the EA or under its control, for preserving them from damage or destruction, or for regulating the opening of sluices or floodgates in connection with any such works. The by-laws require to be confirmed by the relevant Minister and must be made in accordance with the procedure set out in Schedule 26 to the Water Resources Act 1991 which includes the advertising of the by-laws and the giving of notice on any persons carrying out functions under any enactment who appear to be concerned.

17.85 Under section 66 of the Land Drainage Act 1991 an IDB may make such by-laws as they consider necessary for securing the efficient working of the drainage system in their district. Like by-laws made by the EA, such by-laws may regulate the use and prevent the improper use of any watercourses, banks or works vested in the IDB or under their control or for preserving any such watercourses, banks or works from damage or destruction and may regulate the opening of sluices and flood gates in connection with any such works. An IDB may not make by-laws in connection with a main river or the banks of such river. By-laws made by an IDB under section 66 are subject to confirmation by the relevant Minister and must be made in accordance with the procedure set out in Schedule 5 to the Land Drainage Act 1991 which is similar to that contained in Schedule 26 to the Water Resources Act 1991 referred to above.

17.86 The powers in section 66 of the Land Drainage Act 1991 are also exercisable by a local authority for securing the efficient working of the drainage system in their area but only so far as may be necessary for the purpose of preventing flooding or remedying or mitigating any damage caused by flooding. The power may not be exercised by an English county council unless the county council is exercising land drainage powers under the provisions of section 16 of the Land Drainage Act 1991 (see paragraph 17.76 *ante*). The by-laws must be confirmed by the relevant Minister and the procedure for by-laws in section 236 of the Local Government Act 1972 applies.

17.87 Under section 66, it is an offence for a person to act in contravention of, or fail to comply with, any by-law made under section 66 punishable, on summary conviction, to a fine not exceeding level 5 on the standard scale[17] and, if the contravention or failure is continued after conviction, to a further fine not exceeding £40 for every day on which the contravention or failure is so continued. In addition, an IDB or local authority may take any action which may be necessary to remedy the effect of the contravention or failure and recover the expenses reasonably incurred in doing so from the person in default.

17.88 By-laws made under paragraph 5 of Schedule 25 to the Water Resources Act 1991 or under section 66 of the Land Drainage Act 1991 must not conflict with or interfere with the operation of any by-law made by a navigation authority, harbour authority or conservancy authority.

17.89 The above powers to make by-laws, and to apply them, are subject to the general environmental duties of the EA, IDBs and local authorities set out in paragraphs 17.101 and 17.102 *post*.

Financial provisions

Financing of the EA

17.90 For the purposes of its flood defence functions, the EA is a levying body within the meaning of section 74 of the Local Government Finance Act 1988, which provides for the making of regulations authorizing a levying body to issue a levy on local authorities.

Financing of internal drainage boards

17.91 Part IV of the Land Drainage Act 1991 provides for the financing of IDBs. The expenses of the IDBs (including any contributions to the expenses of the EA) are, by section 36 of the Land Drainage Act 1991, insofar as not met by the EA, to be raised by means of drainage rates under Chapter II of Part IV and special levies by virtue of the Local Government Finance Act 1988. Part IV of the Land Drainage Act 1991 makes provision for the apportionment of the rates and for the levying of differential rates by subdividing districts for that purpose. Under section 57 of that Act, the EA has power in certain circumstances, on an application from an IDB, to pay contributions to the IDB. The IDB, if dissatisfied by the EA's response, may appeal to the relevant Minister. Section 58 enables the EA, where it is itself the IDB, to allocate from its revenues received other than as an IDB, a sum corresponding to that which it would have made to the IDB under section 57 if it were not itself the IDB. Section 58 also enables the EA to defray, out of the sums received by it as the IDB, an amount equal to the contribution it could have required the IDB to pay to it, under section 139 of the Water Resources Act

---

17. Level 5 on the standard scale is currently £5,000.

1991, were it not the IDB. IDBs are eligible to receive ministerial grants under section 59 of the Land Drainage Act 1991 (see paragraph 19.95 *post*).

Contributions to the Environment Agency from Internal Drainage Boards

17.92 The EA is under a duty imposed by section 139 of the Water Resources Act 1991 to require every IDB to make such contribution towards the expenses of the EA as the EA considers to be fair. There are exceptions in the case of main internal drainage districts and provisions for appeal.

Special duties of Environment Agency with respect to flood defence revenue

17.93 Section 118 of the Water Resources Act 1991 provides that, subject to certain exceptions, revenue raised by the EA in relation to flood defence and land drainage, shall be spent only in the carrying out of the EA's flood defence functions (which include land drainage) in or for the benefit of the local flood defence district in which it is raised and shall be disregarded in determining the amount of any surplus for the purposes of section 44(4) of the Environment Act 1995 which enables the appropriate Minister to direct the EA to pay to him the whole or part of any surplus on capital or revenue account.

Navigation tolls

17.94 Section 143 of the Water Resources Act 1991 enables the EA (with the consent of the Secretary of State) to levy navigation tolls in respect of navigable waters in England and Wales and so much of the territorial sea adjacent to England and Wales as is included in the area of a regional flood defence committee, where those waters are not under the control of any navigation authority, harbour authority or conservancy authority. The Secretary of State must be satisfied that the cost of the maintenance or works in connection with the waters has been or will be increased as a result of the use of those waters for the purposes of navigation.

Ministerial grants

17.95 Section 59 of the Land Drainage Act 1991 enables Ministers to make grants towards expenditure incurred by IDBs or by other bodies (except the EA) in the exercise of their functions in carrying out drainage schemes. That provision was amended by the Environment Act 1995 to enable grants to be made towards studies to determine whether drainage works should be carried out, obtaining or organising information (including information about natural processes affecting the coastline) to enable the formulation or development of plans with regard to the defence against sea water of any part of the coastline or obtaining, after the carrying out of drainage works, information with respect to the quality or effectiveness, or the effect, on the environment, of the works of any matter of a financial nature relating to the works.

17.96 The relevant Minister may make grants under section 147 of the Water Resources Act 1991 towards expenditure incurred by the EA in the improvement of existing drainage works and the construction of new drainage. Again, these powers were extended by the Environment Act 1995 so that grants could be given to the EA to cover the additional matters set out in paragraph 17.95 *ante*.

17.97 Section 148 of the Water Resources Act 1991 enables Ministers to make grants towards expenditure incurred by the EA in providing or installing apparatus, or carrying out other engineering or building operations, for the purposes of flood warning systems. Further grants powers are contained in section 149 of that Act in respect of the exercise by the EA of its land drainage powers under section 165 of that Act.

17.98 Under section 21 of the Coast Protection Act 1949, the relevant Minister may make grants towards any expenditure incurred by a coast protection authority or by the council of a county or county borough in the carrying out of coast protection work under the enactments relating to highways.

17.99 The current government policy for the appraisal of projects qualifying for grants is set out in Guidance Notes published by the Ministry of Agriculture, Fisheries and Food entitled "Flood and Coastal Defence Project Appraisal Guidance Notes" (February 1995).

Contributions by county councils to coast protection authorities

17.100 Under section 20 of the Coast Protection Act 1949, where the Minister undertakes to make, or makes, a grant under section 21 of the Coast Protection Act 1949 to a maritime district council, the county council within which the maritime district is situated must pay to the maritime district council a contribution towards that expenditure of such amount and payable at such time as may be agreed or, in default of agreement, may be determined by the Minister in accordance with the provisions of that section. In addition, the county council may make contributions towards any expenses incurred by any person other than a maritime district council within the county in respect of coast protection work carried out within the county or appearing to the council to be work for the protection of land within the county. A coast protection authority may contribute towards the cost of carrying out any coast protection work, whether within or outside their area, which appears to them to be work for the protection of land within their area.

General environmental duties

17.101 Section 7 of the Environment Act 1995 and sections 61A and 61B of the Land Drainage Act 1991 require the EA, IDBs and local authorities respectively to contribute to the conservation of nature and the heritage when carrying out their flood defence functions under the relevant Acts, the main duties being:

(a) to further the conservation and enhancement of natural beauty, and conservation of flora, fauna and geological or physiographical features of special interest, so far as may be consistent with the purposes of any enactments relating to their functions and, in the case of the EA, with any guidance given to it under section 4 of the 1995 Act;

(b) to have regard to the desirability of protecting and conserving buildings, sites and objects of archaeological, architectural or historic interest (and in the case of the EA engineering interest);

(c) to have regard to the desirability of preserving public access to areas of woodland, mountains, moor, heath, down, cliff or foreshore and other places of natural beauty, and to buildings, sites and objects of archaeological, architectural or historic interest (and in the case of the EA engineering interest); and

(d) to take into account any effect which proposals would have on the preservation of such public access or on the beauty or amenity of any rural or urban area, or on any flora, fauna, features, buildings, sites or objects.

In addition the EA is required to have regard to any effect which proposals would have on the economic and social well-being of local communities in rural areas.

17.102 Subject to other legislative provisions, the EA is required under section 4(4) of the 1995 Act to discharge its functions towards obtaining the objective of achieving sustainable development in accordance with guidance issued by Ministers. Section 6(1) of the 1995 Act imposes a duty on the EA generally to promote, to such extent as it considers desirable:

(a) the conservation and enhancement of the natural beauty and amenity of inland and coastal waters and of land associated with such waters;

(b) the conservation of flora and fauna which are dependent on an aquatic environment; and

(c) the use of such waters and land for recreational purposes.

17.103 The Acts also contain specific provisions in respect of sites of special interest notified to the EA, IDBs or local authorities by English Nature or the Countryside Council for Wales, and in respect of notified areas within National Parks or the Broads. In summary, operating authorities are required to consult the notifying body before undertaking any potentially damaging works, operations or activities other than in an emergency, in which case the notifying body must be told as soon as practicable.

17.104 Under section 9 of the Environment Act 1995, each relevant Minister may issue, or approve, codes of practice for the purpose of giving practical guidance to the EA with respect to their environmental functions and for promoting desirable practices by the EA with respect to those functions. There is similar power for Ministers to issue codes of practice to IDBs and local authorities under section 61E of the Land Drainage Act 1991. (The Code of Practice referred to in paragraph 17.02 *ante* was issued under these provisions.) Ministers may give directions to an IDB under section 61D of the Land Drainage Act 1991 if they consider that any works, operations or activities carried on by the IDB are likely to destroy or seriously damage flora, fauna, building structures or sites, or objects of archaeological, architectural or historic interest which they consider to be of national or international importance.

17.105 The above statutory environmental duties apply to all flood defence and land drainage related activities carried on by the EA, IDBs and local authorities, and conservation and environmental issues must be taken into account in applying flood defence and land drainage by-laws.

Application of general legislation regulating coastal development

Town and Country Planning legislation

17.106 Coast protection works and new flood defence works generally require planning permission under the Town and Country Planning Act 1990 (see paragraph 17.61 *ante*). However, certain flood defence and land drainage improvement schemes currently have deemed consent under the Town and Country Planning (General Permitted Development) Order 1995 and the equivalent Order in force in Scotland. The development authorized by the 1995 Order is specified in Parts 14 and 15 of Schedule 2 to the Order. Part 14 covers "development by a drainage body in, on or under any watercourse or land drainage works and required in connection with the improvement, maintenance or repair of that watercourse or those works", "drainage body" meaning an IDB or any other body having power to make or maintain works for the drainage of land. Part 15 covers specified development by the EA, for the purposes of their functions, including (*inter alia*) "development in, on or under any watercourse or land drainage works and required in connection with the improvement, maintenance or repair of that watercourse or those works".

17.107 Relevant government guidance on planning is provided by the DoE and Welsh Office to local planning authorities in a Planning Policy Guidance Note on coastal planning known as PPG20 which is described in paragraphs 16.37 to 16.44 *ante*. Further guidance is given by Circular 30/92 issued jointly by the Department of the Environment, the Ministry of Agriculture, Fisheries and Food and the Welsh Office. That Circular advises that local authorities should consult the EA (as successor to the National Rivers Authority), which is a statutory consultee in the preparation of development plans, and, where appropriate, IDBs and should take account of the results of surveys of flood risk areas undertaken by the EA under section 105 of the Water Resources Act 1991 and other information provided by the EA. The Circular also advises that local planning authorities should take account of Ministerial advice on sea level rise and global warming.

17.108 PPG20 and Circular 30/92 state that the Government looks to local authorities to use their planning powers to guide development away from areas that may be affected by flooding or instability, to restrict development that would itself increase the risk of flooding or interfere with the operations of the flood and coastal defence authorities and to seek to minimise development in areas at risk. Planning authorities are required to adopt a precautionary approach.

Environmental assessment

17.109 Flood defence capital works which may have a significant environmental impact are subject to the Town and Country Planning (Assessment of Environmental Effects) Regulations 1988 or, if they are improvements to existing works, to the Land Drainage Improvement Works (Assessment of Environmental Effects) Regulations 1988, as amended by the Land Drainage Improvement Works (Assessment of Environmental Effects) (Amendment) Regulations 1995. Those Regulations implement Council Directive 85/337/EEC on the assessment of the effects of certain public and private projects on the environment. The Regulations require the preparation of an environmental statement of the effects where the impact of these projects is likely to be significant (see further paragraphs 16.65 to 16.74 *ante*).

17.110 Also of relevance to the carrying out of coast protection works are the European Union Directive of 2 April 1979 on the conservation of wild birds (79/409/EEC), known as the Birds Directive, and the Council Directive of 21 May 1992 on the conservation of natural habitats and of wild fauna and flora (92/4/EEC), known as the Habitats Directive, and the UK legislation implementing those Directives. Details of these are set out in paragraphs 18.6 to 18.27 *post*.

Deposit of materials at sea

17.111 Operations for coast protection works and flood defence works which involve the deposit of materials below mean high water mark require a licence under the Food and Environment Protection Act 1985 (see paragraphs 16.52 and 16.53 *ante*).

The Ancient Monuments and Archaeological Areas Act 1979

17.112 The Coast Protection Act 1949, the Water Resources Act 1991 and the Land Drainage Act 1991 contain savings for the Ancient Monuments and

Archaeological Areas Act 1979. See paragraphs 17.43, 17.61 and 17.83 *ante*. So coastal protection or defence works which affect a monument, scheduled under that Act, must be authorized by consent of the Secretary of State under section 2 of that Act and carried out in accordance with that consent. Where works carried out in an area designated as an area of archaeological importance include flooding operations or operations which disturb the ground, notice of the operations must be served in accordance with section 35 of the 1979 Act.

Rights and obligations of private landowners

17.113 At common law a landowner may erect such sea defences as are necessary for the protection of his land on the sea coast. However, he may not interfere with existing sea defences even with a view to protecting his land. In *Symes* v. *Essex Rivers Catchment Board*[18] an owner of land to the seaward side of a sea wall made a gap underneath that wall with the object of letting sea water drain from his land to the landward side of the sea wall. It was held that this was unlawful because sea walls owed their origin to the Crown's prerogative to protect the realm against the incursion of sea water and to interfere with the sea wall would be contrary to public policy at common law. The right to erect coast protection works is now subject to section 16 of the Coast Protection Act 1949 under which the written consent of the coast protection authority is required for the carrying out of any coast protection work other than a work of maintenance or repair (see paragraph 17.30 *ante*).

17.114 Landowners are not under duty at common law to erect, or contribute to the cost of erecting or maintaining, sea defences but may be placed under such an obligation by tenure, custom, prescription, charter, contract or statute. Such obligations are not affected by the flood defence provisions of the Water Resources Act 1991 (see paragraph 17.62 *ante*) nor by the provisions in Part I of the Coast Protection Act 1949 (see paragraph 17.29 *ante*). By section 15(4) of the Coast Protection Act 1949 a coast protection authority is given power to enforce such an obligation and similar powers are conferred on the EA and IDBs by section 21 of the Land Drainage Act 1991 (see paragraphs 17.29 and 17.79 *ante*). The EA and IDBs have power under section 33 of the Land Drainage Act 1991 to commute such obligations (see paragraphs 17.80 and 17.81 *ante*).

17.115 The relevant Ministers are empowered by section 22 of the Land Drainage Act 1991 to make an order authorizing a person interested in land to carry out drainage works. The power is exercisable on application by the landowner concerned who must show that he is of the opinion that the land in question is capable of improvement by drainage works but the works cannot be carried out by reason of the objection or disability of any person whose land

18. *Symes* v. *Essex Rivers Catchment Board* [1936] 3 All E.R. 908, C.A.

would be entered upon, cut through or interfered with by or for the purposes of the works. Notice of the application must be given to all persons not parties to the application whose lands are proposed to be entered upon, cut through or interfered with, to the EA, and to the IDB for any district within which all or any of the proposed works are to be carried out. A public inquiry must be held if objection is made within a prescribed period by any person interested or in any way affected by the proposed works. After considering the report of any such inquiry, the Minister may refuse to authorize the carrying out of the works or may make an order authorizing the carrying out of the works with or without alteration. Compensation is payable to every person interested in land affected by the order who suffers injury by reason of the works, the amount being determined by the Lands Tribunal in case of a dispute. Broadly similar powers are given to the Minister to make an order under section 28(1) of the Coast Protection Act 1949 authorizing a person, other than a coast protection authority, to carry out coast protection works in accordance with a works scheme or a notice served under section 12 of the 1949 Act (see paragraph 17.39 *ante*).

17.116 The owners and occupiers of land on which coast protection works are situated may be required under section 12 of the Coast Protection Act 1949 to maintain or repair them (see paragraphs 17.20 to 17.22 *ante*).

CHAPTER 18

CONSERVATION AND COASTAL MANAGEMENT

18.1 Nature conservation has, in recent years, assumed an important role in development control. Nowhere has this been more noticeable than in the case of coasts and harbours whose natural features and wildlife habitats are now subject to a range of legal restrictions which can have profound effects upon, for example, the ability of a port to expand its activities. At the same time, and partly as a result of the growth in interest in conservation, attention is being focused upon the question of coastal management and, in particular, the scope for interaction between bodies, such as harbour authorities, local authorities and governmental agencies, in achieving an integrated approach to managing the coast. This chapter outlines the main legal mechanisms for achieving conservation, insofar as they relate to coasts and harbours, besides considering the question of coastal management.

Wildlife and Countryside Act 1981

Sites of Special Scientific Interest

18.2 The Wildlife and Countryside Act 1981 contains a procedure for designating areas known as Sites of Special Scientific Interest ("SSSIs") and for regulating the carrying on of activities on those sites. As at 1994, there were 3,794 SSSIs in England, covering 871,065 hectares. Identification and notification of SSSIs in England is carried out by English Nature. Owners and occupiers of an SSSI are given at least three months after the site is notified to make representations or objections (section 28). Unresolved objections are dealt with by the full Council of English Nature, who decide whether or not to confirm the notification. Confirmation must in all cases occur within nine months of notification; otherwise the notification will lapse and the site will no longer be an SSSI.

18.3 The effects of notification of an SSSI are, of themselves, not particularly severe, so far as the owner or occupier is concerned, at least when compared with the effect of designation as a Special Protection Area or Special Area of Conservation (see paragraphs 18.6 to 18.13 *post*). Owners and occupiers have a duty to give English Nature four months' notice in writing if they intend to carry out or permit to be carried out any operation listed in the

233

notification which is likely to change the special interest of the site (section 28(5), (6)). This period is intended to give English Nature time to consider the implications of the proposals and to discuss modifications which might avoid damage to the special interest. The operation may be carried out before four months have elapsed if:

(a) consent has been granted by English Nature;
(b) it is to be carried out under the terms of a management agreement with English Nature;
(c) it has to be undertaken in an emergency; or
(d) it has been authorized by a planning permission granted on an application to the local planning authority (i.e. not as permitted development—see Chapter 14, (section 28(6), (8)).

18.4 After four months, the operation may be carried out in any event, unless (which is rare) the Secretary of State has made a Nature Conservation Order under section 29 which in certain circumstances has the effect of extending the statutory negation period to 12 months. It will be appreciated that operations which constitute development within the meaning of the Town and Country Planning Act 1990 will require planning permission. Development within an SSSI will be subject to special scrutiny by the local planning authority (see PPG9: Nature Conservation (1994) paragraphs 29 to 35). Furthermore, it should be noted that certain forms of development (such as development by harbour authorities on their operational land) will not be permitted development for which planning permission is automatically granted by the General Permitted Development Order if an environmental assessment would be needed. In the case of an SSSI, such an assessment is, clearly, as a general matter more likely to be required than in the case of land which has not been given that classification (see paragraph 16.33 *ante*). Under the Town and Country Planning (General Development Procedure) Order 1995, English Nature must be consulted before a local planning authority grants permission for the development of land in an SSSI. In the case of Wales, the functions of English Nature described in this and the preceding paragraphs are undertaken by the Countryside Council for Wales. In Scotland the relevant body is Scottish Natural Heritage.

Marine nature reserves

18.5 Under section 36 of the Wildlife and Countryside Act 1981 the Secretary of State may designate an area of land covered (continuously or intermittently) by tidal waters, or parts of the sea up to the seaward limits of territorial waters, as a marine nature reserve. The purpose of such designation is to conserve marine flora and fauna or geological or physiographical features; or to allow study of such features. English Nature/Countryside Council for Wales/Scottish Natural Heritage may make by-laws for the protection of marine nature reserves, except where these would interfere with the by-law-making functions of another authority, such as a harbour authority. Currently, the only marine nature reserve is at Lundy Island in the Bristol Channel.

Special protection areas under the Birds Directive

18.6 Two Directives of (what is now) the European Union are of particular importance as regards the conservation of the coast and harbour areas. The Council Directive of 2 April 1979 on the Conservation of Wild Birds (79/409/EEC), known as the Birds Directive, establishes a scheme for the conservation of all species of naturally occurring birds in the wild state in the European territory of the Member States, and covers the protection, management and control of these species, laying down rules for their exploitation (Article 1). Article 2 requires Member States to take the requisite measures to maintain the population of the species referred to in Article 1 at a level which corresponds in particular to ecological, scientific and cultural requirements, while taking account of economic and recreational requirements, or to adapt the population of these species to that level. In the light of these requirements, Article 3 requires Member States to take requisite measures to preserve, maintain or re-establish a sufficient diversity and area of habitats for all the species of birds referred to in Article 1. Amongst the measures specified in Article 3 for preserving, maintaining and re-establishing biotypes and habitats is the creation of "protected areas". Particularly rare and/or vulnerable species are listed in Annex I to the Directive. Article 4 requires Member States to:

"classify in particular the most suitable territories in number and size as special protection areas for the conservation of these species, taking into account their protection requirements in the geographical sea and land area where this Directive applies".

Article 4 also requires Member States to take similar measures for regularly occurring migratory species not listed in Annex I, bearing in mind their need for protection in the geographical sea and land area where the Directive applies, as regards their breeding, moulting and wintering areas and staging posts along their migration routes. To this end, Member States are required to pay particular attention to the protection of wetlands and particularly to wetlands of international importance.

18.7 The importance of the Birds Directive for harbour authorities and others wishing to carry out development or similar activities on the coast lies in the restrictions which apply in respect of the areas known as Special Protection Areas (or "SPAs") designated under Article 4. As originally drafted, the first sentence of Article 4(4) provided that:

"In respect of the protection areas referred to in [Article 4(1) and (2)] above, Member States shall take appropriate steps to avoid pollution or deterioration of habitats or any disturbances affecting the birds, insofar as these would be significant having regard to the objectives of this Article."

In the *Leybucht Dykes* case[1] the EC Commission sought an injunction to prevent dyke-building works which were detrimental to the habitat of birds in an area which had been designated as an SPA. The European Court held that the first sentence of Article 4(1), just quoted, did not enable Germany to amend the boundaries of the SPA (so as to exclude the site of the works) on economic grounds. The economic and recreational interests referred to in Article 2 were not, the Court said, exceptional grounds corresponding to a general interest which was superior to the interest represented by the ecological objective of the Directive. However, the Court held that the need to ensure human safety by preventing flooding and ensuring coastal protection was a superior general interest.

18.8 Concern over the narrowness of the grounds upon which Member States could authorize development adversely affecting an SPA led to the replacement of the first sentence of Article 4(1) by a new set of criteria which permit economic considerations to be taken into account in certain (albeit limited) circumstances. Article 7 of the Council Directive of 21 May 1992 on the Conservation of Natural Habitats and of Wild Fauna and Flora (92/4/EEC), known as the Habitats Directive, replaces the sentence by the obligations set out in Article 6(2), (3) and (4) of the latter Directive, as from the date of implementation of that Directive (30 October 1994, in the case of the United Kingdom) or the date of classification or recognition of the SPA, whichever is later. Article 6(2), (3) and (4) are dealt with at paragraph 18.12 *post*. Briefly stated, however, Member States are allowed to permit projects which (after appropriate environmental assessment) have been found will adversely affect the integrity of the SPA, if the project must be carried out "for imperative reasons of overriding public interest, including those of a social or economic nature". There are two caveats. First, the Member State is required to take all compensatory measures necessary to ensure that the overall coherence of "Natura 2000" is protected, and to inform the Commission of the compensatory measures adopted. Natura 2000 is the proposed European ecological network of SPAs under the Birds Directive and Special Areas of Conservation under the Habitats Directive itself. Second, if (notwithstanding that the site is an SPA designated by reference to the ornithological criteria in the Birds Directive) the site hosts a priority natural habitat type and/or a priority species within the meaning of the Habitats Directive, then the only considerations which may be raised are those relating to human health or public safety, to beneficial consequences of primary importance for the environment or, further to an opinion from the Commission, to other imperative

---

1. *Commission v. Fed. Rep. Germany* Case C57/ 89, 28 February 1991, unreported.

reasons of overriding public interest. The enforcement of these provisions in Great Britain is effected by the Conservation (Natural Habitats &c.) Regulations 1994 (see paragraphs 18.16 to 18.25 *post*).

18.9 In the *Leybucht Dykes* case, the European Court had expressed the view that Member States have a discretion in deciding what sites should be designated as SPAs under Article 4 of the Birds Directive. In the case of *R. v. Secretary of State for the Environment ex parte Royal Society for the Protection of Birds*[2] (the *Lappel Bank* case) the European Court categorically rejected the United Kingdom's argument (which had found favour with the English Court of Appeal) that a Member State may take economic considerations into account in deciding, under Article 4 of the Birds Directive, which are the "most suitable" territories to designate as SPAs. The facts of *Lappel Bank* are that, on 15 December 1993, the Secretary of State for the Environment decided to designate the Medway Estuary and Marshes as an SPA but with the omission of some 22 hectares known as Lappel Bank, which were required by the Port of Sheerness for port expansion. Lappel Bank was the only area into which the Port could realistically have envisaged expanding. The Secretary of State had regard to the significant contribution which the expansion of the Port would make to both the national and local economies and concluded that this outweighed the site's nature conservation value. The Royal Society for the Protection of Birds sought to have the Secretary of State's decision quashed on the ground that he was not entitled, by virtue of the Birds Directive, to have regard to economic considerations when classifying an SPA. Although the RSPB were unsuccessful before both the Divisional Court and the Court of Appeal, the House of Lords sought a preliminary ruling from the European Court as to the interpretation of the Directive. The European Court found in favour of the RSPB. It held that the economic and recreational considerations mentioned in Article 2 of the Directive are irrelevant in deciding which sites should be designated as SPAs and that economic interests cannot correspond to a general interest superior to that represented by the ecological objective of the Directive. Finally, the Court held that, notwithstanding the changes effected by Articles 6(2) to (4) and 7 of the Habitats Directive (see paragraph 18.8 *ante*) when deciding upon the designation of an SPA it is not possible to take account of economic requirements even to the extent that they reflect imperative reasons of overriding public interest of the kind referred to in Article 6(4). Accordingly, if an area qualifies on ornithological grounds for designation as part of an SPA, it must be so designated, even though a project may already be proposed for that site which could be justified on the grounds of economic requirements constituting imperative reasons of overriding public interest.

---

2. Case C44/95, 11 July 1996, unreported.

Special areas of conservation under the Habitats Directive

18.10 The Habitats Directive, to which reference has already been made, was issued on 21 May 1992 with the main aim of promoting the maintenance of biodiversity. This is to be achieved by the designation and protection of a European ecological network of special areas of conservation (SACs) and special protection areas under the Birds Directive, bearing the title of Natura 2000 (see paragraph 18.8 *ante*). The network is to be composed of sites hosting the natural habitat types listed in Annex I to the Directive and habitats of the species listed in Annex II, so as to enable the natural habitat types and species' habitats to be maintained or, where appropriate, restored at a favourable conservation status in their natural range (Article 3(1)). Amongst the habitats listed in Annex I are "sandbanks which are slightly covered by sea water all the time", estuaries, mudflats and sandflats not covered by sea water at low tide, lagoons (a priority habitat type) and large shallow inlets and bays. The criteria for selection of SACs are contained in Annex III to the Directive.

18.11 The process whereby a site is designated as an SAC is complex. Each Member State is required first to notify the European Commission of a list of sites in its territory indicating to which natural habitat types and species in Annexes I and II the sites are host. Then, on the basis of the criteria set out in Annex III, the Commission is required to establish, in agreement with each Member State, a draft list of sites of Community importance drawn from the Member States' list. The list of sites selected as sites of Community importance is then to be adopted by the Commission (within six years of notification of the Directive). Once a site of Community importance has been adopted in accordance with the procedure just mentioned, the Member State must then formally designate the site as an SAC "as soon as possible and within six years at most". Priorities must be established, in the light of their importance, for the maintenance or restoration of a natural habitat type in Annex I or a species in Annex II and for the coherence of Natura 2000, and in the light of the threats of degradation or destruction to which those sites are exposed (Article 4).

18.12 Article 6 of the Directive is of particular importance, since it deals with the consequences of a site being designated as an SAC. Each Member State is required to establish the necessary conservation measures involving, if need be, appropriate management plans specifically designed for the sites or integrated into other development plans, and appropriate statutory, administrative or contractual measures which correspond to the ecological requirements of the natural habitat types and species present on the sites (Article 6(1)). Member States must take appropriate steps to avoid the deterioration in SACs of natural habitats of species as well as disturbance of the species for which the areas have been designated, insofar as such disturbance could be significant in relation to the objectives of the Directive (Article 6(2)). Any plan or project not directly connected with or necessary to the management of the site but likely to have a significant effect thereon (either individually or in combination with other plans or projects) is required to be subject to the appropriate assessment of its implications for the site in view of the site's conservation objectives. In the light of the conclusions of this assessment, the competent national authorities shall agree to the plan or project only after ascertaining that it will not affect the integrity of the site concerned and, if appropriate, after having obtained the opinion of the general public (Article 6(3)). Article 6(4), however, introduces a limited exception allowing a plan or project to be carried out in spite of a negative assessment of its implications for the SAC and in the absence of alternative solutions. Where the plan or project must be carried out for imperative reasons of overriding public interest, including those of a social or economic nature, it may be permitted, provided that the Member State takes all compensatory measures necessary to ensure that the overall coherence of Natura 2000 is protected and it must inform the Commission of the compensatory measures adopted. However, if the SAC hosts a priority natural habitat type (such as a lagoon) and/or a priority species (in each case designated as such in Annex I or II, as the case may be) then the only considerations which may be raised are those relating to human health or public safety, to beneficial consequences of primary importance to the environment or, further to an opinion from the Commission itself, to other imperative reasons of overriding public interest.

18.13 It is important to be aware that Article 6(2) to (4) applies not only to formally designated SACs but also to sites of Community importance which have been placed on a list by the Commission under Article 4(2) (see paragraph 18.11 *ante*).

Ramsar convention on wetlands of international importance especially as waterfowl habitat

18.14 The United Kingdom is a contracting party to the Convention signed in Ramsar, Iran, in February 1971 which seeks to protect wetlands of international importance especially as a waterfowl habitat. Each contracting party is required to designate within its territory suitable areas of wetlands for inclusion in a list to be maintained by the International Union for Conservation of Nature and Natural Resources. Wetlands for this purpose are areas of marsh, fen, peatland or water, whether natural or artificial, permanent or temporary, with water that is static or flowing, fresh, brackish or salt, including areas of marine water the depth of which at low tide does not exceed six metres. Contracting parties are required by Article 3 to formulate and implement their planning so as to promote the conservation of the wetlands included in the list, and as far as possible the "wise use" of wetlands (Article 3(1)).

18.15 Unlike the Birds and Habitat Directives, which are implemented by a specific and wide-ranging set of regulations, Ramsar sites in the United Kingdom have had to look to the town and country planning system for their protection. However, since Ramsar sites in the United Kingdom tend also to be SPAs, they will in any event be subject to the regulations discussed below.

Conservation (Natural Habitats, etc.) Regulations 1994

18.16 The United Kingdom has implemented the Habitats Directive by means of the Conservation (Natural Habitats, etc.) Regulations 1994. These regulations, which came into force on 30 October 1994, apply to:

(a) SACs;
(b) sites of Community importance which have been placed on the list established by the Commission under Article 4(2) of the Habitats Directive (see paragraph 18.11 *ante*);
(c) certain sites hosting a priority natural habitat type or priority species which, in an exceptional case, the Commission finds that the preliminary national list of candidate SACs fails to mention, during the consultation period or pending a decision of the Council of Ministers under Article 5 of the Habitats Directive; and
(d) SPAs designated under the Birds Directive.

Together with SACs, these other sites and areas are referred to in the regulations as "European sites" (regulation 10). Sites which are European sites only by virtue of (c) above are, however, not subject to certain regulations relating to the approval of certain plans and projects, including regulation 48 (as to which see paragraph 18.20 *post*).

18.17 European sites are kept on a register and notified to the appropriate nature conservation body (i.e. English Nature, the Countryside Council for Wales or Scottish Natural Heritage), to owners/occupiers of the relevant land, and to the local planning authorities in which the site (or part) is situated (regulations 11, 12). Provisions in the regulations relating to management agreements, notification of potentially damaging operations and restrictions upon carrying out operations specified in the notification (including the ability to go ahead with the operation after four months) largely follow those in the Wildlife and Countryside Act 1981 in the case of Sites of Special Scientific Interest (which European sites will also be). If the Secretary of State makes a special nature conservation order under regulation 22, specifying operations which appear to him to be likely to destroy or damage the flora, fauna or geographical or physiographical features by virtue of which the land is a European site, the operations cannot be carried out unless either the appropriate nature conservation body has given its written consent or the operation is carried out in accordance with the terms of a management agreement with that body, entered into under regulation 16. Contravention of these restrictions is a criminal offence punishable by a fine.

European marine sites

18.18 The regulations contain a number of special provisions for those European sites which comprise or include any land covered (whether continuously or intermittently) by tidal waters or any part of the sea in or adjacent to Great Britain up to the seaward limit of territorial waters. Insofar as a European site contains such land (known as a "marine area") it constitutes a European marine site (EMS) (regulation 2). The appropriate nature conservation body is empowered by regulation 33 to install markers indicating the existence of an EMS, subject to obtaining coast protection consent under section 34 of the Coast Protection Act 1949 (see Chapter 16). Important functions in respect of EMSs are conferred upon the "relevant authorities" which comprise the following bodies (having existing functions in relation to land or waters within or adjacent to the EMS):

   (a) a nature conservation body;
   (b) a county council, district council, London borough council or, in Scotland, an islands or other council;
   (c) the Environment Agency, a water undertaker or sewerage undertaker, or an internal drainage board;
   (d) a navigation authority within the meaning of the Water Resources Act 1991;
   (e) a harbour authority within the meaning of the Harbours Act 1964;
   (f) a lighthouse authority;
   (g) the Scottish Environmental Protection Agency or a district salmon fishery board;
   (h) a local fisheries committee under the Sea Fisheries Regulation Act 1966 or any authority exercising the powers of such a committee (regulation 5).

18.19 The relevant authorities, or any of them, are empowered by regulation 34 to establish for an EMS a management scheme under which their functions (including any power to make by-laws) are to be exercised so as to secure compliance with the Habitats Directive in relation to the EMS. In England the Secretary of State and the Minister of Agriculture, Fisheries and Food acting jointly (and elsewhere the Secretary of State) may give directions to the relevant authorities or any of them as to the establishment of a management scheme for an EMS. These directions may, *inter alia*, require specified conservation measures to be included in the scheme, appoint one of the relevant authorities to co-ordinate the establishment of the scheme, set time limits within which any steps are to be taken, and provide that the Minister's approval is required before the scheme is established (regulation 35). It is noteworthy that regulations 34 and 35 represent an exception to the Government's policy whereby coastal management schemes are seen as voluntary management between bodies having relevant statutory responsibilities (see paragraph 18.31 *post*).

Adaptation of planning and other controls

18.20 Part IV of the Regulations adopts planning and other controls for the protection of European sites. Regulations 48 and 49 give effect to Article 6(3) and (4) of the Habitats Directive (paragraph 18.12 *ante*). Regulation 48 requires a competent authority, before deciding to undertake or give any consent, permission or other authorization for a plan or project which is likely to have a significant effect on a European site in Great Britain (either alone or in combination with other plans or projects) and which is not directly connected with or necessary to the management of the site, to make an appropriate assessment of the implications of the project for the site. "Competent authority" is widely defined to include any Minister, local authority and statutory undertaker (regulation 6). As a result, a harbour authority will find itself to be a competent authority for the purpose of regulation 48 and (subject to what is said at paragraph 18.23 *post*) it must, therefore, comply with regulations 48 to 53, not only in the case of projects which it is undertaking or planning to undertake, but also in the case of projects which require its approval (e.g. in the form of dredging or works licences). Furthermore, in the case of, e.g., a harbour authority which is proposing a project which is likely to have a significant effect on an SPA or other European site, the local planning authority must operate in accordance with regulations 48 and 49 in deciding whether to grant planning permission for any development comprised in that project (regulation 54).

18.21 Regulation 49 gives effect to Article 6(4) of the Habitats Directive by setting out the circumstances in which a competent authority may agree to the plan or project notwithstanding a negative assessment of the implications for the site (see paragraph 18.12 *ante*). The Secretary of State is given power to prohibit another competent authority from giving their agreement to the plan or project (regulation 49(6)). Any request for the opinion of the European Commission in the case of a site hosting a priority habitat type or priority species must be channelled through the Secretary of State who may decide not to seek the Commission's opinion (regulation 49(3), (4)).

18.22 Regulation 50 requires competent authorities to review plans or projects which they have decided to undertake, or for which they have given consent, upon the site's becoming a European site or, if later, upon the commencement of the regulations. An assessment of the implications of the plan or project must be undertaken in accordance with regulation 48. Following the review, the appropriate authority must affirm, modify or revoke the consent, permission or other authorization which they have granted, depending upon the effect which the plan or project will have. Where no statutory procedures exist for reviewing existing consents etc. (for example, in the case of works or dredging licensed by a harbour authority) the Secretary of State may give directions as to the procedure to be followed (regulation 50(3)). Regulation 51 applies the provisions of regulations 48(5) and (6) and 49 in the case of a review so as to ensure that reviewed plans or projects are permitted to proceed only in the same circumstances as plans or projects which arise after the commencement of the Regulations or the date on which the site becomes a European site.

18.23 It has been seen how, in the example of a harbour authority given at paragraph 18.20 *ante*, more than one competent authority may be involved. Regulation 52 provides for co-ordination in such circumstances by stating that nothing in regulation 48(1) or 50(2) requires a competent authority to assess any implications of a plan or project which would be more appropriately assessed under that provision by another competent authority. The Secretary of State may issue guidance to authorities for the purposes of regulations 48 to 51 as to the circumstances in which an authority may or should adopt the reasoning or conclusions of another competent authority as to whether a plan or project is likely to have a significant effect on a European site or will adversely affect the integrity of a European site. The authorities involved are required to have regard to any guidance so issued. In determining whether a plan or project should be agreed on the grounds of overriding public interest, a competent authority other than the Secretary of State must seek and have regard to the views of the other competent authorities involved.

18.24 Regulation 53 requires the Secretary of State to secure that any necessary compensatory measures are taken to ensure the protection of the overall coherence of Natura 2000, where a plan or project is agreed to (or allowed to proceed following review) notwithstanding a negative assessment of the implications for a European site.

18.25 Regulations 55 to 59 provide for the review of extant planning permissions which have not been completed, as per regulations 50 and 51 (see paragraph 18.22 *ante*). A local planning authority in England and Wales is required to consider whether any adverse effects on the European site could be overcome by planning obligations (that it to say, section 106 agreements) and, if so, to invite those concerned to enter into such obligations. To the extent that they cannot be overcome, the planning consent is to be revoked under the procedure in section 97 of the Town and Country Planning Act 1990, including the payment of compensation (regulation 59).

General development orders

18.26 Chapter 16 showed how statutory undertakers, such as harbour authorities, enjoy certain permitted development rights under the General Permitted Development Order 1995 (or its Scottish equivalent) although, in

England and Wales, those rights, so far as they relate to development on operational land, are removed where the nature of the development is such that it requires an environmental assessment to be carried out (paragraph 16.33 *ante*). The Regulations introduce a separate set of restrictions upon the ability to undertake development permitted by general development order which apply not only to development on operational land but also to development authorized under a private Act or an order under the Harbours Act 1964 (see paragraph 16.31 *ante*). Regulation 60 provides that it shall be a condition of any planning permission granted by general development order, whether made before or after the commencement of the Regulations (30 October 1994), that development which is likely to have a significant effect on a European site (either alone or in combination with other plans or projects) and is not directly connected with or necessary to the management of the site, shall not be begun until the developer has received written notification of the approval of the local planning authority under regulation 62. A corresponding requirement applies in the case of a planning permission granted by such a general development order where the development was begun but not completed before the commencement of the Regulations. The appropriate nature conservation body may be asked to give a written opinion on whether the development is likely to have a significant effect, as mentioned above. An opinion in the negative is conclusive of that question for the purpose of reliance on the planning permission granted by a general development order (regulation 61). Regulation 62 contains the procedure for obtaining the approval of the local planning authority for the purposes of regulation 60. The appropriate nature conservation body is required to be notified. Again, an opinion from that body that the development will not be likely to have a significant effect on the European site will be conclusive. In any other case the local planning authority is required to take account of any representations of the appropriate nature conservation body in making an appropriate assessment of the implications of the development for the site in view of the site's conservation objectives. In the light of the conclusions of that assessment, the local planning authority shall approve the development only after having ascertained that it will not adversely affect the integrity of the site. The developer may appeal to the Secretary of State against an unfavourable determination of the local planning authority (regulation 63).

18.27 Regulations 75 and 79 apply regulations 48 and 49 (see paragraphs 18.20 and 18.21 *ante*) to, respectively, the granting of a pipeline construction order or diversion authorization under the Pipelines Act 1962 and the making of an order under section 1 or 3 of the Transport and Works Act 1992. (Section 3 orders concern, *inter alia*, the authorization of works interfering with public rights of navigation—see paragraph 16.9 *ante*). In each case there is a requirement to review certain authorizations or orders already granted. If necessary, such authorizations and consents may be varied or revoked (regulations 76 to 78 and 80 to 82).

By-laws

18.28 The appropriate nature conservation body is empowered by regulation 28 to make by-laws under section 20 of the National Parks and Access to the Countryside Act 1949 for the protection of a European site. Amongst other matters, such by-laws may prohibit or restrict the entry into or movement within the site of persons, vehicles, boats and animals. By-laws may also prohibit or restrict these, and certain other, activities within areas surrounding or adjoining the site. By-laws may not, however, interfere with the exercise of any functions of statutory undertakers (including harbour authorities) (regulation 29(c)).

Conservation duties of harbour authorities

18.29 Section 48A of the Harbours Act 1964 (which was inserted by the Transport and Works Act 1992) provides that it shall be the duty of a harbour authority in formulating or considering any proposals relating to its functions under any enactment to have regard to:

(a) the conservation of the natural beauty of the countryside and of flora, fauna and geological or physiographical features of special interest;
(b) the desirability of preserving for the public any freedom of access to places of natural beauty; and
(c) the desirability of maintaining the availability to the public of any facility for visiting or inspecting any building, site or object of archaeological, architectural or historic interest;

and to take into account any effect which the proposals may have on the natural beauty of the countryside, flora, fauna or any such feature or facility.

18.30 It should be observed that the duty under section 48A does not amount to a separate statutory function of harbour authorities to further nature conservation etc. but is, rather, in the nature of a set of directions as to what harbour authorities should have regard in exercising their existing functions, such as the duty to improve, maintain and manage their harbour areas. Paragraph 16A of Schedule 2 to the Harbours Act 1964, however, enables a harbour revision order to impose or confer upon harbour authorities duties or powers (including the power to make by-laws) for the conservation of the natural beauty of all or any part of the harbour or of any of the flora, fauna or geological or physiographical features in the harbour or other natural features. Whilst a harbour authority might perhaps be unlikely to promote a harbour revision order to impose upon itself environmental duties which it regards as inimical to its general interests, a third party might seek to do so, if it can demonstrate that it has, or is representative of those having, a substantial interest in the harbour (Harbours Act 1964, section 14(2)(a)). Even then, however, the applicant would have to satisfy the requirement in section 14(2)(b) that the order was:

"desirable in the interests of securing the improvement, maintenance or management of the harbour in an efficient and economical manner or of facilitating the efficient and economic transport of goods or passengers by sea or in the interests of the recreational use of sea-going ships."

A harbour revision order whose environmental provisions significantly impaired the authority's ability to continue to run the undertaking as a commercial enterprise for the shipping of goods and passengers would be unlikely to satisfy this requirement unless the appropriate Minister were to decide that the order would actually facilitate a reduction in the facilities available in the harbour, and that this reduction was desirable on grounds other than those specified in section 14(2)(b) (see section 14(2B)).

Coastal management plans

18.31 The Government's current policies on coastal management are set out in *Managing the Coast: A review of Coastal Management Plans in England and Wales and the powers supporting them*, published by the Department of the Environment and the Welsh Office in October 1993 in fulfilment of a commitment made in response to the 1992 Report of the House of Commons Environment Select Committee on Coastal Zone Protection and Planning. The Government's strategic aim is to promote the sustainable use of the coast, reflecting both its conservation value and the human activities which take place there. Where the coast is of great conservation or recreation value or where there are substantial conflicting uses, integrated management to fulfil that aim may well, in the Government's view, be essential and in such areas "coastal management plans can provide a structured means at the local level of bringing together different interests, ordering priorities and ensuring resources are deployed effectively".

18.32 It should be emphasized that coastal management plans are not intended by the Government to be mandatory. Instead, local authorities and other agencies are expected to work together on a voluntary basis, informed by an understanding of national and regional issues provided by national policy statements (such as planning policy guidance notes) and by bodies such as the Environment Agency, English Nature, the Countryside Council for Wales and Sports Councils. Nor is it intended that coastal management plans should replace the statutory powers and rights of existing bodies. Instead, plans will provide a framework for improved co-operation and understanding between bodies with statutory responsibility which, in turn, should improve the speed and effectiveness of existing decision-making procedures such as statutory development plans, management plans for heritage coasts and other environmentally sensitive areas, pollution control plans of the Environment Agency, harbour authority functions, regulations by Sea Fisheries Committees and national controls over developments below high-water mark (as described in Chapter 16).

18.33 As mentioned in paragraph 18.19 *ante* an exception to the policy that management plans should be voluntary is provided for in regulation 35 of the Conservation (Natural Habitats, &c.) Regulations 1994, whereby the Minister can give directions to the relevant authorities as to the establishment etc. of a management scheme for a European marine site.

18.34 *Managing the Coast* assumes that the leading bodies in creating management plans will be local authorities since they have a wide range of associated responsibilities and powers on land, including traffic management, car parks, footpaths, recreational and visitor facilities, coastal defence and litter as well as discretionary powers to act in the interest of their areas. There will also be close links between coastal management plans and the statutory development plans for which local authorities are responsible under town and country planning legislation. The political accountability of local authorities—and the broad range of expertise which they possess—also influenced the Government's view that they are best placed to assume the leading role in the preparation of management plans. Local authorities will, however, need to work closely with other key agencies such as harbour authorities and the Environment Agency. Wide consultation on the proposed plan is essential, especially in view of the fact that the plan will depend substantially upon voluntary co-operation and self-regulation. Only where the voluntary approach proves to be inadequate will it be appropriate, in the Government's view, to resort to by-laws or other controls. Intensive policing of the many activities falling within the purview of a coastal management plan will in any event often be impractical given the length of the coastline and the limited resources available. However, the Government acknowledge that statutory controls may be necessary in certain cases, particularly where there are problems with jet-skis and other personal water craft or in busy port and harbour areas. Harbour and coastal by-law-making powers are discussed in Chapter 7.

18.35 Responsibility for deciding the content of coastal management plans lies with those responsible for their preparation. *Managing the Coast* states that the content should reflect issues and problems relevant to the area covered and the interests of the many users of the coastal zone, taking into account national policies and existing regulatory systems. In October 1996 the Department of the Environment published a report prepared by Nicholas Pearson Associates entitled *Coastal Zone Management—Towards Best Practice*. This contains advice upon the preparation of coastal management plans based upon initiatives currently underway.

CHAPTER 19

HISTORY OF PILOTAGE LAW BEFORE THE PILOTAGE ACT 1987

Introduction

19.1 In 1514 Henry VIII granted to the Trinity House of Deptford Strond, now usually known simply as "Trinity House", a charter which gave them the powers necessary to control the operations of ship men, pilots and mariners, not only in the River Thames but throughout the country. This charter was subsequently confirmed by Edward VI, Queen Mary, and Queen Elizabeth I. In 1604 James I gave Trinity House a new and more comprehensive charter but in 1647, being under suspicion of having Royalist tendencies, their charter was dissolved by Parliament. After the Restoration, Trinity House received a new charter from Charles II on the same lines as that of James I. In 1685 came the charter of James II which strictly charged that no person was to act as pilot in the "river Thames or any other creek belonging to or running into the same" unless he had first been appointed and authorized by the "masters, wardens and assistants" of Trinity House.

19.2 Beginning in the early 18th century a succession of Acts were passed relating to London Trinity House, although a number of the provisions they contained were of a general nature. Successive general Acts then followed dealing with all pilotage authorities, with the result that by the beginning of the 20th century the confusion that was created by the variance between the general law contained in the public statutes and the special provisions contained in the local Acts became so apparent that in 1911 a Departmental Committee on Pilotage was appointed. The function of this committee was to examine the existing state of the law and to recommend any changes, and the outcome of their inquiry was the passing of the Pilotage Act 1913.

A brief summary of these earlier statutes now follows.

The first Pilotage Acts

19.3 The first Act relating to pilots was the Act 3 Geo. I c. 13 in 1717, the purpose of which was to give to the Dover Trinity House similar powers to those granted by James II to London Trinity House. It made pilotage compulsory for all ships navigating between Dover, Deal or the Isle of Thanet and any places in the "Rivers of Thames and Medway"; and granted exemptions to the master, mate, or part owner of any vessel who was a resident of either Dover, Deal, or the Isle of Thanet. Unlicensed pilots could only be employed if licensed pilots were unavailable, and were heavily fined if they contravened this provision (£40 for a persistent offender), the fines being used to provide for superannuated pilots and the widows of pilots. A scale of charges was laid down and "no greater or other prices" were to be accepted or demanded.

19.4 An Act of 1732 (5 Geo. II c. 20) gave to London Trinity House general confirmation of the powers granted in the charter of James II. Its provisions were generally the same as those in the Act of 1717 except that exemption from compulsory pilotage was extended to vessels engaged in the coal trade.

19.5 In 1808 an Act (48 Geo. III c. 104) was passed setting out the basic scheme whereby London Trinity House became the largest pilotage authority in Great Britain. It reaffirmed the power granted to the London and Dover Trinity Houses in the previous statutes and in addition empowered the London Trinity House to appoint subcommissioners to examine and license pilots at "such ports and places in England as they may think requisite", except in those places where pilotage was already under the control of some statutory authority.

19.6 Although this Act applied principally to the London and Dover Trinity Houses it contained a number of provisions which could be interpreted as having general application. For example, section 51 stated that "no pilot shall be taken to sea beyond the limits of his district by the Commanding Officer of any of His Majesty's ships or by the master of any ship in the Merchant Service" without the consent of the pilot except in cases of "unavoidable necessity". Compensation for being taken to sea in such circumstances was to be paid at the rate of 10 shillings and sixpence per day, a figure which remained unchanged until 1979. It would also appear that it was intended that pilotage should be compulsory in all districts because section 55 stated that "the Master of every ship . . . which shall be conducted by any other person than a duly licensed pilot, within any limits for which any pilots have or shall be appointed by *any lawful authority* shall forfeit double the amount of the sum which would have been demandable for the pilotage . . . ".

19.7 Section 67 of the Act of 1808 stated that it was to remain in force for only four years. Thus, in 1812, a further Act was passed (52 Geo. III c. 39) which repealed, and in the main re-enacted, all the provisions contained in its predecessor. In addition, the right to appoint subcommissioners was extended to the Trinity Houses of Hull and Newcastle. A further important provision was section 30, which stated that the owner or master of a ship would not be answerable for any loss or damage caused by "the incompetence or incapacity of any pilot taken on board . . . under or in pursuance of any provision of this Act".

19.8 In 1825 the Act of 1812 was also repealed, and a new Act (6 Geo. IV c. 125), which contained most of the original provisions, replaced it. Exemptions from compulsory pilotage were again extended, this time to British vessels engaged in a variety of trades, such as vessels trading to either Norway, the Kattegat or Baltic, and vessels "wholly laden with stone from Guernsey, Jersey, Alderney, Sark or Man and being the production thereof". In addition, His Majesty in Council could permit certain vessels not having British Registers to be conducted without pilots. Another important inclusion was contained in section 57 which stated that a pilot who had executed a bond would not be liable beyond the amount stated therein (maximum £100) for any damage arising from "neglect or want of skill".

The Royal Commission of 1836

19.9 In 1836 a Royal Commission appointed in the previous year reported on "the existing laws, regulations and practices under which pilots were appointed, governed, and paid in the British Channel and the several approaches to the Port of London, and also in the navigation connected with the other principal ports in the United Kingdom".[1] With regard to compulsory pilotage it reported that in nearly all the important ports in the United Kingdom all vessels above a certain tonnage, unless specifically exempted and irrespective of nationality, were obliged to receive on board a licensed pilot "if he shall present himself". The report stated that to make pilotage entirely optional would "only hold out a boon to the foolhardy"[2] and recommended that it should be compulsory everywhere with certain specific exemptions. The recommended exemptions were the coasting trade and ships trading between the United Kingdom and foreign ports within 24 hours steaming. It pointed out that to allow too many exemptions would put "too great a charge on the remainder".[3] With regard to pilotage authorities the report commented on their great variety and pointed out that in some ports the regulations they imposed were "inexpedient and onerous"[4] while in others no sufficient regulations had been adopted at all. The report concluded, therefore, that the abuses and complaints that had resulted demonstrated "the want of a superior body to control the acts of local authorities".[5]

19.10 The report also recommended the repeal of all existing Pilotage Acts (including local Acts) and the introduction of a general Act which would be in force throughout the United Kingdom. Trinity House would, in effect, become the central pilotage authority with the power to revise and sanction

1. *Report from the Commissioners appointed to inquire into the Laws and Regulations relating to Pilotage in the United Kingdom* (1836) [56] xxviii.
2. *Ibid.*, p. 17.
3. *Ibid.*, p. 17.
4. *Ibid.*, p. 7.
5. *Ibid.*, p. 7.

by-laws made by local pilotage authorities and to make new by-laws and fix pilotage rates.

19.11 The report appears to have been largely ignored, however, and by an Act passed in 1840 (3 & 4 Vict. c. 48) exemptions were extended to "the subjects of foreign countries having Treaties of Reciprocity with the United Kingdom". In 1853, the Pilotage Law Amendment Act brought about the amalgamation of the London and Cinque Ports pilots under the jurisdiction of the London Trinity House. It also contained a number of general provisions. It stated, for the first time, the powers and duties of pilotage authorities other than Trinity House, empowering them "with the consent of Her Majesty" to determine pilots' qualifications, to make regulations for the government of pilots and of certificated masters and mates, and to fix pilotage rates. They were also empowered to make and extend exemptions from compulsory pilotage and to arrange the limits of pilotage districts. They were required to make full returns to the Board of Trade of various particulars connected with pilotage, and if they failed to do so they were liable to be deprived of their authority, and the power to appoint pilots would be invested in Trinity House. The Board of Trade were empowered to examine and grant pilotage certificates to masters and mates in the event of an authority's refusal to do so.

The Merchant Shipping Act 1854

19.12 In 1854 the Merchant Shipping Repeal Act repealed all previous provisions in public Acts relating to pilotage. It came into force on the same day as the Merchant Shipping Act 1854, Part V of which was devoted to pilotage. It re-enacted most of the general provisions contained in the earlier statutes, and kept alive all provisions contained in local Acts which were not inconsistent with it. Subject to alteration by by-law, compulsory pilotage was to continue in all districts where it was currently in force and similarly all exemptions therefrom were to continue.

19.13 Home Trade passenger ships were to employ qualified pilots unless they had on board masters or mates holding pilotage certificates. Trinity House retained the special position it enjoyed under previous statutes but was not permitted to extend its jurisdiction without the consent of Her Majesty in Council. Pilotage continued to be compulsory in all London and Trinity House outpost districts, and similar exemptions applied to those embodied in the earlier statutes except that they were no longer granted on the basis of reciprocity.

19.14 After the passing of the Merchant Shipping Act 1854 a strong reaction appears to have set in against the principle of compulsory pilotage. In 1860 a select committee of the House of Commons, appointed to inquire into the general state of the shipping industry, recommended that pilotage should be non-compulsory throughout most parts of the British Empire. They added that they had "the most convincing evidence that where the system of voluntary pilotage prevails the supply of pilots is more abundant, their efficiency is no way inferior, and the rates generally lower than at any ports where compulsory pilotage is still in force".[6]

19.15 In 1862, no doubt prompted by the report of the select committee, Parliament's antipathy towards compulsory pilotage began to make itself felt. Under the Merchant Shipping Act Amendment Act the Board of Trade were empowered, in a non-compulsory district in which there was no restriction on the number of licensed pilots, to give a pilotage authority the power to raise rates and additional facilities for their recovery, and also to give them the power to prevent unqualified persons from obtaining licences and to assist qualified persons to obtain licences. They were also empowered to create new pilotage districts.

19.16 Between 1870 and 1888 various select committees examined the problems of pilotage and although they differed in their attitudes towards compulsory pilotage they were all of the opinion that the shipowners' defence of compulsory pilotage in respect of a claim for loss or damage caused by a vessel while under pilotage should be abolished.

19.17 In 1889 the power of the Board of Trade to make provisional orders with respect to pilotage matters was again extended. By the Merchant Shipping (Pilotage) Act they were empowered to extend pilotage districts but the Act specified that in any new district pilotage was to be non-compulsory and there was to be no restriction on the right of duly qualified persons to obtain licences. Also, subject to the condition that pilots were directly represented thereon, pilotage authorities were empowered to suspend or dismiss pilots, and any pilot so dealt with had the right to appeal to a County Court or stipendiary magistrate.

The Merchant Shipping Act 1894

19.18 Part X of the Merchant Shipping Act 1894 repealed and re-enacted practically all the provisions appertaining to pilots in the Merchant Shipping Act 1854; the Merchant Shipping Act Amendment Act 1862; and the Merchant Shipping (Pilotage) Act 1889. Like the Merchant Shipping Act 1854, although it purported to be a consolidating Act, it did not embody or supersede any of the various local Acts relating to particular ports.

The Departmental Committee of 1909

19.19 In July 1909 a Departmental Committee of the Board of Trade was appointed "to inquire as to the present state of law and its administration with

6. As quoted in *Report of Departmental Committee on Pilotage*, Cd. [5571], London, 1911 (Board of Trade), p. 9.

respect to pilotage in the United Kingdom, and as to what changes, if any, are desirable".[7] The committee's report was published in 1911. It described the then existing state of the pilotage law as "chaotic", a condition which, it said, was due to the fact that the statute law relating to pilotage was contained partly in general Acts and partly in local Acts, and to the absence of any definite principle governing pilotage legislation in enactments of either description.

19.20 The report recommended that, in order to achieve the necessary reforms, all the provisions in local Acts, charters, or customs relating to pilotage should be repealed, and in their place should be substituted:

(a) A general Act of Parliament laying down the principles governing pilotage.

(b) Orders of a Central Authority defining the constitution and limits of each pilotage authority.

(c) By-laws of local authorities applying to the particular districts under their control.

19.21 With regard to the general law, one of the most important changes recommended was that pilotage should be compulsory in all districts except in the case of:—vessels whose masters or mates held pilotage certificates; Naval vessels; vessels under 100 tons gross register; vessels passing through a pilotage district. The committee was not unanimous in giving this recommendation, however, and the report contained a minority proposal that compulsory pilotage should remain only in those ports where it already existed.

19.22 The other important change recommended was that the immunity from liability of the shipowner or master for loss or damage occasioned by the fault of a compulsory pilot should be abolished, and that this should be coupled with an alteration in the legal relationship between the master and the pilot.

19.23 The legal relationship between master and pilot was the subject of considerable discussion by the committee and the opinion of those who gave evidence was clearly divided. Lord Gorell, a former President of the Probate, Divorce, and Admiralty Division of the High Court, was of the opinion that "no-one unaccustomed to a particular ship can handle her as her master and officers can",[8] while Sir Kenneth Anderson, Chairman of the Orient Steam Navigation Company, said that "it is obviously better that the actual giving of orders should rest with the man who has the knowledge than with the man who seeks advice".[9] One shipmasters' organization said that "in a district where pilotage is compulsory, the pilot should have sole and complete charge of the ship",[10] while another said that "under no circumstances should a

7. *Report of Department Committee, &c., op. cit.*, p. 1.

8. *Report of Departmental Committee, &c., op. cit.*, Minutes of Evidence, p. 231, question 7445.

9. *Ibid.*, p. 321, question 10077.

10. *Ibid.*, Appendix A, p. 7, *per* Hull British Shipmasters' Association.

master give up charge of his ship or the control of his crew".[11] Pilots, under-standably, were almost unanimous in the view that the pilot should have complete control. A typical view was expressed by the Manchester pilots who said that the pilot's authority "should be absolute in the control of the ship while within his jurisdiction".[12] Having weighed all the evidence the commit-tee recommended that there should be an express provision in the new pilotage legislation that the pilot should be given a subordinate role.

19.24 With regard to pilotage orders and by-laws the report recommended that pilotage commissioners should be appointed for a period of five years to "bring about such changes in the law of pilotage and its administration as may best meet the special requirements of any pilotage district and at the same time, secure, as far as possible, greater uniformity in the general law of pilotage".[13] The report also stated that the Board of Trade was and should remain the central pilotage authority for the United Kingdom, and that the commissioners should be the medium through whom all pilotage questions of an administrative nature should be brought before the central authority for their ultimate decision. Finally, there was a memorandum by the committee's chairman in which he stressed the importance of the continuance of the Pilotage Commissioners or some similar body as an essential part of the organization of the Central Pilotage Authority. He summarized his position as follows:

It is impossible for a department of a central office, where the superintendence of pilotage would only be one out of many subjects under its charge, to possess the technical experience or to give the detailed attention required for the direct control of such questions as are constantly arising in the administration of the law of pilot-age.[14]

The Pilotage Act 1913

19.25 The outcome of the Departmental Committee's report was the Pilotage Act 1913, which was described in its preamble as "an Act to consolidate and amend the Law relating to Pilotage". It was not a completely new Act, therefore, and many of the general provisions which had appeared in the earlier statutes were again re-enacted. While it gave effect to most of the report's recommendations there were several important variations. For exam-ple, despite the committee's emphatic recommendation that the Board of Trade should be the Central Pilotage Authority the Act did not contain any express provision to that effect; indeed the statutory definition of a pilotage authority as stated in the Pilotage Authorities (Limitation of Liability) Act 1936 would appear to have excluded the Board of Trade. Again, although the

11. *Ibid.*, Appendix A, p. 9, *per* Mercantile Marine Association.
12. *Ibid.*, Appendix C, p. 68.
13. *Report of Departmental Committee, &c., op. cit.*, p. 84.
14. *Ibid.*, p. 113.

chairman recommended that the Pilotage Commissioners should become a permanent body the Act provided that they should not continue in office beyond 1922. The intervention of the 1914–1918 war meant that in all probability the greater part of their work was carried out in their last four years of office, as nearly all Pilotage Orders setting up local pilotage authorities were not confirmed by Parliament until 1920 or later. The committee's recommendations on compulsory pilotage were not accepted either, with Parliament preferring the minority proposal that the existing system, with pilotage compulsory in some ports and not in others, should be retained. The Act did give effect to the recommendation abolishing the shipowners' and masters' defence of compulsory pilotage but did not include any specific provision altering or defining the legal relationship between master and pilot, a provision which the committee had regarded as an essential adjunct to such abolition.

19.26 The legislature's failure to give effect to the first three of these recommendations meant, arguably, that little substantial change actually took place. Part 1 of the Act, which was devoted to the revision of the pilotage organization, directed the Board of Trade to institute local inquiries to be held by the Pilotage Commissioners with a view to making the pilotage law at the various ports accessible and, so far as was possible, uniform; and to securing, so far as was practicable, uniformity of administration. This meant, effectively, the abolition of all existing local Acts, charters, customs, etc., and a thorough revision of all Pilotage Orders and by-laws. Whether these aims were achieved, however, is questionable. The provisions relating to compulsory pilotage in nearly all the Pilotage Orders, for example, simply re-enacted the *status quo* with pilotage being compulsory only in those ports where it was compulsory before the passing of the Act. By-laws stating the exemptions from compulsory pilotage were based on no obvious criteria, with ports of similar size and geography having exemptions varying between a few hundred tons and several thousand.

19.27 Some delegated legislation passed at that time even appeared to contradict the general law. The Liverpool Pilotage Order of 1920, for example, reads at times like a local Act of Parliament when one considers such a provision as section 27, which made it an offence for anyone to act as an unlicensed pilot, whereas this only became an offence under the Pilotage Act 1913 after a licensed pilot had offered his services. The same Pilotage Order made it an offence for Liverpool pilots to make claims for salvage without prior consent from the Pilotage Committee, thus setting aside the pilots' rights at common law. Positive Government action as respects the organization of pilotage virtually ceased to exist with the Pilotage Commissioners. The Board of Trade, not having been charged with any continuing duty to initiate legislation, contented itself with its quasijudicial role, acting as arbiter in disputes over by-laws, pilots' licences and pilotage certificates. Any initiative for change had to come from other interested bodies such as pilotage and harbour authorities, shipowners' associations and pilots' organizations. Such a process being inevitably cumbersome no real progress was made for nearly half a century, but eventually sufficient pressure for change from various vested interests and for widely differing reasons had built up to cause the setting up in 1973 of the Steering Committee on Pilotage.

The Steering Committee on Pilotage (SCOP) 1973

19.28 SCOP's terms of reference were "to examine the arrangements for marine pilotage in the United Kingdom with a view to preparing new legislation to supersede the Pilotage Act 1913 . . . ". The outcome of its investigations was a report to the Secretary of State for Trade in 1974 entitled *Marine Pilotage in the United Kingdom.*[15] It contained 29 recommendations, the most significant of which dealt with the subjects of a central pilotage body, compulsory pilotage, and the re-organization of pilotage districts and local pilotage authorities.

19.29 The report recommended the setting up of a Central Pilotage Board appointed by the Secretary of State, consisting of shipowners, serving pilots, port operators and others with nautical, financial, or administrative background, plus a full time staff of 20 to 30 people. It claimed justification for this recommendation on the grounds that such a body would help to create a more flexible pilotage organization, and that it would help to bring about the proposed re-organization in pilotage districts and "the new approach to compulsory pilotage on a broadly consistent basis". SCOP's "new approach" to compulsory pilotage is redolent of the Reports of the Royal Commission of 1836 and the Departmental Committee of 1911. They discovered, not surprisingly, that the system was not based on any consistent principle and recommended that as a general principle pilotage should be compulsory subject to carefully considered local exemptions for areas, small vessels and experienced personnel, and certain general exemptions such as for H.M. ships. In addition, they recommended a "liberal attitude" to the issue of pilotage certificates to masters and first mates of ships which used a port frequently and could demonstrate their familiarity with it by examination. The remaining recommendations dealt with, *inter alia*, the question of pilots' remuneration, qualifications and training, pilotage charges, the amalgamation of small adjacent districts, provisional licences, and the surveying of pilot craft.

19.30 In December 1975 a policy statement by the Government was issued which broadly endorsed all the recommendations of SCOP. Owing to lack of Parliamentary time available to bring in all the new proposals, it recommended that certain developments could take place under the existing legislation on such matters as pilots' qualifications, compulsory pilotage and pilotage

15. Department of Trade. *Marine Pilotage in the United Kingdom. Report to the Secretary of State for Trade by the Steering Committee on Pilotage*, London, 1974.

certificates. It also stated that the Government would in the meanwhile consider, along with interested parties, the action which might be taken in advance of new legislation on remuneration, pensions, training, dues, provisional licences, and pilot craft surveys. Approximately one year later it was announced by the Government that, in view of the unlikelihood of new pilotage legislation being introduced in the foreseeable future, the Secretary of State for Trade had appointed a new Advisory Committee on Pilotage, whose terms of reference were:

To advise the Secretary of State regarding changes in all aspects of pilotage arrangements in the U.K. which can and should be made in advance of new legislation; in particular to progress the re-organization of local pilotage authorities on the general lines endorsed in the Government's Policy Statement of 1975; and to work for early agreement on the content of future pilotage legislation.

The Advisory Committee on Pilotage (ACOP) 1977

19.31 ACOP's recommendations on the content of future pilotage were produced within a few months of their appointment.[16] They expressed the view that SCOP's idea of a central board with executive powers was unnecessary and that any such body should act only in an advisory capacity, the main responsibility for running the pilotage services remaining with the local pilotage authorities. They proposed instead the setting up of a Pilotage Commission, which would perform those functions which of necessity should be carried out centrally, with the basic guidelines of "safeguarding the needs of safe navigation through pilotage, promoting efficient pilotage administration and ensuring fair conditions of service and remuneration for pilots". It was recommended that it should consist of somne 10–14 members including pilots, shipowners, port operators, persons experienced in the administration of pilotage services and others with relevant experience or knowledge. The appointment of staff would be the Commission's responsibility but it was suggested that numbers should be fewer than 10 rather than the 20–30 recommended by SCOP.

19.32 On the question of compulsory pilotage ACOP noted but did not specifically endorse SCOP's recommendation that it should be extended as a general principle subject to carefully considered local and general exemptions. They recommended, *inter alia*, that the designation of compulsory pilotage areas should continue to be by Pilotage Order promoted by local authorities, that the law should be amended to permit compulsory pilotage within closed docks and in respect of vessels passing through a pilotage district, and that the exemptions for coasting vessels should be repealed and replaced by exemptions based on tonnage, length, draught or beam. On the question of general

---

16. Department of Trade. *Report of the Advisory Committee on Pilotage to the Secretary of State for Trade on the content of future pilotage legislation*, London, 1977.

exemptions they recommended that these should be restricted to vessels under 50 tons, with a re-examination of the situation with regard to fishing vessels and H.M. ships. On the question of pilotage certificates it was recommended that their issue should be extended to subjects of European Economic Community States, but any increase in the number of pilotage certificates in a particular district brought about by changes in the law should be monitored by the Pilotage Commission. If necessary, the extended use of pilotage certificates would then be phased in so as to prevent any sudden reduction in the required manning levels of pilots with its consequent adverse effect on their conditions of service.

19.33 ACOP dissented from the view that Trinity House should no longer act as a pilotage authority and recommended its continuance as such in those districts where local interests expressed the wish for it to do so. Other recommendations of ACOP included suggested amendments in the law to permit the employment of an assistant to the pilot, to improve the system of notifying pilots of estimated times of arrival and departure, and to simplify the procedure for fixing pilotage dues.

19.34 In 1979 a Merchant Shipping Act was passed containing 13 sections relating to pilotage and some 27 amendments to the Pilotage Act 1913. It embodied most of ACOP's recommendations but provided that the new Pilotage Commission should have power in certain circumstances to initiate action with regard to the organization of pilotage services and the extension of compulsory pilotage. In 1983 the Pilotage Act 1913 and the pilotage provisions of the Merchant Shipping Act 1979, together with the Pilotage Authorities (Limitation of Liability) Act 1936, were repealed and re-enacted in a consolidating Act entitled the Pilotage Act 1983.

The Pilotage Act 1983

19.35 The Pilotage Act 1983 reproduced most of the provisions of the Pilotage Act 1913 (which had been implemented by pilotage orders made under that Act mainly in the 1920s). However, as indicated above, the Merchant Shipping Act 1979 had introduced important changes and modernized certain provisions. It made clear that pilots licensed by a pilotage authority (as to which see below) could also be employed by the authority although very few were, the great majority being self-employed on the rather special basis subsisting under the Pilotage Act 1913 (and subsequently the Act of 1983) and the orders and by-laws made thereunder.

19.36 The Merchant Shipping Act 1979 had established the Pilotage Commission, comprising representatives of licensed pilots, shipowners, harbour authorities and pilotage authorities and other persons of relevant experience. It was mainly an advisory body but also had the important functions of considering pilotage charges and, as already stated above, powers in certain specified circumstances to promote pilotage orders and by-laws to bring about changes in the organization of the pilotage service.

19.37 Under the Pilotage Act 1983, as under the Act of 1913, the local administration of pilotage was carried out by pilotage authorities. Each pilotage authority administered a pilotage district. Some pilotage authorities administered more than one district and one authority, London Trinity House, was responsible for over 40. There were in total 94 pilotage districts.

19.38 Each pilotage district was established by a pilotage order made under the Pilotage Act 1913 or the Pilotage Act 1983. Each pilotage order designated or constituted the pilotage authority for the district. A pilotage order might include a number of other provisions and might, in particular, provide whether and in what circumstances pilotage was to be compulsory in the district, although this also depended to some extent on the provisions of section 31 of the Pilotage Act 1983 and of by-laws made by the pilotage authority.

19.39 A pilotage order was made by the Secretary of State, under provisions latterly contained in section 9 of the Pilotage Act 1983, on the application of any person interested in the pilotage of any pilotage district or in the operation or administration of the laws relating to pilotage in that district or, in certain circumstances, on the application of the Pilotage Commission. The related procedure was contained in the Pilotage Orders (Applications) Regulations 1980 and could be lengthy. After a pilotage order had been made it was subject to a parliamentary control. If there were no outstanding objections to the order it was subject to annulment in pursuance of a resolution by either House of Parliament. If there were outstanding objections the order was subject to special parliamentary procedure.

19.40 There were, broadly speaking, three different types of pilotage authority as follows:

(a) London Trinity House, which was by far the largest pilotage authority, administered the London Pilotage Districts and over 40 other districts (known as "outport districts"). The administration of the London districts was to a considerable extent delegated to the London Pilotage Committee which included, in addition to five elder brethren of Trinity House, representatives of shipowners, pilots, and harbour authorities. In every other Trinity House district, Trinity House's pilotage functions were to some extent delegated to Sub-Commissioners who, according to the provisions of the pilotage order for the district, generally included representatives of pilots, shipowners and any harbour authority whose harbour was within the district. Mention should also be made of Trinity House, Newcastle, which was the pilotage authority for several small pilotage districts in the North East of England.

(b) In a number of pilotage districts, the relevant pilotage order constituted the local harbour authority as the pilotage authority for the district. Where a harbour authority was also a pilotage authority, the pilotage order usually provided for the establishment of a pilotage committee on which pilots and shipowners as well as the harbour authority were represented, and for certain functions of the authority to be delegated to the committee.

(c) In some pilotage districts the pilotage authority was a body constituted for the purpose by the pilotage order. These *ad hoc* pilotage authorities usually included representatives of local pilots, shipowners, and the local harbour authority or authorities.

19.41 The most important functions of a pilotage authority were the licensing of pilots for its district and, where pilotage was compulsory, granting pilotage certificates to masters and first mates (who were Commonwealth citizens, citizens of the Republic of Ireland or nationals of another member State of the EEC) to enable them, in effect, to pilot a specified ship or ships in the compulsory area. The granting of pilotage licences and certificates was regulated to some extent by the provisions of pilotage by-laws made by the pilotage authority. There were also a number of related provisions in the Pilotage Act 1983, including the right for a licensed pilot to appeal to a court against the suspension or revocation of his licence by the pilotage authority or the refusal or failure of the authority to renew his licence.

19.42 In practice it was very rare for a licensed pilot to lose his licence. There were also rights of appeal to the Secretary of State against the action, or lack of it, by pilotage authorities in relation to the granting of pilotage licences and certificates and the renewal, suspension or revocation of pilotage certificates.

19.43 Other important functions of pilotage authorities were—

(a) The making and enforcement of pilotage by-laws which provided for detailed matters regarding the administration of pilotage within the framework laid down by the Pilotage Act 1983 and the relevant pilotage order.

(b) The making of pilotage charges.

(c) The approval and licensing of pilots' boats.

19.44 The numerous purposes for which pilotage by-laws might be made included determining the qualifications required by candidates for pilots' licences, providing for the "good government" of pilots and apprentices and ensuring their "good conduct and constant attendance to and effectual performance of their duties whether at sea or on shore". Pilotage by-laws had to be submitted to the Secretary of State for confirmation and the procedure could sometimes take a considerable time.

19.45 In most pilotage districts, the by-laws provided for the pilotage charges to be collected by the pilotage authority and distributed to the pilots. Under the Pilotage Act 1983, a pilotage authority might make charges to be paid by persons who made use of the services of pilots licensed for the district. These included charges for the services of a pilot and charges in respect of the cost of providing, maintaining and operating pilot boats, and of other costs in respect of providing and maintaining the local pilotage organization. The Act provided that objections to such charges might be made to the Pilotage Commission by the majority of the pilots licensed for the district, three or more shipowners whose ships navigated in the district, a harbour authority whose area lay within the district or any other person who appeared to the Commission to have a substantial interest in the charges. Upon such an objection, the Commission might cancel or alter the pilotage authority's charges.

CHAPTER 20

CURRENT PILOTAGE LAW

Introduction

20.1 On 1 October 1988 Part I of the Pilotage Act 1987 came into force. 1 October 1988 is therefore "the appointed day" for the purposes of that Act. On that day the legal structure of the marine pilotage service based on the Pilotage Act 1913 and re-enacted in the Pilotage Act 1983 which had lasted, subject to some changes made by the Merchant Shipping Act 1979, for more than 60 years, was swept away and pilotage became a function of harbour authorities.

20.2 The introduction of a basically different, and much simpler, legal structure means that some of the legal authorities on marine pilotage are no longer relevant or must be treated with caution.

20.3 Before discussing the Act of 1987 it seems pertinent to say a little about the statutory definition of "pilot", which remains the same.

20.4 The expression "Pilot" is defined in section 31(1) of the Pilotage Act 1987 as amended by the Merchant Shipping Act 1995 as "any person not belonging to a ship who has the conduct thereof". This was the definition contained in section 742 of the Merchant Shipping Act 1894 which was originally applied for the purposes of the 1987 Act and it applied for the purposes of the pilotage legislation in force before 1 October 1988.

20.5 This definition re-enacted verbatim that contained in the Merchant Shipping Act 1854. Prior to that Act no statutory definition of the word "pilot" existed, but an authoritative opinion as to its meaning was given by Baron Tenterden, an eminent 18th century authority on maritime law, in a treatise on that subject. In it he stated:

The name of a pilot, or steersman, is applied either to a particular officer, serving on board a ship during the course of a voyage, and having the charge of the helm and the ship's route; or to a person taken on board at a particular place for the purpose of conducting a ship through a river, road, or channel, or from or into a port.[1]

---

1. Charles Abbott. *A Treatise of the Law relative to Merchant Ships and Seamen.* 2nd edn., London, 1804, p. 167.

The second part of this definition was considered and held to be accurate by Hill, J., in *The Andoni*.[2]

20.6 In 1916 a case was brought under the Defence of the Realm (Consolidation) Regulations 1914. A Notice to Mariners made under those regulations stated that "all ships . . . whilst navigating in the waters from Gravesend to London Bridge, or vice versa, must be *conducted* by pilots licensed by the London Trinity House". In giving judgment, Bargreave Deane, J., interpreted the verb "to conduct" as follows:

She took her pilot on board at Gravesend for the purpose of being "conducted" by him to London. I think the word "conducted" means that the pilot is in charge under the old system—that is in full charge—and entitled to all the assistance he can get from the master and crew. He is in command.[3]

20.7 In a later case brought under the same regulations this interpretation was reaffirmed by Pickford, L.J., who said:

A regulation having a statutory force which provides that a ship is to be conducted by a pilot does not mean that she is to be navigated under his advice; it means she must be conducted by him . . . .[4]

20.8 The statutory definition of the word "pilot" was alluded to in a more recent case in the House of Lords. Counsel for the respondent had claimed that a vessel which under certain specified circumstances was "not deemed to be navigating in the District", was not therefore being piloted. Lord Widgery, C.J., concurred:

. . . he [counsel for the respondent] contends that if a ship is not navigating then no question of her being piloted can arise. This part of his argument does not derive specifically from the terms of the statute but derives from a common and normal use of language. He says that before anyone can be a pilot, who is defined in section 742 of the Merchant Shipping Act, 1894, as "a person not belonging to a ship who has the conduct thereof", the ship must be navigating. The ship must be in a condition in which the pilot has some function to perform. Accordingly he argues that if by virtue of the byelaw this particular ship is not deemed to be navigating in the district at all, then no person in charge of her, be it the master or anyone else, can be a pilot within the meaning of legislation . . . I have come to the conclusion that Mr Stone's [counsel for the respondent] argument upon this is right.[5]

20.9 It would appear from these judgments, therefore, that a person can only come within the statutory definition of a pilot if he actually has the conduct of the vessel, the verb "to conduct" being synonymous with the verb "to navigate".

20.10 A definitive interpretation of the word "pilot" is also contained in the report of a Royal Commission published in 1968, which investigated all

2. *The Andoni* (1918) 14 Asp. M.L.C. 326, at p. 328.
3. *The Nord* (1916) 13 Asp. M.L.C. 606, at p. 608.
4. *The Mickleham* [1918] P. 166 C.A., at p. 169.
5. *Babbs* v. *Press* [1971] 2 Lloyd's Rep. 383, at pp. 387, 388.

aspects of pilotage in Canada. The definition contained in the Canada Shipping Act 1952 is expressed in words identical to the definition contained in the Merchant Shipping Act 1894 (and now in the Pilotage Act 1987) and the Royal Commission's Report concurs with the general import of the judicial pronouncements stated above. The report analyses the statutory definition of the word "pilot" as follows:

This is composed of two elements:
    (a) having the conduct of the ship, that is the action of navigating the ship;
    (b) not belonging to the ship, that is the relationship towards the ship.
The expression "having the conduct of the ship" is not defined and, therefore, it should be construed in its normal meaning, that is to have charge and control of navigation; in other words, of the movement of the vessel. Hence the substantive "pilot" is synonymous with "navigator" and the verb "to pilot" is equivalent to "to navigate" . . . The verb "to pilot" and the noun expressing the action of piloting, i.e. "pilotage" are synonymous with "to navigate a ship" and "the action of navigating a ship" . . . Therefore, to be a pilot as defined in the Act is not a question of qualification, profession, certificate or licence; it is the fact of actually navigating a vessel (and not of being capable or authorized to navigate a vessel). A pilot, whether licensed or not, ceases to be "pilot" when, for any reason, he is superseded by the Master or by the person in command. Similarly, if anyone is merely used as an adviser and is not entrusted with the navigation of the ship, he is not the pilot of that ship. Therefore the general provisions concerning pilots do not apply to him under such circumstances. The first component of the definition is, therefore, the ordinary sense of the term, i.e. the person who at a given moment is navigating the ship is the pilot at that time. It is by the second component of the definition that the legislature has restricted the general meaning of the term to those navigators who are not part of the normal complement of the crew. Therefore, a "pilot" as defined in the Act in addition to navigating the ship must also be a stranger as far as that ship is concerned.[6]

20.11 A clear understanding of the statutory definition of the word "pilot" is important when the subject of the master-pilot relationship is considered in Chapter 21 *post*.

The Pilotage Act 1987

Which harbour authorities are responsible for pilotage?

20.12 The primary responsibility for the provision of a pilotage service on and after the appointed day (which, as mentioned above, was 1 October 1988) is imposed on a class of harbour authorities described in section 1 of the Act, perhaps a little invidiously, as "competent harbour authorities". For a harbour authority to fall within this class:

(a) they must be a harbour authority as defined in the Harbours Act 1964 or, in Northern Ireland, the Harbours Act (Northern Ireland) 1970, i.e., an authority who manage their harbour under statutory powers;

6. Canada. *Report of Royal Commission on Pilotage.* Ottowa, 1968, Part 1, pp. 23, 24.

(b) they must have statutory powers in relation to the regulation of shipping movements and the safety of navigation within their harbour; powers vested in the harbour master, for example, his power to give directions to ships under section 52 of the Harbours, Docks and Piers Clauses Act 1847, are deemed to be powers exercised by the harbour authority, and the harbour authority's harbour is the area or areas inside the limits of which their statutory powers and duties as a harbour authority are exercisable; and

(c) their harbour must fall within a so-called active former pilotage district, that is to say a pilotage district designated by a pilotage order made under the Pilotage Act 1983, or the legislation which it consolidated (see paragraphs 19.38 and 19.39 *ante*), where at least one act of pilotage was performed in 1984, 1985, 1986 or 1987, or in respect of which a pilotage certificate authorizing a master or first mate to pilot his ship in circumstances in which pilotage was compulsory was in force at any time in any of those years.

20.13 There may be a question of whether the references in section 1 to harbour authorities speak from time to time or whether they refer only to harbour authorities which existed, and complied with the conditions specified in the section, on the appointed day. If the latter view is correct, then a new harbour authority, even if its harbour falls wholly or partly within a former pilotage district and the authority otherwise complies with the conditions specified in section 1, can only become a competent harbour authority by virtue of an order made by the Secretary of State under the power referred to below. However, although it might be argued that this view is in accordance with the general tenor of section 1, the better view is probably that section 1 speaks from time to time. That then is the class of competent harbour authorities described by section 1 of the Act but the section excludes from that class:

(a) regional water authorities and certain other drainage and river authorities (unless they have special powers under local statutes);

(b) a Queen's harbour master, that is to say, the harbour master for a Dockyard Port (within the meaning of the Dockyard Ports Regulation Act 1865), or

(c) any own account operator, that is to say a body which manages a harbour under statutory powers wholly or mainly for the purpose of goods which it, or an associated body, manufactures or produces, for example an oil company which manages its own jetty under statutory powers.

20.14 This class is not, however, immutable. A harbour authority who manage their harbour under statutory powers but are not within the class, for example because the harbour does not fall within a former pilotage district, may apply to the Secretary of State to be added to it and the Secretary of State may by order provide accordingly. The Secretary of State may, again by order, provide that a competent harbour authority shall exercise pilotage functions in an area additional to their own harbour. Such an additional area may be outside the limits of any competent harbour authority or it may comprise another competent harbour authority's harbour. In the latter case, the Secretary of State's order may provide that the other harbour authority shall be excluded from the class of competent harbour authorities. The Secretary of State may only provide under this enabling power for a competent harbour authority to exercise pilotage functions in an additional area if he considers that this is in the interests of efficiency and safety of navigation.

20.15 Before the Secretary of State makes an order under section 1 either to add a harbour authority to the class of competent harbour authorities or to provide for a competent harbour authority to exercise pilotage functions in an additional area, he must inform the persons he considers may be affected by the terms of the proposed order and specify a reasonable time within which they may object.

20.16 If a person objects to an order under section 1 and does not withdraw his objection, then if the Secretary of State makes the order substantially in the form originally proposed, the order as made is subject to special parliamentary procedure (see paragraphs 11.25 to 11.35 *ante*). Otherwise the order as made is subject to the negative resolution procedure—annulment by a resolution of either House of Parliament.

20.17 Still on the subject of which authorities are to be responsible for pilotage, reference is now made to section 11, subsections (2) and (3) and to sections 12 and 13. Under section 11(2), a competent harbour authority may arrange for another competent harbour authority to exercise on their behalf all or any of their pilotage functions, except the primary duty under section 2(1) of keeping under consideration what pilotage services need to be provided and whether and how far pilotage should be compulsory. Arrangements under section 11(2) could therefore provide for one competent harbour authority to stand substantially in the shoes of another, although they could also provide for something short of that.

20.18 Under section 11(3) two or more competent harbour authorities may arrange to discharge any of their pilotage functions jointly. This would enable two or more competent harbour authorities to establish a joint committee which would, in effect, operate as the competent harbour authority to provide pilotage services for their combined harbours and approaches. Joint arrangements under section 11(3) could stop short of complete integration, and, for example, could be limited to the provision and operation of pilot boats.

20.19 Arrangements made under section 11(2) or (3) may be terminated by the giving of reasonable notice to the other party or parties by a competent harbour authority who entered into the arrangements.

20.20 Section 12 enables the Secretary of State to intervene in certain cases where joint arrangements might, *prima facie*, seem appropriate. In particular he may do so where the harbours of two or more competent harbour authorities fall wholly or partly within a single former pilotage district, or where access for ships to the harbour of one competent harbour authority is through the harbour of another.

20.21 He may also intervene where a person other than the competent harbour authority carries on harbour operations within their harbour (for example, a terminal operator); where a person other than the harbour authority carries on harbour operations in a harbour which is not that of a competent harbour authority, access to which is through the harbour of a competent harbour authority; and where the harbour of a competent harbour authority and a dockyard port fall within the same former pilotage district.

20.22 Also under section 12, the Secretary of State may require the competent harbour authorities concerned to provide him with any information he requests about arrangements made or proposed for the provision of pilotage services in the sort of cases mentioned above. If no arrangements have been made or proposed and the Secretary of State considers that these are necessary, he may direct the authorities concerned to make such arrangements—for example, for the harbour authorities in an estuary to establish a joint committee to discharge pilotage functions in their harbours and approaches. If he considers that any arrangements actual or proposed are unsatisfactory, he may direct either that they shall be modified in such ways as he may specify, or that the authorities concerned must make different arrangements. Section 12(4) makes clear that the right mentioned above to withdraw from joint arrangements entered into by agreement does not apply to arrangements made or modified pursuant to a direction by the Secretary of State.

20.23 Section 13 provides for the Secretary of State to determine disputes between competent harbour authorities concerning, among other things, joint arrangements for the discharge of pilotage functions.

20.24 Usually, the authority responsible for the provision of pilotage services at a harbour will be the harbour authority for that harbour, if they are a competent harbour authority, as is the case with most important commercial harbours. But it may be another competent harbour authority by virtue of arrangements under section 11(2), or a joint board or committee by virtue of arrangements under section 11(3).

20.25 If the body managing a harbour are not a competent harbour authority, for example if they are a company which manages the harbour otherwise than under statutory powers, the Secretary of State may by order provide for a competent harbour authority to provide pilotage services there. Even where the harbour authority for a harbour are a competent harbour authority, the Secretary of State may appoint another competent harbour authority to provide pilotage services there if he considers that somewhat drastic step to be necessary in the interests of efficiency and safety of navigation.

General duties for provision of pilotage services

20.26 The general duties for the provision of pilotage services are contained in section 2 of the Pilotage Act 1987. Under section 2(1) each competent harbour authority are required to keep under consideration whether any and if so what pilotage services need to be provided to secure the safety of ships navigating in or in the approaches to their harbour and whether, in the interests of safety, pilotage should be compulsory in any part of that harbour or its approaches. If so, the authority must consider for what ships and in which circumstances pilotage is necessary, and what services should be provided.

20.27 This general duty applies to a competent harbour authority in relation to any additional area for which they have been made responsible by an order under section 1. It cannot be delegated by arrangements under the Act to anyone else—not even another competent harbour authority—but only to a joint committee or board established to carry out the pilotage functions of two or more competent harbour authorities. A question which may arise under subsection (1) of section 2 is what area is comprised in the approaches to a particular harbour. The answer is that this is a question of fact and depends on the circumstances of each case.

20.28 In performing their duty under section 2(1), each competent harbour authority is required by subsection (2) to have particular regard to the hazards involved in the carriage of dangerous goods or hazardous substances by ship.

20.29 Subsection (3) of section 2 imposes on each competent harbour authority the duty of providing such pilotage services as they consider necessary. Under section 11 this duty of providing the pilotage services which a competent harbour authority consider necessary may be the subject of arrangements for the services to be provided on behalf of the competent harbour authority by another competent harbour authority or by an agent (although as described in paragraphs 20.51 and 20.52 *post* in the latter case certain powers must be reserved to the competent harbour authority).

20.30 A case which may still be relevant in this context is *Anchor Line (Henderson Bros.) Ltd. v. Dundee Harbour Trustees*[7] in which it was held that an authority which failed to maintain an adequate service of pilots might incur liability to the owner of a ship which had sustained damage in consequence of the absence of the pilot.

The authorization and engagement of pilots

20.31 Perhaps the most interesting, and certainly the most complicated, part of the 1987 Act is the complex of inter-related provisions dealing with the authorization of pilots, the arrangements under which pilots are to provide

---

7. *Anchor Line (Henderson Bros.) Ltd. v. Dundee Harbour Trustees* (1922) 38 T.L.R. 299.

their services and, if they are employed, the terms of their employment. These provisions are contained in sections 3, 4 and 5 and subsection (1) of section 11 and also in paragraph 2 of Schedule 1.

20.32 The power for competent harbour authorities to authorize persons to act as pilots in their harbours and approaches clearly has analogies with the former power for pilotage authorities under the Pilotage Act 1983 to license pilots for their districts (see paragraph 19.41 *ante*). In each case the purpose is to ensure that pilots have the necessary skill and experience. The difference is that, whereas under the former system a licence in itself enabled a pilot to provide his services as a pilot in the district for which he was licensed, authorization under section 3 must be coupled with arrangements under a contract of employment or otherwise to enable him to act as an authorized pilot in the harbour in question.

20.33 A competent harbour authority's power to authorize pilots for their harbour and the approaches cannot be exercised on their behalf by an agent under section 11(1) (although, as mentioned above it may be exercised by another competent harbour authority or a joint committee pursuant to arrangements under subsections (2) or (3) of section 11).

20.34 Under subsection (1) of section 3, a competent harbour authority may authorize such persons to act as pilots in or in any part of their harbour or the approaches to the harbour as they consider are suitably qualified to act in that capacity. An authorization must specify the area within which it has effect. It may, for example, authorize the pilot to act only in part of the harbour. It may also authorize him to pilot only ships of a particular description and, if so, the authorization must specify that too.

20.35 The authority may determine the qualifications in respect of age, physical fitness, time of service, local knowledge, skill, character and other qualities required from persons applying for authorization. That gives a competent harbour authority a wide discretion as to the qualifications on which they may insist in authorizing pilots, but it is hardly necessary to add that that discretion must be exercised reasonably and with relevant—but only relevant—considerations in mind. With regard to the first authorizations of pilots, a competent harbour authority could require different qualifications from persons who immediately before the appointed day were licensed pilots for any district or who were time-expired apprentice pilots, or recognized assistant pilots. The purpose of that provision was of course to enable a harbour authority's general requirements to be relaxed or modified for people who had substantial recent experience of piloting ships, but a competent harbour authority were not obliged to relax their requirements for such persons, though they could do so on a selective basis.

20.36 During the period of four years beginning on the appointed day a competent harbour authority's discretion as to whom they authorized as pilots was limited by subsections (3) and (4) of section 3. During that period they could not, in the first place, authorize any persons who were not licensed pilots immediately before the appointed day, unless the number of former licensed pilots applying to be authorized and who had the qualifications required by the authority (which might be modified for former licensed pilots) fell short of the number of pilots considered necessary by the authority. In the second place, if during that period the number of suitably qualified persons who were licensed pilots immediately before the appointed day did fall short of the required number, the competent harbour authority could not authorize any persons who were not immediately before the appointed day time-expired apprentice pilots or recognized assistant pilots, unless the number of apprentice and assistant pilots who had the requisite qualifications also fell short of the number required. After that the field was open for suitably qualified people.

20.37 A "time-expired apprentice pilot" was defined as a person who had served the full term of his apprenticeship but was not the holder of a licence under section 12 of the Pilotage Act 1983. A "recognized assistant pilot" was defined as a person who acted as an assistant to pilots in a pilotage district and was recognized as such an assistant by the pilotage authority but was not the holder of a pilot's licence.

20.38 Turning to subsection (4) of section 4, we see that a competent harbour authority may refuse to authorize any person who is not willing to provide his services as a pilot in accordance with the arrangements made for the provision of such services in their area. What those arrangements might be is discussed below but this subsection means, for example, that if the arrangements are that pilots are to be employed by the competent harbour authority, the authority may refuse to authorize a former licensed pilot who insists that he will only provide pilotage services on a self-employed basis.

20.39 Returning to section 3, a competent harbour authority may under subsection (5) suspend or revoke an authorization which they have granted if it appears to them:

(a) that the authorized person has been guilty of any incompetence or misconduct affecting his capability as a pilot;

(b) that the authorized person has ceased to have the qualifications required of persons applying for authorization, or has failed to provide evidence that he continues to have the qualifications—and that includes qualifications in respect of physical fitness;

(c) that the number of persons for the time being authorized by it exceeds the number required to be authorized; or

(d) that it is appropriate to do so by virtue of any alteration in or the termination of any contract or other arrangement under which the services of pilots are provided at the harbour.

20.40 However, the Act provides that a competent harbour authority may not revoke the authorization of a pilot who provides his services under a contract for services (as distinct from a contract of employment) on the grounds that there are too many authorized pilots, except where the authority gave the pilot notice before the appointed day that they proposed in the first place to authorize more pilots than were needed (in order to give surplus pilots who did not wish to retire the opportunity to transfer to another authority), and that they intended to revoke his authorization after allowing him a reasonable period to seek authorization by another competent harbour authority.

20.41 Before suspending or revoking an authorization on the grounds either that a pilot has been guilty of any incompetence or misconduct or that he has ceased to have the required qualifications or has failed to provide evidence that he still has them, a competent harbour authority must give written notice of their intention to the pilot concerned, stating their reasons, and must give him a reasonable opportunity of making representations.

20.42 Where a competent harbour authority suspend or revoke an authorization either on the grounds that there are too many authorized pilots or because of the termination of any contract or other arrangement, they must give the pilot concerned a notice in writing stating the grounds of the suspension or revocation and specifying the length of time for which he had been authorized as a pilot by that authority. This is intended as a formal testimonial to his professional competence.

20.43 Subsection (7) of section 3 makes it an offence for a person who is not an authorized pilot for an area to hold himself out as an authorized pilot. The maximum penalty on summary conviction is a fine at level 5 on the standard scale.

20.44 Again, under section 4, which deals with such matters as the employment of authorized pilots, subsection (2) imposes a duty on a competent harbour authority to offer themselves to employ under a contract of employment any person they authorize as a pilot (apart from pilots who are already employed by them) unless (a) (in the case of the first authorization of pilots by the authority under the Pilotage Act 1987) a majority of the "relevant licence holders" had agreed during the period beginning six months and ending three months before the appointed day that the authority need not offer to employ them; or (b) a majority of the "relevant authorized pilots" have agreed on or after that day that the authority need not do so. A competent harbour authority's duty under section 4(2) cannot be exercised on their behalf by an agent under section 11(1), although it could be exercised by another competent harbour authority or by a joint committee. Subsection (3) of section 4 defines "relevant licence holders" and "relevant authorized pilots".

"RELEVANT LICENCE HOLDERS"

    (a) If the competent harbour authority's harbour fell within more than one former pilotage district (it is believed that the only case of that kind was the harbour of the former Tees and Hartlepool Port Authority), "relevant licence holders" meant the persons who at the time of the agreement that the competent harbour authority need not offer to employ them were holders of pilotage licences for the district which included the area for which the authorizations covered by the agreement were granted.

(b) If the competent harbour authority's harbour fell within a former pilotage district in which another competent harbour authority's harbour also fell (as for example in the case of the harbours in the London district), then the relevant licence holders were the persons who at the time of the agreement that the competent harbour authority need not offer to employ them were holders of pilotage licences for the district and, in the opinion of the Pilotage Commission, were at that time regularly providing their services as pilots within the part of the district in which the harbour in question was situated.

(c) In any other case, the relevant licence holders were all the persons who at the time of the agreement that the competent harbour authority need not offer to employ them, were the licensed pilots for the former pilotage district in which the competent harbour authority's harbour fell.

"RELEVANT AUTHORIZED PILOTS"

These are the people who on and after the appointed day may agree that the competent harbour authority need not offer employment to a pilot whom it authorizes:

(a) If the competent harbour authority's harbour falls within more than one former pilotage district, the relevant authorized pilots are the persons who at the time of the agreement are authorized for the area for which the pilot or pilots concerned are authorized.

(b) In any other case, the relevant authorized pilots are the persons who at the time of the agreement are authorized pilots for the harbour of the competent harbour authority.

20.45 Section 4(1) provides that, subject to subsection (2) (i.e., subject to the competent harbour authority's obligation to offer to employ the pilots whom they authorize unless that obligation is removed by an agreement on the part of a majority of the local pilots), a competent harbour authority may make such arrangements as they consider appropriate for the provision of the services of authorized pilots in their harbour and the approaches, whether under a contract of employment or a contract for services.

20.46 Functions under section 4(1) are not among those which are excluded by section 11(1) from the functions which may be exercised by an agent on behalf of a competent harbour authority. If, therefore, a competent harbour authority make arrangements with a company for that company to exercise pilotage functions on their behalf, these could include giving the company the discretion of deciding under section 4(1) whether to employ the pilots, or to enter into contracts with them under which they would provide their services as self-employed contractors. That situation could, of course, only arise if the majority of the local pilots had agreed to release the competent harbour authority from their obligation under subsection (2) to offer to employ them.

20.47 It should be noted that under section 4(1), a competent harbour authority may employ the pilots they authorize, even where a majority of the local pilots have agreed that the authority need not employ them and would prefer some other arrangement.

20.48 A point which may not be completely clear is whether the obligation to offer to employ an authorized pilot implies a continuing obligation to employ him so long as he remains an authorized pilot, in the absence of an agreement to the contrary by a majority of the relevant authorized pilots. It is thought that the better view is that it does.

20.49 The distinction between a contract of employment and a contract for services can be a fine one. One test which the courts have applied is whether the employer has the right to control the manner of doing the work, but that test is not always correct: *Cassidy* v. *Ministry of Health*.[8] It would not seem to be the appropriate test to apply in the case of marine pilots. An analogous case appears to be that of a master of a ship who is clearly employed by his shipping company. His employer can tell him where to go but not how to navigate (*Gold* v. *Essex County Council*[9]). With regard to the distinction between a contract of employment and a contract for services Stevenson, L.J., said in *Cassidy* v. *Ministry of Health*: "One perhaps cannot get much beyond this: Was the contract a contract of service (i.e., of employment) within the meaning which an ordinary person would give under the words?"

20.50 Subsection (5) of section 4 enables a competent harbour authority to pay into a pilots' benefit fund (which includes the Pilots' National Pension Fund to which most pilots belong) such contributions as may be required by the rules governing the fund in respect of any authorized pilot providing his services under such arrangements as are mentioned in subsection (1).

20.51 Under subsection (1) of section 11, a competent harbour authority may arrange for certain of their pilotage functions to be exercised on their behalf by such other persons as they think fit. A competent harbour authority may also establish such companies as they think fit to exercise those functions on their behalf. The subsection, however, excludes from such arrangements a competent harbour authority's basic statutory functions in relation to pilotage.

20.52 The functions which cannot be exercised by an agent or by a company established by a competent harbour authority are:

---

8. *Cassidy* v. *Ministry of Health* [1951] 2 K.B. 343.
9. *Gold* v. *Essex County Council* [1942] 2 K.B. 293.

(a) the general duty contained in section 2(1) to keep the need for pilotage services under review;

(b) the authorization of pilots under section 3(1);

(c) determining the qualifications to be required from applicants for authorization under section 3(2);

(d) the obligation to offer to employ authorized pilots under section 4(2);

(e) the licensing of pilot boats operated by persons other than the authority under section 6(1)(*b*);

(f) directing that pilotage shall be compulsory under section 7(1);

(g) granting pilotage exemption certificates under section 8(1);

(h) making charges under section 10; and

(i) making payments required by a pilots' compensation scheme under section 28.

As mentioned above, the arrangements which can be made with other competent harbour authorities are more comprehensive.

20.53 Section 5 and paragraph 2 of Schedule 1 provided for a temporary arbitration procedure for resolving disputes between competent harbour authorities and authorized pilots whom they employed. It applied to such disputes which arose during the initial period after the appointed day and also to disputes which arose before that day about terms on which a pilot was to be employed on and after that day. Pilots already employed before the passing of the Act were excluded from this procedure. Section 5 related to the position after the appointed day. It provided that where any dispute arose between a competent harbour authority and an authorized pilot or a person wishing to be authorized:

(a) as to what the terms of any provision in any contract of employment which was to be entered into between them should be; or

(b) whether the terms of any provision in any existing contract of employment between them should be modified,

and that dispute could not be resolved by negotiation between them, the authority or a majority of the authorized pilots for the harbour might refer the dispute to an arbitration panel. The arbitration panel was to consist of three members, one appointed by the Secretary of State, who was the Chairman; one appointed by a body appearing to the Secretary of State to be representative of harbour authorities throughout the United Kingdom; and one appointed by a body appearing to him to be representative of pilots throughout the United Kingdom.

20.54 When a dispute was referred to them the panel were required to determine what the terms of the provision in dispute should be, and the kinds of contracts of employment between the authority and authorized pilots to which their determination was to apply. In making a determination the panel

275

were required to have regard to any general guidance issued by the Secretary of State as to the matters to be considered by them and the Secretary of State specified a number of relevant considerations to which the panel were to have regard.

20.55 Where the arbitration panel made a determination, then subject to any agreement to the contrary between the harbour authority and the authorized pilots and to the effect of any subsequent determination:

> (a) on and after the date on which the determination was made, any contracts of employment between the harbour authority and the pilots of the kinds to which the panel had decided their determination was to apply, which had been entered into before the date of the determination had effect with the substitution of a provision in the terms determined by the panel for any inconsistent provision; and
>
> (b) any such contracts entered into on or after the date of the determination were required to contain a provision in the terms determined by the panel.

20.56 Paragraph 2 of Schedule 1 adapted the procedure under section 5, and applied it to disputes before the appointed day between a competent harbour authority and any person who wished to be authorized by the authority on or after that day.

20.57 Section 5(8) provided that the arbitration procedure should come to an end on such date as the Secretary of State might by order prescribe, but not earlier than the expiry of the period of three years, beginning with the appointed day. Under the Pilotage Act 1987 (Cessation of Temporary Procedure) Order and Regulations 1991 the temporary arbitration procedure described above came to an end on 1 October 1991 and regulations which had been made for the purposes of that procedure were revoked on that day. This Order, however, provided that any arbitration commenced before 1 October 1991 under the temporary arbitration procedure should continue unaffected. Also under the terms of section 5(8) the order bringing the temporary arbitration procedure to an end on 1 October 1991 did not affect the terms of any contract continuing in force at that date.

Compulsory pilotage

20.58 Sections 7, 8 and 15 of the Pilotage Act 1987 deal with the important subject of compulsory pilotage. On the appointed day all existing requirements for pilotage to be compulsory in the Pilotage Act 1983, pilotage orders and pilotage by-laws were abrogated. Instead, under section 7, if a competent harbour authority consider that in the interests of safety they should do so, then they have a duty to direct that pilotage shall be compulsory for ships navigating in, or in any part, of their harbour or the approaches. This power is flexible and discriminating. A pilotage direction:

(a) may apply to all ships (except ships of less than 20 metres in length, fishing boats of less than 47.5 metres in length and, by virtue, respectively, of Crown and Sovereign Immunity, British and foreign warships) or all ships of a description specified in the direction (subject to any specified exceptions);

(b) shall specify the area and circumstances in which it applies;

(c) may specify the circumstances in which an authorized pilot in charge of a ship to which the direction applies is to be accompanied by an assistant who is also an authorized pilot; and

(d) may contain such supplementary provisions as the authority consider appropriate.

20.59 Among other things, it is possible under this power for a competent harbour authority to direct that any ship which has a defect in its hull, machinery or equipment which might materially affect its navigation should be subject to compulsory pilotage (*cf.* the former section 30(3) of the Pilotage Act 1983).

20.60 Where a competent harbour authority consider that pilotage should be compulsory in part of the approaches to their harbour, the limits of their harbour must be extended by a harbour revision order under section 14 of the Harbours Act 1964 to include the area in question before a pilotage direction can become effective in that area. By virtue of provisions of the Interpretation Act 1978 which enabled anticipatory action to be taken in certain circumstances, it was possible for a competent harbour authority who intended to give a pilotage direction in respect of an area outside their harbour on or after the appointed day, to apply before that day for a harbour revision order to extend their limits. If they did so, then if pilotage was already compulsory in the area concerned by virtue of a pilotage order, the harbour revision order had the benefit of an expedited procedure as specified in paragraph 3 of Schedule 1 to the Act.

20.61 A pilotage direction is not subject to appeal, but before giving such a direction a competent harbour authority must consult the owners of ships which customarily navigate in the area which would be affected and any other persons who carry on harbour operations within the harbour, or, in either case, the appropriate representative bodies. A competent harbour authority must arrange for any pilotage direction given by them to be published in such a manner as to bring it to the notice of those persons likely to be interested.

20.62 Section 9 of the 1987 Act requires a competent harbour authority to secure that any ship owned or operated by them in the exercise of their functions otherwise than under the 1987 Act (that is, craft operated by the authority other than pilot boats) is subject to the same obligations as respects pilotage while navigating within their harbour as any other ship.

20.63 It may be pertinent to refer here to section 16 of the 1987 Act which provides that the fact that a ship is being navigated in an area and in circumstances in which pilotage is compulsory for it shall not affect any liability of the owner or master of the ship for any loss or damage caused by the ship or by the manner in which it is navigated. This section re-enacts in a slightly different form the provisions originally contained in section 15(1) of the Pilotage Act 1913 which abolished the defence of compulsory pilotage. For the history of, and the background to, this provision reference should be made to the notes to section 15 of the 1913 Act in Temperley, *Merchant Shipping Acts* (7th edn.) (*British Shipping Laws*, Vol. 21), pp. 362–63. Section 16 is referred to in paragraph 20.85 *post* in the context of liability for damage caused by a ship under compulsory pilotage.

Pilotage exemption certificates

20.64 Section 8 of the Act provides in effect that where pilotage is compulsory the competent harbour authority must, on application by the master or first mate of a ship, grant him a certificate enabling him to navigate that ship (and any other ships specified in the certificate) in the area concerned without a pilot if they are satisfied (by examination or by reference to such other requirements as they may reasonably impose) that his skill, experience and local knowledge are sufficient for the purpose and, if it appears to be necessary in the interests of safety, that he has sufficient knowledge of English.

20.65 However, under section 8(2) a competent harbour authority's requirements for the grant of a certificate must not be unduly onerous having regard to the difficulties and danger of navigation in the harbour. They must not be more onerous than those which the authority require from persons applying to be authorized as pilots.

20.66 If the Secretary of State is satisfied on application made to him by a competent harbour authority that it is appropriate for him to do so by reason of the unusual hazards involved in shipping movements within their harbour, he may direct that during such period (not exceeding three years) as he may specify, the competent harbour authority may refuse to grant pilotage exemption certificates, even in cases where they are satisfied as regards the applicants' skill, experience and local knowledge. If such a direction is given then pilotage exemption certificates already in force in the harbour cease to have effect.

20.67 A pilotage exemption certificate is not to remain in force for more than one year, but may be renewed annually on application by the holder, if the competent harbour authority continue to be satisfied that he is qualified to navigate the ship or ships in question in their harbour. It may be altered so as to refer to different ships if the competent harbour authority are satisfied that the holder is also suitably qualified to navigate those other ships in the harbour.

20.68 Section 8 enables a competent harbour authority to revoke or suspend a pilotage exemption certificate if it appears to them that the holder has been guilty of any relevant incompetence or misconduct. Before doing so, and before refusing to grant or renew a pilotage exemption certificate, a competent harbour authority must give the holder written notice and give him a reasonable opportunity of making representations.

20.69 A competent harbour authority may charge such fees as they consider reasonable to meet their administrative costs in connection with granting, renewing or altering of pilotage certificates and conducting examinations for the purpose.

Failure to comply with pilotage directions

20.70 Section 15 provides that a ship being navigated in an area and in circumstances where pilotage is compulsory by virtue of a pilotage direction must be under the pilotage of an authorized pilot, accompanied by an assistant if that is required by the direction, or under the pilotage of a master or first mate possessing a pilotage exemption certificate for the ship. If any ship is not under such pilotage after an authorized pilot has offered to take charge of the ship, the master is guilty of an offence and liable on summary conviction to a fine not exceeding level 5 on the standard scale.

20.71 Under subsection (3) of section 15, if the master of a ship navigates in an area and in circumstances in which pilotage is compulsory without notifying the competent harbour authority that he proposes to do so, he is guilty of an offence and liable on summary conviction to a fine not exceeding level 2 on the standard scale. This is a new provision. It is still not an offence in itself for a master without a pilotage exemption certificate to navigate his ship without a pilot where pilotage is compulsory unless and until an authorized pilot offers to take charge,[10] but he must now notify the competent harbour authority before doing so.

20.72 With regard to what constitutes an offer by an authorized pilot to take charge of a ship, the cases on what constituted an offer by a licensed pilot under the Pilotage Act 1913 and the Pilotage Act 1983 would still appear to be relevant. In *Babbs* v. *Press*[11] it was claimed that a flag displayed at the Trinity House pilot station at Gravesend constituted an offer of pilotage on the part of the pilots stationed there. Lord Widgery, C.J., did not agree. He said:

An offer to provide pilotage for the purpose of the Pilotage Act (1913) section 30(3) must be an offer made or communicated in relation to the particular movement of the vessel in question . . . Whether or not in a given case an offer has been made relative to the particular movement of the vessel is a question of fact . . . in many instances an offer may be made simultaneously to a number of vessels at the same time . . . On the

10. See *Muller (W.H.) & Co.* v. *Trinity House (Deptford Strond)* [1925] 1 K.B. 166; 16 Asp. M.L.C. 458, although the decision in that case is now in some respects out of date.
11. *Babbs* v. *Press* [1971] 2 Lloyd's Rep. 383.

facts of this case I think the Justices were wholly justified in reaching the conclusion that the presence of the pilot station and its flag two miles down river were not a sufficient offer to the master of the *Matilde* of a licensed pilot at the time when she set off on this short two-mile voyage.

20.73 In *Jenkin* v. *Godwin*[12] it was held that the refusal of a licensed pilot to take charge of a ship in the evening (because he considered it unsafe to proceed on the flood tide 20 minutes before sunset) but to take charge the following morning did not constitute a reasonable offer by the pilot.

20.74 In modern circumstances the normal practice is for the master to ask for a pilot by radio. Failing that, notification (by radio) under section 15(3) that the master proposes to navigate in a compulsory pilotage area will no doubt prompt the speedy dispatch of a pilot to take charge of the ship.

Charges by competent harbour authorities

20.75 Section 10 of the Pilotage Act 1987 authorizes a competent harbour authority to make reasonable charges in respect of the pilotage services provided by them and such charges may include:

    (a) charges for the services of a pilot authorized by the authority;

    (b) charges in respect of any expenses reasonably incurred by a pilot in connection with the provision of his services as a pilot;

    (c) charges by way of penalties payable in cases where the estimated time of arrival or departure of a ship is not notified as required by the authority or the ship does not arrive or depart at the notified time;

    (d) charges in respect of the cost of providing, maintaining and operating pilot boats for the area; and

    (e) charges in respect of any other costs involved in providing and maintaining the pilotage organization provided by the authority.

20.76 Where pilotage is compulsory, a competent harbour authority may also make reasonable charges in respect of a ship which is being navigated by a master or first mate with a pilotage exemption certificate. It was held in *W.H. Muller & Co.* v. *Trinity House (Deptford Strond)*[13] that the reference in the Pilotage Act 1913 to rates of payments to be made in respect of the services of a licensed pilot meant payments for "services rendered" and that a pilotage authority could not therefore impose a charge (by by-law under section 17(1)(*f*) of the 1913 Act) upon a ship when in fact no pilotage services had been performed. This principle may still apply but does not, of course, affect the express power to make reasonable charges in respect of a ship which is being navigated by a master or first mate with a pilotage exemption certificate.

---

12. *Jenkin* v. *Godwin* (1983) 81 L.S.G. 482.
13. *W.H. Muller & Co.* v. *Trinity House (Deptford Strond)* [1925] 1 K.B. 166; 16 Asp. M.L.C. 458.

20.77 Section 10 applies section 31 of the Harbours Act 1964 (see paragraphs 10.16 to 10.21 *ante*) with modifications to enable:

    (a) the owners of ships which customarily navigate in the harbour in question;

    (b) any persons who carry on harbour operations within the harbour; and

    (c) any other harbour authority to whose harbour ships obtain access through that harbour,

or, in any of those cases, persons representatives of them, to object to the Secretary of State against pilotage charges on the grounds:

    (i) that the charge ought to be imposed at a rate lower than that at which it is imposed; or

    (ii) that, according to the circumstances of the case, the charge ought to be imposed (either generally or in circumstances specified in the objection) on ships of a class so specified at a rate lower than that at which it is imposed on others.

20.78 Section 10 differs from the charging provisions of the Harbours Act 1964 in that it combines, in respect of the same charges, a requirement that charges must be reasonable with a statutory objection procedure. The existence of this procedure might be held to exclude application to the courts for a declaration as to whether a charge was reasonable[14] but it seems likely that a shipowner, in addition to his right to object to the Secretary of State, could refuse to pay pilotage charges on the grounds that they were unreasonable with a view to the issue of reasonableness being tested in the court when the harbour authority instituted proceedings to recover the charges.

Accounts

20.79 Section 14 of the 1987 Act relates to the accounts of competent harbour authorities. This section extended the Secretary of State's power to make regulations under section 42 of the Harbours Act 1964 about a statutory harbour undertaker's accounts (as to which see paragraphs 10.81 to 10.93 *ante*) so as to enable the Secretary of State to require a competent harbour authority's statement of accounts relating to pilotage functions to be made available for inspection by the public. The Statutory Harbour Undertakings (Pilotage Accounts) Regulations 1988 made by the Secretary of State under section 42 of the Harbours Act 1964 as extended by section 14 of the 1987 Act:

    (a) Prescribe a competent harbour authority's activities in relation to pilotage as "associated activities" for the purposes of section 42

---

14. See *Gillingham Corporation v. Kent County Council* [1953] Ch. 37.

which must therefore be included in the authority's statement of accounts to be prepared under that section but excludes pilotage activities from the scope of regulation 5 of the Statutory Harbour Undertakings (Accounts, etc.) Regulations 1983, which provide that where a statement of accounts prepared under section 42 relates to associated activities it must include a statement of gross revenue in relation to (all) those activities.

(It seems arguable that a competent harbour authority's pilotage activities are in fact "harbour activities" as defined in section 42, i.e., activities involved in carrying on the authority's statutory harbour undertaking, and should be included in their statement of accounts on that basis, but with the amendment of regulation 5 of the 1983 Regulations, the point is academic.)

 (b) Require a competent harbour authority to show pilotage income and expenditure separately in their accounts.
 (c) Require copies of any statement of accounts identifying pilotage revenue and expenditure to be made available for inspection by the public at all reasonable hours at the registered office of the competent harbour authority and require that authority to make copies available for purchase by members of the public at a reasonable charge.

 20.80 Section 14(3) provides that where a competent harbour authority's pilotage functions are discharged by an agent, the statement of accounts under section 42 of the Harbours Act must still relate to those activities, and the agent must furnish the authority with the requisite information.

Limitation of liability

20.81 It may be helpful to begin by referring briefly to the statutory limitations of liability which formerly applied in relation to pilots and pilotage authorities under the Pilotage Act 1983:

 (a) Under section 17 of the Pilotage Act 1983, a pilotage authority had no vicarious liability for any loss occasioned by any act or default of a pilot whom it had licensed.
 (b) Under section 42 of the 1983 Act a pilot's liability, and that of an authorized assistant, for neglect or want of skill was limited to £100 and the amount of the pilotage charges in respect of the voyage during which the liability arose.
 (c) Also under section 42, the vicarious liability of a pilotage authority for neglect or want of skill on the part of a pilot, or assistant, whom it employed was similarly limited to £100 and the pilotage charges in respect of the relevant voyage.

(d) Under section 55 of the 1983 Act, a pilotage authority had a general right to limit its liability for loss or damage to vessels, goods and other property arising on one distinct occasion, which did not result from its personal act or omission made with intent to cause such loss or recklessly and with the knowledge that such loss would probably result, to the amount of £100 multiplied by the number of licensed pilots for the district at the time when the loss or damage occurred.

(e) Section 58 of the 1983 Act made clear that none of these specific rights to limit liability prejudiced the right of a pilotage authority to limit its liability as a shipowner under section 17 or 18 of the Merchant Shipping Act 1979, e.g., for damage caused by a pilot boat.

20.82 Under section 22 of the Pilotage Act 1987:

(a) Subsection (8) provides that a competent harbour authority shall not be liable for any loss or damage caused by any act or omission of a pilot authorized by them by virtue only of that authorization. That corresponds to section 17 of the 1983 Act.

(b) Subsection (2) limits the liability of any authorized pilot for any loss or damage caused by any act or omission of his while acting as such a pilot to £1,000 and the amount of the pilotage charges in respect of the voyage during which the liability arose. So that corresponds as far as pilots are concerned, to section 42 of the 1983 Act with a reasonable escalation in the amount of the limitation.

(c) Subsection (3) limits the liability of a competent harbour authority for loss or damage to any ship, to any property on board any ship or to any property rights of any kind caused, without the personal act or omission of the authority, by an authorized pilot whom they employ, to £1,000 multiplied by the number of authorized pilots employed by the authority at the date when the loss or damages occurs. Subsection (3) is therefore adapted from the right for pilotage authorities to limit their liability generally contained in section 55 of the 1983 Act, but applies only to vicarious liability for damage to property caused by employed pilots. Subsection (4) limits in the same way the liability of persons providing pilotage services as agents for competent harbour authorities for loss or damage caused by authorized pilots employed by such agents.

(d) Subject to these specific provisions, a competent harbour authority's general right to limit their liability for loss or damage to ships or to property on board ships under section 191 of the Merchant Shipping Act 1900 as amended 1995 applies in relation to pilotage functions. (The amount of that limitation depends on the tonnage of the largest

British ship which, at the relevant time, is, or within the past five years has been, within the harbour, with certain qualifications.) See paragraphs 3.20 and 3.21 *ante*.

20.83 With regard to liability arising from the operation of pilot boats, it appears that a competent harbour authority are entitled to limit their liability as shipowners under the Merchant Shipping Act 1995. Subsection (7) of section 22 of the Pilotage Act 1987 makes clear that the special right to limit vicarious liability for loss or damage caused by an employed pilot does not affect a competent harbour authority's right to limit their liability as ship-owners.

20.84 It appears that the provisions of section 22(3) and (4) of the Pilotage Act 1987 referred to in paragraph 20.82 *ante*, which limit the vicarious liability of a competent harbour authority, or of a person providing pilotage services as an agent for a competent harbour authority, for the negligence of an employed pilot, will seldom be relevant because such vicarious liability will only arise in special circumstances (which are indeed difficult to envisage).

20.85 At common law it has long been held that a pilot when navigating a ship, is the servant of the shipowner. In the case of *The Beechgrove*[15] it was held that a pilot navigating outwith a compulsory district was, in law, the servant of the shipowner. In *Thom* v. *Hutchison Ltd.*[16] it was held that section 15 of the Pilotage Act 1913, which provided that the owner or master of a vessel navigating in circumstances in which pilotage was compulsory was answerable for any loss or damage caused by the vessel or by any fault in the navigation of the vessel as he would be if pilotage was not compulsory (which is substantially reproduced in a different form in section 16 of the Pilotage Act 1987), resulted in a pilot also being the servant of the owner where the vessel was navigating in a compulsory district. This was also held to be the position in *Workington Harbour and Dock Board* v. *Towerfield (Owners)*.[17] In all these cases the pilot was licensed by the pilotage authority but was not employed by the author-ity.

20.86 In the case of *The Esso Bernicia*[18] (which related to an incident in a compulsory district which had occurred in January 1978 when the Pilotage Act 1913 was the governing legislation) the pilot concerned was not only licensed by but, exceptionally at that time, was also employed by, the Shetland Islands Council. The Court nevertheless held that the SIC were not liable for any negligence on the part of the pilot because:

15. *The Beechgrove* [1916] 1 A.C. 364.
16. *Thom* v. *Hutchison Ltd.* (1925) 21 Ll.L.Rep. 169.
17. *Workington Dock and Harbour Board* v. *Towerfield (Owners)* [1951] A.C. 112.
18. *The Esso Bernicia* [1989] A.C. 643.

   (1) the pilot was an independent professional man who navigated the ship as a principal and not as a servant of his general employer; and

   (2) section 15 of the 1913 Act made him the servant of the shipowner for all purposes connected with navigation.

20.87 In the course of his judgment in this case Lord Jauncey also emphasized that, although SIC were empowered to license pilots, there was no statutory provision which either obliged or empowered them to undertake the pilotage of ships or employ pilots. He cited the precedent of *Fowles* v. *Eastern and Australian Steamship Co. Ltd.*[19] where it was held that under the relevant Australian legislation the Government of Queensland had no duty to manage or control ships but merely a duty to license duly qualified pilots. (The express power for pilotage authorities in Britain to employ pilots was originally included in the Merchant Shipping Act 1979. This power was re-enacted in the Pilotage Act 1983 which, as mentioned above, included in section 42 of that Act a provision limiting the vicarious liability of pilotage authorities for the negligence of employed pilots. As also mentioned above, section 22(3) of the 1987 Act was not based so much on section 42 of the 1983 Act as on section 55 of that Act which contained a right for pilotage authorities to limit their liability for damage to property generally but did not refer specifically to damage caused by the negligence of pilots. Section 55 was based on section 1 of the Pilotage Authorities (Limitation of Liability) Act 1936.)

20.88 The Fourth Edition of this book tentatively suggested that the Pilotage Act 1987, by imposing on competent harbour authorities an express duty to provide a pilotage service, might have changed the law as respects the vicarious liability of competent harbour authorities for the negligence of employed pilots. It was thought that this might have resulted in competent harbour authorities being in the business of piloting ships instead of only having a duty to provide competent pilots as in the case of pilotage authorities under the former system.

20.89 However, it was held in the case of *The Cavendish*[20] that the duties expressed in section 2 of the 1987 Act in essence gave statutory definition to duties which were in practice assumed by pilotage authorities under the earlier legislation. As in the case of the former pilotage authorities, the duty of competent harbour authorities is to supply properly authorized pilots for ships. Competent harbour authorities are therefore in the same position as the former pilotage authorities as respects vicarious liability for the negligence of employed pilots. A pilot, whether employed or not, remains the servant of the shipowner while in the course of navigating a ship.

---

19. *Fowles* v. *Eastern and Australian Steamship Co. Ltd.* [1916] A.C. 556.
20. *The Cavendish* [1993] 2 Lloyd's Rep. 292.

Rights of authorized pilots

20.90 Sections 17 to 20 of the Pilotage Act 1987 apply to pilots authorized under that Act provisions similar to those of the Pilotage Act 1983 which related to the rights of licensed pilots and the obligations of masters of ships in relation to such pilots.

20.91 Under section 17(1) an authorized pilot may, within the harbour for which he is authorized, supersede as the pilot of a ship any unauthorized person who has been employed to pilot it. This right does not, however, apply in the approaches to a harbour, even though the competent harbour authority may be obliged to provide pilotage services in them. Similarly, subsections (2) and (4) which, respectively, make it an offence for a master to navigate his ship in any part of a harbour under the pilotage of an unauthorized person without first notifying the competent harbour authority that he proposes to do so, or to knowingly employ or continue to employ an unauthorized person to pilot his ship after an authorized pilot has offered to pilot it, do not apply in the approaches to a harbour, and neither does subsection (3) which makes it an offence for an unauthorized person to pilot a ship within a harbour knowing that an authorized pilot has offered to pilot it.

20.92 So far as pilotage in the approaches to a harbour is concerned the position is, therefore, that, although the competent harbour authority may be providing a service, authorized pilots may be competing with deep sea pilots.

20.93 Subsections (7) and (8) of section 17 enable a competent harbour authority to direct that the rights of authorized pilots and the related obligations of masters shall not apply to certain ship movements for the purpose of changing a ship from one mooring to another or taking it into or out of dock. The circumstances in which such a direction can be given, and the area to which it may apply, are narrowly limited. The effect is to enable harbour authorities to allow dock pilots and watermen to continue to operate where they do so already.

20.94 Under section 18 a pilot may require the master of a ship which he is piloting to declare its draught of water, length and beam and to provide him with other relevant information. This provision is not limited to authorized pilots or to a particular area. It would, therefore, seem to apply to deep sea pilots and indeed to an unauthorized person who pilots a ship within a harbour.

20.95 Section 19 re-enacts the former prohibition on a master taking a pilot out of his area but in terms that an authorized pilot must not, without reasonable excuse, be taken without his consent beyond the point up to which he has been engaged to pilot the ship. This recognizes that the approaches to a harbour are not usually a clearly defined area.

20.96 Section 20 requires the master of a ship to give a pilot facilities for boarding, and subsequently leaving, his ship. Failure to comply with this requirement is an offence punishable on summary conviction by a fine not exceeding level 4 on the standard scale.

Duties of pilots under Merchant Shipping (Port State Control) Regulations 1995 and Merchant Shipping (Reporting Requirements for Ships Carrying Dangerous or Polluting Goods) Regulations 1995

20.97 The duties of pilots under the above Regulations are described in paragraphs 6.34 to 6.36 and 6.44 *ante*.

Misconduct by pilots

20.98 Under section 21 of the 1987 Act if the pilot of a ship:

(a) does any act which causes or is likely to cause the loss or destruction of, or serious damage to, the ship or its machinery, navigational equipment or safety equipment or the death of, or serious injury to, a person on board the ship; or

(b) omits to do anything required to preserve the ship or its machinery, navigational equipment or safety equipment from loss, destruction or serious damage or to preserve any person on board the ship from death or serious injury,

and the act or omission is deliberate or amounts to a breach or neglect of duty or he is under the influence of drink or a drug at the time of the act or omission he is guilty of an offence and liable:

(a) on summary conviction, to imprisonment for a term not exceeding six months or a fine not exceeding the statutory maximum or both; or

(b) on conviction on indictment, to imprisonment for a term not exceeding two years or a fine or both.

Winding up of former pilotage authorities and Pilotage Commission

20.99 Sections 24 to 29 of the Pilotage Act 1987 dealt with the winding up of the former pilotage structure. The Act provided for the Pilotage Commission to play a central role in this process.

20.100 On the appointed day (see paragraph 20.1 *ante*) every pilotage authority within the meaning of the Pilotage Act 1983 ceased to exist as such an authority. Of course, if a body which had been a pilotage authority also had other capacities—if it was, for example, also a harbour authority—it continued to exist in that capacity and if, indeed, it was a competent harbour authority within the meaning of the Act, continued to perform pilotage functions, but in its capacity as a harbour authority. And Trinity House of course continued to exist as a lighthouse authority.

20.101 Perhaps the most important duty imposed on the Pilotage Commission was that contained in sections 24 and 25 of the 1987 Act to prepare and submit to the Secretary of State proposals for a scheme or schemes for the transfer of property, rights and liabilities of pilotage authorities, including liabilities in respect of pensions payable in respect of staff and former staff, and including arrangements as regards pilotage authority staff.

20.102 The Secretary of State was required to make a scheme or schemes giving effect to the proposals submitted to him by the Commission with such modifications as he considered appropriate. Schemes under sections 24 and 25 of the 1987 Act transferring to competent harbour authorities the property, rights, liabilities and staff of the former pilotage authorities were duly made by the Secretary of State after appropriate consultation.

20.103 Section 26 of the 1987 Act provided that the Pilotage Commission should be abolished on such day as the Secretary of State might by order appoint and that not less than six months before that day the Commission should submit to the Secretary of State a scheme for the winding up of the Commission. Such a scheme was duly submitted and implemented by the Secretary of State in accordance with section 26(3). The Pilotage Commission was abolished by order of the Secretary of State under section 26(1) on 30 April 1991.

20.104 Under section 28 of the 1987 Act the Secretary of State made a pilots' compensation scheme to compensate pilots for any loss of employment which they might suffer in consequence of the re-organization of pilotage services under the Act. (The original scheme, made on 27 June 1988, was replaced by a new scheme which came into force on 10 September 1990. The second scheme was substantially the same as the first one but, in consequence of the winding up of the Pilotage Commission, the Commission's functions under the original scheme were performed under the second scheme partly by the Pilots' National Pension Fund Trust Company Limited and partly by the Advisory, Conciliation and Arbitration Service.) These schemes provided that, subject to certain qualifications, any pilot aged between 50 and 65 on the appointed day who was a licensed pilot immediately before that day and who either—

(i) had no arrangements offered to him (whether by way of employment under a contract of employment or otherwise) for the provision of his services as an authorized pilot after the appointed day; or

(ii) had such arrangements made with him which were terminated within three years from the appointed day,

was entitled to a compensation payment calculated in accordance with the scheme (broadly, one year's earnings for pilots aged between 50 and 60 with a progressive reduction in the amount for those aged over 60). No claim for compensation under the Scheme could be made where arrangements for the provision of a pilot's services were terminated on or after 1 October 1991.

20.105 Payments were made by competent harbour authorities via the Pilotage Commission which played an important part in the administration of the scheme and had been responsible for determining any disputes as to entitlement to a payment under the scheme. When the Commission was wound up its administrative functions under the scheme were transferred to the P.N.P.F. Trust Company Limited and its function of determining disputes was transferred to A.C.A.S.

20.106 Competent harbour authorities liable for payments under the scheme were, in the case of a pilot who had no arrangements offered to him immediately after the appointed day, the authority or authorities whose harbour or harbours were situated in the former pilotage district for which the pilot had been licensed and, in the case of a pilot who had arrangements made with him which were terminated within three years from the appointed day, the authority who terminated those arrangements. The scheme provided for the amount of such payments to be apportioned by the Pilotage Commission where more than one harbour authority was involved.

20.107 The scheme provided for the repayment of compensation, or a proportion thereof, if a pilot, after receiving compensation was subsequently authorized by a competent harbour authority within the periods specified in the scheme (but occasional authorization for short periods was permitted without repayment).

20.108 The scheme enabled a competent harbour authority to require the whole or part of any existing fund constituted for the purpose of making payments for loss of employment to pilots working in its harbour to be applied towards payments required to be made by the harbour authority under the pilots' compensation scheme.

20.109 Section 29 of the 1987 Act provided for the funding of the re-organization arrangements. Under this section the Secretary of State made a scheme requiring competent harbour authorities to contribute towards the expenses of the Pilotage Commission in carrying out its functions to facilitate these arrangements. Under section 29(5) a competent harbour authority were authorized to recover certain amounts for which they became liable in consequence of these arrangements, including any sums required to meet obligations or liabilities transferred to or imposed on them by a scheme transferring the property, liabilities and staff of a former pilotage authority (see paragraph 20.101 *ante*), by increasing any charges, dues or fees payable to them.

Pilot boats

20.110 Section 6 of the 1987 Act provides that pilot boats—"ships regularly employed in pilotage services provided by or on behalf of any competent harbour authority"—shall—

    (a) if they are operated by the authority be approved by the authority; and

(b) otherwise (i.e., if they are operated by an agent on behalf of the authority pursuant to arrangements made under section 11) be licensed by the authority.

Section 6 also requires a competent harbour authority to make such other provisions as it considers necessary for the operation of pilot boats.

20.111 The Merchant Shipping (Pilot Boats) Regulations 1991 made by the Secretary of State under powers contained in sections 21 and 22 of the Merchant Shipping Act 1979 require that the design and construction of, the machinery installed in, and the equipment carried in, any boat employed or intended to be employed in pilotage services (a "pilot boat") must comply with standards specified in the Code of Practice entitled *A Code of Practice for the Construction, Survey and Certification of Pilot Boats* issued by the Department of Transport. The Regulations also require that the manning of pilot boats must be in accordance with requirements contained in the Code of Practice (there must normally be at least two crew members).

20.112 The Regulations also require pilot boats to be surveyed at regular intervals by a marine surveyor nominated by the Secretary of State and for the "Certifying Authority" (the Secretary of State or any other person or organization authorized by him) to issue a Pilot Boat Certificate in respect of a pilot boat following a satisfactory report of its survey. A Pilot Boat Certificate is valid for a period not exceeding four years and may be suspended by the Secretary of State if he is notified by the surveyor that the boat is not fit for sea service or that the competent harbour authority or (if the boat is not owned by them) the owner of the boat has or have failed to take any corrective action which in the opinion of the surveyor is necessary to secure that it complies with the standards specified in the Regulations.

20.113 The Regulations impose certain responsibilities on the competent harbour authority, any other person who owns a pilot boat and the master of a pilot boat. These include the duty to ensure that the pilot boat does not operate unless it has a valid Pilot Boat Certificate. The Regulations also provide for offences and penalties where their requirements are not complied with.

Deep sea pilotage certificates

20.114 A deep sea pilotage certificate relates to the competence of a person to act as a pilot in respect of any part of the sea falling outside the harbour of a competent harbour authority. It is a recommendation to masters of ships but does not entitle the holder to supersede any other person as the pilot of a ship. In short, it has no legal force. Section 23 of the 1987 Act enables the Secretary of State to authorize any body appearing to him to be competent to do so to grant deep sea certificates in respect of such part of the sea falling outside the harbour of any competent harbour authority as he may specify. Any body for the time being so authorized may grant a deep sea certificate to any person on application by him if they are satisfied (by examination or by reference to such criteria as they may reasonably impose) that he is qualified to act as a pilot of a ship for the area in respect of which the body is authorized to grant deep sea certificates.

20.115 Since, as indicated in paragraph 20.91 *ante* an authorized pilot is not entitled to supersede any other person piloting a ship in the approaches to a harbour as distinct from the harbour itself authorized pilots and deep sea pilots could, at least in theory, be competing with each other in the approaches to a harbour.

20.116 Before the appointed day for the coming into force of the main provisions of the 1987 Act deep sea pilotage certificates had been granted by such pilotage authorities as were authorized to do so by pilotage orders made under the Pilotage Act 1913 or the Pilotage Act 1983 and related to parts of the sea outside a pilotage district. Paragraph 6 of Schedule 1 to the 1987 Act requires the Secretary of State, on application by any body which immediately before the appointed day was authorized, as mentioned above, to grant deep sea pilotage certificates, to authorize that body to grant such certificates under section 23. This would, in particular, relate to Trinity House. Paragraph 6 also provides that any deep sea pilotage certificate granted to any person pursuant to a pilotage order which is in force immediately before the appointed day in respect of any area shall continue in force during the period for which it was granted and may, on application by him, be renewed by any body authorized under section 23 to grant deep sea pilotage certificates in respect of the whole or part of the area concerned.

CHAPTER 21

DIVISION OF CONTROL BETWEEN
MASTER AND PILOT

21.1 Before 1913 the owner or master of a ship being navigated in circumstances in which pilotage was compulsory was not answerable for any loss or damage occasioned by the fault of a compulsory pilot. This situation led to a profusion of cases coming before the courts where an almost unending stream of litigants attempted to attach either blame or exculpation to pilots in order to avoid the payment of costly damages. The result was that hardship was frequently inflicted on innocent persons whose property had received damage, and the Departmental Committee of 1911 strongly recommended that the defence of compulsory pilotage should be abolished.

21.2 The Pilotage Act 1913 achieved this purpose by making the shipowner answerable for any loss or damage "caused by the vessel or by any fault of the navigation of the vessel" whether pilotage was compulsory or not,[1] and as a consequence since the shipowner had to meet the cost in either event, the question as to whether either the master or the pilot was responsible for damage has, since 1913, been largely academic. The pre-1913 cases on the relationship between master and pilot may therefore no longer be of much practical importance but it still seems worthwhile to examine them, as well as more recent cases, as indicating the views expressed by the courts of what this relationship should be. Before doing so there will be a brief examination of the general attitudes which masters and pilots have towards each other, with particular reference to their respective attitudes to the division of responsibility.

General attitudes of masters and pilots

21.3 The atmosphere on a ship's bridge during the pilotage operation is usually one of cordial professionalism and mutual respect between master and pilot. Any personal views which the master might have about pilots in general, and vice versa, are confined well below the surface and only very rarely

---

1. Pilotage Act 1913, section 15(1), Pilotage Act 1983, section 35, and now Pilotage Act 1987, section 16.

manifest themselves in open mistrust or hostility. These attitudes are never-theless of some importance, as they are generally symptomatic of a basic misunderstanding of the legal relationship between the master and the pilot—a misunderstanding caused by vaguely worded legislation and the fact that since 1913 the superior courts have seldom had occasion to give judgment on this particular aspect of the law. The respective views of the master and pilot are now considered.

The master's view

21.4 From his earliest days at sea the master has seen the expression "pro-ceeding to master's instructions and pilot's advice" written in the deck log on each occasion that a pilot has been on board, and he accepts this as docu-mentary proof that he is personally responsible for all the acts and omissions of the pilot, a conviction which is frequently shared by his employers.

21.5 The amount of freedom which the master gives to the pilot varies considerably between masters. Generally speaking, the masters of smaller coasting vessels have a greater tendency to overrule or ignore a pilot's instruc-tions than those in larger vessels. Masters of large foreign-going vessels are inclined to assume a more passive attitude, carefully observing but seldom interfering with the manoeuvring of the vessel. This difference in attitude is undoubtedly the result of the difference in background and training between the two types of master. The coasting master is called upon to perform his own pilotage duties in a number of ports with which he is familiar and therefore usually considers himself to be fairly skilled in basic ship handling. Also, by virtue of the type of trade in which he is engaged, the coasting master will frequently visit several ports in the course of a week. The master of a large vessel engaged on long international voyages, however, is seldom called upon to conduct his own vessel into or out of port, and the interval between such operations is usually much greater. It does not follow, however, that the foreign-going master has a greater faith in the ability of pilots than his coasting counterpart; he simply feels himself powerless to intervene through lack of local knowledge and lack of experience in practical ship handling.

21.6 In ports where pilotage is not compulsory, the coasting master's confidence in the ability of pilots will be reflected to a certain extent in his decision whether or not to employ them. The master of the larger foreign-going vessel, on the other hand, even if not compelled by law to take a pilot will usually feel compelled by expediency and, on occasions when casualties occur, will regard himself as the innocent victim of a system over which he has no control. Such masters are quite indifferent as to whether pilotage in a par-ticular port is compulsory or not.

21.7 Irrespective of the legal position, masters are generally resigned to the fact that they will be held to blame by their owners for damage occasioned while under pilotage. The majority of incidents involving damage do not come before the courts, and in these cases blame is usually apportioned after an informal investigation by the owners. Disciplinary measures against the master can take several forms; he might be penalized financially by the forfeiture of his safe navigation bonus, although this is a practice which appears to be dying out; he might be demoted to first mate; and on some occasions might be dismissed from the company. Even in circumstances where no disciplinary action is taken, the master usually feels that damage sustained by any vessel under his command is a blot on his record, and it is often resented.

The pilot's view

21.8 Pilots generally dislike interference in the conduct of the ship by the master. They interpret it as an imputation of incompetence by a person not fully qualified to judge and frequently attribute accidents to the master's unwarranted intrusion. They feel that whatever a person's sea-going experience, when he first becomes a pilot a minimum period of basic training is essential. Pilots believe, having undergone this extensive period of training in what they consider to be a highly specialized field, that in circumstances where there is no time for consultation and "instant" decisions are required the pilot is the person who is best qualified to appraise the situation. They consider that the master's duty is to advise the pilot of the handling characteristics of the vessel and to ensure that the crew carry out the pilot's instructions. The same view has been expressed by pilots with previous command experience.

21.9 The term "adviser", which is frequently applied to the pilot, is considered to be derogatory and contrary to the actual situation on board ship. They see it as a word which underrates their professional skill and casts the pilot in the role of a passive onlooker, watching the master navigate his ship into port and only offering opinions when they are asked for, or when they appear to be required. They also feel that the label "adviser" has been an impediment to them when conducting negotiations regarding their remuneration.

Division of control under statute law

21.10 Although the Pilotage Acts 1913 and 1983 made no specific references to the duties of a pilot the general implication was that the pilot did not act simply as an adviser but was responsible for the navigation of the ship. When navigating in a compulsory pilotage area, for example, the master of a ship was obliged to "give the charge of piloting" to any licensed pilot for the district who offered his services. The courts generally took the view that the master was entitled to take control of the vessel if he considered the pilot to be incompetent, but that if an accident ensued he would have to justify his action. In the case of *The Tower Field*,[2] for example, Lord Norman said:

The master is not merely entitled but bound to point out to the compulsory pilot that he may be mistaken in an opinion he has formed (*The Tactician*).[3] He is also entitled, in order to avoid immediate peril, to take the navigation out of the hands of the pilot, but if he does so he must be prepared to show justification (*The Prinses Juliana*).[4]

The court held in this case that of those on board the ship the pilot was solely to blame.

21.11 In *The Prinses Juliana* case cited above, Bucknill, J., said:

. . . if the master sees fit to take the navigation out of the hands of the pilot and countermands his orders, he must satisfy the court that he was justified in so doing, and that the action which he took was at all events more calculated to avoid a collision than the manoeuvre which he countermanded.[5]

21.12 In a collision case heard in 1952 the defendant was a master and part owner of a vessel which caused a collision in the entrance to Dover Harbour. The collision was caused by the pilot's admitted negligence in disregarding a local signal and the master sought to limit his liability as part owner on the ground that the accident occurred without his actual fault or privity. The plaintiffs contended that the master had contributed to the accident because, *inter alia*, he had failed to acquaint himself beforehand with the local regulations. Wilmer, J., however, granted a limitation decree and in giving his decision said:

It would be, in my judgment, putting too much upon a master, and would be asking him to exercise more than ordinary care, to regard him as being under a duty to know all the local signals when he has a pilot on board, or to expect him to be ready to query the pilot's actions in relation to such signals. In my judgment, on such matters of purely local knowledge, a master exercising ordinary and reasonable care is entitled to rely on the guidance which he obtains from the local pilot.[6]

21.13 In the case of *The Saltero* the pilot was instructed by the harbour master to arrive off the dock entrance at 10 minutes after high water. Because the only two available tugs had a previous commitment the pilot proceeded to navigate the vessel slowly up the approach channel in anticipation of the tugs meeting him at a certain distance along it. At approximately seven minutes after high water the pilot observed the two tugs engaged in towing a submarine, whereupon he stopped the engines. Three minutes later the vessel grounded and broke her back on the falling tide. It was held in this case that the grounding of the *Saltero* was due solely to the negligence of the pilot in that

2. *Tower Field (Owners)* v. *Workington Harbour and Dock Board* (H.L.) (1950) 84 Ll.L.Rep. 233, at p. 259.
3. *The Tactician* [1907] P. 244; 10 Asp. M.L.C. 534.
4. *The Prinses Juliana* [1936] P. 139; 54 Ll.L.Rep. 234.
5. *The Prinses Juliana* (1936) 18 Asp. M.L.C. 614, at p. 619.
6. *The Hans Hoth* [1952] 2 Lloyd's Rep. 341 at p. 349.

it was necessary to hold back; in that it was unseamanlike to lose steerage way while on the port side of the channel; and that through his own inobservance he failed to appreciate the danger of grounding.[7]

21.14 The Pilotage Act 1987 refers throughout to "piloting" and "pilotage". Section 31 of the 1987 Act as amended by the Merchant Shipping Act 1995 defines "pilot" in the same terms as the definition of that expression in the former section 742 of the Merchant Shipping Act 1894 (see paragraph 20.4 *ante*) and provides that "pilotage" shall be construed accordingly. As the definitions of "master" and "pilot" have not been substantially changed it seems unlikely, therefore, that the respective duties of the master and pilot have been affected by the change in legislation.

The master's liability

21.15 The courts have never ruled as to whether the master is legally responsible for the pilot's mistakes but the weight of authoritative opinion seems to lie in favour of the view that the master is not responsible for damage incurred when the navigation of the vessel is in the hands of the pilot. MacLachlan, for example, says:

At common law the pilot, being appointed by the owners, or their servant the master, is their agent, and they are responsible for damage done by the ship while under his charge. How far the master, as having employed him, may be considered in the light of a principal, and answerable in that capacity for his acts, may be doubtful; but as master merely, notwithstanding the dictum of Mansfield, C.J., the better opinion seems to be that he is not responsible while the ship is in the hands of the pilot, if he takes care that the pilot's orders are promptly obeyed by the crew.[8]

21.16 The *dictum* of Mansfield, C.J., referred to by MacLachlan was given in the case of *Bowcher* v. *Noidstrom*. In this case the pilot of the defendant master's vessel ordered the crew to board the plaintiff's vessel to cut free the jib boom which had pierced the defendant's mainsail. An action for trespass was brought against the master who happened to be asleep at the time of the incident. With respect to the master's liability, Mansfield, C.J., was of the opinion that although there was a pilot on board, the pilot did not represent the ship, and the master was still answerable for every trespass.[9] In a later case, however, in which an action was brought against the owner of a ship for the negligence of a pilot employed by both himself and the master, it was held that the pilot was a competent witness for the defendant although he had not been released by the master "because the captain could not be responsible for the misconduct of the pilot".[10]

---

7. *The Saltero* [1958] 2 Lloyd's Rep. 232.
8. *MacLachlan's Treatise on the Law of Merchant Shipping*, 7th edn., London, 1932, p. 211.
9. *Bowcher* v. *Noidstrom* (1809) 127 E.R. 954.
10. *Aldrich* v. *Simmons* (1816) 171 E.R. 451.

21.17 Marsden's opinion on this subject is as follows:

As regards the responsibility of the master when a pilot is on board, whether by compulsion of law or by the master's or owner's choice, it seems clear that for a collision caused by the fault of the pilot the master is not answerable, if the pilot has been placed in charge of the ship properly and in the ordinary course of navigation.[11]

21.18 Marsden cites Chancellor Kent as an authority who also doubts the judgment of Mansfield, C.J.

The pilot, while on board, has the exclusive control of the ship. He is considered as master *pro hac vice*, and if any loss or injury be sustained in the navigation of the vessel while under the charge of the pilot, he is answerable, as strictly as if he were a common carrier, for his default, negligence, or unskilfulness; and the owner would also be responsible to the party injured for the act of the pilot, as being the act of his agent. Though some doubt has been raised by the dictum of Ch.J.Mansfield in *Bowcher* v. *Noidstrom*, yet the weight of authority, and the better reason is, that the master, in such a case, would not be responsible as master, though on board, provided the crew acted in regular obedience to the pilot.[12]

21.19 Marsden also cites the case of *Stort* v. *Clement*, but this case should be treated with some circumspection as on this occasion the pilot was also the ship's sailing master and a member of the ship's company. As such he would not come within the present definition of a pilot but rather within an earlier definition which did not preclude persons belonging to the ship. His position, however, was analogous with the modern pilot, for, by their terms of his commission, the sailing master was entrusted with the navigation of the ship under the command of his superior officer. In this case an action was brought against the pilot for running down a brig belonging to the plaintiff, and it was stated by Lord Kenyon that although the pilot might be obliged to act in obedience to the orders of the lieutenant, yet if in this case the accident had happened through the defendant's misconduct, he was answerable. It was proved, however, that the lieutenant had instructed him to conduct the ship in a particular manner, in consequence of which the accident occurred.[13]

21.20 In Canada the Royal Commission on pilotage gave the following opinion on the subject of the master's liability:

Whilst the master always retains his responsibility for the safety of the ship, his responsibility in the sense of liability is not absolute. Either civilly, criminally, or with respect to the safety of navigation, he is answerable only for his own acts, mistakes, negligence or omissions. At civil law he is merely a servant of the owner and he does not incur personally any civil responsibility for any damage caused by a pilot's error in which he did not participate or which he could not have prevented.[14]

---

11. Marsden: *The Law of Collisions at Sea. British Shipping Laws*, vol. 4 (11th edn., London, 1961), para. 69.
12. James Kent: *Commentaries on American Law*, vol. 3 (3rd edn., 1836), p. 176.
13. *Stort* v. *Clement* (1792) 170 E.R. 109.
14. Canada. *Report of Royal Commission, &c., op. cit.*, Part 1, p. 27

21.21 It would seem from the authorities cited, therefore, that the master does not incur any personal liability for the actions of the pilot while the latter has the conduct of the ship. The pilot, however, does not supersede the master in his command of the ship, and if the master decides to overrule the pilot's directions the responsibility is transferred to him.

The pilot's liability

21.22 Before the Pilotage Act 1987 came into force the pilot's personal liability was limited to £100, plus the amount of pilotage charges in respect of the voyage during which the liability arose. Under the 1987 Act the figure of £100 has increased to £1,000.

21.23 Because of this strict limitation on personal liability actions against pilots have been rare. Nevertheless actions against pilots for personal negligence have occasionally taken place, although not in recent years. In *The Octavia Stella*, for example, a pilot was held solely to blame for damage caused by a vessel grounding on some oyster beds[15] and in the case of *Stort* v. *Clement, ante*, the judge made it clear that the pilot would have been answerable if the accident had been caused by his negligence. Again, in the case of *London School Board* v. *Lardner*, it was held that the pilot had given an incorrect helm order and he was ordered to pay damages of £75.[16]

21.24 A pilot whose negligence results in someone's death may be convicted of manslaughter. In the case of *R.* v. *Spence* it was alleged that a boat was run down and life was lost because a foreign helmsman had misunderstood the pilot's instructions and put the helm the wrong way. In giving his instructions to the jury Lord Denman, C.J., said:

The law is, that if the prisoner has produced the death by any conduct of his, he is guilty of manslaughter. It appears to me that he was the person guiding and directing the vessel, and that he is responsible for its management. It is extremely unfortunate that he did not, in the first instance, make the foreigners understand such simple directions as starboard and larboard. You will consider whether there was some negligence upon the part of the prisoner, in not making the foreigners understand thoroughly. I take your opinion whether he was guilty of negligence in this respect, and whether that negligence caused the death. If you think so, you will find him guilty.

The defendant was found not guilty on the facts.[17]

Judicial attitude to "divided authority"

21.25 The attitude of the courts to the master–pilot relationship is based on precedents created more than a century ago, the guiding principle of which has been throughout that the paramount danger to a ship under pilotage is that created by a "divided authority". Attention was drawn to this danger on

---

15. *The Octavia Stella* (1887) 6 Asp. M.L.C. 182.
16. *London School Board* v. *Lardner. The Times*, 20 February 1884.
17. *R.* v. *Spence* (1846) 1 Cox C.C. 352.

innumerable occasions, but was perhaps put most succinctly by Dr Lushington in the case of *The Peerless* in 1860:

There may be occasions on which the master of a ship is justified in interfering with the pilot in charge, but they are very rare. If we encourage such interfering, we should have a double authority on board, a *divisum imperium*, the parent of all confusion, from which many accidents and much mischief would probably ensue. If the pilot is intoxicated, or is steering a course to the certain destruction of the vessel, the master no doubt may interfere and ought to interfere, but it is only in urgent cases.[18]

21.26 It would appear, however, from what has been deduced so far, that the legal relationship between the master and the pilot is based on principles which are contradictory:

(i) that division of authority is inimical to the safety of navigation;
(ii) that the pilot, by definition, has the conduct of the ship;
(iii) that the master, by definition, has command or charge of the ship, a definition which specifically excludes the pilot.[19]

21.27 In order to reconcile these apparent inconsistencies it becomes necessary to:

(i) differentiate between the expressions "to conduct a ship" and "to be in command of a ship"; and
(ii) draw up a code of procedure for vessels under pilotage based upon legal decisions, which defines the respective duties of the master and the pilot.

With regard to the first of these requirements it is evident that confusion as to the difference in meaning between these two terms is not confined to the layman. The words of Bargreave Deane, J., for example, in the case of *The Nord* would indicate that he considered the two expressions to be synonymous when he said: "I think the word 'conducted' means that the pilot is in charge . . . he is in command."[20]

21.28 The Canadian Royal Commission, however, drew a very careful distinction between the two expressions thus:

"To conduct a ship" must not be confused with being "in command of a ship". The first expression refers to an action, to a personal service being performed; the second to a power. The question whether a pilot has control of navigation is a question of fact and not of law. The fact that a pilot has been given control of the ship for navigational purposes does not mean that the pilot has superseded the master. The master is, and remains, in command; he is the authority aboard. He may, and does, delegate part of his authority to subordinates and to outside assistants whom he employs to navigate his ship, i.e., pilots. A delegation of power is not an abandonment of authority, but one way of exercising authority.[21]

18. *The Peerless* (1860) 167 E.R. 16, at p. 17.
19. Merchant Shipping Act 1995, s. 313(1).
20. *The Nord* (1916) 13 Asp. M.L.C. 606, at p. 608.
21. Canada. *Report of Royal Commission, &c., op. cit.,* Part 1, pp. 26–27.

21.29 With regard to the second requirement, having established that both the pilot and the master have active roles to play, it becomes essential that the duties of both should be clearly defined in order to minimize the dangers which are inherent in the "divided authority" situation. These respective duties are now considered.

Division of control under case law

21.30 What, then, are the respective duties of the master and pilot? The answer to this question lies mainly in the body of case law dating from the mid 19th century up to the effective date of the repeal of section 633 of the Merchant Shipping Act 1894, during which period it was possible for a shipowner to escape liability for damage when such damage was caused by a compulsory pilot. In order to rebut a defence of compulsory pilotage it was necessary to prove that there was contributory negligence on the part of the servants (i.e., the master and crew), and in many cases, therefore, it became necessary for the courts to distinguish between "pilot's duties" and "master's duties"; that is, to determine which components of the pilotage operation came within the master's jurisdiction and which came within that of the pilot. From a careful study of these cases it is possible to break down the pilotage operation into its constituent parts and to attribute responsibility for them either to the master or to the pilot. In studying these cases it is necessary to bear in mind that many of them took place more than a century ago and they should be considered in that light, and for this reason many of the cases which deal exclusively with the handling of sailing vessels have been omitted. On the other hand, despite the fact that the design of the power-driven vessel has changed considerably since its first appearance, the basic concept has remained unchanged, namely the provision of motive power by means of screw propulsion, and the provision of turning power by means of a rudder. Similarly, although sophisticated navigational aids have been produced, in recent years the basic technique of navigation in close waters is roughly the same—the direction-finding power of the compass has been improved by the gyroscope, the echo-sounder has replaced the hand lead but its function is precisely the same, and the look-out has been augmented, but not replaced by, the radar.

21.31 It should also be noted that nearly all the cases cited are concerned with compulsory pilotage, and it cannot be automatically assumed that the courts would assign the same degree of responsibility to the pilot if he was employed voluntarily. At the same time, in many of these cases it was a matter of considerable legal argument whether pilotage was compulsory for the ships concerned owing to the multifarious exemptions which were then available, and frequently the first task of the court was to rule upon this point before the defence of compulsory pilotage could be put forward. It would be difficult to see, therefore, how in practice a pilot's whole approach to the task of navigating a ship could vary depending on whether the particular ship concerned had employed him voluntarily or by compulsion, especially when this was, and still is, frequently in dispute.

Master's duty to employ a pilot

21.32 A master is only legally bound to employ pilots in areas where pilotage is compulsory (assuming that neither he nor his first mate has a pilotage exemption certificate under section 8 of the Pilotage Act 1987). A master can, however, be held to blame for not employing a pilot, even when pilotage is not compulsory, if it can be shown that his failure to do so caused or contributed to an accident. This can be deduced from the judgment given in the case of a vessel which was exempt from compulsory pilotage and which caused a collision in the River Thames. It was held by the court that the vessel was negligent for proceeding without a pilot in that the absence of a pilot or similarly informed person was a dominant cause of the vessel's negligent navigation.[22]

21.33 In practice, given the choice, a ship's master might be motivated by a variety of factors when deciding whether or not to employ a pilot, with "local knowledge" not necessarily being on the top of his list of priorities. Masters of small coasting vessels are frequently under pressure from their owners to keep the employment of pilots to a minimum. Some owners allegedly pay their masters a bonus for doing their own piloting, while others might require a written explanation if a master employs a pilot in a given port on more than a specified number of occasions. Some coasting masters take a pride in handling their own vessels and resent the imposition of compulsory pilotage upon them, while others seek every excuse to take pilots and see compulsory pilotage as a means of shifting their responsibilities. There is a feeling among some masters that if they do not employ pilots retaliatory action will be taken, and they will be kept waiting if they require pilots on subsequent occasions. Some also believe that ships carrying pilots are shown favourable treatment by port officials and they therefore take pilots on sufferance.

General duties of master and pilot

21.34 Before dealing in detail with the various aspects of the pilotage operation, it is worth noting some general remarks which have been made by judges on the subject of the respective duties of master and pilot:

---

22. *The Alletta* [1965] 2 Lloyd's Rep. 479.

Per Baron Parke:

The duties of the master and the pilot in many respects are clearly defined. Although the pilot has charge of the ship, the owners are most clearly responsible to third persons for the sufficiencies of the ship and her equipments, the competency of the master and crew, and their obedience to the orders of the pilot in everything that concerns his duty, and under ordinary circumstances we think that his commands are to be implicitly obeyed. To him belongs the whole conduct of the navigation of the ship, to the safety of which it is important that the chief direction should be vested in one only.[23]

Per Brett, L.J.:

The duty of a pilot in England is too well known and too universally applied to require any enactment with regard to it at all. It is to regulate the navigation of the ship, and to conduct it so far as the course of the ship is concerned. He has no other power on board the ship; he has no power over the discipline of the ship, he has no power over the cargo on board; he has no power with regard to the various matters which are necessary to enable him to perform his duty; he cannot place a man on the look-out, or regulate the place at which the look-out man shall be on board the ship. He has nothing to do but to control the navigation.[24]

Per Lord Alverstone, C.J.:

I think the cardinal principle to be borne in mind in these cases . . . is that the pilot is in sole charge of the ship, and that all directions as to speed, course, stopping and reversing and everything of that kind are for the pilot . . . But side by side with that principle is the other principle that the pilot is entitled to the fullest assistance of a competent crew, of a competent look-out, and a well-found ship.[25]

Per Bargreave Deane, J.:

I have to . . . lay down what I think is the true principle as to the duty of ship's officers and crew towards the pilot, and . . . unless the man is incompetent in the sense of being ill or the worse for drink, or something of that sort which justifies force majeure, the officers of the vessel have no right to take control of the navigation out of the hands of the pilot, yet he is entitled to every assistance which can be rendered to him by those on board the ship.[26]

21.35 There is no absolute need for the master to be on the bridge throughout the entire period in which the pilot is on board. In the case of *The Umsinga*, for example, where a collision occurred when the master was momentarily below, Sir Samuel Evans said:

It is easy to conceive cases in which . . . a master must be on the bridge before it can be rightly said that all the assistance which the law requires to be given to the pilot by the master and the crew is given, and in which his absence might be evidence of negligence of default . . . But, in my opinion, it cannot be held as a matter of law, or as an inflexible rule of good navigation that the master must be there, or that his absence amounts to default for which his owners are liable, when he provides a competent officer, or where there are no special circumstances of difficulty, or no special matters within his knowledge of which he ought to be ready to inform the pilot . . .

---

23. *The Christiana* (1850) 13 E.R. 841.
24. *The Guy Mannering* (1882) 4 Asp. M.L.C. 553, at p. 554.
25. *The Tactician* (1907) 10 Asp. M.L.C. 534, at p. 537.
26. *The Ape* (1914) 12 Asp. M.L.C. 487, at p. 489.

It is beside the question to inquire whether the master, if on the bridge, might . . . have caused the pilot to avoid the collision. If he is not there, and is not bound by the law, or by the rules of good navigation to be there, the court cannot surmise what he would have done if he was there.[27]

Legal meaning of "interference"

21.36 Many of the pre-1913 Act cases turned on the question of the master's right to interfere with the pilot's instructions. In these cases the master could be found to have contributed to the accident, thus destroying his owners' defence of compulsory pilotage, in one of two ways:

(i) by interfering with the pilot when there was no just reason for doing so, or

(ii) by failing to interfere with the pilot when the evidence showed that there was just reason for doing so.

21.37 Dr Lushington defined "interference" as follows:

I should never go to the length of saying that the mere suggesting to the pilot on the part of the master to take in this sail, or otherwise to keep as near the South Sand light, and vice versa, or to bring the ship up, was interfering, in the legal acceptation of the term, with the duties of the pilot; illegal interference is of a different description. If, for example, in this case the boatswain had called out to the men below to starboard the helm, or if the master had called out to port the helm, it would be interference; but it would not be interference to consult the pilot, or to suggest to him the measures pursued were not proper, or that other measures would in all probability be attended with greater success.[28]

21.38 Thus, in the case of *The Oakfield* where the pilot gave, at the suggestion of the master, an improper order which brought about a collision with a vessel at anchor, it was held that the master's intervention did not transfer the responsibility of the pilot to the master. The judge justified his decision as follows:

There is a conflict as to how this order to starboard came to be given, but the pilot admits that the words proceeded from his lips. To excuse himself he says he was merely carrying out the captain's order, and that it was not his order at all. I cannot accept that explanation. I feel convinced that the true solution of the case is, that when the *Duchess of Albany* was first seen there was no doubt as to whether she was or was not at anchor, that the captain very likely did strongly express an opinion that it would be safe and proper to starboard and go across her bows, that the pilot adopted that view and gave the order which brought about the collision.[29]

21.39 In another case where the master, for the benefit of the crew, merely repeated the pilot's instructions, it was held that the pilot was responsible for

---

27. *The Umsinga* (1912) 12 Asp. M.L.C. 174, at p. 176.
28. *The Lochlibo* (1850) 166 E.R. 978, at p. 985.
29. *The Oakfield* (1886) 5 Asp. M.L.C. 575, *per* Sir James Hannen, at p. 577.

the manoeuvre carried out as a result even though the actual order proceeded from the master's lips.[30]

21.40 Interference by the master, therefore, must be of a positive nature either in the form of a direct order in the absence of any order being given by the pilot; or in the form of a direct revocation of an order given by the pilot, and the pilot who acts, contrary to his better judgment, on the mere advice or suggestion of the master may be held liable if an accident follows as a result.

21.41 In practice, interference comes in a variety of guises, of which "covert interference" is perhaps the most harmful. On board small vessels, for example, when entering or leaving port the master is often the only member of the ship's company on the bridge, and he not only steers the vessel but is responsible for engine movements as well. In the circumstances the pilot's instructions are frequently modified by the master. A request for "half astern" will often produce a movement of "full astern" and when altering course the master will frequently begin to steady the vessel before the pilot wishes to do so. This type of interference is more difficult to detect in vessels fitted with modern navigational aids such as bow-thrusts and variable pitch propellers, which are operated by the master with fingertip control, and in some cases the vessels concerned are fairly large. Here, a pilot who is unaware of what the master is doing, might attribute a sudden movement of the vessel caused by the surreptitious application of a bow thrust to the effect of wind or tide and take counteraction which is inappropriate. A further disadvantage of such vessels is that no written record is kept of movements so that in the event of an accident the facts would be difficult to prove.

21.42 When manoeuvring a vessel alongside a jetty or into a lock the dangers of a divided command are intensified, and it is in this critical part of the operation that damage is most likely to be incurred. Here, since split-second timing is essential, there is little opportunity for consultation or advice, and yet it is at this point that the master, if he is that way inclined, is most likely to interfere. It is here also that the contrast between coasting and foreign-going masters is most sharply defined, with the former sometimes attempting to take over the operation completely. In those smaller vessels where the master also doubles as helmsman, he suffers from the disadvantage of having his field of vision considerably reduced, and the master who wishes to supervise the berthing operation himself has to spend his time oscillating between the bridge wing and the helm.

21.43 On board foreign vessels, where the master is often the only member of the ship's company with a knowledge of English, the language barrier provides a useful smoke-screen for covert interference. Here, when a pilot gives an instruction the master, if he thinks a different movement is required, will give his own instructions in the vernacular, with the result that the pilot

---

30. *The Admiral Boxer* (1857) 166 E.R. 1090.

can never be sure that his orders are properly being carried out. In these cases, where the master not only interprets the pilot's instructions but censors them as well, the dangers of a divided authority are obviously exacerbated.

Keeping a look-out

21.44 It has been stated in general terms that it is the responsibility of the master and crew to keep a proper look-out and to pass on all relevant information to the pilot. This has been interpreted in the widest possible sense by the courts and includes the reporting of all circumstances and incidents which might influence the pilot's actions, and not merely the sighting of lights, buoys, beacons, etc. In the case of *The Batavier*, for example, a steamer which was proceeding up a river under the control of a pilot caused such a swell that a barge laden with coal was sunk. It was held that the steamer was to blame for failing to stop in time to avoid the accident. Although the pilot was to blame for failing to check the speed the owners were liable because it appeared in evidence that neither the swell nor the barge had been seen from the steamer, and that therefore there was not a good look-out.[31]

21.45 Keeping a look-out also means the reporting of all material facts even if the pilot is in a position where he ought to be able to see things clearly for himself. In the case of *The Alexander Shukoff*, for example, a pilot was navigating a vessel at full speed in narrow waters among a large number of other vessels and the course taken was such that it must have been obvious to the master that a dangerous situation was developing. It was held in this case that it was the master's duty to call the pilot's attention to the risk, and that he was not justified in doing nothing. Lord Birkenhead, L.C., said;

In circumstances which called for the greatest care and fullest assistance he [the pilot] was left to his own observation. It is obvious from his own explanation that he was not fully aware of the position and intentions of both these vessels at the time of the collision. It may be (though I am not satisfied on this point) that he ought to have been aware, but a pilot's duty is that of controlling the navigation of the ship and his attention must at times be concentrated on some particular fact. He is entitled to have the assistance of a look-out and timely reports of material incidents.[32]

In the same case Lord Molton said:

The defendants say that the pilot ought to have found these things for himself and that, therefore, they are excused for having omitted to report them to him. Now it must be remembered that the pilot has many things to think of, especially where . . . he is leaving port in company with other vessels and new incidents may at any moment arise. He needs, therefore, to be in a position of feeling that he can give his whole attention to his duties of management secure that all relevant occurrences will be duly reported to him.[33]

---

31. *The Batavier* (1854) 164 E.R. 218.
32. *The Alexander Shukoff* (1920) 15 Asp. M.L.C. 122, at p. 125.
33. *Ibid.*, at p. 130.

21.46 If, however, it can be shown that the pilot was at all times fully aware of all the circumstances leading up to a collision, it would seem that the absence of an efficient look-out would not necessarily constitute evidence of contributory negligence on the part of the ship. In the case of *The Kamouraska*, for example, which ran down a torpedo-boat in the River Thames while under the control of a pilot, Viscount Finlay in the House of Lords said:

> . . . He must have been, from his own observation, perfectly aware of the torpedo-boat and her movements at all material times. Under these circumstances it is not easy to see how, even if there had been an omission on the part of the lookout . . . to report the torpedo-boat, this omission could have contributed to the accident, as the pilot was throughout in full possession of all the facts himself.[34]

21.47 In practice, the quality of the look-out (in the broad sense of the term) varies from ship to ship and it is almost impossible to generalize on this point. There is an understandable reluctance on the part of the master to point out what is apparently obvious, and in good visibility the pilot is usually expected to observe things for himself. In thick weather, on the other hand, the pilot is usually given adequate assistance.

The observance of Collision Regulations

21.48 As far as the question as to whether the master or the pilot is responsible for the observance of the Collision Regulations is concerned, it would appear that this would depend on the type of regulation involved, i.e., whether it concerns the exhibition of navigation lights, the use of sound signals, or the observance of the steering and sailing rules. In the case of *The Ripon*, for example, the vessel concerned was under tow and dropping stern foremost in the Humber with the tide, and was eventually brought athwart the tide to go into the dock. She was showing, in addition to the regulation masthead and sidelights, a white light showing astern, which had been placed there on the pilot's instructions. The exhibition of such a light was contrary to the Collision Regulations which were in force at that time. Another vessel coming down the Humber collided with the *Ripon*. Although the blame was admitted by the other vessel it was held that the *Ripon* was also to blame, as it was impossible to say that the improper exhibition of a stern light had not contributed to the collision. It was held that as the master had permitted an infringement of the regulations the defence of compulsory pilotage failed. Butt, J., justified his decision as follows:

> It is clear that a master should not allow a light to be improperly carried as to cause an infringement of the regulations. Suppose for example a pilot for some reason chose to order a green light to be carried on the port side, it would be impossible to say that this should be allowed by the master. The latter must consider for himself whether the law

---

34. *The Kamouraska* (1920) 2 Ll.L.Rep. 125, 299, at p. 300.

in respect to lights is being infringed, and if it is he must take steps to stop such infringement.[35]

Sound signals

21.49 The law regarding the making of sound signals is unclear. In the case of *The Saint Paul* it was left open as to whether the master ought to call the attention of the pilot to the fact that sound signals (in this case fog signals) ought to be given, and also the point was left open as to whether the responsibility for giving such signals rests with the pilot or the master.[36] The first point, but not the second, seems to have been resolved in the case of *The Elysia*. In this case a vessel which was at anchor in the River Mersey and showing anchor lights was being attended by a tug which was stemming the tide but was not made fast to the vessel. The tug was showing the proper lights for a vessel under way and her green light was open to an upcoming steamship, under the control of a pilot, in such a position that the latter thought he was approaching a vessel under way showing a green light. It was held that although the pilot could not properly complain of being misled by the green light, the master had contributed to the accident because, *inter alia*, he knew what the pilot was doing and had failed to call his attention to the fact that no sound signal had been given. The President of the court, Sir Samual Evans, said:

The master himself knew what the pilot was doing, and notwithstanding these three different orders to the helm, he did not call the attention of the pilot to the fact that he had not ordered any sound signals to be given. If sound signals had been given what would have happened? No answer would have been given . . . but some signal could be given . . . that the *Explorer* was not in a position to alter her course at all. In this way it would have been brought to the notice of those on the *Elysia* . . . that this vessel was at anchor. Then the collision might have been avoided at the last.[37]

Private sound signals

21.50 The courts do not approve of the use of private sound signals between pilots in contravention of the Collision Regulations, but the position of the master in such a situation is unclear. In the case of *The Century* for example, Hewson, J., said:

Whatever may be the understanding between pilots . . . in regard to the use of manoeuvring signals . . . these signals are signals which mean nothing more and nothing less than "I am directing my course to starboard" . . . and those signals mean nothing else. The danger of using such signals to convey any other meaning is this: though it may be understood between local people . . . to strangers using the port it can invite the

35. *The Ripon* (1885) 10 P.D. 65, at p. 69.
36. *The Saint Paul* (1908) 11 Asp. M.L.C. 169.
37. *The Elysia* (1912) 12 Asp. M.L.C. 198, at p. 202.

greatest misunderstanding. The custom of a port does not override the regulations. The regulations are paramount and must be upheld.[38]

21.51 With regard to the steering and sailing rules, it was held in the case of *The Argo* that although the pilot had taken a vessel on the port side of the fairway contrary to the Collision Regulations, the master was not responsible for failing to overrule the pilot. Dr Lushington justified his decision as follows:

I have said on many occasions . . . that a master has no right to interfere with the pilot, except in cases of the pilot's intoxication or manifest incapability, or in cases of danger which the pilot does not foresee, or in cases of great necessity. The master of the *Argo* says "It is not my province to take notice of the ship, or on what shore she is navigating. She may be taken here or there, while she is in charge of the pilot, without my knowing the cause; there may be reason under water why the pilot does it. All my duty is, to take care that all the pilot's orders are promptly and properly obeyed"; and I think he says so rightly.[39]

21.52 Here again, however, pilots will be censured by the courts if they contravene the regulations simply to honour some private arrangements with their colleagues. In the case of *The Hjortholm*, for example, where it was revealed that there was a private practice among Swansea pilots to pass starboard to starboard in the entrance channel under certain circumstances, Langton, J., said:

It has been said times without number that as to practices among pilots—understandings or customs of this kind—which are not enshrined in rules and by-laws, and which are in contravention of rules and by-laws, that they are not matters of which this Court can take the slightest notice.[40]

And in a similar case involving Liverpool pilots, Willmer, L.J., said:

What I would say about it is this, that if any such practice does exist among pilots in the River Mersey the sooner it is discontinued the better . . . the duty of a down coming vessel . . . is to obey rule 25 of the Collision Regulations . . . and to keep to her own starboard side.[41]

Criminal liability for infringement of Collision Regulations

21.53 So far as criminal liability for infringement of the Collision Regulations is concerned, until recently it appeared from the terms of section 419(2) of the Merchant Shipping Act 1894 that the pilot could not be guilty of an offence under this provision and that the master would only be guilty of a criminal offence if the infringement was caused by his wilful default. See also the case of *Henry Broadshaw* v. *Alan Ewat James* (*The Tiger*) in which it was held that for

38. *The Century* [1963] 1 Lloyd's Rep. 99, at pp. 102–103.
39. *The Argo* (1859) 166 E.R. 1217, at p. 1218.
40. *The Hjortholm* (1935) 52 Ll.L.Rep. 223, at p. 228.
41. *The Santander* [1966] 2 Lloyd's Rep. 77, at p. 83.

the master to be guilty of an offence under section 419(2) there must be *mens rea* on his part.[42] However, the Merchant Shipping (Distress Signals and Prevention of Collisions) Regulations 1983, made under sections 21 and 22 of the Merchant Shipping Act 1979, which came into force on 1 June 1983, repealed (*inter alia*) section 419 of the Merchant Shipping Act 1894 and provided in regulation 5(1) that "where any of these Regulations is contravened, the owner of the vessel, the master and any person for the time being responsible for the conduct of the vessel shall each be guilty of an offence. . .". Regulation 6 of the Merchant Shipping (Distress Signals and Prevention of Collisions) Regulations 1996, which are the regulations now in force, is in similar terms. It appears therefore that a pilot may now be criminally liable for an infringement of the Collision Regulations. Regulation 6(2) of the 1996 Regulations provides that it shall be a defence for any person charged with an infringement of the Collision Regulations that he took all reasonable precautions to avoid the commission of the offence.

Whether to proceed

21.54 It would appear that the courts, in most cases, take the view that the pilot should decide whether or not it is prudent to proceed in bad weather conditions. Thus in a case where the court had to decide upon the wisdom of taking a vessel through the Downs in bad weather, the judge said:

It was contended at the bar that in this case the impropriety of sailing through the Downs was so manifest that the captain ought to have refused, in spite of the pilot's opinion, to permit the ship to proceed. But we cannot assent to this. It would be very dangerous to hold that there can be any divided authority in the ship with reference to the same subject, and whether the ship was to anchor or to proceed was a matter which we think belonged exclusively to the pilot to decide.[43]

21.55 Similarly, in the case of *The Oakfield*, which was involved in a collision with a vessel at anchor in the River Mersey in poor visibility, Sir James Hannen said:

I think if there was such a state of obscurity owing to fog as would give rise to a plain prospect of danger, the master could in those circumstances throw the whole responsibility on the pilot if he ordered the vessel to get under way. But in this case it is said that the circumstances did not give rise to such a plain prospect of danger, for although the weather was admittedly foggy, yet vessels might be seen at a very considerable distance; the evidence is, from 300 yards to half a mile. If vessels can be seen at such a distance as that, then it is a question for the pilot to determine whether it was wise to weigh anchor, and the master would be relieved from responsibility. The pilot knows all the local dangers and knows as it were by instinct where he may go and where he may not go. It is therefore obvious that the master would leave it to the pilot to judge whether it would be safe to proceed in such a state of weather.[44]

---

42. *The Tiger* [1983] 1 All E.R. 12.
43. *Pollock* v. *M'Alpin* (1851) 13 E.R. 945, *per* Lord Kingsdown, at p. 946.
44. *The Oakfield* (1886) 5 Asp. M.L.C. 575, at p. 576.

21.56 In practice, where the possibility of causing serious damage through attempting to dock or sail a vessel in strong winds arises, the master usually accepts the decision of the pilot. In borderline cases, particularly involving large vessels, he prefers to err on the side of caution and will often cancel the operation without consulting the pilot. It is very rare, in these circumstances, for a master to insist on proceeding when it is contrary to the pilot's view that it would be imprudent to do so. In fog also, the master almost invariably accepts the judgement of the pilot, but again he usually prefers to err on the side of caution.

21.57 The question also arises in tidal ports where the danger of having insufficient water presents itself, particularly on a falling tide. Here again the master is usually willing to accept the decision of the pilot, although pilots have occasionally been known to have been persuaded against their better judgement by over-zealous masters anxious to "catch the tide".

Anchoring

21.58 This is generally within the purview of the pilot. In *The Octavia Stella* a vessel under the control of a compulsory pilot was brought to anchor at high water in a position which was not usually used by a vessel of her size and draught. At low water the vessel grounded and damaged some oyster beds, the existence of which were known to the pilot. In an action brought by the lessee of the oyster beds against the pilot and master it was held that the pilot alone was liable for anchoring the vessel in that position.[45] Similarly, in the case of *The George*, where a vessel approaching an anchorage in the dark ran down a vessel at anchor, it was held that the position in which a vessel brought up was entirely within the province of the pilot. It was also held in this case that the time of letting go was to be decided by the pilot.[46] In the case of *The Agricola* it was held that when a vessel is taking up her berth in a dock the time and the manner of dropping the anchor is exclusively within the pilot's province.[47]

21.59 In the case of *The Rigborgs Minde*, a schooner proceeding through the Humber Dock, Hull, collided with a flyboat, and the latter was damaged by the fluke of her anchor, which had been placed in a certain position prior to letting go. It was held that the damage was caused by the fault of the pilot alone. Brett, M.R., summed up as follows:

It is next said that the *Rigborgs Minde* did not manage her sternrope properly, that she came up the dock fast and should have had a check rope to the dolphins, and that her anchor was wrongly and improperly slung, and that when the final order to let go was given, that it was done in an unseamanlike manner. But all these matters, with the exception of the last, are connected with the navigation of the ship by way of steering her course, and attention to them is within the pilot's duty . . . Assuming that anything

45. *The Octavia Stella* (1887) 6 Asp. M.L.C. 182.
46. *The George* (1845) 166 E.R. 800.
47. *The Agricola* (1843) 2 Wm. Rob. 10.

done wrongly up to the moment of letting go the anchor was the fault of the pilot alone, anything done after that moment would be, no doubt, the fault of the crew.[48]

21.60 Similarly, it was held in the case of *The Monte Rosa* that if damage is caused by the anchor, so placed by the pilot's authority, then the fault lies with him, notwithstanding the fact that the position of the anchor is in breach of a port rule.[49]

21.61 It frequently occurs that a vessel approaching or leaving a port is delayed through tidal conditions, weather conditions, or other similar causes, and is obliged to anchor for a period of time. It has been held by the courts that on such occasions vessels in a compulsory pilotage district are still under the directions of the pilot while at anchor. In the case of *The City of Cambridge*, for example, where a vessel parted her cable in the River Mersey and subsequently collided with another vessel, it was held to be the duty of the pilot to decide upon the length of cable at which the vessel rides, and when the vessel swings to the tide to superintend that manoeuvre and to give any helm orders that may be necessary. It was also held that the pilot should not leave the bridge before the vessel is fully swung and if the vessel sheers and parts her cable as a result of insufficient length, or as a result of failure to regulate the helm, the pilot is solely responsible provided that the watch on the bridge takes the right manoeuvre to counteract the sheer. Also under these circumstances the necessity for letting go a second anchor is within the discretion of the pilot and that manoeuvre should also be superintended by him. If the pilot is below at the time, the officer of the watch is justified in calling the pilot before giving any orders to bring up the vessel provided she is not in imminent danger.[50]

21.62 In the case of *The Princeton*, where the vessel concerned dragged her anchor and collided with another vessel, it was held that the pilot ought to have let go a second anchor and should also have realized the state of affairs for himself despite an alleged bad look-out.[51] Again, in the case of *The Northampton*, the vessel concerned also dragged her anchor and collided with another vessel. It was held that this collision also could have been avoided by dropping a second anchor and for failing to do this the pilot was solely to blame.[52] In the case of *The Massachusetts*, on the other hand, which collided in similar circumstances to the two preceding incidents, it was held that the owners had contributed to the accident because it was shown that the anchor was too light to hold the ship.[53]

21.63 If, however, a vessel is not anchored temporarily to await weather or tide, but is anchored in her final position in the port, then the pilot is not to blame for accidents which occur some considerable time after he has left the

---

48. *The Rigborgs Minde* (1883) 8 P.D. 132, at pp. 135–136.
49. *The Monte Rosa* (1892) 7 Asp. M.L.C. 326.
50. *The City of Cambridge* (1874) 2 Asp. M.L.C. 193, 239.
51. *The Princeton* (1878) 3 Asp. M.L.C. 562.
52. *The Northampton* (1853) 164 E.R. 88.
53. *The Massachusetts* (1842) 166 E.R. 612.

ship. In the case of *The Woburn Abbey*, for example, a pilot anchored the vessel in her berth, and several days later she swung and hit the *British Trident* which had anchored before her. It was held that at the time of the collision the pilot was no longer in compulsory charge of the vessel and it was for those on board to make themselves aware of any impending danger.[54]

Speed

21.64 It would appear from reported cases that the speed at which a vessel should proceed is within the province of the pilot. In *The Maria*, for example, Dr Lushington said:

> . . . it would be a most dangerous doctrine to hold, except under most extraordinary circumstances, that the master could be justified in interfering with the pilot in his proper vocation . . . If no order was given to ease the steamer, the fault was in the pilot, not in the master.[55]

21.65 Similarly, in the case of *The Batavier*, Dr Lushington said that with regard to the speed at which the vessel was going, it appeared to him that the pilot was solely to blame,[56] and in the case of *The Calabar*, Sir James W. Colville said that it was within the province of the pilot in giving directions for the navigation of a steam vessel to determine the rate of speed at which she should proceed.[57]

21.66 In practice, if the master has any criticism to make of the vessel's speed, it is usually in circumstances when it appears to him that she is approaching a lock or a jetty too quickly. Sometimes, of course, such criticism is shown by subsequent events to be justified, but it is more often made through lack of knowledge of the local tides and currents, under the effects of which a vessel might be in more danger through approaching too slowly. Some masters adopt a more subtle approach and attempt to induce the pilot to proceed with less speed by over-emphasizing the weakness of his vessel's engines when moving astern.

Navigating with radar

21.67 It would appear from the judgment given in the case of *The Fina Canada* that provided a radar watch is being kept by an efficient officer who passes on all "relevant" information to the pilot, the latter is not bound to keep a radar watch himself. In this case Hewson, J., said:

> As the *Fina Canada* progressed towards the Medway buoy, the pilot was in charge of the navigation, and on the bridge with him were the master, the senior chief officer

---

54. *The Woburn Abbey* (1869) 20 L.T. 621.
55. *The Maria* (1839) 166 E.R. 508, at p. 514.
56. *The Batavier* (1854) 164 E.R. 218, at p. 221.
57. *The Calabar* (1868) L.R. 2 P.C. 238, at p. 241.

(who kept the radar watch), and the second and third officers, who were on the starboard and port wings respectively. There were no other officers and seamen on the forecastle head. At no time did the pilot look in the radar. The radar watch was kept exclusively by the chief officer. It was kept continuously by him, except for two brief visits to the chartroom to consult the chart. This officer, who struck me as being efficient and responsible, reported what he observed to the pilot and master. In such conditions as we are considering in this case, when reliance is placed upon radar, it cannot be too strongly emphasized that a continuous radar watch should be kept by one person experienced in its use, as this officer was, and further, that such a person should keep those in charge of the navigation informed of all matters relevant to the safe handling of the ship.[58]

21.68 In the same case in the Court of Appeal, Willmer, L.J., concurred with this view.[59] It should be noted, however, that radar was being used in this case primarily for the purpose of collision avoidance. If the radar was being used mainly for navigational purposes in (say) a narrow river it would be difficult to see how a ship's officer, who possessed no local knowledge, could accurately distinguish between "relevant" and "irrelevant" information. It might be appropriate at this point to note the views of the Canadian Royal Commission on the subject of the use of radar by pilots:

With the aid of various electronic instruments, the pilot is now provided with means which are constantly being improved to "see" when visual means fail but this electronic "sight" has its limitations, and the images and information provided differ from what is seen by the naked eye. Therefore, to take advantage of these technical developments, pilots must acquire the necessary knowledge and skill to understand and use these instruments. The strange images that appear on the radar screen should be as familiar to the pilot as the land features in time of clear visibility and such local knowledge must form part of the qualifications of pilots today.[60]

21.69 The practical situation in these circumstances varies from ship to ship. When navigating in fog some masters will commandeer the radar set completely and simply pass on any information they think the pilot might require, while others will leave it almost entirely to the pilot. A properly recognized procedure is the exception rather than the rule in these cases.

---

58. *The Fina Canada* [1962] 2 Lloyd's Rep. 113, at p. 117.
59. *Ibid.* [1962] 2 Lloyd's Rep. 445, at p. 450.
60. Canada. *Report of Royal Commission, &c., op. cit.*, Part 1, p. 44.

CHAPTER 22

DIVISION OF CONTROL BETWEEN SHIP AND TUGS

22.1 In a port which is regularly used by medium and large sized vessels, and particularly in a port which contains an enclosed docks system, there is usually a permanently based fleet of tugs available to assist in the berthing and manoeuvring of these vessels. Through being closely involved with each other over a period of time, a working relationship is usually built up between the port's pilots and tug masters which is based on mutual understanding and trust. The tug master who "knows his pilot" will, by intelligent anticipation, position his tug so as always to be ready to give instant assistance. From similar experience, the pilot will know which tugs are more powerful or manoeuvrable than the others, and will therefore be in a position to deploy them in his best advantage.

22.2 Unfortunately, however, accidents involving vessels under tow do sometimes occur, and are usually caused either by a collision between the tug and tow; or between the tug or tow and another vessel or a stationary object such as a pier or dock wall. This chapter examines the courts' decisions relating to such incidents, and, in the same manner as in the previous chapter, attempts to break down the towing operation into its constituent parts with a view to apportioning responsibility between the ship and the tugs.

Responsibility for hiring tugs

22.3 In 1860 Dr Lushington held that in "ordinary circumstances" the responsibility for engaging a tug rested with the master and not with the pilot. He qualified his judgment, however, as follows:

I am speaking of the ordinary case where a tug is employed for accelerating speed and for completing the voyage in a short time for the benefit of the owners . . . It may be different in cases where a ship is in distress, and if it is a critical question whether to employ a tug or not. Those are cases in which the master ought to attend to the pilot's voice.[1]

22.4 In modern times tugs are rarely, if ever, employed simply to expedite a ship's passage, and Dr Lushington's proposition clearly belongs to the days

1. *The Julia* (1860) 15 E.R. 284, at p. 288.

of sail. Today, tugs are mainly employed to manoeuvre large vessels into confined spaces where their absence, particularly in adverse weather conditions, would give rise to the danger of colliding with piers or other vessels, or to the danger of grounding. In more exceptional circumstances tugs are employed when vessels are suffering from some mechanical deficiency such as the breakdown of engines or steering gear.

22.5 In practice, the decision to employ tugs is normally taken by the master or agent who sometimes, if in doubt, will consult the pilot beforehand. On occasions where their advice has not been sought pilots are frequently critical of these decisions and claim that they are often hampered by tugs when they are unnecessary and are often obliged to perform difficult manoeuvres without tugs when their assistance would be useful.

Division of control—a general rule

22.6 The following general proposition was laid down by Dr Lushington in the case of *The Gipsey King* in 1847:

. . . a vessel in charge of a licensed pilot, whilst in tow of a steam tug is, under ordinary circumstances, to be considered as navigated by the pilot in charge. That if the course pursued by the steam tug is in conformity with his directions, and a collision takes place, the pilot is responsible, and not the owners of the vessel or of the steam tug. If on the contrary, the steamer disregarded the directions of the pilot, and the collision was occasioned by her misconduct, the owner of the ship would, in that case be responsible.[2]

22.7 In a later case, however, Dr Lushington made one exception to this rule, that exception being the case of a ship being shifted from one dock to another, at night and in thick weather, the ship herself being without motive power. He said in this case:

As regards the *Borussia* it will be a question whether it was expedient to move such a vessel, by means of a steam-tug, in anything like thick weather? She was in charge of a pilot; but it is not pretended that his presence can excuse the master from his responsibility; the circumstances are quite different from those of a vessel in tow of a steam-tug in broad daylight, where the tug ought to obey the orders of the pilot.[3]

Tug master's right to interfere

22.8 The master of a tug is in the same position as any other ship's master when confronted with a case of manifest incompetence on the part of the pilot. In the case of *The Duke of Manchester* Dr Lushington said:

It is, I conceive, the duty of the master to observe the conduct of the pilot, and in the case of palpable incompetency, whether arising from intoxication or ignorance or any other cause, to interpose his authority for the preservation of the property of his

2. *The Gipsey King* (1847) 166 E.R. 858.
3. *The Borussia* (1856) 166 E.R. 1037, at p. 1038.

employers . . . So in the case of a steamer which has a vessel in tow with a licensed pilot on board, if the master of the steamer sees the pilot is incompetent to direct the course of the vessel, is he blindly to follow his orders and allow a valuable property, and still more valuable lives, to be imperilled? I never laid down such a proposition.[4]

Making fast

22.9 When making fast while under way, it would appear to be the duty of the tug to keep clear and avoid collision. In the case of *Contest* v. *Age* a collision with the tow occurred shortly after the tug had taken a hawser from the forecastle and made it fast to the towing hook. Hill, J., in finding that there had been no negligence on the part of the tow said:

Tugs which are making fast to a ship necessarily take upon themselves the main burden of keeping clear; and there are many ways in which careless handling of the tugs may, in the very close quarters in which they have to work, bring themselves into contact with the ship.[5]

22.10 In a similar case, in which a tug was rammed while making fast to a ship and subsequently sank, it was claimed by the owners of the tug that the accident had been caused by the ship deviating from her course shortly before the collision occurred. Here, again, however, Hill, J., found that there was no negligence on the part of the tow. In this case he said that "if there was a slight deflection involved in keeping course that was a thing which the tug must expect and be prompt to follow".[6]

22.11 This does not mean, however, that those on board the tow can completely ignore the presence of the tug when she is making fast. In the case of *Harmony* v. *Northborough* the tug, which was already fast on the *Northborough's* port bow, was ordered by the pilot to transfer to the starboard quarter. She cast off and was attempting to re-secure on the starboard quarter, as directed, when the pilot put the ship's engines ahead. The propeller then struck the tug which sank shortly afterwards. In this case the pilot was held to be negligent for using the engines before ensuring that the tug was out of danger. In giving judgment, the President of the court said:

The pilot seemed to me to put on the *Harmony* the absolute duty, under the circumstances of her relation with the *Northborough*, to look out for her own safety. There is no unilateral duty of that kind in the relations of tug and tow. Each of them has to exercise proper care.[7]

---

4. *The Duke of Manchester* (1846) 166 E.R. 833, at p. 837.
5. *Contest* v. *Age* (1923) 17 Ll.L.Rep. 172, at pp. 173–174.
6. *Assistance and Others* v. *Lagarto* (1923) 17 Ll.L.Rep. 264.
7. *The Harmony* v. *The Northborough* (1923) 15 Ll.L.Rep. 119, *per* Sir Henry Duke, at p. 120.

Extent of pilot's authority in directing course of tug

22.12 The precise extent to which a pilot should go in giving instructions to the tug is not clear. In the case of *The Energy* a barque with a pilot on board was being towed by a steam tug which ported her helm and passed across the bows of a brig under way, causing a collision between the brig and the barque. It was revealed in evidence that the pilot gave no orders to the tug either before or after she ported her helm. It was held by the court that the tug was to blame for attempting to tow the barque across the bows of the brig, but that the pilot had contributed to the accident by failing to give proper instructions to the tug.[8] In the case of *The Sinquasi*, on the other hand, a collision was caused by a tug executing a wrong manoeuvre, and it was held by the court that the fact that the pilot had not given instructions to the tug prior to the collision did not relieve the owners of the ship from liability. In this case the judge said that it was not necessary that the pilot "should be giving orders perpetually for every movement of the helm of the tug".[9] Again, in the case of *Smith etc.* v. *The St. Lawrence Tow Boat Company* it was decided that a tug towing a sailing vessel is responsible for the course of both vessels, so long as no orders are given by the person in charge of the tow. The court stated that although the tug is the motive power, she is under the control of the person in charge of the vessel being towed.[10]

Extent of pilot's control over engine movements of tug

22.13 In the case of a vessel proceeding up the Manchester Ship Canal the stern tug collided with a barge which was going in the opposite direction. After the collision the port propeller of the tug was improperly kept turning with the result that it struck the barge several times until she finally sank. It was held by Willmer, J., that the pilot was not at fault for failing to instruct the tug to stop her engines. He gave his reasons as follows:

No pilot can possibly be expected to control the individual engine manoeuvres of his two tugs. The evidence shows that in practice the detailed manoeuvres of the tug are, and must be, left to the discretion of the tug master, the duty of the pilot being confined to giving general directions, such as to start or stop towing, or to tow in this or that direction. I do not see how a pilot on the bridge of a large ship can possibly be expected to direct the engine movements of a stern tug, operating some three or four hundred feet behind him, and mostly out of sight, or even to know how the engines of the tug are working at any particular moment.[11]

---

8. *The Energy* (1870) L.R. 3 A. & E. 48.
9. *The Sinquasi* (1880) 4 Asp. M.L.C. 383, *per* Sir Robert Phillimore, at p. 384.
10. *Smith and Others* v. *The St. Lawrence Tow Boat Company* (1873) 2 Asp. M.L.C. 41.
11. *Trishna (Owners, master and crew)* v. *M.S.C. Panther and Ericbank (Owners)* [1957] P. 143, at p. 147.

Swinging

22.14 When a ship is swinging with the assistance of tugs it is the duty of the stern tug to keep herself off the ship's propeller and to have her tow rope properly secured. In the case of a ship which was attempting to swing to starboard with the aid of tugs, it was revealed that at the start of the operation the stern tug was made fast on the ship's starboard quarter with her tow rope secured to the forward bitts instead of the main hook. When instructed to tow on the port quarter she moved under the stern of the ship and at that moment the pilot put the ship's engines astern with the result that she struck the tug. It was held by Hill, J., that the tug should have shifted her rope to the main hook before passing under the ship's stern, in which event the collision would have been avoided. He summed up as follows:

In general, when a tug is acting as this tug was doing as the stern tug of the ship, it must be the business of the tug to keep herself clear of the ship. The tug knows that the steamer is turning. She knows that in doing that the steamer will very likely move her engines ahead and astern as required, and in this the tug master knew that the steamer was moving her engines ahead and astern. I am advised that the proper handling of this tug, in order to carry out the manoeuvre of assisting the turning of the steamer, required that the tug should not continue to hang on to the ship by the rope to the forward bitts, but that it should be placed on the towing hook in proper time to carry out the manoeuvre.[12]

Where tow is in imminent danger

22.15 In a situation of impending peril to the ship, a tug is bound to endeavour to save her, especially when instructed to do so by the pilot. Thus, in the case where a ship was entering a dock with a tug lashed alongside, and was forced by the tide into close proximity to a landing stage with the tug nearest the stage, it was held that it was the tug's duty to hold on and go ahead as the pilot had instructed. In this case the tug struck the landing stage and was damaged, and it was held by the court that the tug was entitled to full compensation for damage and a salvage award.[13]

When navigating in fog

22.16 In a case where a vessel, with a pilot on board, was being towed by a tug in a river where, due to dense fog, neither bank of the river could be seen, it was held that it was negligent on the part of both vessels to proceed under such circumstances. It was also held that it was the duty of the pilot to order the tug to stop in order that the vessel under tow could come to anchor.[14]

---

12. *The Alexandra (Newport and South Wales) Docks and Railway Company* v. *Cape Colony* (1920) 4 Ll.L.Rep. 116, at p. 118.
13. *The Saratoga* (1861) 167 E.R. 140.
14. *Smith and Others* v. *The St. Lawrence Tow Boat Company* (1873) 2 Asp. M.L.C. 41.

CHAPTER 23

DIVISION OF CONTROL BETWEEN SHIP AND HARBOUR MASTER

23.1 When a ship is navigating within the limits of a harbour authority she is subject to a certain degree of control by the harbour master or his assistants. Disputes occasionally arise as to the wisdom or practicability of instructions given by harbour officials and on such occasions the pilot invariably plays a prominent part. The question therefore arises as to what extent the harbour master is entitled to interfere in the navigation of a vessel when she is within his jurisdiction and this chapter examines the harbour master's powers under the present law.

Harbour master's statutory powers

23.2 As indicated in Chapter 6 *ante*, a harbour master derives his power to control the movement of shipping chiefly from the provisions contained in, or incorporated by, the local Acts and statutory orders of his authority. Until fairly recently the provisions in question were usually those of sections 52 and 53 of the Harbours, Docks and Piers Clauses Act 1847 which were incorporated with the special legislation of nearly all harbour authorities (and still frequently are). Under the first of these sections the harbour master is entitled to give directions for, *inter alia*:

regulating the time in which and manner in which any vessel shall enter into, go out of, or lie at the harbour, dock, or pier, and within the prescribed limits, if any, and its position, mooring or unmooring, placing and removing, whilst therein;

and under section 53:

. . . any master of a vessel who, after notice of any such direction by the harbour master served upon him, shall not forthwith regulate such vessel according to such direction shall be liable to a penalty not exceeding (now in most cases level 3 on the standard scale).

23.3 At most major ports, these provisions of the Harbours, Docks and Piers Clauses Act have now been superseded by more flexible and sophisticated powers to regulate the movement, etc., of vessels (for example, sections 111 and 112 of the Port of London Act 1968). However, except that the harbour master's power to give directions is in somewhat wider terms, and is

321

geared to some extent to the implementation of "general directions" given by the harbour authority, the principles as respects the division of control between ship and harbour master appear to be essentially the same as where sections 52 and 53 of the 1847 Act apply.

Judicial decisions

23.4 In most court cases dealing with the harbour master's powers it has been decided that, unless there was manifest evidence that obedience to a harbour master's instructions would lead to an accident, those instructions had to be obeyed. In *Reney* v. *Magistrates of Kirkcudbright*, for example, where a vessel ran on to a sandbank in consequence of a mistake as to the state of the tide by the harbour master, Halsbury, L.C., said:

> to say that the harbour master's authority is limited, or that a person is at liberty to disregard the orders of the harbour master, who has by law power to give orders . . . would be, to my mind, a most dangerous principle to establish. A double authority would be in many cases fatal. Those who have the power to give orders have the right to consider that they will be obeyed.[1]

23.5 It was held in the above case that the accident was caused by the negligence of the harbour master, but it should be noted that the vessel was not at the time under the control of a licensed pilot but was being navigated by the master with the assistance of two local fishermen who were employed as "advisers". It would be reasonable to assume that, if there had been a licensed pilot on board to whose certain knowledge the grounding was inevitable, the court might have held that he was entitled to disregard the harbour master's instructions, as the judgment in the following cases might indicate.

23.6 In the case of *Taylor* v. *Burger*, where an accident was caused, *inter alia*, by a steamer disobeying an order from the harbour master to go astern, Halsbury, L.C., modified his view on the subject, while adhering to the principle that there should be no divided authority with reference to the same subject:

> . . . a man is not blindly to run into danger or encounter wilfully what would result in a collision if he could see that it must take place. I suppose that no one would contend that obedience to an order should be carried to the extent of leading to an inevitable disaster. The broad proposition must be admitted that you must not knowingly run into danger by the order of a harbour master or any one else. That assumes the fact that a disaster must happen. I adhere to what I said in *Reney* v. *Magistrates of Kirkcudbright* that if it was once supposed that a person acting under the orders of a harbour master is to exercise his own judgment whether or not the harbour master's orders are most consistent with prudence, and then refuse to obey the order given, that would lead to very serious consequences indeed.[2]

---

1. *Reney* v. *Magistrates of Kirkcudbright* (1892) 7 Asp. M.L.C. 221, at p. 222.
2. *Taylor* v. *Burger and Another* (1898) 8 Asp. M.L.C. 364, at p. 365.

23.7 In 1936, in the case of *The Framlington Court*, the ship involved was attempting to move stern first out of the Greenland Dock entrance, in the River Thames. The dock master was supervising the manoeuvre by virtue of his powers under section 160 of the Port of London (Consolidation) Act 1920 (now repealed and replaced by section 113 of the Port of London Act 1968) which stated that every master should navigate his vessel in accordance with the dock master's instructions, and was liable to a fine of £20 (now level 2 on the standard scale) if he failed to do so. On this occasion the dock master instructed the ship to leave the dock, despite the fact that the entrance was obstructed by a flotilla of barges, and the pilot responded to the order by putting the engines astern. When the dock master realized that a collision was likely to occur he first signalled the ship to stop her engines, and then to put them ahead in order to reduce her sternway. When, however, one of the barges drifted close to the stern of the ship he signalled to the pilot to stop the engines. This instruction was not carried out immediately and the ship's propeller struck the barge, causing damage to three of its blades. The owners of the ship brought an action against the Port of London Authority on the ground that the dock master was negligent in (a) failing to remove the barges, which was within his powers, and (b) ordering the vessel to leave the dock when the entrance was obstructed. The defendants claimed, *inter alia*, that having instructed the vessel to leave, the dock master was under no obligation to give any further instructions and that those that he did give were only in the nature of voluntary advice.

23.8 The court held that although the dock master had been negligent in ordering the vessel to leave the dock, those on board the ship had contributed to the accident by failing to stop the engines in sufficient time. Referring to the subject of divided authority, Langton, J., said:

As far as this court is concerned there is only one control about the safety of a ship; I have laid it down again and again. When ships are coming out of dock, the dock master gives the orders and the pilot is bound to obey them, but he is not bound to obey an order which will take his ship into danger. It is for him to decide whether he is taking his ship into danger or not. That is as I have understood the law ever since I have practised it. It will take a good deal to shift me from that conviction. There is no dual control at all. That does not preclude all these other points. You may get a case . . . in which a dock master gives an order and the range is so short that there is no negligence on the part of the pilot in not taking some other step. We have not finished with this matter when we have finished with dual control. It does not mean that a dock master has only to give an order, and if anything goes wrong it is the pilot's fault . . . A pilot must have a reasonable chance.[3]

23.9 In referring to the contention that the dock master was not under a continuing obligation to supervise the manoeuvre once he had given the ship permission to leave, he said:

3. *United British Steamship Co. Ltd.* v. *Port of London Authority (The Framlington Court)* (1936) 56 Ll.L.Rep. 200, at p. 203.

For my part I cannot accept the contention that the dock master who continues in these circumstances to give orders to the ship within the prescribed limits can divest himself either of authority or of responsibility. He may not be under an obligation to direct the ship's movements when leaving his dock, but if he elects to give orders these orders must be obeyed and the dock authority must shoulder the responsibility if these orders given within the scope of his authority are negligent and improper.[4]

23.10 A harbour master has a general duty towards the collective safety of the ships within his harbour. It was held in the case of the *Excelsior*[5] that it was reasonable for the harbour master to give an instruction which placed one ship in possible danger in order to secure the safety of the remainder.

23.11 It should be noted that section 53 of the Harbours, Docks and Piers Clauses Act specifically states that the master is personally liable to a fine for any infringement of the provisions contained in section 52, and to that extent he must also be responsible for the actions of the pilot. The by-laws of most pilotage authorities contained a provision that the master is to comply with the directions of the harbour master in connection with the docking or undocking of any ship, though in the light of the decision given in the case above this would appear to be superfluous. In practice, the extent to which the harbour master chooses to exercise his powers varies considerably. In some ports he simply gives ships permission to enter or leave the dock, while in others he directs all movements of the ship.

4. *The Framlington Court, ante,* at p. 208.
5. See *The Excelsior,* paragraph 6.5 *ante.*

APPENDIX A

SECTION 37 OF THE DOCKS AND HARBOURS ACT 1966 AS AMENDED BY THE TRANSPORT AND WORKS ACT 1992

Power of harbour authorities to acquire a harbour business or shares in a harbour business

37—(1) Subject to the provisions of this section, a harbour authority, not being one of the Boards,[1] may acquire by agreement any business or undertaking which consists wholly or mainly of the carrying out of activities relating to harbours or of the provision, maintenance or operation of any such depot as is mentioned in the last foregoing section,[2] or so much of any business or undertaking as consists of the carrying out of activities relating to harbours or of the provision, maintenance or operation of any such depot.

(2) Subject as aforesaid, a harbour authority, not being one of the Boards, may subscribe for or acquire any securities of a body corporate which is wholly or mainly engaged or which it is proposed should become wholly or mainly engaged in carrying out activities relating to harbours or in providing, maintaining or operating any such depot.

(2A) Nothing in subsection (2) above shall be construed as authorising a harbour authority to delegate to another body any function which it could not delegate apart from that subsection.

(4) In this section "securities", in relation to a body corporate, means any shares, stock, debentures, debenture stock, and any other security of a like nature, of the body corporate.

1. The reference to the Boards now applies only to the British Waterways Board.
2. The depots referred to are inland clearance depots.

APPENDIX B

PORT AUTHORITY CONSTITUTION ORDER

THE PORT OF TYNE AUTHORITY (CONSTITUTION) REVISION ORDER 1974

Made — 8th February 1974
Laid before Parliament — 26th March 1974
Coming into Operation — 21st May 1974

The Secretary of State for the Environment,[1] in exercise of the powers conferred by section 15 of the Harbours Act 1964 and now vested in him and of all other powers enabling him in that behalf, and on a representation made to him by the National Ports Council, hereby makes the following order:—

PART I. PRELIMINARY

Citation and commencement

1. This Order may be cited as the Port of Tyne Authority (Constitution) Revision Order 1974 and shall come into operation on the date fixed in accordance with the Statutory Orders (Special Procedure) Acts 1945 and 1965.

Interpretation

2.—(1) In this Order, unless the context otherwise requires, the following expressions have the respective meanings hereby assigned to them:—

"the Authority" means the Port of Tyne Authority;

"the new constitution date" means the first day of the third month after the expiry of the month current at the commencement of this order;

"the Port" has the same meaning as in the Port of Tyne Reorganisation Scheme 1967.

(2) The Interpretation Act 1889 shall apply for the interpretation of this order as it applies for the interpretation of an Act of Parliament.

1. When this order was made the powers originally conferred by the Harbours Act 1964 on "the Minster of Transport" and now vested in the Secretary of State for Transport were vested in the Secretary of State for the Environment.

327

APPENDIX B

The new constitution

3.—(1) On and after the new constitution date the Authority shall consist of:—

(a) a chairman and not less than six and not more than seven other members appointed by the Secretary of State,

(b) the general manager of the Authority for the time being, and

(c) (as from the time when officers of the Authority are appointed to serve as members thereof in accordance with paragraph 2 of the Schedule to this order) not less than two and not more three other full-time officers of the Authority appointed on the occasion of the first appointment of such officers under the said paragraph 2 by the members referred to in sub-paragraphs (a) and (b) above on subsequent occasions by the Authority.

(2) The Secretary of State shall consult the Council[2] on the appointments to be made under paragraph (1)(a) above and shall also consult the chairman on such appointments other than that of the chairman. The Council, in considering the appointments which are the subject of such consultation, shall themselves consult with such bodies, being bodies which, in the Council's opinion, are likely to be substantially affected by the way in which the functions of the Authority are discharged or which appear to the Council to be representative of interests likely to be so affected, as the Council consider appropriate. Before making the first appointments under the said paragraph (1)(a) (including that of chairman) the Secretary of State shall also consult the person then holding office as chairman of the Authority.

(3) In selecting persons for appointment as members of the Authority the Secretary of State shall—

(a) select persons who appear to him to have wide experience of, and to have shown capacity in, one or more of the matters mentioned in paragraph (4) below or to have in some other respect knowledge or experience that would be of value to the Authority in the discharge of their functions, and

(b) have regard to the desirability of having members who are familiar with the area served by the port.

(4) The matters referred to in paragraph (3)(a) above are—

(a) the management of harbours;

(b) shipping or other forms of transport;

(c) industrial, commercial or financial matters;

(d) administration;

(e) the organisation of workers; and

(f) environmental matters affecting the area of the Port.

Appointment and terms of office of members appointed by Secretary of State

4.—(1) The Secretary of State shall appoint the first members to be appointed by him under article 3(1)(a) above before the new constitution date and each member so appointed shall come into office on that date and, subject to the provisions of Schedule 1 to the Port of Tyne Reorganisation Scheme 1967, shall continue in office until either the end of June 1976 or the end of June 1977 as the Secretary of State may specify when he makes the appointment. The members of the Authority holding office immediately before the new constitution date shall go out of office on that date.

---

2. The National Ports Council which was abolished by the Transport Act 1981. That Act also provided that any statutory requirement to consult the NPC should cease to have effect.

(2) A member subsequently appointed by the Secretary of State under the said article 3(1)(a) shall, unless appointed to fill a casual vacancy, come into office on the 1st July following his appointment and, subject to the provisions of Schedule 1 to the Port of Tyne Reorganisation Scheme 1967, shall continue in office until the end of June in either the second or third year thereafter as the Secretary of State may specify when he makes the appointment. A member appointed by the Secretary of State may specify when he makes the appointment and, subject as aforesaid, shall continue in office until the end of June occurring within four years after that date which the Secretary of State may specify when he makes the appointment.

Incidental provisions relating to Authority

5. On and after the new constitution date the provisions of the Schedule to this Order shall have effect with respect to the members and proceedings of the Authority (in addition to the provisions of Schedule 1 to the Port of Tyne Reorganisation Scheme 1967 which are not repealed by this Order).

Repeal of certain provisions relating to existing constitution etc.

6. On the new constitution date articles 5 and 6 of, and paragraphs 1 to 5, the words "Except in the case of the first appointments made under this Scheme" in paragraph 9 and paragraph 14 of Schedule 1 to, the Port of Tyne Reorganisation Scheme 1967 shall be repealed and paragraph 7 of the said Schedule 1 shall have effect as if for the words "31st December" there were substituted the words "30th June".
Signed by authority of the Secretary of State
8th February 1974.

John Peyton,
Minister for Transport Industries,
Department of the Environment.

SCHEDULE. INCIDENTAL PROVISIONS WITH RESPECT TO THE AUTHORITY

1. The first meeting of the Authority after the new constitution date shall be convened by the chairman of the Authority for such date and at such place as he may fix and the chairman shall make arrangements for notice of that meeting to be sent by post to each of the other members of the Authority appointed by the Secretary of State and to the general manager of the Authority.

2. At the first meeting of the Authority after the new constitution date the members appointed by the Secretary of State and the general manager of the Authority (or as many of them as are present) shall, as the first item of business, appoint not less than two and not more than three other full-time officers of the Authority to serve as members thereof.

3. The Authority shall at their first meeting after the new constitution date and subsequently at their first meeting after 30th June in each year appoint one of their number (being a member appointed by the Secretary of State) to be deputy chairman and the deputy chairman shall, unless he resigns his office or ceases to be a member of the Authority, continue in office until the next annual appointment of a deputy chairman.

4. On a casual vacancy occurring in the office of deputy chairman of the Authority the vacancy shall be filled by the appointment by the Authority of one of their number (being a member appointed by the Secretary of State) at a meeting held as soon as practicable after the vacancy occurs and the person so appointed shall hold office until the date on which the person in whose place he is appointed would ordinarily have retired and shall then retire.

5. A full-time officer of the Authority other than the general manager who is appointed to serve as a member thereof under paragraph 2 of this Schedule or subsequently by the Authority shall hold and vacate his office as a member at the discretion of the Authority but may at any time resign his membership by notice in writing given to the chairman of the Authority. If such a member shall cease to be a full-time officer of the Authority he shall thereupon cease to be a member of the Authority but the termination by the Authority of the appointment as a member thereof of a full-time officer other than the general manager shall be without prejudice to his appointment as an officer of the Authority.

6. At meetings of the Authority the quorum shall be five.

7. Subject to the provisions of this Schedule and of Schedule 1 to the Port of Tyne Reorganisation Scheme 1967 the Authority shall have power to regulate their own procedure.

APPENDIX C

GENERAL DUTIES AND POWERS

I. SECTION 9 OF TRANSPORT ACT 1981

General duties of Associated British Ports

9.—(1) It is the duty of Associated British Ports to provide port facilities at its harbours to such extent as it may think expedient.

(2) Associated British Ports shall have due regard to efficiency, economy and safety of operation as respects the services and facilities provided by it and its subsidiaries.

(3) In the performance of its functions Associated British Ports shall have regard to the interests in general of its employees and the employees of its subsidiaries.

(4) This section does not impose any form of duty or liability enforceable, either directly or indirectly, by proceedings before any court.

II. SECTION 5 OF PORT OF LONDON ACT 1968

General duties and powers

5.—(1) It shall be the duty of the Port Authority to take such action as they consider necessary or desirable for or incidental to the improvement and conservancy of the Thames.

(1A) The Port Authority shall have power to provide, maintain, operate and improve such port and harbour services and facilities in, or in the vicinity of, the Thames as they consider necessary or desirable and to take such action as they consider incidental to the provision of such services and facilities.

(2) The Port Authority shall have power either themselves or by arrangement between themselves and another person to take such action as the Port Authority consider necessary or desirable whether or not in, or in the vicinity of, the Thames—

    (a) for the purpose of discharging or facilitating the discharge of any of their duties, including the proper development or operation of the undertaking;

    (b) for the provision, maintenance and operation of—

        (i) warehousing services and facilities;

        (ii) services and facilities for the consignment of goods on routes which include the port premises;

(c) for the purpose of turning their resources to account so far as not required for the purposes of the undertaking.

(3) Particular powers conferred or particular duties laid upon the Port Authority by this Act shall not be construed as derogating from each other or from the generality of subsection (1), (1A) and (2) of this section.

APPENDIX D

LICENSING OF WORKS

ARTICLES 18–22 OF THE SEALINK (TRANSFER OF NEWHAVEN HARBOUR) HARBOUR REVISION ORDER 1991

Restriction of works and dredging

18.—(1) Subject to paragraph (3) below, no person other than the Company[1] shall—

(a) construct, alter, renew or extend any works; or

(b) dredge;

on, under or over tidal land below the level of high water[2] in the transferred harbour[3] unless he is licensed so to do, in the case of works by a works licence and in the case of dredging by a dredging licence, nor except upon the terms and conditions, if any, upon which the licence is granted and in accordance with plans, sections and particulars approved in pursuance of article 20 or, as the case may require, article 21, of this Order.

(2) The Company may by notice require a person who contravenes this article to remove, abate or rectify, within a reasonable time specified in the notice, any work, operation or omission to which the contravention relates, and to restore the site thereof to its former condition; and if he fails to comply with the notice the Company may carry out the works so required and may recover the reasonable cost of so doing from that person.

(3) Nothing in this article shall apply to—

(a) any operations or works specifically authorised by any enactment; or

(b) any operations or works of a statutory undertaker.[4]

1. Defined in the order as Newhaven Port and Properties Limited who by virtue of the order became harbour authority for Newhaven Harbour.
2. Defined in the order as the level of mean high-water springs.
3. Defined in the order as Newhaven Harbour.
4. "Statutory undertaker" is defined in the order as—
    (a) any person who is a statutory undertaker for the purposes of the Town and Country Planning Act 1990;
    (b) any other person who exercises functions under the Land Drainage Act 1976;
    (c) a coast protection authority within the meaning of section 1 of the Coast Protection Act 1949;
    (d) any operator of a telecommunication code system (which has the same meaning as in the Telecommunications Act 1984).

(4) Any person who without reasonable excuse contravenes this article shall be guilty of an offence and liable on summary conviction to a fine not exceeding level 3 on the standard scale.

Control of certain operations and works of statutory undertakers

19.—(1) This article applies to any operations or works in the transferred harbour of a statutory undertaker on, under or over tidal waters or tidal land below the level of high water in the transferred harbour, not being operations or works which are specifically authorised by any enactment.[5]

(2) Subject to paragraph (3) below, a statutory undertaker shall not carry out any operations or works to which this article applies unless it has given notice of its intention to do so to the Company and has supplied the Company with such particulars as it may reasonably require.

(3) Where, in an emergency, it is impracticable to give notice as required by paragraph (2) above, the statutory undertaker concerned shall inform the Company of the operations or works as soon as reasonably practicable.

(4) Any operations or works to which this article applies shall be carried out subject to any directions which may from time to time be given by the Company to the statutory undertaker concerned, being directions such as in the opinion of the Company are necessary for the avoidance of danger and the prevention, so far as reasonably possible, of interference with navigation in the carrying out of such operations or works.

(5) Any person who without reasonable excuse contravenes this article shall be guilty of an offence and liable on summary conviction to a fine not exceeding level 3 on the standard scale.

Licensing of works

20.—(1) The Company may upon such terms and conditions as it thinks fit grant to any person a licence to construct, alter, renew or extend any works in the transferred harbour on, under or over tidal waters or tidal land below the level of high water, notwithstanding any interference with public rights of navigation or other public rights by such works as constructed, altered, renewed or extended.

(2) Application for a works licence shall be made in writing to the Company and shall—

(a) be accompanied by plans, sections and particulars of the works to which the application relates;

(b) specify whether the applicant holds such rights in, under or over land as are necessary to enable him to enjoy the benefits of the licence and, if not, the action taken to enable him to obtain such rights if the licence is granted; and, in granting a licence, the Company may require modifications in the plans, sections and particulars so submitted.

(3) The Company may require an applicant for a works licence, on making his application, to pay a reasonable fee in respect of the administrative expenses of dealing with the application; and different fees may be specified in relation to different cases or different classes of cases.

(4)(a) On receipt of an application for a works licence the Company shall serve on the National Rivers Authority a copy of the application and all plans, sections and particulars incident thereto;

5. "enactment" is defined in the order as any Act or any order or scheme made under an Act.

334

(b) The Company shall consider such observations as the National Rivers Authority may submit to the Company within six weeks after service on the National Rivers Authority of the application and particulars as aforesaid, and shall not grant a works licence before the expiry of that period;

(c) In granting any works licence in response to such an application the Company shall impose on the applicant such terms and conditions as give effect to such reasonable requirements to prevent pollution of any watercourse, to safeguard it against damage or to secure that its efficiency for land drainage purposes is not impaired, as the National Rivers Authority may, within the said period, make in any observations to the Company;

(d) The provisions of subparagraph (c) above are subject to the Company's duty under article 22(5) of this Order to give effect to any decision or requirement given or made by the Secretary of State under article 22(4) of this Order.

(5) Where the Company refuses to grant a works licence which has been applied for it shall give reasons in writing for its refusal.

(6) Where the Company grants a works licence upon terms or conditions or requires any modifications in the plans and particulars, it shall give reasons in writing for the terms and conditions imposed or the modifications required.

(7) If within three months from the receipt of the application under paragraph (2) above the Company does not grant a works licence it shall be deemed to have refused the application.

(8) Articles 13 to 17 of this Order[6] shall apply in relation to the holder of a works licence as respects the works which are authorised by the licence as they do in relation to the Company as respects tidal works.

(9) In the carrying out of operations in pursuance of a works licence, the holder of the licence shall not—

(a) interfere with, damage or otherwise injuriously affect any apparatus belonging to or maintained by any statutory undertaker; or

(b) do anything which will obstruct or impede any work relating to the inspection or repair of any such apparatus;

without the consent of the statutory undertaker concerned.

Licence to dredge

21.—(1) The Company may upon such terms and conditions as it thinks fit grant to any person a licence to dredge in any part of the transferred harbour.

(2) Application for a dredging licence shall be made in writing to the Company and shall be accompanied by plans, sections and particulars defining the nature, extent and manner of the operations to be carried out in the exercise of the powers granted by the licence, and in granting any such licence the Company may require modifications in the plans, sections and particulars so submitted.

(3) Article 20(3), (4), (5), (6) and (7) of this Order shall apply in relation to a dredging licence as it applies in relation to a works licence.

(4) Any materials (other than wreck within the meaning of Part IX of the Act of 1894) taken up or collected by means of dredging in pursuance of a dredging licence shall be the property of the holder of the licence and he may use, sell or otherwise dispose of or remove or deposit the materials as he thinks fit;

Provided that no such material shall be laid down or deposited in any place below the level of high water except in such a position as may be approved by the Secretary of State and subject to such conditions and restrictions as he may impose.

6. These are provisions to ensure that tidal works do not become a danger to navigation.

APPENDIX D

(5) The grant of a dredging licence shall not confer statutory authority for the carrying out of the operations covered by the licence.

(6) Paragraph (9) of article 20 of this Order shall apply in relation to the carrying out of operations in pursuance of a dredging licence as it applies in relation to the carrying out of operations in pursuance of a works licence.

Appeals in respect of works or dredging licence

22.—(1) An applicant for a works licence or a dredging licence who is aggrieved by—

(a) a refusal of the Company to grant a licence; or
(b) any terms or conditions subject to which the licence is granted; or
(c) any modifications required by the Company in the plans, sections and particulars submitted by the applicant;

may within 28 days from the date on which the Company notifies the applicant of their decision or the date on which the Company is, under article 20(7) or 21(3) of this Order, deemed to have refused the application, appeal to the Secretary of State.

(2) An appeal under paragraph (1) above shall be made by notice in writing stating the grounds of the appeal.

(3) A person who appeals under paragraph (1) above shall give to the Company notice of his appeal accompanied by a copy of his statement of appeal; and the Company shall, within 28 days of the receipt of the notice, be entitled to furnish to the Secretary of State its observations on the appeal.

(4) On an appeal under this article the Secretary of State may—

(a) dismiss the appeal; or
(b) require the Company to grant the licence or, as the case may be, to give its approval upon such terms or conditions and with such modifications (if any) of plans, sections and particulars as the Secretary of State may specify.

(5) The Company shall give effect to any decision or requirement given or made by the Secretary of State under paragraph (4) above.

APPENDIX E

NAVIGATION

SECTIONS 42–45 OF MEDWAY PORTS AUTHORITY ACT 1973[1]

Provision against danger to navigation

42.—(1) In case of injury to or destruction or decay of a tidal work or any part thereof the Authority shall forthwith notify Trinity House and shall lay down such buoys, exhibit such lights and take such other steps for preventing danger to navigation as Trinity House shall from time to time direct.

(2) If the Authority fail to notify Trinity House as required by this section or to comply in any respect with a direction given under this section they shall be liable on summary conviction to a fine not exceeding the prescribed sum and on conviction on indictment to a fine.

Abatement of works abandoned or decayed

43.—(1) Where a tidal work is abandoned, or suffered to fall into decay, the Secretary of State may by notice in writing require the Authority at their own expense either to repair and restore the work or any part thereof, or to remove the work and restore the site thereof to its former condition, to such an extent and within such limits as the Secretary of State thinks proper.

(2) Where a work consisting partly of a tidal work and partly of works of the Authority on or over land above the level of high water is abandoned or suffered to fall into decay and that part of the work on or over land above the level of high water is in such condition as to interfere or to cause reasonable apprehension that it may interfere with the right of navigation or other public rights over the foreshore, the Secretary of State may include that part of the work, or any portion thereof, in any notice under this section.

(3) If, on the expiration of thirty days from the date when a notice under this section is served upon the Authority, they have failed to comply with the requirements of the notice, the Secretary of State may execute the works specified in the notice and any expenditure incurred by him in so doing shall be recoverable from the Authority as a simple contract debt.

---

1. The functions of the Medway Ports Authority under these sections have been transferred to Medway Ports Limited by section 2(2)(b) of the Ports Act 1991 on the relevant Scheme under that Act taking effect. Medway Ports Limited have been re-named Port of Sheerness Limited.

APPENDIX E

Survey of tidal works

44. The Secretary of State may at any time if he deems it expedient order a survey and examination of a tidal work or of the site upon which the Authority propose to construct a tidal work, and any expenditure incurred by the Secretary of State in any such survey and examination shall be recoverable from the Authority as a simple contract debt.

Permanent lights on tidal works

45.—(1) The Authority shall exhibit on each tidal work every night from sunset to sunrise such lights, if any, and take such other steps for the prevention of danger to navigation as Trinity House shall from time to time direct

(2) If the Authority fail to comply in any respect with a direction given under this section they shall be liable on summary conviction to a fine not exceeding the prescribed sum and on conviction on indictment to a fine.

APPENDIX F

WRECKS

I. SECTION 252 OF MERCHANT SHIPPING ACT 1995

Powers of harbour and conservancy authorities in relation to wrecks

252.—(1) Where any vessel is sunk, stranded or abandoned in, or in or near any approach to, any harbour or tidal water under the control of a harbour authority or conservancy authority in such a manner as, in the opinion of the authority, to be, or be likely to become, an obstruction or danger to navigation or to lifeboats engaged in lifeboat service in that harbour or water or approach thereto, that authority may exercise any of the following powers.

(2) Those powers are—

    (a) to take possession of, and raise, remove or destroy the whole or any part of the vessel and any other property to which the power extends;

    (b) to light or buoy the vessel or part of the vessel and any such other property until it is raised, removed or destroyed; and

    (c) subject to subsections (5) and (6) below, to sell, in such manner as the authority think fit, the vessel or part of the vessel so raised or removed and any other property recovered in the exercise of the powers conferred by paragraph (a) or (b), above;

    (d) to reimburse themselves, out of the proceeds of the sale, for the expenses incurred by them in relation to the sale.

(3) The other property to which the powers conferred by subsection (2) above extend is every article or thing or collection of things being or forming part of the equipment, cargo, stores or ballast of the vessel.

(4) Any surplus of the proceeds of a sale under subsection (2)(c) above shall be held by the authority on trust for the persons entitled thereto.

(5) Except in the case of property which is of a perishable nature or which would deteriorate in value by delay, no sale shall be made under subsection (2)(c) above until at least seven days notice of the intended sale has been given by advertisement in a local newspaper circulating in or near the area over which the authority have control.

(6) At any time before any property is sold under subsection (2)(c) above, the owner of the property shall be entitled to have it delivered to him on payment of its fair market value.

(7) The market value of property for the purposes of subsection (6) above shall be that agreed on between the authority and the owner or, failing agreement, that determined by a person appointed for the purpose by the Secretary of State.

APPENDIX F

(8) The sum paid to the authority in respect of any property under subsection (6) above shall, for the purposes of this section, be treated as the proceeds of sale of the property.

(9) Any proceeds of sale arising under subsection (2)(c) above from the sale of a vessel and any other property recovered from the vessel shall be treated as a common fund.

(10) This section is without prejudice to any other powers of a harbour authority or conservancy authority.

II. SECTIONS 46 AND 47 OF MEDWAY PORTS AUTHORITY ACT 1973[1]

Powers with respect to disposal of wrecks

46.—(1) In its application to the Authority, section 252 of the Merchant Shipping Act, 1995, shall have effect—

  (a) subject to the provisions of section 47 (Protection of Crown interests in wrecks) of this Act; and

  (b) in relation to a vessel sunk, stranded or abandoned before as well as after the passing of this Act.

(2) Subject to subsection (3) of this section, and to any enactment for the time being in force limiting his liability, the Authority may recover as a simple contract debt from the owner of any vessel in relation to which they have exercised their powers under the said section 252 any expenses reasonably incurred by them under that section in relation to that vessel which are not reimbursed out of the proceeds of sale (if any) within the meaning of those sections.

(3) Except in a case which is, in the opinion of the Authority, a case of emergency, subsection (2) of this section shall not apply in relation to any vessel unless, before exercising in relation to that vessel any of the powers conferred on them by the said section 252, other than the power of lighting and buoying, the Authority have given to the owner of the vessel not less than forty-eight hour's notice of their intention to do so; and if before the notice expires they receive from the owner counter-notice in writing that he desires to dispose of the vessel himself, and no direction is served in respect of the vessel under paragraph (b) of subsection (2) of the said section 47 he shall be at liberty to do so, and the Authority shall not exercise the powers aforesaid in relation to that vessel until the expiration of seven days from the receipt of the counter-notice and of any further continuous period thereafter during which the owner of the vessel proceeds with the disposal thereof with all reasonable diligence and in compliance with any directions for the prevention of interference with navigation which may be given to him by the Authority.

(4) Notice under subsection (3) of this section to the owner of any vessel may be served by the Authority either by delivering it to him or by sending it to him by registered post or the recorded delivery service addressed to him at his last known place of business or abode in the United Kingdom, or, if the owner or any such place of business or abode is not known to the Authority or is not in the United Kingdom, by

1. The functions of the Medway Ports Authority under these sections have been transferred to Medway Ports Limited by section 2(2)(b) of the Ports Act 1991 on the relevant Scheme under that Act taking effect. Medway Ports Limited have been re-named Port of Sheerness Limited.

displaying the notice at the principal office of the Authority for the period of its duration.

(5) Except in the case which is, in the opinion of the Authority, a case of emergency, the Authority shall, before raising, removing or destroying under the powers conferred upon them by the said section 252 any vessel sunk, stranded or abandoned in the port or in or near any approach thereto and within a distance of 200 yards of any sub-aqueous cable belonging to or used by the Post Office, give to the Post Office in writing as long notice as is practicable of their intention to do so.

(6) In this section the expression "owner" in relation to any vessel means the person who was the owner of the vessel at the time of the sinking, stranding or abandonment thereof.

Protection of Crown interests in wrecks

47.—(1) Without prejudice to section 308 of the Merchant Shipping Act, 1995, the powers conferred on the Authority by section 252 of the said Act of 1995 shall not be exercisable—

(a) in relation to any vessel sunk, stranded or abandoned by design by or under the orders of a person acting on behalf of Her Majesty or an officer or servant of the Crown acting in the course of his duty as such;

(b) except with the consent of the Secretary of State for Defence, which may be given with or without such a direction as is referred to in paragraph (b) of subsection (2) of this section, in relation to any vessel which is not excluded from the exercise of those powers by virtue of being a vessel belonging to Her Majesty but which, at the time when the vessel was sunk, stranded or abandoned—

(i) had been required to be placed at the disposal of Her Majesty or of a government department; and

(ii) was appropriated to the service, under the direction and control of the Secretary of State for Defence, of Her Majesty's ships of war.

(2) The Authority shall give notice in writing to the Secretary of State for Defence and to the Secretary of State for Trade and Industry[2] of any decision of the Authority to exercise in relation to any vessel referred to in paragraph (b) of subsection (1) of this section any of the powers aforesaid other than the power of lighting and buoying and, except in a case which is in the opinion of the Authority a case of emergency, shall not proceed with the exercise thereof—

(a) except with the consent of the Secretary of State for Defence and the Secretary of State for Trade and Industry before the expiration of a period of fourteen days from the giving of the notice; or

(b) if before the expiration of the said period there is served on the Authority a direction by the Secretary of State for Defence or the Secretary of State for Trade and Industry that those powers shall not be exercised in relation to that vessel except in such a case as aforesaid;

and where, in any such case as aforesaid, the Authority proceed to exercise those powers without the consent and before the expiration of the period mentioned in paragraph (a) of this subsection or after a direction has been served on them as aforesaid, they shall not in the exercise of those powers use any explosives and, if, before the expiration of the period aforesaid, such a direction as aforesaid is served on

2. Now the Secretary of State for Transport.

them, shall not be entitled to exercise the power of sale conferred by the said section 252 or the power conferred by subsection (2) of section 46 (Powers with respect to disposal of wrecks) of this Act:

Provided that—

(i) the Authority shall not be required to give notice under this subsection in respect of any vessel in respect of which they have received a consent under paragraph (b) of subsection (1) of this section, but any direction such as is referred to in paragraph (b) of this subsection accompanying that consent shall be deemed for the purposes of this subsection and of subsection (3) of the said section 46 to have been duly served under paragraph (b) of this subsection;

(ii) the prohibition on the use of explosives imposed by this subsection shall not apply to the use for cutting away the superstructure of a vessel of such small explosive charges as may for the time being be approved by the Secretary of State for the purposes of this proviso.

(3) Without prejudice to the powers of sale conferred on the Authority by the said section 252, the Authority shall hold and dispose of any wreck within the meaning of Part IX of the said Act of 1995 raised, removed or recovered under that section, and any surplus proceeds of sale within the meaning of that section, in accordance with such directions (if any) as may be given to them by the receiver of wreck; and on exercising the said power of sale in the case of any property the Authority shall discharge any sums payable in respect of that property by way of duties of customs or excise and any sums so discharged shall be deemed to be expenses incurred by the Authority under that section.

(4) Any limitation on the powers of the Authority in relation to any vessel arising by virtue of subsection (1) or subsection (2) of this section shall not operate to authorise the exercise in relation to that vessel of the powers conferred on Trinity House by section 253 of the said Act of 1995.[3]

III. SECTION 56 OF HARBOURS, DOCKS AND PIERS CLAUSES ACT 1847

Harbour masters may remove wrecks, etc.

56.—The harbour master may remove any wreck or other obstruction to the harbour, dock, pier, or the approaches to the same, and also any floating timber which impedes the navigation thereof, and the expense of removing any such wreck, obstruction, or floating timber shall be repaid by the owner of the same; and the harbour master may detain such wreck or floating timber for securing the expenses, and on non-payment of such expenses, on demand, may sell such wreck or floating timber, and out of the proceeds of such sale pay such expenses, rendering the overplus, if any, to the owner on demand.

---

3. This section confers powers to raise wrecks etc. on the appropriate general lighthouse authority in cases where there is no harbour authority with powers for the purpose.

IV. SECTIONS 121 AND 122 OF PORT OF LONDON ACT 1968

Removal of obstructions other than vessels

121.—(1) The Port Authority may remove—
  (a) anything, other than a vessel, causing or likely to become an obstruction or impediment in any part of the Thames or in a dock;
  (b) anything, other than a vehicle, causing or likely to become an obstruction or impediment to the proper use of a towpath on the Thames.

(2) (a) If anything removed by the Port Authority under subsection (1) of this section is so marked as to be readily identifiable as the property of any person, the Port Authority shall within one month of its coming into their custody give notice, as required by subsection (5) of this section, to that person and if possession of the thing is not retaken within the period specified in, and in accordance with the terms of, the notice it shall at the end of that period vest in the Port Authority.

(b) If anything removed by the Port Authority under subsection (1) of this section which is not so marked is not within three months of its coming into the custody of the Port Authority proved to the reasonable satisfaction of the Port Authority to belong to any person, it shall thereupon vest in the Port Authority.

(3) The Port Authority may at such time and in such manner as they think fit dispose of anything referred to in paragraph (b) of subsection (2) of this section which is of a perishable nature or the custody of which involves unreasonable expense or inconvenience notwithstanding that it has not vested in the Port Authority under this section, and if it is sold the proceeds of sale shall be applied by the Port Authority in payment of the expenses incurred by them under this section in relation to the thing, and any balance—
  (a) shall be paid to any person who within three months from the time when the thing came into the custody of the Port Authority proves to the reasonable satisfaction of the Port Authority that he was the owner thereof at that time; or
  (b) if within the said period no person proves his ownership at the said time, shall vest in the Port Authority.

(4) If anything removed under this section—
  (a) is sold by the Port Authority and the proceeds of sale are insufficient to reimburse the Port Authority for the amount of the expenses incurred by them in the exercise of their powers of removal; or
  (b) is unsaleable;
the Port Authority may recover as a debt in any court of competent jurisdiction the deficiency or the whole of the expenses, as the case may be, from the person who was the owner at the time when the thing removed came into the custody of the Port Authority or who was the owner at the time of its abandonment or loss.

(5) A notice given under paragraph (a) of subsection (2) of this section shall specify the thing removed and state that upon proof of ownership to the reasonable satisfaction of the Port Authority possession may be retaken at a place named in the notice within the time specified in the notice, being not less than fourteen days after the date when the notice is served.

(6) The Port Authority shall not under the powers of this section remove anything placed or constructed by a local authority or statutory undertakers under the provisions of a statute or of a consent or licence given or issued by the Port Authority thereunder.

(7) In subsection (6) of this section—

"local authority" means the council of a county, district or London borough, the Common Council of the City of London, the Thames Water Authority[4] and an authority established under section 10 (joint arrangements for waste disposal functions) of the Local Government Act 1985.

"statutory undertaker" means a person authorised by statute to carry on any undertaking for the supply of electricity, gas or water.

Removal of projections

122.—(1) In this section—

"projection" means anything which projects over the Thames and includes stairs and any tree, bush or other plant but does not include any such thing authorised by or under statute or by a works licence to be placed or constructed.

(2) (a) If any projection is a danger to the navigation of the Thames, the Port Authority may remove it and recover the expenses of removal from the owner or occupier of the land on which the projection was situated as a debt in any court of competent jurisdiction.

(b) Before exercising their powers under this subsection the Port Authority shall, if it is reasonably practicable to do so, give notice of their intention to the owner and occupier of the land on which the projection is situated.

(c) In proceedings to recover expenses under paragraph (a) of this subsection the court may inquire whether the Port Authority might reasonably have proceeded instead under subsection (3) of this section, and, if the court determines that the Port Authority might reasonably have proceeded instead under the said subsection (3), the Port Authority shall not recover the expenses.

(3) (a) If any projection is an obstruction or inconvenience to the navigation of the Thames but not a danger thereto, the Port Authority may by notice in writing require the owner or occupier of the land on which the projection is situated to remove the projection within such time, not being less than seven days, as may be specified in the notice.

(b) If a person to whom notice is given under paragraph (a) of this subsection fails to comply with the notice within the time stated in the notice, or, if he appeals and the appeal is not allowed, within the time stated in the notice or such other time as the court may substitute therefor, the Port Authority may themselves remove the projection and recover the expenses of removal from the person on whom the notice was served as a debt in any court of competent jurisdiction.

(4) A notice under paragraph (a) of subsection (3) of this section shall have annexed to it a copy of this section.

(5) A person aggrieved by a notice served by the Port Authority under subsection (3) of this section may appeal to a magistrates' court.

(6) This section is subject to section 84 (Replacement of marked landing places) of this Act.

---

4. The Thames Water Authority has now been abolished and its functions divided between its successor company under the Water Act 1989 and the Environment Agency.

DIRECTIONS TO VESSELS

SECTIONS 20-27 OF MEDWAY PORTS AUTHORITY ACT 1973[1]

General directions to vessels in the port and the Medway approach area

20.—(1) The Authority may, after consultation in each case with the pilotage authority and the Chamber of Shipping of the United Kingdom,[2] give directions for the purpose of promoting or securing conditions conducive to the ease, convenience or safety of navigation in the port and the Medway approach area and, without prejudice to the generality of the foregoing, for any of the following purposes:—

    (a) for designating areas, routes or channels in the port or the Medway approach area which vessels are to use or refrain from using for movement or mooring;

    (b) for securing that vessels move only at certain times or during certain periods;

    (c) for prohibiting—

        (i) entry into or movement in the port or the Medway approach area by vessels at times of poor visibility due to the weather or to the presence of dust or smoke; and

        (ii) entry into the port or the Medway approach area by a vessel which for any reason would be, or be likely to become, a danger to other vessels in the port or the Medway approach area;

    (d) requiring the master of a vessel to give to the harbour master information relating to the vessel reasonably required by the harbour master in order to effect the objects of this subsection.

(2) Directions given under subsection (1) of this section may apply—

    (a) to all vessels or to a class of vessels designated, or the designation of which is provided for, in the direction;

    (b) to the whole of the port of the Medway approach area or to a part designated, or the designation of which is provided for, in the direction; and

    (c) at all times or at times designated, or the designation of which is provided for, in the direction;

---

1. The functions of the Medway Ports Authority under these sections have been transferred to Medway Ports Limited by section 2(2)(b) of the Ports Act 1991 on the relevant Scheme under that Act taking effect. Medway Ports Limited have been re-named Port of Sheerness Limited.
2. Now the General Council of British Shipping.

and every direction made under this section shall specify the extent of its application in relation to the matters referred to in paragraphs (a), (b) and (c) of this subsection.

(3) The Authority may, after consultation with the pilotage authority and the Chamber of Shipping of the United Kingdom,[3] revoke or amend directions given under this section.

Special directions to vessels in the port and the Medway approach area

21.—(1) A direction under this section may be given for any of the purposes set out in subsection (2) of this section by the harbour master to a vessel anywhere in the port or the Medway approach area and to a vessel prior to its entering the port from a dock.

(2) A direction under this section may be given for any of the following purposes:—

    (a) requiring a vessel to comply with a requirement made in or under a general direction;

    (b) regulating or requiring for the ease, convenience or safety of navigation the movement, mooring or unmooring of a vessel;

    (c) regulating for the safety of navigation the manner in which a vessel takes in or discharges cargo, fuel, water or ship's stores.

Directions to vessels at the docks

22.—(1) The Authority may give directions applicable to all vessels, or to a specified class of vessels, at the docks, for the purpose of ensuring the safety of vessels at the docks, preventing injury to persons at, or to property at, or forming part of, the docks or of securing the efficient conduct of the business carried on at the docks and, without prejudice to the generality of the foregoing, such directions may relate to—

    (a) the movement, berthing or mooring of a vessel;

    (b) the dispatch of its business at the dock;

    (c) the disposition or use of its appurtenances or equipment;

    (d) the use of its motive power;

    (e) the embarking or landing of passengers;

    (f) the loading or discharging of cargo, fuel, water or ship's stores;

    (g) the use of ballast.

(2) The harbour master may give a direction requiring the removal from a dock of a vessel if—

    (a) it is on fire;

    (b) it is in a condition where it is liable to become immobilized or waterlogged, or to sink;

    (c) it is making an unlawful or improper use of the dock;

    (d) it is interfering with the use of the dock by other vessels, or is otherwise interfering with the proper use of the dock or the dispatch of business therein;

    (e) the removal is necessary to enable maintenance or repair work to be carried out to the dock or to an adjacent part of the dock.

(3) The harbour master may give a direction to a vessel at the docks for the following purposes:—

    (a) any of the purposes referred to in subsection (1) of this section;

---

3. Now the General Council of British Shipping.

(b) requiring the vessel to comply with a general direction made under this section.

(4) In this section reference to a vessel at a dock includes reference to a vessel entering or about to enter a dock and to a vessel leaving or having just left a dock.

Publication of general directions

23.—(1) Notice of the giving of a general direction and of any amendment or revocation of a general direction shall, except in case of emergency, be published by the Authority once in Lloyd's List and Shipping Gazette newspaper or some other newspaper specializing in shipping news, and, if the notice relates to the giving or amendment of a general direction, shall state a place at which copies of the direction may be inspected and bought and the price thereof.

(2) In an emergency, notice of the giving of a general direction or of any amendment or revocation of a general direction may be given in any manner the harbour master considers appropriate.

Manner of giving special directions

24. A special direction may be given in any reasonable manner considered appropriate.

Master's responsibility to be unaffected

25. The giving of a general direction or a special direction shall not diminish or in any other way affect the responsibility of the master of the vessel to which the direction is given in relation to his vessel, persons on board, its cargo or any other person or property.

Failure to comply with directions

26.—(1) The master of a vessel who fails to comply with a general or special direction shall be liable to a fine not exceeding the prescribed sum.

(2) It shall be a defence to the master of a vessel charged with an offence under subsection (1) of this section to prove that he had reasonable ground for supposing that compliance with the direction in question would be likely to imperil his vessel or any person for whom he is responsible or that in the circumstances compliance was impracticable.

Enforcement of directions

27.—(1) Without prejudice to any other remedy available to the Authority, if a special direction is not complied with within a reasonable time, the harbour master may, where practicable, put persons aboard the vessel to carry out the direction or may otherwise cause the vessel to be handled in accordance with the direction.

(2) If there is no one on board a vessel to attend to a special direction, the harbour master may proceed as if the direction had been given and not complied with:

Provided that the powers of this subsection shall not be exercised—

    (a) in relation to a vessel other than a lighter, unless after reasonable inquiry has been made the master cannot be found; or

(b) in relation to a lighter, unless it is obstructing the access to or exit from a dock or otherwise interfering with navigation.

(3) Expenses incurred by the Authority in the exercise of the powers conferred by subsection (1) of this section shall be recoverable by the Authority as a simple contract debt.

APPENDIX H

BY-LAWS

I. SECTION 83 OF HARBOURS, DOCKS AND PIERS CLAUSES ACT 1847

83. Byelaws may be made for all or any of the purposes herein named.—The undertakers may from time to time make such byelaws as they shall think fit for all or any of the following purposes; (that is to say,)

For regulating the use of the harbour, dock, or pier:

For regulating the exercise of the several powers vested in the harbour master:

For regulating the admission of vessels into or near the harbour, dock or pier, and their removal out of and from the same, and for the good order and government of such vessels whilst within the harbour or dock, or at or near the pier:

For regulating the shipping and unshipping, landing, warehousing, stowing, depositing, and removing of all goods within the limits of the harbour, dock, or pier, and the premises of the undertakers:

For regulating (with the consent of the Commissioners of Her Majesty's Customs) the hours during which the gates or entrances or outlets to the harbour, dock, or pier shall be open:

For regulating the duties and conduct of all persons, as well [as] the servants of the undertakers as others, not being officers of Customs or Excise, who shall be employed in the harbour, dock, or pier, and the premises of the undertakers:

For regulating the use of fires and lights within the harbour, dock, or pier, and the premises belonging thereto, and within any vessel being within the harbour or dock, or at or near the pier, or within the prescribed limits (if any):

For preventing damage or injury to any vessel or goods within the harbour or dock, or at or near the pier, or on the premises of the undertakers:

For regulating the use of the cranes, weighing machines, weights and measures belonging to the undertakers, and the duties and conduct of all weighers and meters employed by them:

For regulating the duties and conduct of the porters and carriers employed on the premises of the undertakers and fixing the rates to be paid to them for carrying any goods, articles, or things from or to the same:

And the undertakers may from time to time, as they shall think fit, repeal or alter any such byelaws: Provided always, that such byelaws shall not be repugnant to the laws of that part of the United Kingdom where the same are to have effect, or the provisions of this or the special Act; and such byelaws shall be reduced into writing, and have affixed thereto the common seal of the undertakers, if they be a body corporate, or the signatures of the undertakers, or two of them, if they be not a body corporate, and, if affecting other persons than the officers or servants of the undertakers shall be confirmed and published as herein provided.

II. SECTION 78 OF MEDWAY PORTS AUTHORITY ACT 1973[1]

General byelaws

78. Subject to the provisions of this Act, the Authority may make byelaws for all or any of the following purposes:—

(a) for regulating the use, operation and superintendence of the port and the docks, berths, wharves, quays, piers, jetties, staiths, warehouses, sheds, landing places, locks, sluices, equipment, works and conveniences (including moorings) in the port;

(b) for regulating the admission to movement and berthing within, and the departure of vessels from, the port, or the removal of vessels, and for the good order and government of vessels whilst within the port;

(c) for regulating the shipping and unshipping, landing, warehousing, stowing, depositing and removing of goods within the limits of the port, and at the premises of the Authority;

(d) for regulating the navigation, berthing and mooring of vessels within the port and their speed and manner of navigation, and the use of tugs within the port;

(e) for preventing damage or injury to any vessel, goods, vehicle, plant, machinery, property or persons within the port, or on the premises of the Authority;

(f) for regulating the conduct of all persons in the port, not being members of a police force or officers or servants of the Crown whilst in the exercise of their duties;

(g) for regulating the placing and maintenance of moorings;

(h) for preventing and removing obstructions or impediments within the port;

(i) for prohibiting or regulating the discharge or deposit of ballast, ashes, refuse, rubbish or other material (including any polluting liquid) in the port;

(j) for regulating the use of ferries within the port;

(k) for regulating the use of yachts, sailing boats, rowing boats, pleasure craft and other small craft and the holding of regattas and other public events within the port;

(l) for regulating the launching of vessels within the port;

(m) for prohibiting persons working or employed in or entering the port, or any part thereof, from smoking therein;

(n) for regulating or preventing the use of fires and lights within the port and the premises belonging thereto, and within any vessel within the port;

(o) for regulating traffic on railways within the port and the use of locomotives thereon;

(p) for regulating the movement, speed and parking of vehicles within the port;

1. The functions of the Medway Ports Authority under this section have been transferred to Medway Ports Limited by section 2(2)(b) of the Ports Act 1991 on the relevant Scheme under that Act taking effect. Medway Ports Limited have been re-named Port of Sheerness Limited.

(q) for regulating the exercise of the powers vested in the harbour master.

III. MODEL GENERAL HARBOUR BY-LAWS

The   Port/Harbour Authority, in exercise of the powers conferred by section/article   of the   Act/ Order 19   and of all other powers them enabling, hereby make the following byelaws.

Title and commencement

1. These byelaws may be cited as the   Byelaws 19   and shall come into operation on the expiration of 28 days from the date of confirmation thereof by the Secretary of State.

[*Note: the period of 28 days referred to in by-law 1 may be varied in some cases.*]

Application

2. These byelaws shall apply to all parts of the port/harbour the limits of jurisdiction of which are set forth in the Schedule hereto and to the harbour premises/dock estate as defined in byelaw 3 hereof.

[*Note: in some cases it may be useful to annexe to the prints of the by-laws, on an informal basis, a map indicating the limits of jurisdiction.*]

Interpretation

3. In these byelaws, unless the context otherwise requires, the following words or expressions have the meanings hereby respectively assigned to them "the Authority" means the   Port/Harbour Authority as defined by section/ article   of   the   Act/ order   ;

"Collision Regulations" means regulations for the prevention of collisions made under section 85 of the Merchant Shipping Act 1995;

"diving operations" means commercial diving operations;

"goods" means all articles and merchandise of every description and includes fish, livestock and animals;

"the harbour master" means the person appointed as such pursuant to section/ article   of the   Act/Order 19   and includes his authorised deputies, assistants and any other person authorised by the Authority to act in that capacity;

"the harbour premises/dock estate" means the docks, quays, jetties, stages and all other works, land and buildings for the time being vested in or occupied or administered by the Authority;

"hovercraft" means a vehicle which is designed to be supported when in motion wholly or partly by air expelled from the vehicle to form a cushion of which the boundaries include the ground, water or other surface beneath the vehicle;

[*Note: the definition of "hovercraft" is similar to that set out in section 4 of the Hovercraft Act 1968.*]

"jet craft" means any watercraft (not normally used in navigation and not being a structure which by reason of its concave shape provides buoyancy for the carriage of persons or goods) propelled by a jet engine or other mechanical means of propulsion and steered either:—

    (a) by means of a handlebar operated linkage system (with or without a rudder at the stern); or

    (b) by the person or persons riding the craft using his or their body weight for the purpose; or

    (c) by a combination of the methods referred to respectively in (a) and (b) above.

[*Note: Whether it is appropriate to include this definition depends on the circumstances of the particular harbour (the term "jet craft" is suggested for use in by-laws since "jet ski" is a trade name). In the recent case of Steadman v. Schofield and Another,[2] Mr Justice Sheen held that a jet ski was not a vessel within the meaning of section 742 of the Merchant Shipping Act 1894,[3] i.e. was not "any ship or boat or any other description of vessel used in navigation". In the course of his judgment his Lordship observed that in his opinion a boat conveyed the concept of a structure which by reason of its concave shape provided buoyancy for the carriage of persons or goods. He also expressed the view that "navigation" was not synonymous with movement on water and meant planned or ordered movement from one place to another.*]

"master" when used in relation to any vessel means any person having the command, charge or management of the vessel for the time being;

"owner" when used in relation to goods includes any consignor, consignee, shipper or agent for the sale, receipt, custody, loading or unloading and clearance of those goods and includes any other person in charge of the goods and his agent in relation thereto; and when used in relation to a vessel includes any part owner, broker, charterer, agent or mortgagee in possession of the vessel or other person or persons entitled for the time being to possession of the vessel [and when used in relation to a vehicle includes any part owner or agent or person having charge of the vehicle for the time being].

[*Note: the definition of "owner" is not used in relation to vehicles in this code and will only be necessary, therefore, where individual authorities propose additional by-laws which require the definition to extend to vehicles.*]

"quay" means any quay, wharf, jetty, dolphin, landing stage or other structure used for berthing or mooring vessels, and includes any pier, bridge, roadway or footway immediately adjacent and affording access thereto;

"sail board" means a raft with a sail or sails designed to be operated by a person or persons standing upright thereon;

[*Note: Whether it is appropriate to include this definition depends on the circumstances at the particular harbour. It would appear that the views expressed by Mr Justice Sheen in his judgment in the case of Steadman v. Schofield and Another (see the Note to the definition of "jet ski") about the nature of a jet ski would also apply to sail boards and that they are not therefore boats nor used in navigation.*]

"small vessel" means any vessel of less than 20 metres in length or a sailing vessel and for the purposes of this definition "sailing vessel" means a vessel designed to carry sail, whether as the sole or as a primary or supplementary means of propulsion;

"vehicle" includes any vehicle propelled on rails, any machinery on wheels or caterpillar tracks, trailers, caravans and mobile homes and includes a hovercraft or any other amphibious vehicle;

---

2. *Steadman v. Schofield and Another* [1992] 2 Lloyd's Rep. 163.

3. Repealed by the Merchant Shipping Act 1995. The relevant definition of "ship" is now contained in section 313 of the Merchant Shipping Act 1995.

"vessel" [*Note: it is suggested that the first choice for this definition should be that which is included in a harbour authority's own legislation; the second choice should be that which is included in the Collision Regulations (viz. " 'vessel' includes every description of water craft, including non-displacement craft and seaplanes, used or capable of being used as a means of transportation on water"); the third choice is that which follows and was devised to extend to unusual but navigable objects found in some harbours, such as oil rigs, but the third choice should only be adopted where the authority are dealing, or anticipate that they will deal, with such unusual objects*] means a ship, boat, raft or water craft of any description and includes non-displacement craft, seaplanes and any other thing constructed or adapted for floating on or being submersed in water (whether permanently or temporarily) and a hovercraft or any other amphibious vehicle.

[*Note: With regard to the inclusion of jet craft and/or sail boards in the definition of "vessel", the definition in the harbour authority's own legislation might or might not include them, according to its terms, but probably in most cases would not. The second choice of definition mentioned above probably would not include them but the third would appear to do so. However, most of the model by-laws relating to vessels do not seem applicable, for practical reasons, to jet craft or sail boards. It is suggested that if it is desired that any by-law relating to vessels should apply to jet craft and/or sail boards (in addition to by-laws 44 and 45 which deal respectively with the regulations of these craft) a specific reference to jet craft and/or sail boards should be included in the by-law in question.*]

Application of Collision Regulations

4. Insofar as the rules contained in Schedule 1 to the Merchant Shipping (Distress Signals and Prevention of Collisions) Regulations 1996 do not apply within the harbour by virtue of Rule 1 (a) of the said Schedule 1, the like rules shall so apply as part of these byelaws but subject to the other provisions of these byelaws [and references in these byelaws to the Collision Regulations shall include references to the said rules as applied by this byelaw].

[*Note: generally, the Collision Regulations apply of themselves within harbours. Although by-laws applying the Collision Regulations are not uncommon they are usually unnecessary. Furthermore, such a by-law may well result in a breach of the Collision Regulations being treated as a breach of the by-laws rather than as an offence under the Merchant Shipping Acts with the consequence that the maximum penalty will be substantially reduced. It has, however, been held by the courts that the Collision Regulations do not apply of themselves in landlocked artificial channels.[4] Where, therefore, a harbour, or part of it, consists of such a channel a by-law on the lines of the above may be appropriate. The words in square brackets at the end should not, of course, be included unless the other by-laws refer to the Collision Regulations.*]

PART II—NAVIGATION

Vessel movements

5. The master of a vessel shall give prior notice to the harbour master of the vessel's arrival at, departure from or movement within, the harbour.

[*Note: the general requirements of this by-law overlap more specific requirements to give notice of entry which apply to certain vessels, e.g. the requirements for such notice contained in the Dangerous Substances in Harbour Areas Regulations 1987.*]

---

4. *The Hare* [1904] P. 331.

APPENDIX H

Declaration of particulars of vessel

6. The master of a vessel arriving at the harbour shall, if required by the harbour master, furnish to him a declaration in the form to be obtained from him containing a correct statement of the tonnage and draught of the vessel, its last port of call, ownership and destination, and particulars of its cargo.

Vessels to navigate with care

7. The master shall navigate his vessel with such care and caution and at such speed and in such manner as not to endanger the lives of or cause injury to persons or damage to property and as not to obstruct or prejudice the navigation, manoeuvring, loading or discharging of vessels or cause unnecessary damage to moorings, river banks or other property.

Speed of vessels

8. Except with permission of the harbour master and, subject to byelaw 7 and the Collision Regulations, the master of a vessel shall not cause or permit the vessel to proceed at a speed greater than   knots.

Small vessels not to obstruct fairway

9. The master of a small vessel which is not confined to a fairway shall not make use of the fairway so as to cause obstruction to other vessels which can navigate only within the fairway.

Vessels not to be made fast to navigation buoys or marks

10. The master of a vessel shall not make fast his vessel to or lie against any buoy, beacon or mark used for navigational purposes.

Notification of collisions, etc.

11. The master of a vessel which—
    (a) has been involved in a collision with any vessel or property, or has been sunk or grounded or become stranded in a harbour area; or
    (b) by reason of accident, fire, defect or otherwise is in such a condition as to affect its safe navigation or to give rise to danger to other vessels or property; or
    (c) in any manner gives rise to an obstruction to a fairway;
shall as soon as reasonably practicable report the occurrence to the harbour master (and as soon as practicable thereafter) provide the harbour master with full details in writing and where the damage to a vessel is such as to affect or be likely to affect its seaworthiness the master shall not move the vessel except to clear the fairway or to moor or anchor in safety, otherwise than with the permission and in accordance with the directions of the harbour master.

PART III—BERTHING AND MOORING

Provision of proper fenders

12. The master and the owner of a vessel shall ensure that it is provided with a sufficient number of fenders adequate for the size of their vessel and, when berthing and leaving or lying at a quay or against other vessels, the master shall cause the vessel

354

to be fended off from that quay, or those other vessels so as to prevent damage to that quay, those other vessels or any other property.

Vessels to be properly berthed

13. The master of a vessel shall at all times keep his vessel properly and effectively moored when berthed or lying at any quay.

Vessels adrift

14. The master of a vessel which parts from its moorings shall as soon as possible report the same to the harbour master.

Access to and egress from vessels

15. The master and the owner of a vessel (other than a small vessel) while berthed alongside a quay shall provide and maintain a sufficient and proper gangway for the access and egress of all persons having lawful business on the vessel and shall during the hours of darkness provide sufficient lighting to illuminate the whole length of the gangway.

Sufficiency of crew

16. Except with the permission of the harbour master, the master of a vessel shall at all times when his vessel is within the harbour ensure that his vessel is capable of being safely moved and navigated and that there are sufficient crew or other competent persons readily available—
   (a) to attend to his vessel's moorings;
   (b) to comply with any directions given by the harbour master for the unmooring, mooring and moving of his vessel; and
   (c) to deal, so far as reasonably practicable, with any emergency that may arise.

Vessels to be kept in a movable condition

17.—(1) The master of a vessel shall not, except where his vessel is lying aground, take any steps to render his vessel incapable of movement without first notifying the harbour master and, subject as aforesaid, shall at all times keep his vessel so loaded and ballasted and in such condition that it is capable of being safely moved.

(2) Where a vessel is at any time not capable of being safely moved by means of its own propulsive machinery, the master or owner shall as soon as reasonably practicable inform the harbour master forthwith and give to him any further information which the harbour master may reasonably require.

Use of engines while vessel moored or berthed

18. The master of a vessel which is moored at a quay or attached to any mooring device shall not permit the engines of his vessel to be worked in such a manner as to cause unnecessary injury or damage to the bed or banks of the harbour or to any other vessel or property.

APPENDIX H

Vessels not to make fast to unauthorised objects

19. No person shall make a vessel fast to any post, quay, ring, fender or any other thing or place not assigned for that purpose.

Access across decks

20. The master of a vessel alongside a quay or alongside any vessel already berthed within the harbour shall, if required so to do by the harbour master, give free access across the deck of his vessel for persons and goods to and from vessels berthed alongside his vessel.

Lost anchor, cable or propeller

21. The master of a vessel which has slipped or parted from or lost any anchor, chain, cable or propeller shall—
   (a) as soon as reasonably practicable give to the harbour master notice thereof and, if possible, of the position of the anchor, chain, cable or propeller and, if the harbour master so directs, shall cause it to be recovered as soon as reasonably practicable;
   (b) in the case of an anchor or propeller leave a buoy to mark the position thereof if this is known.

PART IV—GOODS AND ROAD AND RAIL TRAFFIC

Requirements as to handling and movement of goods in the harbour

22.—(1) The owner of any goods loaded or discharged at the harbour shall ensure that the goods are removed therefrom as soon as practicable and in any case within 48 hours unless the Authority or the harbour master otherwise agrees.

(2) The owner of any goods shall comply with such directions as the harbour master may from time to time give for regulating the time, place and manner of discharging, loading or otherwise bringing into or removing those goods from the harbour premises/dock estate.

Precaution against goods, etc., falling into harbour waters or the Authority's premises

23. The master of a vessel and a person undertaking the loading of cargo into, or the discharging of cargo from, a vessel shall use or cause to be used such methods as the harbour master may direct for the prevention of any cargo, dunnage, ballast or other materials from falling or escaping into the waters of the harbour or onto the premises of the Authority.

Obstruction or interference at harbour premises/dock estate

24. No person shall—
   (a) except with the permission of the harbour master, deposit or place on any part of the harbour premises/dock estate any goods or park any vehicle so as to obstruct any road, [railway], building, mooring place, plant, machinery or apparatus or the access thereto; or
   (b) without lawful authority, use, work, move or tamper with any plant, machinery, equipment or apparatus at the harbour premises/dock estate.

Safe driving of vehicles

25. No person shall drive or otherwise operate a vehicle in the harbour premises/dock estate without due care and attention or without reasonable consideration for other persons using the harbour premises/dock estate.

Speed limit for vehicles

26. No person shall allow a vehicle to proceed anywhere in the harbour premises/dock estate at a speed greater than   miles per hour in the case of road vehicles, and   miles per hour in the case of vehicles on rails.

Supervision of vehicles

27. A person having charge of a vehicle in the harbour premises/dock estate shall at all times comply with any directions of the harbour master with respect to the loading, discharging, manoeuvring and removal thereof and shall not, without the permission of the harbour master—

(a) leave the vehicle unattended anywhere within the harbour premises/dock estate; or

(b) take it into any shed or working area.

Loads not to leak, spill or drop

28. The owner, driver or other person having charge of a vehicle in the harbour premises/dock estate shall not permit any substance to leak, spill or drop from the vehicle.

[*Note: vehicles transporting fish in bulk would find it difficult, if not impossible, to comply with this byelaw. The defence of due diligence or reasonable excuse contained in byelaw 49(3) would probably prevent a conviction in the case of such vehicles. A port which trades in fish should consider whether to adopt this byelaw at all or adopt it subject to the following qualification—*

"(2) This byelaw shall not apply to any spillage from a vehicle in which fish are being transported in bulk where that spillage could not have been reasonably prevented".]

Loads to be secured

29. The owner, driver or other person having charge of a vehicle in the harbour premises/dock estate shall ensure that any load carried thereon or therein is adequately supported and secured where appropriate and that it complies with all such statutory restrictions on the weight of goods to be so carried as are applicable on public roads.

Refuelling, etc., of vehicles

30. No person shall within the harbour premises/dock estate charge or recharge any vehicle with, or empty it of, fuel except with the permission of the harbour master or at a place designated by the Authority for that purpose.

Precedence of locomotives, etc.

31. A person driving or otherwise operating a road vehicle within the harbour premises/dock estate shall give way to any locomotive, railway rolling stock or other rail vehicle.

APPENDIX H

Driving on weighbridges

32. No person shall drive or otherwise operate a vehicle across any weighbridge within the harbour premises/dock estate except for the purpose of weighing the vehicle.

Accidents to be reported

33. Any person driving or otherwise operating a vehicle involved in an accident in the harbour premises/dock estate whereby any injury is caused to any person or any damage is caused to any property, shall stop the vehicle and report the accident to the harbour master and shall give his name and address to the harbour master. The requirements of this byelaw are without prejudice to any reporting obligations under the Reporting of Injuries, Diseases and Dangerous Occurrences Regulations 1985.

PART V—GENERAL

Inspection facilities, etc., to be made available to harbour master

34. The master of a vessel shall so far as may be required by the harbour master in the exercise of his duties, afford the harbour master access to any part of the vessel and provide all reasonable facilities for its inspection and examination.

Navigation under influence of drink or drugs prohibited

35. A person shall not navigate any vessel in the harbour whilst under the influence of drink or drugs to such an extent as to be incapable of taking proper control of the vessel.

Vessels not to be fumigated without permission

36. The master or owner of a vessel shall not cause or permit it to be fumigated without the prior permission of the harbour master.

Laying down moorings, buoys and other tackle

37.—(1) No person shall lay down any mooring, buoy, or similar tackle without a licence or prior consent in writing of the Authority/harbour master nor except in accordance with such conditions as the Authority/harbour master may impose.

(2) A mooring, buoy or similar tackle shall as soon as reasonably practicable forthwith be removed by its owner or any other person claiming possession of it if the harbour master so directs. Without prejudice to byelaw 52 if a direction by the harbour master under this paragraph is not complied with the harbour master may himself remove the mooring, buoy or tackle in question and the amount of the cost he incurs in so doing may be recovered by the Authority from the owner of the mooring, buoy, or tackle as a debt in any court of competent jurisdiction.

Dumping in harbour water prohibited

38. No person shall deposit or throw into the waters of the harbour any rubbish or other material whatsoever or place it in a position that it can fall, blow or drift into the harbour.

Drift or trawling nets not to obstruct vessels

39. No person shall cast or place any drift, trawl or other net in such a position as to be likely to become an obstruction or danger to any property including in particular, but without prejudice to the generality of the foregoing, any vessel or mooring.

No dragging or grappling without permission

40. Without prejudice to byelaw 21, no person shall drag or grapple for any material or article nor remove the same from the bed of any water area of the harbour without the written consent of the harbour master.

Vessels to have names marked on them

41. The owner of a vessel which is not registered as a ship under the Merchant Shipping Act 1894 or the Merchant Shipping Act 1983 and marked accordingly shall ensure that the vessel is marked conspicuously with its name or other means of identification and harbour of origin (if any) unless exempted from this requirement by the Authority.

Abandonment of vessels prohibited

42.—(1) No person shall abandon a vessel on the banks or shore of the harbour.

(2) For the purposes of paragraph (1) of this byelaw, a person who leaves a vessel on the banks or shore of the harbour in such circumstances or for such period that he may reasonably be assumed to have abandoned it shall be deemed to have abandoned it there unless the contrary intention is shown.

Water skiing, aquaplaning, etc.

43.—(1) No person shall engage or take part in water skiing or aquaplaning except with the written permission of the Authority given either specifically or generally and only in such areas as may be designated by the Authority and in accordance with such reasonable conditions as the Authority may impose.

(2) A master whilst using his vessel for the purpose of towing a water skier or a person aquaplaning shall have on board at least one other person capable of taking charge of the vessel and of giving such assistance as may be reasonably required during the towing and in the recovery of the water skier and shall carry—

(a) for each person on board or being towed a life jacket manufactured in accordance with the appropriate British Standards Specification or a personal buoyancy aid of the Ship and Boat Builders' National Federation approved type, two hand held distress signals and a fire extinguisher; and

(b) for each person water skiing or aquaplaning, a rescue quoit with line or other sufficient hand thrown rescue device.

(3) No person shall engage in kiting or parachute towing in the harbour without the prior written consent of the Authority given either specifically or generally and in accordance with such reasonable conditions as may be imposed by the Authority.

Jet craft

44. No person shall operate or cause to be operated a jet craft except with the written permission of the Authority given either specifically or generally and only may be designated by the Authority and in accordance with such reasonable conditions as the Authority may impose.

APPENDIX H

[*Note: As mentioned in the Note to the definition of "jet craft" in by-law 3, it appears that such a craft is not normally used in navigation. It seems therefore that a jet craft is not entitled to take advantage of the public right of navigation in tidal waters which subsists at common law. On that basis, this by-law would not be open to challenge on the grounds that it infringes the public right of navigation.*]

Sail boards

45. No person shall operate or cause to be operated a sail board [in the fairway] [within the area coloured pink on the plan annexed to these byelaws].

Diving operations

46. No diving operation shall be carried out except with the written consent of the harbour master.

Assistance to fire and other services

47. The master of a vessel shall give every reasonable facility and assistance to the fire, police, ambulance and other emergency services for dealing with, alleviating or preventing any emergency.

Fire precautions

48. The master of a vessel shall take all reasonable precautions for the prevention of accidental fire or accidents by fire.

Obstruction of officers of the Authority

49. No person shall intentionally obstruct any officer or employee of the Authority in the execution of his duties.

Meetings

50. Except with the consent of the harbour master, no person shall within the harbour premises/dock estate—
    (a) take part in any general meeting; or
    (b) gather together with other persons, or deliver any address to an audience or gather together any persons whereby any work or business at the harbour or the control, management or use of the harbour is, or is likely to be, obstructed, impeded or hindered.
This byelaw shall not apply to any meeting held for the purposes of, or in connection with requirements under, the Health and Safety at Work etc. Act 1974 or any regulations made under that Act.
[*Note: this by-law should be invoked with caution in that the discretion which it confers on a harbour authority could lay the Authority open to criticism on the grounds of discrimination or bias.*]

Unauthorised trading prohibited

51. No person shall engage by way of trade, in buying or selling any goods or property in the harbour premises/dock estate without the written consent of the Authority.

[*Note: before making the above by-law an authority should consider the following points of difficulty:—*

(1) The by-law could amount to an unreasonable infringement of a person's right to trade and, for this reason, the by-law has been limited to the harbour premises or dock estate but, in certain circumstances, it could also apply throughout a totally enclosed harbour.

(2) In the case of Parker v. Bournemouth Corporation (1902) 86 L.T. 449, 18 T.L.R. 372, it was held that it was unreasonable for the defendant Corporation to seek to regulate the selling or hawking of any article on their beach or foreshore by a by-law which provided that no person should sell, etc., any article except in pursuance of an agreement with the Corporation and in such part or parts of the beach and foreshore as the Corporation should by notice from time to time appoint and that the by-law was bad since it gave the Corporation power to make any agreement they chose without regard to the question of reasonableness or otherwise and because it reserved to the Corporation a right to refuse to give a licence to any particular person.]

Penalties

52.—(1) Any person who contravenes or otherwise fails to comply with any of these byelaws or any condition, requirement or prohibition imposed by the Authority or the harbour master in the exercise of the powers conferred upon them or him by these byelaws shall be guilty of an offence and be liable, on conviction before a court of summary jurisdiction, to a fine not exceeding level 4 on the standard scale and, in the case of a continuing offence, a further fine not exceeding £   for each day during which the offence continues after conviction therefor.

[*Note: Level 4 on the standard scale is the maximum penalty which, under section 57 of the Criminal Justice Act 1988, may be imposed for the contravention of harbour by-laws. However, in practice, level 3 on that scale is usually the maximum penalty which the Secretary of State will endorse save in exceptional cases. The provision for a further fine in the case of a continuing offence is not within the by-law-making powers of many harbour authorities.*]

(2) Where the commission by any person of an offence under these byelaws is due to the act or default of some other person, that other person shall be guilty of an offence; and that other person may be charged with, and convicted of, the offence by virtue of this byelaw whether or not proceedings for the offence are taken against any other person.

(3) In any proceedings for an offence under these byelaws, it shall be a defence for the person charged to prove—

    (a) that he took all reasonable precautions and exercised all due diligence to avoid the commission of such an offence; or

    (b) that he had a reasonable excuse for his act or failure to act.

(4) If in any case the defence provided by paragraph (3)(a) of this byelaw involves the allegation that the commission of the offence was due to the act or default of another person, the person charged shall not, without leave of the court, be entitled to rely on that defence unless, within a period ending seven clear days before the hearing, he has served on the prosecutor a notice in writing giving such information identifying or assisting in the identification of that person as was then in his possession.

Revocation

53. The   Byelaws made   are hereby revoked.

SCHEDULE. LIMITS OF JURISDICTION

APPENDIX I

DANGEROUS GOODS

SECTIONS 67 AND 68 OF FORTH PORTS AUTHORITY ORDER 1969[1]

As to entry of dangerous goods

67.—(1) The Authority may—

    (a) refuse entry into the port premises of any goods which in their opinion would endanger or be liable to endanger persons or property; or

    (b) permit the entry of any such goods subject to compliance with such terms and conditions (including the part or parts of the port premises where such entry is permitted) as they think fit.

(2) The Authority shall publish a schedule of such goods—

    (a) entry of which is forbidden by them; and

    (b) entry of which is permitted by them only upon terms and conditions specified in the schedule.

(3) A person who after publication of the schedule referred to in subsection (2) of this section—

    (a) brings or causes or permits to be brought into the port premises any goods the entry of which is forbidden; or

    (b) fails in relation to any goods brought into the port premises to comply with any terms or conditions imposed by the Authority under subsection (1) of this section;

shall—

    (i) be guilty of an offence and liable to a fine not exceeding the prescribed sum, and on conviction on indictment, to a fine; and

    (ii) indemnify the Authority against all claims, demands, proceedings, costs, damages and expenses which may be made against or recovered from or incurred by the Authority in consequence of the commission of the offence;

and the Authority may remove the goods in question and may recover from the owner or offender the costs of such removal and of placing or storing the goods elsewhere.

Notice before entry of dangerous goods

68.—(1) Except in case of emergency, the owner or master of a vessel—

    (a) which it is intended to bring into the port carrying dangerous goods; or

---

1. The functions of the Forth Ports Authority under these sections have been transferred to Forth Ports PLC by section 2(2)(b) of the Ports Act 1991 on the relevant Scheme under that Act taking effect.

363

    (b) which is within the port and on which it is intended to place dangerous
        goods;

shall, not less than twenty-four hours before that vessel enters the port or before the dangerous goods are placed on board, as the case may be, give notice to the harbour master of the nature and quantity of the dangerous goods in question and, if such notice is not given, the owner or master of the vessel shall be guilty of an offence and liable to a fine not exceeding the prescribed sum.

    (2) Where the owner or master of a vessel is charged with an offence under subsection (1) of this section it shall be a defence to prove that he did not know and could not with reasonable diligence have ascertained the nature of the goods in respect of which the proceedings are taken.

CHAPTER IA OF PART VI OF MERCHANT SHIPPING ACT 1995

Waste reception facilities at harbours

General

130A.—(1) The Secretary of State may by regulations make such provision as he considers appropriate in relation to—

(a) the provision at harbours in the United Kingdom of facilities for the reception of waste from ships (in this Chapter referred to as "waste reception facilities"); and

(b) the use of waste reception facilities provided at such harbours.

(2) In making the regulations, the Secretary of State shall take into account the need to give effect to provisions—

(a) which are contained in any international agreement mentioned in section 128(1) which has been ratified by the United Kingdom; and

(b) which relate to waste reception facilities.

(3) Sections 130B to 130D make further provision with respect to the regulations that may be made under this section.

Waste management plans

130B.—(1) The regulations may make provision requiring a harbour authority for a harbour in the United Kingdom—

(a) in such circumstances as may be prescribed, to prepare a plan with respect to the provision and use of waste reception facilities at the harbour; and

(b) to submit the plan to the Secretary of State for approval.

(2) The regulations may make provision requiring a person—

(a) if directed to do so by the Secretary of State, to prepare a plan with respect to the provision and use of waste reception facilities at any terminals operated by him within a harbour which is in the United Kingdom and is specified in the direction; and

(b) to submit the plan to the Secretary of State for approval.

(3) For the purposes of this Chapter—

(a) "terminal" means any terminal, jetty, pier, floating structure or other works within a harbour at which ships can obtain shelter or ship and unship goods or passengers; and

(b) a person operates a terminal if activities at the terminal are under his control.

(4) In the following provisions of this section, "waste management plan" means a plan of a description mentioned in subsection (1) or (2) above.

(5) The regulations may make provision with respect to the form and content of waste management plans and may in particular require such plans to include—

(a) proposals as to the information to be provided about waste reception facilities to those who are expected to use them;

(b) proposals designed to ensure that adequate provision will be made for the disposal of waste deposited in waste reception facilities; and

(c) proposals about how costs incurred in established and running waste reception facilities will be recovered.

(6) The regulations may require a person preparing a waste management plan to have regard to such matters as the Secretary of State may prescribe or in a particular case direct.

(7) The regulations may make provision as to the procedures to be followed in connection with waste management plans and may in particular—

(a) require a person preparing a waste management plan to consult such persons as the Secretary of State may prescribe or in a particular case direct;

(b) enable the Secretary of State to approve waste management plans with or without modification or to reject such plans;

(c) enable the Secretary of State, if he is satisfied that a person who is required to prepare a waste management plan is not taking any steps necessary in connection with the preparation of the plan, to prepare such a plan;

(d) require harbour authorities and persons operating terminals to implement waste management plans once approved, or to take such steps as the Secretary of State may in a particular case direct for the purpose of securing that approved plans are implemented;

(e) enable waste management plans, in such circumstances as may be prescribed, to be withdrawn, altered or replaced.

Charges for and use of waste reception facilities

130C.—(1) The regulations may make provision enabling a statutory harbour authority, on levying ship, passenger and goods dues, to impose charges for the purpose of recovering the whole or a part of the costs of the provision by or on behalf of the authority of waste reception facilities at the harbour.

(2) The regulations may make provision requiring the master of a ship—

(a) if reasonably required to do so by a Departmental officer, or

(b) in such other circumstances as may be prescribed,

to deposit any waste carried by the ship, or any prescribed description of such waste, in waste reception facilities provided at a harbour in the United Kingdom.

(3) The regulations may make provision—

(a) for the reference to arbitration of questions as to whether requirements made under regulations made in pursuance of subsection (2)(a) above were reasonable and

(b) for compensation to be payable by the Secretary of State where a requirement is found to have been unreasonable.

(4) The regulations may make—

(a) provision prohibiting the imposition by persons providing waste reception facilities at harbours in the United Kingdom of charges for the depositing of waste, or any prescribed description of waste, in the facilities; or

(b) provision authorising the imposition by such persons of such charges subject to such restrictions as may be prescribed.

(5) The regulations may provide for charges to be imposed by virtue of subsection (4)(b) above—

(a) even though the charges are for the depositing of waste in compliance with a requirement imposed by virtue of subsection (2) above; and

(b) even though charges are also imposed by virtue of subsection (1) above.

(6) Subsections (7) to (9) below apply if the regulations make provision enabling a statutory harbour authority to impose charges of a description mentioned in subsection (1) above.

(7) The regulations may require information about the charges to be published in a way that is designed to bring the charges to the notice of persons likely to be affected.

(8) The regulations may provide for the charges to be reduced at the instance of the Secretary of State following the making of an objection by a person of a prescribed description.

(9) Regulations made by virtue of subsection (8) above may in particular make provision which corresponds to that made by section 31(3) to (12) of the Harbours Act 1964.

(10) The regulations may make provision as to the recovery of any charges imposed by virtue of this section.

Supplementary

130D.—(1) The regulations may provide that where a person contravenes a requirement under the regulations he is guilty of an offence and is liable—

   (a) on summary conviction, to a fine not exceeding the statutory maximum, and

   (b) on conviction on indictment, to imprisonment for a term not exceeding two years or to a fine or to both.

(2) The regulations may—

   (a) provide for exemptions from any provision of the regulations;

   (b) provide for references in the regulations to any specified document to operate as references to that document as revised or re-issued from time to time;

   (c) make different provision for different cases;

   (d) include such incidental, supplemental and transitional provision as appears to the Secretary of State to be expedient.

(3) Regulations under section 130A which contain any provision of a description mentioned in section 130C (whether or not they also contain other provision) shall not be made unless a draft of the statutory instrument containing the regulations has been laid before and approved by a resolution of each House of Parliament.

(4) A statutory instrument containing regulations under section 130A to which subsection (3) above does not apply (including regulations which revoke provision of a description mentioned in section 130C but do not contain any other provision made by virtue of section 130C) shall be subject to annulment in pursuance of a resolution of either House of Parliament.

Interpretation of Chapter IA

130E. In this Chapter—

   "prescribe" means prescribe by regulations;

   "ship, passenger and goods dues" has the same meaning—

      (a) in relation to Great Britain, as in the Harbours Act 1964; and

      (b) in relation to Northern Ireland, as in the Harbours Act (Northern Ireland) 1970;

   "waste reception facilities" has the meaning given by section 130A(1).

PROVISIONS OF HARBOURS ACT 1964 CONTAINING ENABLING POWERS AND PROCEDURE FOR HARBOUR REVISION AND EMPOWERMENT ORDERS

Minister's powers, on application of harbour authorities, or others, to make orders for securing harbour efficiency, etc.

14.—(1) Subject to the provisions of this section and to the following provisions of this Act, there may, in relation to a harbour which is being improved, maintained or managed by a harbour authority in the exercise and performance of statutory powers and duties, be made by the appropriate Minister an order (in this Act referred to as a "harbour revision order") for achieving all or any of the objects specified in Schedule 2 to this Act.

(2) Subject to the next following section, a harbour revision order shall not be made in relation to a harbour by the appropriate Minister—

(a) except upon written application in that behalf made to him by the authority engaged in improving, maintaining or managing it or by a person appearing to him to have a substantial interest or body representative of persons appearing to him to have such an interest; and

(b) unless the appropriate Minister is satisfied that the making of the order is desirable in the interests of securing the improvement, maintenance or management of the harbour in an efficient and economical manner or of facilitating the efficient and economic transport of goods or passengers by sea or in the interests of the recreational use of sea-going ships.

(2A) The objects for achieving all or any of which a harbour revision order may be made in relation to a harbour include repealing superseded, obsolete or otherwise unnecessary statutory provisions of local application affecting the harbour, or consolidating any statutory provisions of local application affecting the harbour; and subsection (2)(b) of this section does not apply to an order in so far as it is made for objects mentioned in this subsection.

(2B) Nothing in subsection (2)(b) of this section shall prevent the making of an order for facilitating—

(a) the closing of part of the harbour,

(b) a reduction in the facilities available in the harbour, or

(c) the disposal of property not required for the purposes of the harbour,

if the appropriate Minister is satisfied that the making of the order is desirable on grounds other than those specified in that subsection.

(3) A harbour revision order may include all such provisions as appear to the appropriate Minister to be requisite or expedient for rendering of full effect any other provision of the order and any supplementary, consequential or incidental provisions appearing to him to be requisite or expedient for the purposes of, or in connection

with, the order, including, but without prejudice to the generality of the foregoing words, penal provisions and provisions incorporating, with or without modifications, any provision of the Lands Clauses Acts or any other enactment and provisions for excluding or modifying any provision of any Act or of any instrument made under any Act (including this Act) and for repealing any statutory provision of local application affecting the harbour to which the order relates; but no penal provision of a harbour revision order shall be so framed as to permit of a person's being punished otherwise than on his conviction or as to permit—

(a) on his being summarily convicted, of the infliction on him of a penalty other than a fine or of—

    (i) in the case of an offence triable either summarily or on indictment, the infliction on him of a fine exceeding the prescribed sum within the meaning of section 32 of the Magistrates' Courts Act 1980 or section 289B of the Criminal Procedure (Scotland) Act 1975;

    (ii) in the case of an offence triable only summarily, the infliction on him of a fine exceeding level 4 on the standard scale or, in the case of a continuing offence, a daily fine exceeding £50 for each day on which the offence continues after conviction;

(b) on his being convicted on indictment, of the infliction on him of a penalty other than a fine.

(4) In the case of a harbour revision order that provides for the establishment of a body as the harbour authority for the harbour to which the order relates in lieu of the existing one, references in paragraphs 2 to 17 of Schedule 2 to this Act to the authority (except in the case of the reference in paragraph 3 the references, other than the second, in paragraph 5 and the second reference in paragraph 11) shall be construed as referring to the body established by the order as the harbour authority, and in the said excepted case shall be construed as referring to the existing one.

(4A) Where two or more harbours are being improved, maintained or managed by the same harbour authority or by harbour authorities which are members of the same group, a harbour revision order may relate to more than one of the harbours; and for this purpose two authorities are members of the same group if one is a subsidiary (within the meaning of the Companies Act 1985) of the other or both are subsidiaries of another company (within the meaning of that Act).

(5) Where a harbour revision order includes provision for the compulsory acquisition of land, there must, in the case of each parcel of land proposed to be acquired compulsorily, be annexed to the order a map of a scale not less than 1:2,500 on which the boundaries of that parcel are plainly delineated.

(5A) Where a harbour revision order includes provision for extinguishing or diverting a public right of way over a footpath or bridleway, there must be annexed to the order a map of a scale not less than 1:2,500 on which the path or way concerned, and in the case of a diversion the new path or way, are plainly delineated.

(7) In this section and in Schedule 2 to this Act "the appropriate Minister", in the case of an order to be made in relation to a harbour not being a fishery harbour or a marine work means the Minister,[1] in the case of an order to be made in relation to a fishery harbour means the Minister of Agriculture, Fisheries and Food, and in the case of an order to be made in relation to a marine work means the Secretary of State.

---

1. "the Minister" is defined in the Harbours Act 1964 as the Secretary of State for Transport.

Ministers' powers to make, of their own motion, orders for limited purposes for securing harbour efficiency

15.—(1) If, with respect to a harbour, the appropriate Minister is satisfied, that a harbour revision order ought to be made for the purpose of achieving, in relation to the harbour, either or both of the following objects, namely,—

(a) reconstituting the harbour authority by whom the harbour is being improved, maintained or managed or altering their constitution; and

(b) regulating (in whole or to a less extent) the procedure of, or of any committee of, the authority and fixing the quorum at a meeting of, or of any committee of, the authority;

he may, if he is satisfied as mentioned in subsection (2)(b) of the last foregoing section, make the order despite the fact that no application to him for the making of it is forthcoming from the authority engaged in improving, maintaining or managing the harbour or from such person or representative body as is mentioned in subsection (2)(a) of that section.

(2) . . .

(3) In this section "the appropriate Minister", in relation to a harbour not being a fishery harbour or a marine work means the Minister, in relation to a fishery harbour means the Minister of Agriculture, Fisheries and Food, and in relation to a marine work means the Secretary of State.

Ministers' powers, on application of intending undertakers, or others, to make orders conferring powers for improvement, construction etc., of harbours

16.—(1) In a case where a person is desirous of securing the achievement of any of the following objects, namely,—

(a) the improvement, maintenance or management of a harbour (whether natural or artificial) navigated by sea-going ships (not being a fishery harbour or a marine work) or of a port, haven, estuary, tidal or other river or inland waterway so navigated (not being a fishery harbour or marine work);

(b) the construction of an artificial harbour navigable by sea-going ships or an inland waterway so navigable, other than a harbour or waterway which, in the opinion of the Minister and the Secretary of State, will, on completion, be a marine work; and

(c) the construction, improvement, maintenance or management of a dock elsewhere than at a fishery harbour or marine work or of a wharf elsewhere than at such a harbour or work;

but neither he nor any other person has powers, or sufficient powers, to secure it, or to do so effectively, he may make a written application to the Minister for the making by him of an order conferring on the applicant, some other designated person or a body to be constituted for the purpose by the order (according as may be specified in the application) all such powers (including, in particular, power to acquire land compulsorily and to levy charges other than ship, passenger and goods dues) as are requisite for enabling that object to be achieved.

(2) In a case where a person is desirous of securing the achievement of either or both of the following objects, namely,—

(a) the improvement, maintenance or management of a fishery harbour; and

(b) the construction, improvement, maintenance or management of a dock at a fishery harbour or of a wharf at such a harbour;

but neither he nor any other person has powers, or sufficient powers, to secure it, or to do so effectively, he may make a written application to the Minister of Agriculture, Fisheries and Food for the making by him or such an order as aforesaid.

(3) In a case where a person is desirous of securing the achievement of any of the following objects namely,—

(a) the improvement, maintenance or management of a marine work, being a harbour (whether natural or artificial) navigated by sea-going ships or being a port, haven, estuary, tidal or other river or inland waterway so navigated;

(b) the construction of an artificial harbour navigable by sea-going ships which, in the opinion of the Minister and the Secretary of State, will, on completion, be a marine work or an inland waterway so navigable which, in the opinion of the Minister and the Secretary of State, will, on completion, be a marine work; and

(c) the construction, improvement, maintenance or management of a dock at a marine work or of a wharf at such a work;

but neither he nor any other person has powers, or sufficient powers, to secure it, or to do so effectively, he may make a written application to the Secretary of State for the making by him of such an order as is mentioned in subsection (1) of this section.

(4) An order under this section is in this Act referred to as a "harbour empowerment order".

(5) Neither the Minister, nor the Minister of Agriculture, Fisheries and Food nor the Secretary of State shall make a harbour empowerment order unless he is satisfied that the making thereof is desirable in the interests of facilitating the efficient and economic transport of goods or passengers by sea or in the interests of the recreational use of sea-going ships.

(6) A harbour empowerment order may include all such provisions as appear to the Minister of the Crown by whom it is made to be requisite or expedient for giving full effect to any provision included in the order by virtue of the foregoing provisions of this section and any supplementary, consequential or incidental provisions appearing to him to be requisite or expedient for the purposes of, or in connection with, the order, including but without prejudice to the generality of the foregoing words, penal provisions and provisions incorporating, with or without modifications, any provision of the Lands Clauses Acts or any other enactment and provisions for excluding or modifying any provision of any Act or of any instrument made under any Act (including this Act); but no penal provision of a harbour empowerment order shall be so framed as to permit of a person's being punished otherwise than on his conviction or as to permit—

(a) on his being summarily convicted, of the infliction on him of a penalty other than a fine or of—

(i) in the case of an offence triable either summarily or on indictment, the infliction on him of a fine exceeding the prescribed sum within the meaning of section 32 of the Magistrates' Courts Act 1980 or section 289B of the Criminal Procedure (Scotland) Act 1975;

(ii) in the case of an offence triable only summarily, the infliction on him of a fine exceeding level 4 on the standard scale or, in the case of a continuing offence, a daily fine exceeding £50 for each day on which the offence continues after conviction;

(b) on his being convicted on indictment, of the infliction on him of a penalty other than a fine.

(7) Where a harbour empowerment order includes provision for the compulsory acquisition of land, there must, in the case of each parcel of land proposed to be acquired compulsorily, be annexed to the order a map of a scale not less than 1:2,500 on which the boundaries of that parcel are plainly delineated.

(7A) Where a harbour empowerment order includes provision for extinguishing or diverting a public right of way over a footpath or bridleway, there must be annexed to the order a map of a scale not less than 1:2,500 on which the path or way concerned, and in the case of a diversion the new path or way, are plainly delineated.

Procedure for making harbour revision and empowerment orders, and substitution thereof, in general for provisional orders

17.—(1) The provisions of Schedule 3 to this Act shall have effect as follows with respect to the procedure for making harbour revision and empowerment orders:—

(a) Part I of that Schedule shall have effect with respect to the procedure for making harbour revision orders upon application therefor to the Secretary of State;

(b) Part II of that Schedule shall have effect with respect to the procedure for the making of harbour revision orders by the Secretary of State of his own motion;

(g) Part I of that Schedule shall, subject to the modifications specified in Part VII thereof, have effect with respect to the procedure for the making of harbour empowerment orders by the Secretary of State;

and the said Parts I, II and VII shall have effect with respect to the procedure for the making of orders by the Minister of Agriculture, Fisheries and Food with the substitution, except in paragraph 6(2), of references to him for references to the Secretary of State.

(2) Neither the Minister nor the Minister of Agriculture, Fisheries and Food nor the Secretary of State shall make a harbour revision or empowerment order including provision authorising the compulsory acquisition of land unless it also includes provision for the payment of compensation in respect of the acquisition.

(2A) Neither the Secretary of State nor the Minister of Agriculture, Fisheries and Food shall make a harbour revision or empowerment order which provides for extinguishing a public right of way over a footpath or bridleway unless he is satisfied—

(a) that an alternative right of way has been or will be provided, or

(b) that the provision of an alternative right of way is not required.

(2B) Neither the Secretary of State nor the Minister of Agriculture, Fisheries and Food shall make a harbour revision or empowerment order which provides for diverting a public right of way over a footpath or bridleway unless he is satisfied that the path or way will not be substantially less convenient to the public in consequence of the diversion.

SCHEDULE 2. OBJECTS FOR WHOSE ACHIEVEMENT HARBOUR REVISION ORDERS MAY BE MADE

1. Reconstituting the harbour authority by whom the harbour is being improved, maintained or managed or altering their constitution, or establishing, as the harbour authority, in lieu of the existing one, an existing body designated in that behalf or a body constituted for the purpose.

2. Regulating (in whole or to a less extent) the procedure of, or of any committee of, the authority and fixing the quorum at a meeting of, or of any committee of, the authority.

3. Varying or abolishing duties or powers imposed or conferred on the authority by a statutory provision of local application affecting the harbour, being duties or powers imposed or conferred for the purposes of—

(a) improving, maintaining or managing the harbour;

(b) marking or lighting the harbour, raising wrecks therein or otherwise making safe the navigation thereof; or

(c) regulating the carrying on by others of activities relating to the harbour or of activities on harbour land.

4. Imposing or conferring on the authority, for the purpose aforesaid, duties or powers (including powers to make byelaws), either in addition to, or in substitution for, duties or powers imposed or conferred as mentioned in paragraph 3 above.

5. Transferring from the authority to another or to the authority from another all or any of the property vested in, as the case may be, the authority or that other and held for the purposes of the harbour and, so far as they relate to the transferred property, all or any of the duties and powers imposed and conferred on, as the case may be, the authority or that other by a statutory provision of local application affecting the harbour.

6. Settling (either for all purposes or for limited purposes) the limits within which the authority are to have jurisdiction or altering (either for all purposes or for limited purposes) such limits as previously settled.

7. Conferring on the authority power to acquire (whether by agreement or compulsorily) land described in the order, being land required by them for the purpose of its being used as the site of works that they have, or will by virtue of the order have, power to execute or for some other purpose of the harbour.

7A. Extinguishing or diverting public rights of way over footpaths or bridleways for the purposes of works described in the order or works ancillary to such works.

7B. Extinguishing public rights of navigation for the purposes of works described in the order or works ancillary to such works, or permitting interference with the enjoyment of such rights for the purposes of such works or for the purposes of works carried out by a person authorised by the authority to carry them out.

8. Authorising justices of the peace to appoint, on the nomination of the authority, persons to act as constables within any limits within which the authority have jurisdiction in relation to the harbour and within one mile outside any such limits, and to dismiss persons appointed by virtue of this paragraph, and conferring on persons so appointed, while acting within any such limits as aforesaid or within one mile outside any such limits, the powers which a constable has within his constablewick.

8A. Enabling the authority to close part of the harbour or to reduce the facilities available in the harbour.

9. Empowering the authority to dispose of property vested in them and held for the purposes of the harbour which is no longer required for those purposes.

9A. Empowering the authority (alone or with others) to develop land not required for the purposes of the harbour with a view to disposing of the land or of interests in it, and to acquire land by agreement for the purpose of developing it together with such land.

9B. Empowering the authority to delegate the performance of any of the functions of the authority except—

(a) a duty imposed on the authority by or under any enactment;

(b) the making of byelaws;

(c) the levying of ship, passenger and goods dues;

(d) the appointment of harbour, dock and pier masters;

(e) the nomination of persons to act as constables;

(f) functions relating to the laying down of buoys, the erection of lighthouses and the exhibition of lights, beacons and sea-marks, so far as those functions are exercisable for the purposes of the safety of navigation.

10. Empowering the authority to borrow money, with or without limitation with respect to the amount that may be borrowed or the time or manner in which the power may be exercised.

11. Empowering the authority to levy at the harbour charges other than ship, passenger and goods dues or varying or abolishing charges (other than as aforesaid) levied by them at the harbour.

12. Securing the efficient collection of charges levied by the authority at the harbour and specifying the times at which and the persons by whom such charges are to be paid.

13. Regulating the application of moneys in the nature of revenue received by the authority and securing that the financial affairs of the authority are properly managed.

14. Varying or extinguishing any exemption from charges levied by the authority at the harbour or any other right or privilege enjoyed thereat.

15. Securing the welfare of the authority's officers and servants and empowering the authority to provide, or secure the provision of, pensions, gratuities and other like benefits for or in respect of their officers and servants.

16. Extending the time within which anything is required or authorised by a statutory provision of local application affecting the harbour to be done in relation to the harbour by the authority or fixing a time within which anything authorised by the order to be so done must be done.

16A. Imposing or conferring on the authority duties or powers (including powers to make byelaws) for the conservation of the natural beauty of all or any part of the harbour or of any of the fauna, flora or geological or physiographical features of the harbour and all other natural features.

17. Any object which, though not falling within any of the foregoing paragraphs, appears to the appropriate Minister to be one the achievement of which will conduce to the efficient functioning of the harbour.

SCHEDULE 3. PROCEDURE FOR MAKING HARBOUR REVISION AND EMPOWERMENT ORDERS

PART I. PROCEDURE FOR MAKING HARBOUR REVISION ORDERS ON APPLICATION TO THE SECRETARY OF STATE (AS SET OUT), AND FOR THE MAKING OF HARBOUR EMPOWERMENT ORDERS BY THE SECRETARY OF STATE (SUBJECT TO PART VII)

A1. In this Part of this Schedule "the Directive" means Council Directive No. 85/337/EEC on the assessment of the effects of certain public and private projects on the environment; and "project" has the meaning given by article 1 of the Directive.

A2.—(1) A person may not make an application for a harbour revision order which, directly or indirectly, authorises any project unless—

    (a) he has given the Secretary of State prior notice of his intention to make the application, and

    (b) the Secretary of State has responded under sub-paragraph (3) or, as the case may be, (4) below.

(2) Sub-paragraph (3) below applies where it appears to the Secretary of State that a proposed application of which he is notified under sub-paragraph (1)(a) above relates to—

    (a) a project which falls within Annex I to the Directive, or

    (b) a project which falls within Annex II to the Directive the characteristics of which require that it should be made subject to an environmental assessment.

(3) The Secretary of State shall direct the proposed applicant to supply him in such form as he may specify with the information referred to in Annex II to the Directive to the extent—

    (a) that it is relevant to any stage of the procedure set out in this Part and to the specific characteristics of the project to which the proposed application relates and of the environmental features likely to be affected by it; and

    (b) that (having regard in particular to current knowledge and methods of assessment) the proposed applicant may reasonably be required to gather that information, and including at least—

        (i) a description of the project comprising information on the site, design and size of the project;

        (ii) a description of the measures envisaged in order to avoid, reduce and, if possible, remedy significant adverse effects;

        (iii) the data required to identify and assess the main effects which the project is likely to have on the environment; and

        (iv) a non-technical summary of the information mentioned in paragraphs (i) to (iii) above.

(4) Where sub-paragraph (3) above does not apply in relation to a proposed application of which the Secretary of State is notified under sub-paragraph (1)(a) above, he shall forthwith notify the proposed applicant accordingly.

1. An application for a harbour revision order must be accompanied by not less than six copies of a draft of the proposed order and not less than six copies of any map or maps which, if the order is made in the form of the draft, will be required to be annexed to it.

1B. Such fees as may be determined by the Secretary of State shall be payable on the making of an application for a harbour revision order.

3.—(1) Where an application for a harbour revision order has been duly made to the Secretary of State, the following shall be conditions precedent to the taking by him of any steps (otherwise than under this paragraph) in the matter of the application, that is to say—

    (a) compliance with any directions given under paragraph A2(3) above in response to the notice of intention to make the application;

    (b) compliance with the requirements mentioned in paragraph (a) of sub-paragraph (2) below; and

    (c) compliance with such of the requirements mentioned in paragraphs (b) to (d) of that sub-paragraph as are applicable in the circumstances.

(2) The requirements referred to above are as follows—

    (a) there must be published by the applicant by *Gazette* and local advertisement and (if so required by the Secretary of State) by such other means as the Secretary of State may specify, a notice stating that application has been made to him for the making of the order and whether information has been supplied under paragraph A2 above and containing a concise summary of the proposed order, a copy of any information supplied under paragraph A2 above and (if provision is proposed to be included therein authorising the execution of works or the compulsory acquisition of land) a general description of the nature of the works and the land on which their execution is proposed to be authorised or, as the case may be, of the land whose compulsory acquisition is proposed to be authorised, naming a place where a copy of the draft of the proposed order and (if the application for the order was accompanied by copies of a map or maps) a copy of that map or, as the case may be, copies of those maps may be seen at all reasonable hours and stating that any person who desires to make to the Secretary of State objection to the application should do so in writing (stating the grounds of his objection) before the expiration of the period of forty-two days from the date (specifying it) of the first local advertisement;

(b) if provision is proposed to be included in the order authorising the compulsory acquisition of land, there must, in the case of each parcel of land whose compulsory acquisition is proposed to be authorised, be served by the applicant on every owner, lessee and occupier (except a tenant for a month or any period less than a month) of that parcel a notice stating that application has been made to the Secretary of State for the making of the order with the inclusion therein of provision authorising the compulsory acquisition of that parcel (describing it), naming a place where a copy of the draft of the proposed order and a copy (on the like scale) of the map that accompanied the application therefor on which the boundaries of that parcel are delineated may be seen at all reasonable hours and stating that, if the person served desires to make to the Secretary of State objection to the application so far as regards the inclusion in the order of provision authorising the compulsory acquisition of that parcel, he should do so in writing (stating the grounds of his objection) before the expiration of the period of forty-two days from the date on which the notice is served on him;

(ba) If provision is proposed to be included in the order extinguishing or diverting a public right of way over a footpath or bridleway the applicant shall—

    (i) serve on every local authority for the area in which the path or way is situated a notice stating the effect of the provision, naming a place where a copy of the draft of the proposed order (and of any relevant map accompanying the application for the order) may be seen at all reasonable hours and stating that, if the local authority desire to make to the Secretary of State objection to the inclusion of the provision in the order, they should do so in writing (stating the grounds of their objection) before the expiration of the period of forty-two days from the date on which the notice is served on them;

    (ii) cause a copy of the notice to be displayed in a prominent position at the ends of so much of any path or way as would by virtue of the order cease to be subject to a public right of way;

and for the purposes of this sub-paragraph, "local authority" means, in England, a county council, a district council, a London borough council, the Common Council of the City of London, the Council of the Isles of Scilly, a parish or community council and a parish meeting of a parish not having a separate parish council, in Wales, a county council, a county borough council and a community council and, in Scotland, a regional, island or district council; council constituted under section 2 of the Local Government etc. (Scotland) Act 1994;

(c) if the applicant is not the harbour authority, there must be served by the applicant on that authority a copy of the draft order together (if the application for the order was accompanied by copies of a map or maps) with a copy of that map, or copies of those maps, and, in any event, with a notice stating that application has been made to the Secretary of State for the making of the order and that, if the authority desire to make to the Secretary of State objection to the application, they should do so in writing (stating the grounds of their objection) before the expiration of the period of forty-two days from the date on which the notice is served on them;

(d) if the Secretary of State so requires, there must, on any person specified by him, and within such time as may be so specified, be served by the applicant the like documents as are required to be served in compliance with sub-paragraph (c) above where it applies.

377

3A. The Secretary of State shall furnish such bodies appearing to him to have environmental responsibilities as he thinks fit with any information supplied under paragraph A2 above and shall consult such bodies.

4.—(1) Where the proper notices concerning an application for the making of a harbour revision order have been published under paragraph 3 above, and all persons required thereunder to be served in the case of the application with notices and other documents have been properly served therewith, and the time for the due making to the Secretary of State of objection to the application has elapsed, the following provisions of this paragraph shall have effect.

(3) If objections to the application were duly made to the Secretary of State and have not been withdrawn, the Secretary of State, unless he decides that the application shall not proceed further,—

    (a) in the case of an objection so far as regards the inclusion in the draft order of a provision authorising the compulsory acquisition of a parcel of land, shall either cause an inquiry to be held with respect to the objection or afford to the objector an opportunity of appearing before and being heard by a person appointed by the Secretary of State for the purpose;

    (b) in the case of any other objection, shall cause an inquiry to be held with respect thereto, unless he is of opinion that it is frivolous or too trivial to warrant the holding of an inquiry with respect to it.

(4) Where an objector to the application avails himself of an opportunity of being heard afforded to him in pursuance of sub-paragraph (3)(a) above, the Secretary of State shall afford to the applicant, and to any other persons to whom it appears to the Secretary of State expedient to afford it, an opportunity of being heard on the same occasion.

(5) After considering—

    (a) the objections (if any) made and not withdrawn;

    (b) any information supplied under paragraph A2(3)(b) above;

    (c) the result of any consultation under paragraph 3A above; and

    (d) the report of any person who held an inquiry and any person appointed for the purpose of hearing an objector,

the Secretary of State may decide—

    (i) not to make the order applied for; or

    (ii) to make it in the form of the draft submitted to him or (subject to the restrictions imposed by sub-paragraph (6) below and by paragraph 6 below) in that form but subject to such modifications as he thinks fit.

(6) Where the Secretary of State proposes to make the order applied for with modifications which appear to him substantially to affect the character of the order as applied for, he shall take such steps as appear to him to be sufficient and reasonably practicable for informing the applicant and other persons likely to be concerned, and shall not make the order until such period for consideration of, and comment upon, the proposed modifications by the applicant and those other persons as he thinks reasonable has elapsed; nor shall he, unless all persons interested consent, so make the order as to authorise the compulsory acquisition of any land that was not described in the draft submitted to him as being land subject to be acquired compulsorily.

(7) the Secretary of State may disregard for the purposes of this paragraph an objection to the application unless it states the grounds on which it is made, and may disregard for those purposes such an objection so far as regards the inclusion in the draft order of a provision authorising the compulsory acquisition of land if he is satisfied that the objection relates exclusively to matters which can be dealt with by the tribunal by whom compensation in respect of the acquisition will fall to be assessed in default of agreement.

4ZA. Where it appears to the Secretary of State that the application relates to:
(a) a project which falls within Annex I to the Directive, or
(b) a project which falls within Annex II to the Directive the characteristics of which require that it should be subject to environmental assessment,
the Secretary of State shall publish in such manner as he thinks fit his decision whether or not to make an order and the reasons and considerations upon which his decision was based, including a statement that the matters referred to in paragraph 4(5) above have been taken into consideration.

4A.—(1) The provisions of this paragraph have effect where the Secretary of State makes—
(a) a harbour revision order relating to a harbour in England and Wales; or.
(b) a harbour empowerment order relating to a harbour or to works to be carried out in England or Wales,
and, in either case, the order authorises the compulsory purchase of land.

(2) Where this paragraph has effect in relation to an order, it shall be subject to special parliamentary procedure to the same extent as it would be, by virtue of section 18 or 19 of the Acquisition of Land Act 1981 (or by virtue of paragraph 5 or 6 of Schedule 3 to that Act) (National Trust land, commons etc.) if the purchase were authorised by an order under section 2(1) of that Act.

4B.—(1) The provisions of this paragraph apply to—
(a) a harbour revision order relating to a harbour in Scotland, or
(b) a harbour empowerment order relating to a harbour or to works to be carried out in Scotland,
where the order authorises the compulsory acquisition of land.

(2) Where this paragraph applies to an order, the order shall be subject to special parliamentary procedure to the same extent as it would be, by virtue of section 1(2)(b) of the Acquisition of Land (Authorisation Procedure) (Scotland) Act 1947 (land forming part of a common or open space or held inalienably by the National Trust for Scotland), if the purchase were authorised by an order under section 2(1) of that Act.

5. So soon as may be after a harbour revision order has been made, the applicant for it—
(a) shall publish by *Gazette* and local advertisement a notice stating that the order has been made and naming a place where a copy thereof (and, if a map or maps is or are annexed to the order, a copy of that map or, as the case may be, copies of those maps) may be inspected at all reasonable hours and further stating, in the case of an order which is not subject to special parliamentary procedure, the date on which it came or will come into operation;
(b) shall, if not the harbour authority, serve on that authority a copy of the order, together (if a map or maps is or are annexed to it) with a copy of that map or, as the case may be, copies of those maps;
(c) shall serve a copy of the order, together (if a map or maps is or are annexed to it) with a copy of that map or, as the case may be, copies of those maps, on each person on whom, in compliance with a requirement imposed by virtue of paragraph 3(d) above, a copy of the draft of the order as submitted to the Secretary of State was served.

6.—(1) Where application is made to the Secretary of State for a harbour revision order which includes provision authorising the compulsory acquisition of land which includes land which has been acquired by statutory undertakers for the purposes of their undertaking, then if on a representation made to the appropriate Minister before the expiration of the period of forty-two days from the date of the first local advertisement of notice that the application has been so made that Minister is satisfied—

(a) that any of the said land is used for the purposes of the carrying on of their undertaking, or

(b) that an interest in any of the said land is held for those purposes,

the order shall not be so made as to authorise the acquisition of any land as to which the Minister is satisfied as aforesaid except land as to which he is satisfied that its nature and situation are such—

(i) that, without serious detriment to the carrying on of the undertaking, it can be acquired and not replaced, or

(ii) that, if acquired, it can, without such detriment as aforesaid, be replaced by other land belonging to, or available for acquisition by, the undertakers,

and certifies accordingly.

(2) In this paragraph the following expressions have the meanings hereby assigned to them respectively, that is to say:—

"statutory undertakers" means any person authorised by an Act (whether public, general or local) or by an order or scheme made under or confirmed by an Act to carry on any such undertaking as follows, that is to say,—

(a) a railway, light railway, tramway or road transport undertaking;

(b) an undertaking the activities whereof consist in—

(i) the maintenance of a canal;

(ii) the conservation or improvement of a river or other inland navigation;

(iii) the improvement, maintenance or management of a harbour (whether natural or artificial), port, haven or estuary, a dock (whether used by sea-going ships or not) or a wharf, quay, pier, jetty or other place at which ships (whether sea-going or not) can ship or unship goods or embark or disembark passengers; or

(iv) the provision and maintenance of a lighthouse; or

(c) an undertaking for the supply of electricity, gas, hydraulic power or water.

PART II. PROCEDURE FOR THE MAKING OF HARBOUR REVISION ORDERS BY THE SECRETARY OF STATE OF HIS OWN MOTION

7. Where the Secretary of State proposes to make, of his own motion, a harbour revision order, he shall, before doing so—

(a) publish by *Gazette* and local advertisement and by such (if any) other means as he thinks fit a notice stating that he proposes to make the order, containing a concise summary of the provisions to be embodied in it, naming a place where a copy of the draft of the proposed order may be seen at all reasonable hours and stating that any person who desires to make to him objection to the proposal should do so in writing (stating the grounds of his objection) before the expiration of the period of forty-two days from the date (specifying it) of the first local advertisement;

(b) serve on the harbour authority and on such (if any) other persons as he thinks ought to have notice of the proposal a copy of the draft of the proposed order together with a notice stating that he proposes to make the order and that if the person served desires to make to the Secretary of State objection to the proposal he should do so in writing (stating the grounds of his objection) before the expiration of the period of forty-two days from the date on which the notice is served on him.

8.—(1) Where effect has been given to paragraph 7 above in the case of a proposal of the Secretary of State to make, of his own motion, a harbour revision order, and the time for the due making to the Secretary of State of objection to the proposal has elapsed, the following provisions of this paragraph shall have effect.

(3) If objections to the proposal that were duly made to the Secretary of State have not been withdrawn, he shall, unless he decides to proceed no further in the matter, cause an inquiry to be held with respect to each objection so made and not withdrawn unless in his opinion it is frivolous or too trivial to warrant the holding of an inquiry with respect thereto.

(4) After considering the objections (if any) made and not withdrawn, and the reports of any person who held an inquiry and any person appointed for the purpose of hearing an objector, the Secretary of State, unless he decides not to make the order, may make it in the form of the draft or (subject to the restriction imposed by sub-paragraph (5) below) in that form but subject to such modifications as he thinks fit.

(5) Where the Secretary of State proposes to make the order subject to modifications which appear to him substantially to affect the character of the order as originally proposed to be made, he shall take such steps as appear to him to be reasonably practicable for informing persons likely to be concerned and shall not make the order until such period for consideration of, and comment upon, the proposed modifications by those persons as he thinks reasonable has elapsed.

(6) The Secretary of State may disregard for the purposes of this paragraph an objection to the proposal unless it states the grounds on which it is made.

9. So soon as may be after a harbour revision order has been made by the Minister of his own motion he shall publish by *Gazette* and local advertisement a notice stating that the order has been made and naming a place where a copy thereof may be inspected at all reasonable hours, and shall serve a copy of the order on every person on whom notice of the proposal to make the order was served in compliance with the requirement imposed by paragraph 7(b) above.

PART VII. MODIFICATIONS SUBJECT TO WHICH PART I IS TO HAVE EFFECT
WITH RESPECT TO PROCEDURE FOR THE MAKING OF HARBOUR
EMPOWERMENT ORDERS BY THE SECRETARY OF STATE

14.—(1) The modifications subject to which part I of this Schedule is, by virtue of section 17(1)(g) of this Act, to have effect with respect to the procedure for the making of harbour empowerment orders by the Secretary of State are those set out in the following provisions of this paragraph.

(2) For references to a harbour revision order there shall be substituted references to a harbour empowerment order.

(3) For the reference, in paragraph 3, to the requirements of sub-paragraphs (b) to (d), there shall be substituted a reference to the requirements of sub-paragraphs (b) to (c), and for sub-paragraphs (c) to (d) of that paragraph, there shall be substituted the following sub-paragraph:—

"(c) if the Secretary of State so requires, there must, on any person specified by him, be served by the applicant a copy of the draft order together (if the application for the order was accompanied by a copy of a map or copies of maps) with a copy of that map, or copies of those maps, and, in any event, with a notice stating that application has been made to the Secretary of State for the making of the order and that, if the person served desires to make to the Secretary of State objection to the application, he should do so in writing (stating the grounds of his objection) before the expiration of the period of forty-two days from the date on which the notice is served on him".

(4) Sub-paragraph (b) of paragraph 5 shall be omitted, and for the reference, in sub-paragraph (c) of that paragraph, to paragraph 3(d), there shall be substituted a reference to paragraph 3(c).

AVIATION AND MARITIME SECURITY ACT 1990

PART III. PROTECTION OF SHIPS AND HARBOUR AREAS AGAINST ACTS OF VIOLENCE AS AMENDED

General purposes

Purposes to which Part III applies

18.—(1) The purposes to which this Part of this Act applies are the protection against acts of violence—

(a) of ships, and of persons or property on board ships, and

(b) of harbour areas, of such persons as are at any time present in any part of a harbour area and of such property as forms part of a harbour area or is at any time (whether permanently or temporarily) in any part of a harbour area.

(2) In this Part of this Act "act of violence" means any act (whether actual or potential, and whether done or to be done in the United Kingdom or elsewhere) which either—

(a) being an act done in Great Britain, constitutes, or

(b) if done in Great Britain would constitute,

the offence of murder, attempted murder, manslaughter, culpable homicide or assault, or an offence under section 18, 20, 21, 22, 23, 24, 28 or 29 of the Offences against the Person Act 1861, under section 2 of the Explosive Substances Act 1883 or under section 1 of the Criminal Damage Act 1971 or, in Scotland, the offence of malicious mischief.

(3) In this Part of this Act "harbour area" means—

(a) the aggregate of—

(i) any harbour in the United Kingdom in respect of which there is a harbour authority within the meaning of the Merchant Shipping Act 1995, and

(ii) any land which is adjacent to such a harbour and which is either land occupied by the harbour authority or land in respect of which the harbour authority has functions of improvement, maintenance or management, or

(b) any hoverport which does not form part of any area which falls within paragraph (a)(i) or (ii) above.

Powers of Secretary of State

Power of Secretary of State to require information

19.—(1) The Secretary of State may, by notice in writing served on any of the following persons—

(a) the owner, charterer, manager or master of—
   (i) a British ship, or
   (ii) any other ship which is in, or appears to the Secretary of State to be likely to enter, a harbour area,

(b) a harbour authority,

(c) any person who carries on harbour operations in a harbour area, and

(d) any person who is permitted to have access to a restricted zone of a harbour area for the purposes of the activities of a business carried on by him,

require that person to provide the Secretary of State with such information specified in the notice as the Secretary of State may require in connection with the exercise by the Secretary of State of his functions under this Part of this Act.

(2) A notice under subsection (1) above shall specify a date (not being earlier than seven days from the date on which the notice is served) before which the information required by the notice in accordance with subsection (1) above is to be furnished to the Secretary of State.

(3) Any such notice may also require the person on whom it is served, after he has furnished to the Secretary of State the information required by the notice in accordance with subsection (1) above, to inform the Secretary of State if at any time the information previously furnished to the Secretary of State (including any information furnished in pursuance of a requirement imposed by virtue of this subsection) is rendered inaccurate by any change of circumstances (including the taking of any further measures for purposes to which this Part of this Act applies or the alteration or discontinuance of any measures already being taken).

(4) In so far as such a notice requires further information to be furnished to the Secretary of State in accordance with subsection (3) above, it shall require that information to be furnished to him before the end of such period (not being less than seven days from the date on which the change of circumstances occurs) as is specified in the notice for the purposes of this subsection.

(5) Any person who—
   (a) without reasonable excuse, fails to comply with a requirement imposed on him by a notice under this section, or
   (b) in furnishing any information so required, makes a statement which he knows to be false in a material particular, or recklessly makes a statement which is false in a material particular,
commits an offence.

(6) A person guilty of an offence under subsection (5) above is liable—
   (a) on summary conviction, to a fine not exceeding the statutory maximum;
   (b) on conviction on indictment, to a fine or to imprisonment for a term not exceeding two years or to both.

(7) A notice served on a person under subsection (1) above may at any time—
   (a) be revoked by a notice in writing served on him by the Secretary of State, or
   (b) be varied by a further notice under subsection (1) above.

Designation of restricted zones of harbour areas

20.—(1) A harbour authority may, and shall if so requested in writing by the Secretary of State, apply to the Secretary of State for the designation of the whole or any part of the harbour area as a restricted zone for the purposes of this Part of this Act.

(1A) A harbour operator may, and shall if so requested in writing by the Secretary of State, apply to the Secretary of State for the designation of the whole or any part of the operating area as a restricted zone for the purposes of this Part of this Act.

(2) An application under subsection (1) or (1A) above shall be in such form, and accompanied by such plans, as the Secretary of State may require.

(3) If the Secretary of State approves an application under subsection (1) or (1A) above with or without modifications, he shall designate the restricted zone accordingly.

(4) Before approving an application with modifications, the Secretary of State shall consult the applicants.

(5) If a person is requested in writing by the Secretary of State to make an application under subsection (1) or (1A) above within a specified period but fails to do so within that period, the Secretary of State may designate the whole or any part of the harbour area or, as the case may be, of the operating area as a restricted zone.

(6) The whole or any part of a harbour area or, as the case may be, of an operating area may be designated as a restricted zone, or part of a restricted zone, for specified days or times of day only.

(7) The Secretary of State shall give notice to the person who made, or was requested to make, the application of any designation under this section and the designation of the restricted zone shall take effect on the giving of the notice.

(8) Where the whole or any part of a harbour area or, as the case may be, of an operating area has been designated under this section as a restricted zone—
    (a) subsections (1) to (7) above also have effect in relation to any variation of the designation, and
    (b) the designation may at any time be revoked by the Secretary of State.

(9) In this Part of this Act "harbour operator" means a person who—
    (a) carries on harbour operations in a harbour area, and
    (b) is designated for the purposes of this Part by an order made by the Secretary of State;
and "operating area" means, in relation to that person, so much of the harbour area as is under his control.

(10) An order under subsection (9) may be revoked by a subsequent order.

Power to impose restrictions in relation to ships

21.—(1) For purposes to which this Part of this Act applies, the Secretary of State may give a direction in writing to a harbour authority or to the owner, charterer, manager or master of a British ship, or of any other ship which is in a harbour area, requiring that person—
    (a) not to cause or permit persons or property to go or be taken on board any ship to which the direction relates, or to come or be brought into proximity to any such ship, unless such searches of those persons or that property as are specified in the direction have been carried out by constables or by other persons of a description specified in the direction, or
    (b) not to cause or permit any such ship to go to sea unless such searches of the ship, as are specified in the direction have been carried out by constables or by other persons of a description so specified.

(2) For purposes to which this Part of this Act applies, the Secretary of State may give a direction in writing to the owner, charterer, manager or master of—
    (a) a British ship, or
    (b) any other ship which is in a harbour area,
requiring him not to cause or permit the ship, to go to sea unless such modifications or alterations of the ship, or of apparatus or equipment installed in or carried on board the ship, as are specified in the direction have first been carried out, or such additional apparatus or equipment as is so specified is first installed in or carried on board the ship.

(3) In giving any direction under subsection (2) above, the Secretary of State shall allow, and shall specify in the direction, such period as appears to him to be reasonably required for carrying out the modifications or alterations or installing or obtaining the additional apparatus or equipment in question; and the direction shall not take effect before the end of the period so specified.

(4) Subject to the following provisions of this Part of this Act, a direction given to an owner, charterer or manager of a ship under subsection (1) or (2) above may be given so as to relate either to all the ships falling within that subsection of which at the time when the direction is given or at any subsequent time he is the owner, charterer or manager or only to one or more such ships specified in the direction; and a direction given to a harbour authority under subsection (1) above may be given so as to relate either to all ships which at the time when the direction is given or at any subsequent time are in any part of the harbour area, or to a class of such ships specified in the direction.

(5) Subject to the following provisions of this Part of this Act, a direction under subsection (1) above may be given so as to relate—
   (a) either to all persons or only to one or more persons, or persons of one or more descriptions, specified in the direction, and
   (b) either to property of every description or only to particular property, or property of one or more descriptions, so specified.

(6) Subject to the following provisions of this Part of this Act, any direction given under this section to any person not to cause or permit anything to be done shall be construed as requiring him to take all such steps as in any particular circumstances are practicable and necessary to prevent that thing from being done.

(7) A direction may be given under this section to a person appearing to the Secretary of State to be about to become such a person as is mentioned in subsection (1) or (2) above, but a direction given to a person by virtue of this subsection shall not take effect until he becomes a person so mentioned and, in relation to a direction so given, the preceding provisions of this section shall apply with the necessary modifications.

(8) Any person who, without reasonable excuse, fails to comply with a direction given to him under this section is guilty of an offence and liable—
   (a) on summary conviction, to a fine not exceeding the statutory maximum;
   (b) on conviction on indictment, to a fine or to imprisonment for a term not exceeding two years or to both.

(9) Where a person is convicted of an offence under subsection (8) above, then, if without reasonable excuse the failure in respect of which he was convicted is continued after the conviction, he is guilty of a further offence and liable on summary conviction to a fine not exceeding one-tenth of level 5 on the standard scale for each day on which the failure continues.

Power to require harbour authorities to promote searches in harbour areas

22.—(1) For purposes to which this Part of this Act applies, the Secretary of State may give a direction in writing to—
   (a) a harbour authority, or
   (b) a harbour operator,
requiring that person to use his best endeavours to secure that such searches to which this section applies as are specified in the direction are carried out by constables or by other persons of a description specified in the direction.

(2) The searches to which this section applies, in relation to a harbour area, are searches—
   (a) of the harbour area or any part of it,

(b) of any ship which at the time when the direction is given or at any subsequent time is in the harbour area, and

(c) of persons and property (other than ships) which may at any time be in the harbour area.

(2A) The searches to which this section applies, in relation to an operating area, are searches—

(a) of the operating area or any part of it,

(b) of any ship which at the time when the direction is given or at any subsequent time is in the operating area, and

(c) of persons and property (other than ships) which may at any time be in the operating area.

(3) Where a direction under this section to a harbour authority is for the time being in force, then, subject to subsections (4) and (5) below, if a constable or any other person specified in the direction in accordance with this section has reasonable cause to suspect that an article to which this subsection applies is in, or may be brought into, any part of the harbour area, he may, by virtue of this subsection and without a warrant, search any part of the harbour area or any ship, vehicle, goods or other moveable property of any description which, or any person who, is for the time being in any part of the harbour area, and for that purpose—

(a) may enter any building or works in the harbour area, or enter upon any land in the harbour area, if need be by force,

(b) may go on board any such ship and inspect the ship,

(c) may stop any such ship and, for so long as may be necessary for that purpose, prevent it from being moved, and

(d) may stop any such vehicle, goods, property or person and detain it or him for so long as may be necessary for that purpose.

(3A) Subsection (3) above applies in relation to a direction under this section to a harbour operator as it applies in relation to a direction to a harbour authority, but as if the references to the harbour area (or to any part of the harbour area) were references to the operating area (or any part of the operating area).

(4) In the case of premises used only as a private dwelling any power to search or enter conferred by subsection (3) above may not be exercised except—

(a) under the authority of a warrant issued by a justice of the peace; and

(b) by a constable who is a member of a body of constables maintained—

(i) in England, Scotland or Wales by a police authority or an authority which has entered into an agreement with the Police Complaints Authority under section 96(1) of the Police and Criminal Evidence Act 1984; or

(ii) in Northern Ireland, by the Police Authority for Northern Ireland or an authority which has entered into an agreement with the Independent Commission for Police Complaints for Northern Ireland under Article 16 of the Police (Northern Ireland) Order 1987.

(5) If, on an application made by a constable, a justice of the peace is satisfied that there are reasonable grounds for suspecting that an article to which subsection (3) above applies is in any premises used only as a private dwelling, he may issue a warrant authorising a constable to enter and search the premises.

(6) Subsection (3) above applies to the following articles—

(a) any firearm, or any article having the appearance of being a firearm, whether capable of being discharged or not,

(b) an explosive, any article manufactured or adapted (whether in the form of a bomb, grenade or otherwise) so as to have the appearance of being an explosive, whether it is capable of producing a practical effect by explosion or not, or any article marked or labelled so as to indicate that it is or contains an explosive, and

(c) any article (not falling within either of the preceding paragraphs) made or adapted for use for causing injury to or incapacitating a person or for destroying or damaging property, or intended by the person having it with him for such use, whether by him or by any other person.

(7) Any person who—

(a) without reasonable excuse, fails to comply with a direction given to him under this section, or

(b) intentionally obstructs a person acting in the exercise of a power conferred on him by subsection (3) above,

commits an offence.

(8) A person guilty of an offence under subsection (7) above is liable—

(a) on summary conviction, to a fine not exceeding the statutory maximum;

(b) on conviction on indictment, to a fine or to imprisonment for a term not exceeding two years or to both.

(9) Where a person is convicted of an offence under subsection (7)(a) above, then, if without reasonable excuse the failure in respect of which he was convicted is continued after the conviction, he is guilty of a further offence and liable on summary conviction to a fine not exceeding one-tenth of level 5 on the standard scale for each day on which the failure continues.

(10) Subsection (3) above has effect without prejudice to the operation, in relation to any offence under this Act—

(a) in England and Wales, of sections 17, 24 and 25 of the Police and Criminal Evidence Act 1984 (which confer power to arrest without warrant and to enter premises for the purpose of making an arrest) or of section 3 of the Criminal Law Act 1967 (use of force in making arrest etc.), or

(b) in Scotland, of any rule of law relating to the power to arrest without warrant, or

(c) in Northern Ireland, of Articles 19, 26 and 27 of the Police and Criminal Evidence (Northern Ireland) Order 1989 or of section 3 of the Criminal Law Act (Northern Ireland) 1967.

Power to require other persons to promote searches

23.—(1) For purposes to which this Part of this Act applies, the Secretary of State may give a direction in writing to any person who—

(a) carries on harbour operations in a harbour area, or

(b) is permitted to have access to a restricted zone of a harbour area for the purposes of the activities of a business carried on by him,

requiring him to use his best endeavours to secure that such searches to which this section applies as are specified in the direction are carried out by constables or by other persons of a description specified in the direction.

(1A) A direction may not be given under this section to—

(a) a harbour authority, or

(b) a harbour operator.

(2) The searches to which this section applies are—

(a) in relation to a person falling within subsection (1)(a) above, searches—

(i) of any land which he occupies within the harbour area, and

(ii) of persons or property which may at any time be on that land; and

(b) in relation to a person falling within subsection (1)(b) above, searches—

(i) of any land which he occupies outside the harbour area for the purposes of his business, and

(ii) of persons or property which may at any time be on that land.

(3) Any person who, without reasonable excuse, fails to comply with a direction given to him under this section is guilty of an offence and liable—

(a) on summary conviction, to a fine not exceeding the statutory maximum;

(b) on conviction on indictment, to a fine or to imprisonment for a term not exceeding two years or to both.

(4) Where a person is convicted of an offence under subsection (3) above, then, if without reasonable excuse the failure in respect of which he was convicted is continued after the conviction, he is guilty of a further offence and liable on summary conviction to a fine not exceeding one-tenth of level 5 on the standard scale for each day on which the failure continues.

General power to direct measures to be taken for purposes to which Part III applies

24.—(1) Subsection (2) below applies to—

(a) any person who is the owner, charterer or manager of one or more ships which—
   (i) are British ships, or
   (ii) are in a harbour area,

(b) any harbour authority,

(c) any person other than a harbour authority who carries on harbour operations in a harbour area, and

(d) any person who is permitted to have access to a restricted zone of a harbour area for the purposes of the activities of a business carried on by him.

(2) Subject to the following provisions of this section, the Secretary of State may give a direction in writing to any person to whom this subsection applies requiring him to take such measures for purposes to which this Part of this Act applies as are specified in the direction—

(a) in the case of a direction given to a person as the owner, charterer or manager of a ship, in respect of all the ships falling within subsection (1)(a) above of which (at the time when the direction is given or at any subsequent time) he is the owner, charterer or manager, or in respect of any such ships specified in the direction,

(b) in the case of a direction given to a harbour authority, in respect of the harbour area,

(c) in the case of a direction given to a person as a person falling within subsection (1)(c) above, in respect of the harbour operations carried on by him, and

(d) in the case of a direction given to a person as a person who is permitted to have access to a restricted zone as mentioned in subsection (1)(d) above, in respect of such activities carried on by that person in that zone as are specified in the direction.

(3) Without prejudice to the generality of subsection (2) above, the measures to be specified in a direction given under this section to any person to whom that subsection applies may include the provision by that person of persons charged with the duty (at such times as may be specified in the direction)—

(a) where the direction is given to a person as the owner, charterer or manager of ships, of guarding the ships against acts of violence,

(b) where the direction is given to a harbour authority, of guarding the harbour area, or persons or property (including ships) in any part of the harbour area, against acts of violence,

389

(c) where the direction is given to a person as falling within subsection (1)(c) above, of guarding against acts of violence any ship in the harbour area which is for the time being under his control, or

(d) where the direction is given to a person as falling within subsection (1)(d) above, of guarding—

　　(i) any land outside the harbour area occupied by him for the purposes of his business, any vehicles or equipment used for those purposes and any goods which are in his possession for those purposes, and

　　(ii) any ship which is for the time being under his control,

for purposes to which this Part of this Act applies.

(4) A direction given under this section may be either of a general or of a specific character, and may require any measures specified in the direction to be taken at such time or within such period as may be so specified.

(5) A direction under this section—

(a) shall not require any search (whether of persons or of property), and

(b) shall not require the modification or alteration of any ship, or of any of its apparatus or equipment, or the installation or carriage of additional apparatus or equipment, or prohibit any ship from being caused or permitted to go to sea without some modification or alteration of the ship or its apparatus or equipment or the installation or carriage of additional apparatus or equipment.

(6) A direction may be given under this section to a person appearing to the Secretary of State to be about to become a person to whom subsection (2) above applies, but a direction given to a person by virtue of this subsection shall not take effect until he becomes a person to whom subsection (2) above applies and, in relation to a direction so given, the preceding provisions of this section shall apply with the necessary modifications.

(7) Any person who—

(a) without reasonable excuse, fails to comply with a direction given to him under this section, or

(b) intentionally interferes with any building constructed or works executed on any land in compliance with a direction under this section or with anything installed on, under, over or across any land in compliance with such a direction,

commits an offence.

(8) A person guilty of an offence under subsection (7) above is liable—

(a) on summary conviction, to a fine not exceeding the statutory maximum;

(b) on conviction on indictment, to a fine or to imprisonment for a term not exceeding two years or to both.

(9) Where a person is convicted of an offence under subsection (7)(a) above, then, if without reasonable excuse the failure in respect of which he was convicted is continued after the conviction, he is guilty of a further offence and liable on summary conviction to a fine not exceeding one-tenth of level 5 on the standard scale for each day on which the failure continues.

(10) The ownership of any property shall not be affected by reason only that it is placed on or under, or affixed to, any land in compliance with a direction under this section.

Supplemental provisions with respect to directions

Matters which may be included in directions under sections 21 to 24

25.—(1) A direction under subsection (1) of section 21 or under section 22 or 23 of this Act may specify the minimum number of persons by whom any search to which the direction relates is to be carried out, the qualifications which persons carrying out any such search are to have, the manner in which any such search is to be carried out, and any apparatus, equipment or other aids to be used for the purpose of carrying out any such search.

(2) A direction under subsection (2) of section 21 of this Act may specify the qualifications required to be had by persons carrying out any modifications or alterations, or the installation of any additional apparatus or equipment, to which the direction relates.

(3) A direction under section 24 of this Act may specify—

    (a) the minimum number of persons to be employed for the purposes of any measures required by the direction to be taken by the person to whom it is given, and the qualifications which persons employed for those purposes are to have, and

    (b) any apparatus, equipment or other aids to be used for those purposes.

(4) Where a direction under any of the preceding provisions of this Part of this Act requires searches to be carried out, or other measures to be taken, by constables, the direction may require the person to whom it is given to inform the chief officer of police for the police area in which the searches are to be carried out or the other measures taken that the Secretary of State considers it appropriate that constables should be duly authorised to carry, and should carry, firearms when carrying out the searches or taking the measures in question.

(5) Nothing in subsections (1) to (4) above shall be construed as limiting the generality of any of the preceding provisions of this Part of this Act.

(6) In this section "qualifications" includes training and experience.

(7) In the application of this section to Northern Ireland for the words in subsection (4) above from "chief officer" to "measures taken" there are substituted the words "chief constable of the Royal Ulster Constabulary".

Limitations on scope of directions under sections 21 to 24

26.—(1) Without prejudice to section 25(4) of this Act, a direction shall not require or authorise any person to carry a firearm, except to the extent necessary for the purpose of removing any firearm found pursuant to a search under section 22 of this Act from the restricted zone and delivering the firearm to a person authorised to carry it.

(2) A direction shall not have effect in relation to any ship used in naval, customs or police service.

(3) A direction shall not have effect in relation to any ship which is registered outside the United Kingdom and of which the owner is the Government of a country outside the United Kingdom, or is a department or agency of such a Government, except at a time when any such ship is being used for commercial purposes or is for the time being allocated by that Government, department or agency for such use.

(4) A direction (except in so far as it requires any building or other works to be constructed, executed, altered, demolished or removed) shall not be construed as requiring or authorising the person to whom the direction was given, or any person acting as his employee or agent, to do anything which, apart from the direction, would constitute an act of violence; but nothing in this subsection shall restrict the use of such force as is reasonable in the circumstances (whether at the instance of the person to whom the direction was given or otherwise) by a constable, or its use by any other person in the exercise of a power conferred by section 22(3) of this Act.

(5) In so far as a direction requires anything to be done or not done at a place outside the United Kingdom—

    (a) it shall not have effect except in relation to British ships, and

(b) it shall not have effect so as to require anything to be done or not done in contravention of any provision of the law (whether civil or criminal) in force at that place, other than any such provision relating to breach of contract.

(6) In so far as a direction given to a harbour authority or to any person mentioned in section 24(1)(c) or (d) of this Act requires a building or other works to be constructed, executed, altered, demolished or removed on land outside the harbour area, or requires any other measures to be taken on such land, the direction shall not confer on the person to whom it is given any rights as against a person having—

(a) an interest in that land, or

(b) a right to occupy that land, or

(c) a right restrictive of its use;

and accordingly, the direction shall not be construed as requiring the person to whom it is given to do anything which would be actionable at the suit or instance of a person having such interest or right in his capacity as a person having that interest or right.

(7) Nothing in this section shall be construed as derogating from any exemption or immunity of the Crown in relation to the provisions of this Part of this Act.

(8) In this section "direction" means a direction under section 21, 22, 23 or 24 of this Act.

General or urgent directions under sections 21 to 24

27.—(1) A direction given to any person under section 21, 22, 23 or 24 of this Act need not be addressed to that particular person, but may be framed in general terms applicable to all persons to whom such a direction may be given or to any class of such persons to which that particular person belongs.

(2) If it appears to the Secretary of State that an exception from any direction given under any of those sections is required as a matter of urgency in any particular case he may, by a notification given (otherwise than in writing) to the person for the time being subject to the direction, authorise that person to disregard the requirements of the direction—

(a) in relation to such ships or class of ships, in relation to such harbour area or part of a harbour area, in relation to such land outside a harbour area, in relation to such activities or in relation to such persons or property or such description of persons or property, and

(b) on such occasion or series of occasions, or for such period,

as he may specify; and the direction shall have effect in that case subject to any exceptions so specified.

(3) Any notification given to any person under subsection (2) above with respect to any direction shall cease to have effect (if it has not already done so)—

(a) if a direction in writing is subsequently given to that person varying or revoking the original direction, or

(b) if no such direction in writing is given within the period of thirty days beginning with the date on which the notification was given, at the end of that period.

(4) Any notification given under subsection (2) above shall be regarded as given to the person to whom it is directed if it is given—

(a) to any person authorised by that person to receive any such direction or notification,

(b) where that person is a body corporate, to the secretary, clerk or similar officer of the body corporate, and

(c) in any other case, to anyone holding a comparable office or position in that person's employment.

Objections to certain directions under section 24

28.—(1) This section applies to any direction given under section 24 of this Act which—
  (a) requires a person to take measures consisting of or including the construction, execution, alteration, demolition or removal of a building or other works, and
  (b) does not contain a statement that the measures are urgently required and that accordingly the direction is to take effect immediately.

(2) At any time before the end of the period of thirty days beginning with the date on which a direction to which this section applies is given, the person to whom the direction is given may serve on the Secretary of State a notice in writing objecting to the direction, on the grounds that the measures specified in the direction, in so far as they relate to the construction, execution, alteration, demolition or removal of a building or other works—
  (a) are unnecessary and should be dispensed with, or
  (b) are excessively onerous or inconvenient and should be modified in a manner specified in the notice.

(3) Where the person to whom such a direction is given serves a notice under subsection (2) above objecting to the direction, the Secretary of State shall consider the grounds of the objection and, if so required by the objector, shall afford to him an opportunity of appearing before and being heard by a person appointed by the Secretary of State for the purpose, and shall then serve on the objector a notice in writing either—
  (a) confirming the direction as originally given, or
  (b) confirming it subject to one or more modifications specified in the notice under this subsection, or
  (c) withdrawing the direction;
and the direction shall not take effect until it has been confirmed (with or without modification) by a notice served under this subsection.

Enforcement notices

29.—(1) Where an authorised person is of the opinion that any person has failed to comply with any general requirement of a direction given to him under section 21, 22, 23 or 24 of this Act, the authorised person may serve on that person a notice (in this Part of this Act referred to as an "enforcement notice")—
  (a) specifying those general requirements of the direction with which he has, in the opinion of the authorised person, failed to comply, and
  (b) specifying, subject to section 30 of this Act, the measures that ought to be taken in order to comply with those requirements.

(2) For the purposes of this section a requirement of a direction given by the Secretary of State under section 21, 22, 23 or 24 of this Act is a "general requirement" if the provision imposing the requirement—
  (a) has been included in two or more directions given to different persons (whether or not at the same time), and
  (b) is framed in general terms applicable to all the persons to whom those directions are given.

(3) If an enforcement notice is served under this section on the owner, charterer or manager of a ship, then (whether or not that service is effected by virtue of section 45(8) of this Act) an authorised person may serve on the master of the ship—
  (a) a copy of the enforcement notice and of the direction to which it relates, and

(b) a notice stating that the master is required to comply with the enforcement notice,

and, if he does so sections 31, 32 and 33 of this Act shall have effect as if the enforcement notice had been served on him as well as on the owner, charterer or manager of the ship.

Contents of enforcement notice

30.—(1) An enforcement notice may specify in greater detail measures which are described in general terms in those provisions of the direction to which it relates which impose general requirements, but may not impose any requirement which could not have been imposed by a direction given by the Secretary of State under the provision under which the direction was given.

(2) An enforcement notice may be framed so as to afford the person on whom it is served a choice between different ways of complying with the specified general requirements of the direction.

(3) Subject to subsection (4) below, an enforcement notice which relates to a direction given under section 21 of this Act must require the person to whom the direction was given not to cause or permit things to be done as mentioned in subsection (1)(a) or (b) or (2) of that section, as the case requires, until the specified measures have been taken.

(4) In serving an enforcement notice which relates to a direction under section 21(2) of this Act, the authorised person shall allow, and shall specify in the notice, such period as appears to him to be reasonably required for taking the measures specified in the notice; and the notice shall not take effect before the end of the period so specified.

(5) An enforcement notice which relates to a direction given under section 22, 23 or 24 of this Act must either—
  (a) require the person to whom the direction was given to take the specified measures within a specified period which—
    (i) where the measures consist of or include the construction, execution, alteration, demolition or removal of a building or other works, must not be less than thirty days beginning with the date of service of the notice, and
    (ii) in any other case, must not be less than seven days beginning with that date; or
  (b) require him not to do specified things, or cause or permit specified things to be done, until the specified measures have been taken.

(6) Subject to section 33(2) of this Act, an enforcement notice requiring a person not to cause or permit anything to be done shall be construed as requiring him to take all such steps as in any particular circumstances are practicable and necessary to prevent that thing from being done.

Offences relating to enforcement notices

31.—(1) Any person who, without reasonable excuse, fails to comply with an enforcement notice served on him is guilty of an offence and liable—
  (a) on summary conviction, to a fine not exceeding the statutory maximum;
  (b) on conviction on indictment, to a fine.

(2) Where a person is convicted of an offence under subsection (1) above, then, if without reasonable excuse the failure in respect of which he was convicted is continued after the conviction, he is guilty of a further offence and liable on summary conviction

to a fine not exceeding one-tenth of level 5 on the standard scale for each day on which the failure continues.

(3) Any person who intentionally interferes with any building constructed or works executed on any land in compliance with an enforcement notice or with anything installed on, under, over or across any land in compliance with such a notice is guilty of an offence and liable—

    (a) on summary conviction, to a fine not exceeding the statutory maximum;

    (b) on conviction on indictment, to a fine.

Objections to enforcement notices

32.—(1) The person on whom an enforcement notice is served may serve on the Secretary of State a notice in writing of his objection to the enforcement notice, specifying the grounds of the objection.

(2) Any notice of objection under subsection (1) above must be served—

    (a) where the enforcement notice specifies measures falling within section 30(5)(a)(i) of this Act, before the end of the period of thirty days beginning with the date on which the enforcement notice was served, or

    (b) in any other case, before the end of the period of seven days beginning with that date.

(3) The grounds of objection to an enforcement notice are—

    (a) that the general requirements of the direction which are specified in the notice for the purposes of section 29(1)(a) of this Act have been complied with,

    (b) that the notice purports to impose a requirement which could not have been imposed by a direction given under the provision under which the direction to which the notice relates was given, or

    (c) that any requirement of the notice—

        (i) is unnecessary for complying with the general requirements specified as mentioned in paragraph (a) above and should be dispensed with, or

        (ii) having regard to the terms of those general requirements, is excessivly onerous or inconvenient and should be modified in a manner specified in the notice of objection under subsection (1) above.

(4) Where the person on whom an enforcement notice is served serves a notice under subsection (1) above objecting to the enforcement notice, the Secretary of State shall consider the grounds of the objection and, if so required by the objector, shall afford to him an opportunity of appearing before and being heard by a person appointed by the Secretary of State for the purpose, and shall then serve on the objector a notice in writing either—

    (a) confirming the enforcement notice as originally served, or

    (b) confirming it subject to one or more modifications specified in the notice under this subsection, or

    (c) cancelling the enforcement notice.

(5) An enforcement notice to which an objection has been made under subsection (1) above—

    (a) if it contains such a requirement as is mentioned in section 30(3) or (5)(b) of this Act, shall continue to have effect as originally served until it has been cancelled, or it has been confirmed subject to modification by a notice under subsection (4) above, and

    (b) in any other case, shall not take effect until it has been confirmed (with or without modification) by a notice under subsection (4) above.

APPENDIX L

Enforcement notices: supplementary

33.—(1) An enforcement notice served on any person—

(a) may be revoked by a notice served on him by an authorised person, and

(b) may be varied by a further enforcement notice.

(2) Sections 25 and 26 of this Act apply to an enforcement notice as they apply to the direction to which the notice relates.

(3) The ownership of any property shall not be affected by reason only that it is placed on or under or affixed to, any land in compliance with an enforcement notice.

(4) Where an authorised person has served an enforcement notice specifying the general requirements of a direction with which the person on whom it is served has, in the opinion of the authorised person, failed to comply, the person on whom the notice is served shall not be taken, for the purposes of section 21(8), 22(7), 23(3) or 24(7) of this Act, to have failed to comply with the direction by reason of the matters specified in the notice.

(5) Subsection (4) above does not apply in relation to any proceedings commenced before the service of the enforcement notice.

(6) Where an enforcement notice has been served in relation to a direction, the fact that the notice specifies certain general requirements of the direction as those with which the person on whom the notice is served has, in the opinion of the authorised person, failed to comply shall not in any proceedings be evidence that any other requirement of the direction has been complied with.

(7) In this section "direction" means a direction under section 21, 22, 23 or 24 of this Act.

Operation of directions under Part III in relation to rights and duties under other laws

34.—(1) In subsections (2) to (4) below references to a direction are references to a direction under section 21, 22, 23 or 24 of this Act as the direction has effect subject to any limitation imposed on its operation—

(a) by section 26 of this Act, or

(b) by any exemption or immunity of the Crown;

and any reference in those subsections to compliance with a direction is a reference to compliance with it subject to any limitation so imposed.

(2) In so far as a direction requires anything to be done or not done in the United Kingdom, the direction shall have effect notwithstanding anything contained in any contract (whether a United Kingdom contract or not) or contained in, or having effect by virtue of, any other Act or any rule of law; and accordingly no proceedings (whether civil or criminal) shall lie against any person in any United Kingdom court by reason of anything done or not done by him or on his behalf in compliance with a direction.

(3) In so far as a direction requires anything to be done or not done at a place outside the United Kingdom, the direction shall have effect notwithstanding anything contained in any contract (whether a United Kingdom contract or not); and accordingly, where a direction is inconsistent with anything in such a contract, it shall (without prejudice to any proceedings in a court other than a United Kingdom court) be construed as requiring compliance with the direction notwithstanding that compliance would be in breach of that contract.

(4) No proceedings for breach of contract shall lie against any person in a United Kingdom court by reason of anything done or not done by him or on his behalf at a

place outside the United Kingdom in compliance with a direction, if the contract in question is a United Kingdom contract.

(5) Subsections (1) to (4) above have effect in relation to an enforcement notice as they have effect in relation to a direction under section 21, 22, 23 or 24 of this Act.

(6) In this section "United Kingdom court" means a court exercising jurisdiction in any part of the United Kingdom under the law of the United Kingdom or of part of the United Kingdom, and "United Kingdom contract" means a contract which is either expressed to have effect in accordance with the law of the United Kingdom or of part of the United Kingdom or (not being so expressed) is a contract the law applicable to which is the law of the United Kingdom or of part of the United Kingdom.

Detention of ships

35.—(1) Where an authorised person is satisfied that the owner, charterer, manager or master of a ship has failed to comply with—

    (a) a direction given to him under section 21 or 24 of this Act in respect of that ship, or

    (b) an enforcement notice which has been served on him in respect of that ship and which relates to such a direction,

and the authorised person certifies in writing to that effect, stating particulars of the non-compliance, the ship may be detained until the authorised person otherwise directs.

(2) Where the authorised person does not himself detain the ship, he shall deliver the certificate to the officer detaining the ship.

(3) On detaining the ship, the authorised person or other officer shall deliver to the master of the ship a copy of the certificate.

(4) Section 284 of the Merchant Shipping Act 1995 (enforcement of detention of ships) applies in the case of detention under this section as if it were authorised or ordered under that Act.

Inspection of ships and harbour areas

36.—(1) For the purpose of enabling the Secretary of State to determine whether to give a direction to any person under any of sections 21 to 24 of this Act, or of ascertaining whether any such direction or any enforcement notice is being or has been complied with, an authorised person shall have power, on production (if required) of his credentials, to inspect—

    (a) any British ship,

    (b) any other ship while in a harbour area,

    (c) any part of any harbour area, or

    (d) any land outside a harbour area which is occupied for the purposes of a business by a person who—

        (i) carries on (or appears to the authorised person to be about to carry on) harbour operations in a harbour area for the purposes of that business, or

        (ii) is permitted (or appears to the authorised person to be about to be permitted) to have access to a restricted zone of a harbour area for the purposes of the activities of that business.

(2) An authorised person inspecting a ship or any part of a harbour area or any land outside a harbour area under subsection (1) above shall have power—

    (a) to subject any property found by him on the ship (but not the ship itself or any apparatus or equipment installed in it) or, as the case may be, to subject that part of the harbour area or any property found by him there or on that land, to such tests.

(b) to take such steps—

(i) to ascertain what practices or procedures are being followed in relation to security, or

(ii) to test the effectiveness of any practice or procedure relating to security, or

(c) to require the owner, charterer, manager or master of the ship, the harbour authority, the occupier of the land or any harbour operator to furnish to him such information,

as the authorised person may consider necessary for the purpose for which the inspection is carried out.

(3) Subject to subsection (4) below, an authorised person, for the purpose of exercising any power conferred on him by subsection (1) or (2) above in relation to a ship, in relation to a harbour area or in relation to any land outside a harbour area, shall have power—

(a) for the purpose of inspecting a ship, to go on board it and to take all such steps as are necessary to ensure that it is not moved, or

(b) for the purpose of inspecting any part of a harbour area, to enter any building or works in the harbour area or enter upon any land in the harbour area, or

(c) for the purpose of inspecting any land outside a harbour area, to enter upon the land and to enter any building or works on the land.

(4) The powers conferred by subsection (3) above shall not include power for an authorised person to use force for the purpose of going on board any ship, entering any building or works or entering upon any land.

(5) Any person who—

(a) without reasonable excuse, fails to comply with a requirement imposed on him under subsection (2)(c) above, or

(b) in furnishing any information so required, makes a statement which he knows to be false in a material particular, or recklessly makes a statement which is false in a material particular,

commits an offence.

(6) A person guilty of an offence under subsection (5) above is liable—

(a) on summary conviction, to a fine not exceeding the statutory maximum;

(b) on conviction on indictment, to a fine or to imprisonment for a term not exceeding two years or to both.

Offences relating to security of ships and harbour areas

False statements relating to baggage, cargo etc.

37.—(1) Subject to subsection (3) below, a person commits an offence if, in answer to a question which—

(a) relates to any baggage, cargo or stores (whether belonging to him or to another) that is or are intended for carriage by sea—

(i) by a British ship, or

(ii) by any other ship to or from the United Kingdom, and

(b) is put to him for purposes to which this Part of this Act applies—

(i) by any of the persons mentioned in subsection (2) below,

(ii) by any employee or agent of such a person in his capacity as employee or agent, or

(iii) by a constable,

he makes a statement which he knows to be false in a material particular, or recklessly makes a statement which is false in a material particular.

(2) The persons referred to in subsection (1)(b) above are—

(a) a harbour authority,

(aa) a harbour operator,

(b) the owner, charterer or manager of any ship, and

(c) any person who—

(i) is permitted to have access to a restricted zone of a harbour area for the purposes of the activities of a business carried on by him, and

(ii) has control in that restricted zone over the baggage, cargo or stores to which the question relates.

(3) Subsection (1) above does not apply in relation to any statement made by an authorised person in the exercise of the power conferred by section 36(2)(b) of this Act.

(4) A person guilty of an offence under subsection (1) above is liable on summary conviction to a fine not exceeding level 5 on the standard scale.

(5) In this section—

"cargo" includes mail;

"ship" does not include a ship used in naval, customs or police service; and

"stores" means any goods intended for sale or use in a ship, including fuel and spare parts and other articles of equipment, whether or not for immediate fitting.

False statements in connection with identity documents

38.—(1) Subject to subsection (4) below, a person commits an offence if—

(a) for the purpose of, or in connection with, an application made by him or another for the issue of an identity document to which this subsection applies, or

(b) in connection with the continued holding by him or another of any such document which has already been issued,

he makes to any of the persons specified in subsection (3) below, to any employee or agent of such a person or to a constable, a statement which he knows to be false in a material particular, or recklessly makes to any of those persons, to any such employee or agent or to a constable, a statement which is false in a material particular.

(2) Subsection (1) above applies to any identity document which is to be or has been issued by any of the persons specified in subsection (3) below in accordance with arrangements the maintenance of which is required by a direction given by the Secretary of State under section 24 of this Act.

(3) The persons referred to in subsection (1) above are—

(a) a harbour authority,

(aa) a harbour operator,

(b) the owner, charterer or manager of any ship, and

(c) any person who is permitted to have access to a restricted zone of a harbour area for the purposes of the activities of a business carried on by him.

(4) Subsection (1) above does not apply in relation to any statement made by an authorised person in the exercise of the power conferred by section 36(2)(b) of this Act.

(5) A person guilty of an offence under subsection (1) above is liable on summary conviction to a fine not exceeding level 5 on the standard scale.

APPENDIX L

Unauthorised presence in restricted zone

39.—(1) A person shall not—

    (a) go, with or without a vehicle or vessel, onto or into any part of a restricted zone of a harbour area except with the permission of the competent authority or a person acting on behalf of that authority and in accordance with any conditions subject to which that permission is for the time being granted, or

    (b) remain in any part of such a restricted zone after being requested to leave by the competent authority or a person acting on behalf of that authority.

(2) Subsection (1)(a) above does not apply unless it is proved that, at the material time, notices stating that the area concerned was a restricted zone were posted so as to be readily seen and read by persons entering the restricted zone.

(2A) A constable or any person acting on behalf of the competent authority may use such force as is reasonable in the circumstances to remove from a restricted zone a person remaining in it in contravention of subsection (1)(b) above.

(2B) For the purposes of this section the competent authority in relation to a restricted zone is—

    (a) if the zone was designated on the application of a harbour authority, that authority; and

    (b) if the zone was designated on the application of a harbour operator, that operator.

(3) A person who contravenes subsection (1) above without lawful authority or reasonable excuse is guilty of an offence and liable on summary conviction to a fine not exceeding level 5 on the standard scale.

Offences relating to authorised persons

40.—(1) A person who—

    (a) intentionally obstructs an authorised person acting in the exercise of a power conferred on him by or under this Part of this Act, or

    (b) falsely pretends to be an authorised person,

commits an offence.

(2) A person guilty of an offence under subsection (1)(a) above is liable—

    (a) on summary conviction, to a fine not exceeding the statutory maximum;

    (b) on conviction on indictment, to a fine or to imprisonment for a term not exceeding two years or to both.

(3) A person guilty of an offence under subsection (1)(b) above is liable on summary conviction to a fine not exceeding level 5 on the standard scale.

Sea cargo agents

Sea cargo agents

41.—(1) The Secretary of State may be regulations made by statutory instrument make provision, for purposes to which this Part of this Act applies, in relation to persons (in this section referred to as "sea cargo agents") who carry on a business of handling cargo which is to be delivered (whether by them or any other person) to the owner, charterer or manager of any ship for carriage by sea from any harbour area.

(2) Regulations under this section may, in particular—

    (a) enable the Secretary of State to maintain a list of sea cargo agents who are approved by him for purposes related to maritime security, to include the name of a sea cargo agent on that list, on application being made to the

400

Secretary of State in accordance with the regulations, if he is satisfied as to such matters as are specified in the regulations, and to remove the name of any person from that list in such circumstances as are so specified,

(b) provide that any provision of this Part of this Act which applies in relation to persons who are permitted to have access to a restricted zone of a harbour area for the purposes of the activities of a business (including any such provision which creates a criminal offence) shall also apply, with such modifications as are specified in the regulations, in relation to sea cargo agents included on any such list,

(c) amend sections 37(2) and 38(3) of this Act by including references to sea cargo agents included on any such list,

(d) make provision (including any such provision as is mentioned in paragraphs (a) to (c) above) relating to a class of sea cargo agents specified in the regulations and not to other sea cargo agents,

(e) make different provision for different cases, and

(f) make such incidental, supplementary or transitional provision as the Secretary of State considers necessary or expedient in consequence of any provision made by the regulations.

(3) Before making any regulations under this section the Secretary of State shall consult organisations appearing to him to represent persons affected by the proposed regulations.

(4) Any statutory instrument containing regulations under this section shall be subject to annulment in pursuance of a resolution of either House of Parliament.

(5) Without prejudice to the generality of sections 21 and 24 of this Act, the exemptions that may be included in any direction given to an owner, charterer, manager or master of a ship under section 21 or 24 which requires the carrying out of searches of cargo, or the taking of any other measures in relation to cargo, include exemptions from such requirements in relation to cargo received from any sea cargo agent included on any list maintained by the Secretary of State under regulations under this section or from any sea cargo agent falling within a class of such sea cargo agents specified in the direction.

(6) In this section—

"cargo" includes stores and mail;

"carriage by sea" does not include carriage by any ship used in naval, customs or police service; and

"stores" means any goods intended for sale or use in a ship, including fuel and spare parts and other articles of equipment, whether or not for immediate fitting.

Reporting of certain occurrences

Duty to report certain occurrences

42.—(1) For purposes to which this Part of this Act applies, the Secretary of State may by regulations made by statutory instrument require such persons as are specified in the regulations to make a report to him, in such manner and within such period as are so specified, of any occurrence of a description so specified.

(2) Before making any regulations under this section, the Secretary of State shall consult organisations appearing to him to represent persons affected by the proposed regulations.

(3) Regulations under this section may—

(a) provide that any person who, in making a report required by the regulations, makes a statement which he knows to be false in a material particular, or recklessly makes a statement which is false in a material particular, is to be guilty of an offence and liable—

> (i) on summary conviction, to a fine not exceeding the statutory maximum;
>
> (ii) on conviction on indictment, to a fine or to imprisonment for a term not exceeding two years or to both; and

(b) provide for persons to be guilty of an offence in such other circumstances as may be specified in the regulations and to be liable on summary conviction to a fine not exceeding level 5 on the standard scale.

(4) Regulations under this section may require the reporting of occurrences taking place outside the United Kingdom only if those occurrences relate to British ships.

(5) Any statutory instrument containing regulations under this section shall be subject to annulment in pursuance of a resolution of either House of Parliament.

General supplemental provisions

Compensation in respect of certain measures taken under Part III

43.—(1) The provisions of this section have effect where, in compliance with a direction under section 24 of this Act or in compliance with an enforcement notice, the person to whom the direction was given or on whom the notice was served takes any measures consisting of the construction, execution, alteration, demolition or removal of a building or other works on land either within or outside a harbour area.

(2) If the value of any interest in that land to which a person is entitled is depreciated in consequence of the taking of those measures, or the person having such an interest suffers loss in consequence of them by being disturbed in his enjoyment of any of that land, he is entitled to compensation equal to the amount of the depreciation or loss.

(3) If any land other than the land on which the measures are taken is injuriously affected by the taking of those measures, any person having an interest in that other land who suffers loss in consequence of its being injuriously affected is entitled to compensation equal to the amount of the loss.

(4) Any compensation to which a person is entitled under this section shall be payable to him by the person by whom the measures in question were taken.

(5) The provisions of Schedule 2 to this Act have effect for the purposes of this section; and subsections (1) to (4) above have effect subject to the provisions of that Schedule.

Annual report by Secretary of State as to notices and directions under Part III

44.—(1) The Secretary of State shall, on or before 31st January in each year, lay before each House of Parliament a report stating the number of notices served by him under section 19 of this Act, the number of directions given by him under sections 21, 22, 23 and 24 of this Act and the number of enforcement notices served by authorised persons during the period of twelve months which expired with the preceding December.

(2) Each such report shall deal separately with notices served under section 19 of this Act, directions given under section 21 of this Act, directions given under section 22 of this Act, directions given under section 23 of this Act, directions given under section 24 of this Act and enforcement notices, and, in relation to each of those matters, shall show separately—

> (a) the number of notices or directions which, during the period to which the report relates, were served on or given to persons as being, or as appearing to

the Secretary of State to be about to become, owners, charterers, managers or masters of ships,

(b) the number of notices or directions which during that period were served on or given to persons as being, or as appearing to the Secretary of State to be about to become, harbour authorities,

(c) the number of notices or directions which during that period were served on or given to persons as being, or as appearing to the Secretary of State to be about to become, persons carrying on harbour operations in a harbour area, and

(d) the number of notices or directions which during that period were served on or given to persons as being, or as appearing to the Secretary of State to be about to become, persons permitted to have access to a restricted zone of a harbour area for the purposes of the activities of a business.

(3) Each such report shall also show separately the number of copies of enforcement notices which during that period were served on masters of ships under section 29(3) of this Act.

Service of documents

45.—(1) This section has effect in relation to any notice, any document containing a direction and any other document authorised or required by any provision of this Part of this Act to be served on or given to any person.

(2) Any such document may be given to or served on any person—

(a) by delivering it to him, or

(b) by leaving it at his proper address, or

(c) by sending it by post to him at that address, or

(d) by sending it to him at that address by telex or other similar means which produce a document containing the text of the communication.

(3) Any such document may, in the case of a body corporate, be given to or served on the secretary, clerk or similar officer of that body.

(4) For the purposes of this section and section 7 of the Interpretation Act 1978 (service of documents by post) in its application to this section, the proper address of any person to whom or on whom any document is to be given or served is his usual or last known address or place of business (whether in the United Kingdom or elsewhere), except that in the case of a body corporate or its secretary, clerk or similar officer it shall be the address of the registered or principal office of that body in the United Kingdom (or, if it has no office in the United Kingdom, of its principal office, wherever it may be).

(5) In the case of a person registered under any of the United Kingdom registration provisions as the owner of any ship so registered, the address for the time being recorded in relation to him in the register in which the ship is registered shall also be treated for the purposes of this section and section 7 of the Interpretation Act 1978 as his proper address.

(6) If the person to or on whom any document mentioned in subsection (1) above is to be given or served his notified the Secretary of State of an address within the United Kingdom, other than an address determined under subsection (4) or (5) above, as the one at which he or someone else on his behalf will accept documents of the same description as that document, that address shall also be treated for the purposes of this section and section 7 of the Interpretation Act 1978 as his proper address.

(7) Any document mentioned in subsection (1) above shall, where there are two or more owners registered under any of the United Kingdom registration provisions, be treated as duly served on each of those owners—

(a) in the case of a ship in relation to which a managing owner is for the time being registered under registration regulations, if served on that managing owner, and

(b) in the case of any other ship, if served on any one of the registered owners.

(8) Where an enforcement notice is to be served under section 29 of this Act on the owner, charterer or manager of a ship, it shall be treated as duly served on him if it is served on the master of the ship in question, but (except as provided by section 29(3) of this Act) the master shall not be obliged by virtue of this subsection to comply with the notice.

(9) Where any document mentioned in subsection (1) above is to be served (for the purposes of subsection (8) above or otherwise) on the master of a ship, it shall be treated as duly served if it is left on board that ship with the person being or appearing to be in command or charge of the ship.

(10) In this section "the United Kingdom registration provisions" means Part II of the Merchant Shipping Act 1995 or any Order in Council under section 1 of the Hovercraft Act 1968.

Interpretation of Part III

46.—(1) In this Part of this Act, except in so far as the context otherwise requires—

"act of violence" shall be construed in accordance with section 18(2) of this Act,

"article" includes any substance, whether in solid or liquid form or in the form of a gas or vapour,

"authorised person" means a person authorised in writing by the Secretary of State for the purposes of this Part of this Act,

"British ship" means a ship which—

(a) is registered in the United Kingdom under Part II of the Merchant Shipping Act 1995 or any Order in Council under section 1 of the Hovercraft Act 1968, or

(b) is not registered under the law of any country and is entitled to be registered in the United Kingdom under Part II of the Merchant Shipping Act 1995,

"constable" includes any person having the powers and privileges of a constable,

"employee", in relation to a body corporate, includes officer,

"enforcement notice" has the meaning given by section 29(1) of this Act,

"explosive" means any article manufactured for the purpose of producing a practical effect by explosion, or intended for that purpose by a person having the article with him,

"firearm" includes an airgun or air pistol,

"harbour" has the same meaning as in the Merchant Shipping Act 1995,

"harbour area" has the meaning given by section 18(3) of this Act,

"harbour authority" means—

(a) a harbour authority within the meaning of the Merchant Shipping Act 1995, or

(b) the manager of any hoverport which does not form part of an area mentioned in section 18(3)(a)(i) or (ii) of this Act.

"harbour operations" means—

(a) the marking or lighting of a harbour or any part of it;

(b) the berthing or dry docking of a ship or the towing or moving of a ship into or out of or within the harbour area;

404

(c) the transportation, handling or warehousing of goods within the harbour area;

(d) the embarking, disembarking or movement of passengers within the harbour area.

"harbour operator" has the meaning given by section 20(9) of this Act,

"hoverport" has the same meaning as in the Hovercraft Act 1968,

"manager", in relation to a hoverport, means the person by whom the hoverport is managed,

"master" has the same meaning as in the Merchant Shipping Act 1995,

"measures" (without prejudice to the generality of that expression) includes the construction, execution, alteration, demolition or removal of any building or other works (whether on dry land or on the seabed or other land covered by water), and also includes the institution or modification, and the supervision and enforcement, of any practice or procedure,

"naval service" includes military and air force service,

"operating area" has the meaning given by section 20(9) of this Act,

"owner", in relation to a ship registered in the United Kingdom or in any other country, means registered owner,

"property" includes any land, buildings or works, any ship or vehicle and any baggage, cargo or other article of any description,

"ship" includes hovercraft and every other description of vessel used in navigation.

(2) Any power to give a direction under any provision of this Part of this Act includes power to revoke or vary any such direction by a further direction.

(2A) In this Part of this Act "restricted zone" means an area designated under section 20 of this Act and references to a restricted zone of a harbour area include references to a restricted zone which is or is part of an operating area.

(3) For the purposes of this Part of this Act a person is permitted to have access to a restricted zone of a harbour area if he is permitted to enter that zone or if arrangements exist for permitting any of his employees or agents to enter that zone.

INDEX

411

INDEX

INDEX

ERRATUM

DOUGLAS & GEEN ON
THE LAW OF HARBOURS, COASTS AND PILOTAGE

FIFTH EDITION

The words "subject to 9.47" should be omitted from the
first line of paragraph 9.45 on page 97.

|L|LP|